D1570777

THE CRITICAL
RESPONSE TO
ISHMAEL REED

Recent Titles in
Critical Responses in Arts and Letters

THE CRITICAL RESPONSE TO ISHMAEL REED

ભ

Edited by
Bruce Allen Dick

With the assistance of Pavel Zemliansky

Critical Responses in Arts and Letters, Number 31
Cameron Northouse, Series Adviser

GREENWOOD PRESS
Westport, Connecticut • London

Library of Congress Cataloging-in-Publication Data

The critical response to Ishmael Reed / edited by Bruce Allen Dick
  with the assistance of Pavel Zemliansky.
     p. cm.—(Critical responses in arts and letters, ISSN
1057–0993 ; no. 31)
  Includes bibliographical references and index.
  ISBN 0–313–30025–9 (alk. paper)
    1. Reed, Ishmael, 1938– —Criticism and interpretation. 2. Afro-
Americans in literature. I. Dick, Bruce, 1953–
II. Zemliansky, Pavel. III. Series.
PS3568.E365Z63   1999
813′.54—dc21   98–31018

British Library Cataloguing in Publication Data is available.

Library of Congress Catalog Card Number: 98–31018
ISBN: 0–313–30025–9
ISSN: 1057–0993

First published in 1999

Greenwood Press, 88 Post Road West, Westport, CT 06881
An imprint of Greenwood Publishing Group, Inc.

Printed in the United States of America

The paper used in this book complies with the
Permanent Paper Standard issued by the National
Information Standards Organization (Z39.48–1984).

10 9 8 7 6 5 4 3 2

Lorenzo Thomas. "The Black roots are back." Rev. of *Mumbo Jumbo*. *The Village Voice* 15 March 1973: 19+. Reprinted by permission.

Robert Elliot Fox. "Blacking the Zero: Toward a Semiotics of Neo-Hoodoo." Reprint from *Black American Literature Forum* (*African American Review*) Volume 18, Number 3. Fall 1984: 95-99. Copyright ©1984 Indiana State University. Reprinted by permission.

Mark Shadle. "A Bird's-Eye View: Ishmael Reed's Unsettling of the Score by Munching and Mooching on the Mumbo Jumbo Work of History." *The North Dakota Quarterly* Winter 1986, 18-29. Reprinted by permission.

Neil Schmitz. "Neo-HooDoo: The Experimental Fiction of Ishmael Reed." *Twentieth Century Literature* April 1974: 126-140. Reprinted by permission.

Barbara Smith. "Recent Fiction: *The Last Days of Louisiana Red*." Rev. of *The Last Days of Louisiana Red*. *The New Republic* 23 November 1974: 53-54. Reprinted by permission.

Lorenzo Thomas. "Two Crowns of Thoth: A Study of Ishmael Reed's *The Last Days of Louisiana Red*." *Obsidian* II.3 1976: 5-25. Reprinted by permission.

Reginald Martin. "The *Freelance Pallbearer* Confronts the *Terrible Threes*: Ishmael Reed and the New Black Aesthetic Critics." *MELUS* 14 Summer 1987: 35-49. Reprinted by permission.

Joe David Bellamy. "Ishmael Reed: *Flight to Canada*." Rev. of *Flight to Canada*. *Fiction International* 6/7 1976: 148-149. Reprinted by permission.

Henry Louis Gates, Jr. "*Flight to Canada*." Rev. of *Flight to Canada*. *The Journal of Negro History* 63 January 1978: 78-81. Reprinted by permission.

Edmund White. "A Fantasia on Black Suffering." Rev. of *Flight to Canada*. *The Nation* 18 September 1976: 247-249. Reprinted with permission from *The Nation* magazine. © The Nation Company, L.P.

Greil Marcus. "From the Shadows." Originally published as "Uncle Tom Redux." Rev. of *Flight to Canada*. *The Village Voice* 15 November 1976: 49-50. Reprinted by permission.

Peter Nazareth. "Heading Them Off at the Pass." *Toronto South Asian Review* Vol. 4, No. 3, Spring 1986, 1-10. Reprinted by permission.

Joye Mercer. "The Improvisations of an 'Ethnic Gate Crasher.'" *The Chronicle of Higher Education* 17 February 1993: A6-A7. Copyright © *The Chronicle of Higher Education*. Reprinted by permission.

Excerpts from Ishmael Reed's *The Free-Lance Pallbearers, Yellow Back Radio Broke-Down, Mumbo Jumbo, The Last Days of Louisiana Red, Flight to Canada, The Terrible Twos, Reckless Eyeballing, Japanese by Spring, Chattanooga, Conjure, A Secretary of the Spirits,* and *catechism of a neoamerican hoodoo church* are reprinted with the permission of Barbara Lowenstein Associates and Ishmael Reed.

Contents

Contents

Series Foreword

Critical Responses in Arts and Letters is designed to present a documentary history of highlights in critical reception to the body of work of writers and artists and to individual works that are generally considered to be of major importance. The focus of each volume in this series is basically historical. The introductions to each volume are themselves brief histories of the critical response an author, artist, or individual work has received. This response is then further illustrated by reprinting a strong representation of the major critical reviews and articles that collectively have produced the author's, artist's or work's critical reputation.

The scope of *Critical Responses in Arts and Letters* knows no chronological or geographical boundaries. Volumes under preparation include studies of individuals from around the world and in both contemporary and historical periods.

Each volume is the work of an individual editor, who surveys the entire body of criticism on a single author, artist, or work. The editor then selects the best material to depict the critical response received by an author or artist over his/her entire career. Documents produced by the author or the artist may also be included when the editor finds that they are necessary to a full understanding of the materials at hand. In circumstances where previous, isolated volumes of criticism on a particular individual or work exist, the editor carefully selects material that better reflects the nature and directions of the critical response over time.

In addition to the introduction and the documentary section, the editor of each volume is free to solicit new essays on areas that may not have been adequately dealt with in previous criticism. For volumes on living writers and artists, new interviews may be included again at the discretion of the volume's editor. The volumes also provide a supplementary bibliography and are fully indexed.

While each volume in *Critical Responses in Arts and Letters* is unique, it is also hoped that in combination they form a useful, documentary history of the critical response to the arts, and one that can be easily and profitably employed by students and scholars.

Cameron Northouse

Chronology

1938   Born on 22 February in Chattanooga, Tennessee, to Thelma V. Coleman and Henry LeNoir.

1942   Moves to Buffalo, New York, with Thelma Coleman Reed and her new husband, Bennie Stephen Reed.

1952   Writes jazz column in *Empire State Weekly*, an African American newspaper in Buffalo.

1952-
1954   Attends Buffalo Technical High School.

1955   Attends an international convention of the YMCA in Paris.

1956   Graduates from East High School, Buffalo, New York.

1957   Performs in *Mooney's Kid Don't Cry* and Jean Anouilh's *Antigone*.

1958-
1960   Attends Millard Fillmore College and the University of Buffalo.

1960   Marries Priscilla Rose Thompson; daughter Timothy Bret Reed is born.

1962   Moves to New York City.

1963   Joins *Umbra* magazine; participates in *Umbra* workshops; *Umbra* publishes poem "Time and the Eagle"; also publishes in the *Liberator*; Reed and Priscilla Rose Thompson separate.

1964   Poem "The Arse Belching Muse" published in the last issue of *New Masses*; meets dancer Carla Blank.

1965   Appears on "The Jazz Poets" from Folkways Records; published in
        "Poets of Today"; serves as editor of *Advance*, a Newark newspaper.

1966   Teaches at St. Mark's in the Bowery prose workshop.

1967   *The Free-Lance Pallbearers*, a novel, is published; moves to Berkeley
        and begins teaching at the the University of California at Berkeley;
        contributes to *Where Is Vietnam?: American Poets Respond*; edits *The
        Rise, Fall and . . . ? of Adam Clayton Powell* under pseudonym Emmett
        Coleman.

1968   *Yellow Back Radio Broke-Down*, a novel, is published; teaches at the
        University of Washington, Seattle.

1970   *catechism of d neoamerican hoodoo church,* a collection of poetry, is
        published; divorces Priscilla Rose Thompson; marries Carla Blank;
        contributes to *Amistad I: Writings on Black History and Culture*; edits
        with introduction and contributes to *19 Necromancers from Now*.

1971   Helps to found *Yardbird*; contributes to *The Black Aesthetic*.

1972   *Mumbo Jumbo*, a novel, is published; *Conjure*, a collection of poems, is
        published; founds Reed, Cannon, and Johnson publishing.

1973   *Chattanooga*, a volume of poetry, is published; nominated for a
        National Book Award in Fiction for *Mumbo Jumbo* and a National
        Book Award in poetry for *Conjure*; nominated for a Pulitzer Prize in
        poetry for *Conjure.*

1974   *The Last Days of Louisiana Red*, a novel, is published; wins the John
        Simon Guggenheim Memorial Award for fiction and a National
        Endowment fellowship for creative writing; wins the National Institute
        for Arts and Letters Awards for best non-commercial novel of 1974.

1975   Wins the National Institute of Arts and Letters Award/Rosenthal
        Foundation Award for *Louisiana Red*; teaches at the State University of
        New York at Buffalo.

1976   *Flight to Canada*, a novel, is published; helps to found the Before
        Columbus Foundation; wins the Poetry in Public Places Award;
        collaborates on bicentennial mystery play, *The Lost State of Franklin*;
        publishes *Y'Bird* and *Quilt Magazine*, 1976-1980.

1977   Daughter Tennessee Reed is born; denied tenure by the English
        Department at UC Berkeley; attends NYU Conference on "The New
        American Novel" in Paris.

1978   *A Secretary to the Spirits*, a volume of poetry, is published; *Shrovetide
        in Old New Orleans*, a collection of essays, is published; wins the
        Lewis Michaux Award and the American Civil Liberties Award; co-
        edits *Yardbird Lives*; organizes first American Book Awards.

1979   Teaches at Yale and SUNY Buffalo.

1980   Teaches at Dartmouth College.

1981   *The Wild Gardens of the Loup Garou*, opera based on poetry of Reed
        and Colleen McElroy and music composed by Carman Moore,
        premiers at the Lenox Arts Festival; *Mother Hubbard*, a play, has
        staged reading at New York's Actors' Studio.

1982   *The Terrible Twos*, a novel, is published; *God Made Alaska for the
        Indians: Selected Essays*, is published.

1983   Teaches at Columbia University; the album *Conjure* is released by
        American Clave Records and released by Pangea Records.

1986   *Reckless Eyeballing*, a novel, is published.

1987   Teaches at Harvard and is made an associate fellow of the Harvard
        Signet Society.

1988   *New and Collected Poems* is published; *Writin' Is Figtin': Thirty-Seven
        Years of Boxing on Paper*, a collection of essays, is published; *Hubba
        City*, a play, premieres at Berkeley's Black Repertory Theatre.

1989   *The Terrible Threes*, a novel, is published; teaches at the University of
        California at Santa Barbara and the University of Washington, Seattle;
        Conjure II released; *Savage Wilds*, a play, runs at the Zephyr Theatre in
        San Francisco.

1990   *Savage Wilds* runs at the Nuyorican Poets Cafe in New York City;
        publishes *Konch*.

1991   Serves as co-editor of *The Before Columbus Foundation Fiction
        Anthology*.

1993   *Japanese by Spring*, a novel, and *Airing Dirty Laundry*, a collection of
        essays, are published.

1994   *The Preacher and the Rapper,* a play, opens at the Nuyorican Poets
        Cafe.

1995   *Conjure I* and *II* reissued by Rounder Records; receives honorary
        doctorate in letters from the State University of New York at Buffalo.

1996   *Hubba City*, a play, opens at the Nuyorican Poets Cafe.

1997   *Hubba City*, *The Preacher and the Rapper*, and *Savage Wilds,*
        published in *Action: Nuyorican Poets Cafe Theater Festival*, Miguel
        Algarin, ed.; *C Above C Above High C,* a play, opens at Nuyorican
        Poets Cafe; edits *MultiAmerica*.

1998   Receives Lila Wallace--Readers' Digest Writers' Award; receives
        honorary degree from Johnson C. Smith, Charlotte, North Carolina;
        Gethsemane Park, a gospera, performed by Black Repertory Theater in
        Berkeley; *Hubba City*, directed by Carla Blank, performed by Arrow
        Smith Academy, Berkeley, California; receives MacArthur Genius
        Award.

Introduction

Since the publication of *The Free-Lance Pallbearers*, his first novel, in 1967, Ishmael Reed has received more critical attention than almost any other contemporary African American male writer. Despite Reed's ongoing conviction that he and other black male artists have been misrepresented and virtually ignored in the press, scholars, students, journalists, fellow writers, and other assorted groups have studied his work. *Ishmael Reed: A Primary and Secondary Bibliography*, by Elizabeth and Thomas Settle, lists over 540 reviews, articles, and interviews related to Reed's writings. Published in 1982, this valuable research tool covers only half of Reed's professional career. More recent bibliographies contain dozens of other entries, including several books, on Reed's more recent work.[1]

The majority of this criticism has centered on Reed's literary innovations and what he once called his "Neo-HooDoo" aesthetic, which "draws from other art forms, like music, painting, film--out of my experience and Afro-American folklore" (Dick and Singh ix). Since the 1970s, many articles and book reviews have focused on Reed's commitment to multiculturalism. Additional criticism has concentrated on Reed's views on gender and how they help define his fiction, his relationship to other writers, and his contentious and changing position as a black man in a traditionally hostile, racist environment. These varied critical perspectives have moved Reed to the cultural forefront and placed him prominently in both African American and American literature.

The Critical Response to Ishmael Reed centers primarily on Reed's nine published novels. Organized by decades, it includes book reviews and essays devoted to these novels, as well as a recent interview in which Reed discusses his novels in progress: *The Terrible Fours*, the third book of the *Terribles* trilogy, and *Making a Killing*, a narrative centering on the O. J. Simpson trial. This emphasis on Reed's fiction is not intended to diminish the importance of his other writing. Reed's numerous publications force any editor to decide on which materials to include. Known primarily as a novelist, Reed is a prototypical postmodern writer who has worked in a variety of literary forms.

In addition to his nine books of fiction, he has produced five volumes of poetry, four collections of essays, and three plays. In 1973, *Conjure* (1972), his first book of poems, was nominated for both a National Book Award and a Pulitzer Prize. By 1988, when his *New and Collected Poems* appeared, Reed had received numerous other honors, including the Poetry in Public Places Award for his poem "From the Files of Agent Franklin." In 1994, he was awarded the Langston Hughes Medal commemorating his lifetime achievements in literature.

While his essays have failed to win the broad recognition his novels and poetry have received, they have made Reed's reputation as a candid social critic. *Airing Dirty Laundry* (1993) in particular distinguished Reed as a writer willing to challenge the status quo. Recently Reed's dramatic efforts have garnered close scrutiny, especially his latest productions at the Nuyorican Poets Cafe in New York City. Three of his plays were published by Scribner's in 1997. Reed also has written for newspapers, magazines, anthologies, scholarly journals, opera, radio, television, and film. In addition, he has published a number of unknown writers from many backgrounds. One of his most ambitious ventures has been the Before Columbus Foundation, a multi-ethnic publishing house he co-founded in 1976 that advocates a "post provincial America" and an awareness of "disparate cultures" (Dick and Singh xii). Like his numerous writings, these publishing projects have received widespread recognition and contributed to Reed's overall reputation as a committed, highly productive artist.

Reed's fiction forms the nucleus of his oeuvre and continues to attract the most critical attention. To date, Reed has published a science fiction fantasy (*The Free-Lance Pallbearers*, 1967), a Western (*Yellow Back Radio Broke-Down*, 1969), two detective mysteries (*Mumbo Jumbo*, 1972, and *The Last Days of Louisiana Red*, 1974*)*, a neo-slave narrative (*Flight to Canada*, 1976), two political parodies (*The Terrible Twos*, 1982, and *The Terrible Threes*, 1989*)*, a trickster tale addressing contemporary questions on gender and race (*Reckless Eyeballing*, 1986), and a satire on modern academia (*Japanese by Spring*, 1993). The reaction to this unusual assortment of novels has varied considerably, ranging from skepticism, ridicule, and condemnation to respect and high praise. Writing in 1969, establishment critic Irving Howe characterized Reed's early fiction as "humor columns in high-school papers" (141) and dismissed it as unworthy of serious debate. On the other hand, less than a decade later, Henry Louis Gates, Jr., wrote that "Reed's novels consistently manage to consolidate disparate, seemingly unrelated characteristics of black written and unwritten formal expression, and thereby to redefine for us the very possibilities of the novel as a literary form" (*Flight* 79). Dozens of other writers have commented on Reed's novels. Ranging between the extremes of Howe and Gates, critical reaction has contributed significantly to Reed's reputation as an innovative and provocative novelist.

No clearly defined pattern distinguishes the critical reception of Reed's fiction. While all of his novels have been reviewed, some have attracted more scholarly attention than others. *Mumbo Jumbo* and *Flight to Canada* are generally considered Reed's most important works, and scholars most often turn to these two novels to discuss his literary achievements. Conversely, *The Terrible Twos* and *The Terrible Threes* remain virtually unexamined. Because of attacks from feminist reviewers, *Reckless Eyeballing* has yet to receive the critical attention it deserves. Several scholars have analyzed *Pallbearers* and *Yellow Back Radio Broke-Down*, but most of their treatments have appeared in retrospectives published several years after *Mumbo Jumbo* solidified Reed's literary reputation. Scholars often have paired *Mumbo Jumbo* with *The Last Days of Louisiana Red* because both books fall under the "whodunit" mystery genre and share the same protagonist. While some critics have considered *Louisiana Red* Reed's first "reactionary" treatment of women and the precursor to *Eyeballing*, undoubtedly Reed's most controversial novel and the book that earned him the wrath of feminists, others have identified Reed's fourth novel (along with *Mumbo Jumbo*) as Reed's "conservative" reaction to the militant black literature of the 1960s. *Japanese by Spring* is generally considered an "insider's book" on academe, but at least one critic has convincingly argued that it revises several ideas in *Eyeballing* and might best be read in conjunction with that novel. With this latest publication, many enthusiasts now identify Reed to the left of center (especially considering his ongoing association with multiculturalism) and argue that his biting commentary on academia accurately reflects the absurd battles over political correctness taking place on many college campuses today.

Yet as this collection points out, "left" and "right" and "conservative" and "liberal" are distinctions that do not apply well to Reed's fiction. As he has proven repeatedly, the tenor of the times does not necessarily determine *what* Reed writes. No one tells him *how* to write or *when* to tone down his attack. Basically Reed is concerned with artistic freedom, especially in today's climate when so much contemporary American literature is swayed by political fashion. Since *Pallbearers*, he has cultivated his own unique aesthetic, combining satire and parody, comedy and fantasy, African and African American religion, as well as myth, history, film, television, and other forms of popular culture. As a writer who has experimented in many forms and genres and chosen postmodernism over protest and naturalism, he defies popular academic conceptions of what American writers, particularly black American male writers, ought to be.

Reed is also interested in exploring the hybridity and shared "Americanness" of all Americans. There is "no such thing as Black America or White America," he argues in *Airing Dirty Laundry*. "America is a land of distant cousins," bonded by history, culture, and blood (273). Reed applauds the increasingly multi-cultural texture of America and openly challenges the myopic attitude that refuses to see this reality. While he celebrates his African American heritage, he also opposes any form of essentialism that assumes one party line or viewpoint.

Intellectually courageous, he is as prone to censure black male critics for imposing a form on black writers as he is to chastise white feminists he feels fail to acknowledge the patterns of exclusion and discrimination that limit the lives of all non-white males in the United States. The criticism gathered here addresses these concerns and more. While the responses vary over decades, collectively they document Reed's forty-year career as an innovator willing to broaden artistic standards and as a chronicler of the times.

1960s

Reed's first two novels were published in the late 1960s, at a time when most American literature was still being judged by an Eastern cultural establishment operating under sometimes narrow and rigid artistic criteria. In a 1968 interview with Walt Shepperd, Reed chided those critics who he felt asserted the power of definition over his art. When "a black man tries to be a satirist, tries to look at the whole universe, *The New York Review of Books. . .The New York Times*, all these cats get uptight" (Shepperd 9). In a later interview he argued that "white writers have more freedom to be avant garde, to be experimental, than black writers do" (Helm 146), and that black writers are expected to "be conservative" and "write conventional novels" (146). Reed suggests in the same interview that both black and white critics want "blacks to write about how much they suffer" (147). If Reed's criticisms are accurate, and there seems to be ample evidence that some of them remain valid even in the 1990s, it is not surprising that his first two novels received mixed reviews.

The *New York Times* and other major newspapers overlooked *The Free-Lance Pallbearers*. However, smaller presses did review the novel, including the *East Village Other*, a paper Reed had co-founded several years earlier while living in New York City. Allan Katzman, its editor, called *Pallbearers* "a great book" and a novel "worth waiting for" (Settle 38). The book also received favorable reviews from Toni Cade Bambara and from such varied publications as *Publishers' Weekly, Book World*, the *Nation*, and the *Village Voice* (38-41). An anonymous reviewer at *Kirkus Review*, on the other hand, dismissed the work as "diarrhea of the typewriter" (37); other negative press came from the *Oklahoman*, the *Boston Globe*, the *Times Literary Supplement*, and the *Washington Star* (39, 41). Keneth Kinnamon, whose review for *Negro Digest* is included in this volume, offered one of the most balanced reactions. He praised Reed's "mastery of idiom" and "bizarre imagination" but questioned Reed's "scattergun technique," which Kinnamon felt "dispers[ed] rather than concentrat[ed]" Reed's "satiric energy" (18).

Irving Howe's review, also included in this collection, appeared in *Harper's* magazine two years after *Pallbearers*. It denounced Reed's narrative, along with *Yellow Back Radio Broke-Down*, his second novel, in a single paragraph. Howe, who had promoted Richard Wright during the 1940s as the prototypical

African American writer, found nothing inspiring--and certainly nothing humorous--about Reed's fiction. "I read him without a guffaw, without a laugh, without a chuckle, without the shade of a smile" (141), Howe wrote. He ended with a sarcastic quip: "[Reed] may intend his books as a black variation of Jonathan Swift, but they emerge closer to the commercial cooings of a Captain Kangeroo" (141).

Reed's response to Howe is also included in this volume under the title "Books in Black." Reed condemned not only Howe's "flippant, nasty, arrogant comments" (6) but also Howe's remarks comparing *Pallbearers* to Swift. "Perhaps I intended the books to be a variation of Afro-American novelists Wallace Thurman and George Schuyler," Reed wrote, "but it seems that Howe is illiterate of Afro-American literature written prior to 1938; a fact which raises serious doubts about his ability to intelligently evaluate this novelistic tradition which dates back to 1854" (6). For Reed, Howe was "only moonlighting" (Domini 134) when he critiqued African American literature and incapable of reviewing a novel which challenged the socio-realistic tradition of Wright. This counterattack represents the first of several that Reed has leveled over the years against unfavorable reviews.

In "*The Free-Lance Pallbearers* or the Dialectics of Shit," French scholar Michel Fabre offers a thorough and insightful analysis of the verbal inventions and linguistic achievements in *Pallbearers,* which many first-time readers either overlooked or dismissed as cartoon silliness. Fabre disagrees with critical perspectives that label Reed's novel "crazy," "incoherent," and "freewheeling" (12). To him, the book is "consistently structured" and provides a "counter-discourse" to the "prostituted language" and other "static [linguistic] systems" that are the main targets of Reed's derision" (5). Fabre includes a helpful comparison to Ralph Ellison's *Invisible Man* (as have other critics), but also emphasizes that such parallels in no way "detract" from Reed's "profound originality" (13). For Fabre, Reed's word play and constant punning question the function of language in fiction and offer a refreshing alternative to the neo-realism that has dominated so much of twentieth-century African American writing.

The reviews for *Yellow Back Radio Broke-Down* initiated the innumerable comparisons, likening Reed to Allen Ginsberg, Terry Southern, Norman Mailer, Ken Kesey, Kurt Vonnegut, Kenneth Patchen and Donald Barthelme, among others. Few critics compared Reed to other African American writers, whose popular tradition Reed argues he has inherited since his early days as a writer. While some reviewers called the novel "propaganda" and others dismissed it as "confusing," "nonsense," and "a failure"(Settle 41-49), most critics recognized Reed's creative word play, sense of humor, and unique style, and subsequently endorsed the book as a promising second novel.

In a second essay included in this volume, Fabre argues that structurally *Yellow Back* "represents a major innovation from *Pallbearers*" ("Postmodernist"

173). Fabre explains that *Yellow Back* is much more adventuresome and can be "decoded simultaneously on several wavelengths from BC to the present" (173). Like many other critical articles and reviews of *Yellow Back*, Fabre's essay highlights the telling literary discussion between the Loop Garou Kid, a black voodoo cowboy and the novel's protagonist, and Bo Schmo, the leader of a gang of socio-realists determined to destroy him. After Bo calls Loop a crazy "dada nigger . . . given to fantasy" and an artist obsessed with "esoteric bullshit" (178), Loop replies:

> What if I write circuses. No one says a novel has to be one thing. It can be anything it wants to be, a vaudeville show, the six o'clock news, the mumblings of wild men saddled by demons. (178)

These possibilities are "fair descriptions of Reed's fiction," Fabre writes, but he finds the "novel's declaration of independence vis-a-vis its author" (178) more revealing. That is, "the novel is said to become anything *it* wants to (not anything its author wants it to), as if it were gifted with a sort of autonomy" (178). In *Yellow Back* Reed conflates centuries, makes language out of noise, resurrects slang, and combines meaning, "possibly making his second novel his richest attempt . . . at reflecting critically upon the possibilities of fiction in the post-modern age" (187).

1970s

The 1970s marked Reed's most productive decade, and he solidified his literary reputation throughout these years. With *Mumbo Jumbo* and *Flight to Canada*, he broadened his HooDoo aesthetic, merging a variety of unconventional sources into a unified whole. He also began exploring other cultures and realized that embracing disparate viewpoints merely expanded one's own limited perspective.

Mumbo Jumbo, Reed's most celebrated novel, has been translated into Spanish, French, Italian, and Japanese and continues to be read and discussed. Unlike his first two novels, the book received national coverage from major newspapers, including a front-page review by Alan Friedman in the *New York Times Book Review*. For Friedman, whose review is part of this collection, *Mumbo Jumbo* is "a satire on the unfinished race between the races in America and throughout history. It is a book of deliberate unruliness, sophisticated incongruity, a dazzling maze of black-and-white history and fantasy, in-jokes and outrage, erudition and superstition" (1). The novel is "sterner stuff than anything in his earlier books" because it is "something a good deal more than a novel" (22), including an "unholy cross between the craft of fiction and witchcraft" (1). Reed appreciated Friedman's coverage (one of the rare times he has complimented the *NYTBR*) because Friedman "went out to the sources, which is all you can ask from a critic" (Young 43).

For Lorenzo Thomas, whose review is also included in this collection, *Mumbo Jumbo* is a big novel. Like Reed's earlier fiction, this book begins "with a willing disruption of belief in the imitation society of America"("Black" 19). On the surface it is a "who dunnit" story that satirizes countless historical and cultural figures, including Moses, Freud, Carl Van Vechten, Hugh Hefner, and Nat Hentoff. It is also a novel that offers an offensive and discourteous explanation for some of twentieth-century American history. It is a "HooDoo narrative" which exposes "the crisis of a culture that refuses to acknowledge itself" (19). Thomas, an early member of the Umbra Workshop, which Reed claims "taught" him his "voice" and "embarrassed [him] into writing . . . [his] own way" (Dick and Singh xi), makes comparative references to William Burroughs and Richard Brautigan, but he also feels that *Mumbo Jumbo* is part of the African diasporic tradition that does not compromise itself to Europeanism. It is "pure inner attainment. Bebop. Sound science"--a book that makes Reed "probably the best Black writer in America today" ("Black" 19).

The novel did get its share of negative reviews, as Reed points out in a "self-interview" originally published in *Black World.* He mentions that "one of the 'Sister' critics thought [the novel] was muddled" ("Writer" 67). Reed explains, in a sarcastic tone that foreshadows the ongoing confrontations he has had with some black women writers and feminist critics, that "I get my strongest criticism from some of the 'Sisters.' I guess this is because they want me to improve and do better, god bless them" (67).

This volume contains four essays on *Mumbo Jumbo*: a previously unpublished "ecocritical reading"by Lisa Slappey; an article by Mark Shadle; "Neo-HooDoo: The Experimental Fiction of Ishmael Reed," Neil Schmitz's seminal essay which has been both praised and criticized by other Reed scholars; and Robert Elliot Fox's "Blacking the Zero: Toward a Semiotics of Neo-Hoodoo."[2] Slappey states her premise up-front: "I intend to show that Ishmael Reed connects the suppression of indigenous nature-based religions, in particular Vodoun, with global colonialism and environmental abuse." She sees the novel as an "ongoing war on cultural identity" and focuses her attention on Osiris, an Egyptian deity linked to the natural world, and Papa LaBas, the book's chief protagonist--"the Legba character from the African tradition, the trickster houngan who serves as intermediary between the spiritual and material worlds." One of Reed's main points is that all people "could free themselves from various forms of oppression if only they would acknowledge" their "pagan roots." Shadle acknowledges the critical contributions made by other scholars, but argues that their positions are either too literal and look "for a consensus of revisionist history," or are too figurative and concerned primarily with "uncovering the illusions and allusions of [Reed's] literary structures" (18). His view is more "suggestive" and focuses on Reed as "an old fashioned triadist," reflecting what Shadle calls a "'multiverse' we try to share (as opposed to a 'universe' we simultaneously 'duel' over in an attempt to dominate)" (18). He

xxvi   Introduction

cites numerous references to support his "triadic" emphasis, including criticism by Fox, one of the first scholars to seriously examine Reed's fiction. Most Reed enthusiasts would agree with Shadle's contention that "it is hard to imagine *Mumbo Jumbo* not remaining near the center of [Reed's] work, 'philosophically speaking'" (27).

Schmitz examines Reed's first three novels and describes *Mumbo Jumbo* as "an ingenious dissertation . . . with a program for the revival of" African American art (136). Schmitz also sees Reed's fiction as highly problematic, especially when it advocates "Neo-HooDoo as a literary mode" separate from "those decreative and self-reflexive fictive modes" (127) of his white contemporaries. "One can invent myths, invoke legends, change his name and dress," Schmitz argues, "but he cannot will himself into language" (127). Reed, he feels, mistakenly identifies his forms as "narrative legends taken from an oral tradition" when in fact they are "popular forms of the Western and the Gangster Novel" (132). In the final assessment, *Mumbo Jumbo* "is not mumbo jumbo at all" (138) but rather another attempt at the "linguistic despair" (139) of William Burroughs or the metafiction one finds in Thomas Pynchon, Donald Barthelme, Robert Coover, and other contemporary American novelists.

In "Blacking the Zero," Fox examines how Neo-HooDooism in *Mumbo Jumbo* explodes "linear patterns of thought and creativity" (95). Reed's interest is to "deconstruct the cultural totalitarianism of Western civilization" by reasserting the "questions which the text of history has sidestepped" (96). Fox writes:

> [Reed] is dealing not only with the *phenomenon* of possession (consciousness ridden by forces or concepts) and the *act* of possession--the reclamation of lost, scattered, or denied areas of experience and traditions(s). Reed, through a deliberate strategy of anachronism, multimedia devices, footnotes, bibliographies, and the like, opens up his texts, allowing dispossessed history to enter. (96)

In 1974, one year after *Mumbo Jumbo* had been nominated for a National Book Award, Reed published *The Last Days of Louisiana Red*, his fourth novel. Like its predecessor, this book focuses on the adventures of Papa LaBas, ace detective and HooDoo priest, who is hired to solve a murder in New Orleans. Unlike *Mumbo Jumbo*, however, *Louisiana Red* drew hostile reactions, especially from feminists who were angered by Reed's characterizations of some women. In a review for the *New Republic*, reprinted in this volume, Barbara Smith criticized Reed's "joking contempt toward women, particularly black women" (54). Although she praised Reed's "comic irony" and unique ability to interweave "fantastic verbal absurdities with the familiar absurdities of everyday life" (53), she labeled his remarks about women "frighteningly distorted" (54). "When he satirizes the women's movement," Smith writes, Reed "falls back on the tired stereotype of feminists as man-hating dykes. The method for subduing these 'fierce, rough-looking women' is attack and rape" (54). Smith concludes, "As a critic I found *The Last Days of Louisiana Red* brilliant. As a black woman I am not nearly so enthusiastic" (54).

Reed addressed this kind of criticism as early as 1976 in an interview with Stanley Crouch. After Crouch pointed out that some readers saw *Louisiana Red* as "an extremely reactionary book, one that proposes the beating of recalcitrant women, [and] opposes women's liberation" ("Interview" 102-103), Reed countered:

> There are characters in the book who have viewpoints . . . Now there are patriarchs all over the place. You can't say that just because some movement comes along that all these people should . . . fold their tents and go away someplace. They're not going to go away. Such people in my books exist in the world. And they're based upon my experience . . . But these intellectuals try to dismiss things from the world. (102)

When Crouch answers that the criticism is focused more specifically on the Papa LaBas character, Reed responds:

> I pointed out many times this is the messenger at the crossroads, between different realities. And he also unites the past and present. You read a textbook of the characteristics of a Legba figure. Legba does those things, and he has those points of view. The African religions were patriarchal. The Haitian culture is patriarchal. Many of the African cultures we come from are patriarchal cultures. So I am just abiding by these ideas. (103-104)

Reed concludes by claiming there is a greater "variety of women in my books than men in the books being written by some feminists I can name" (104). Apparently his remarks did little to appease Smith and others. As Michele Wallace points out in an essay included in this volume, Smith and Reed eventually went head-to-head on a special edition of the television program *Tony Brown's Journal* to debate the topic of victimization among black men and women.

In "The *Freelance Pallbearer* Confronts the *Terrible Threes*: Ishmael Reed and the New Black Aesthetic Critics," Reginald Martin examines another group of readers who attacked *Louisiana Red* and some of Reed's subsequent fiction. Martin focuses particular attention on Houston Baker, Addison Gayle, and Amiri Baraka. While Baker accused Reed of betraying the black aesthetic movement, which he argues had helped discover Reed, Gayle criticized Reed for, among other things, distorting relationships between black men and women. Baraka dismissed Reed as a conservative and as part of the black middle class which had undermined the Black Arts Movement of the 1960s. All three critics looked on Reed's fourth novel as either insensitive to "the disadvantaged" (38) or as an attack on black nationalism and art targeted specifically at blacks. As

Martin points out, Reed was quick to retaliate, referring to his new adversaries as "educated native priest[s]" (38) and "romantic heroes of the left" (46).

For Lorenzo Thomas, *Louisiana Red* is Reed at his consummate best. The book parallels *Mumbo Jumbo* and, in classic Reed style, blends "Reed's historical understanding of corporate Christianity, voodoo, and the Black Power movement in all its Californian extremity. The book," as Thomas points out in "Two Crowns of Thoth: A Study of Ishmael Reed's *The Last Days of Louisiana Red*," "also includes Reed's studies of politics, religion, and mythology in ancient Egypt and Greece" (12). In his highly poetic style, Thomas discusses Antigone, André Breton, and other subjects alongside Reed, while arguing that the "heart" of the novel "is Reed's hearty denunciation of what he considers mistaken steps along the road to Black liberation" (14). Thus Eldridge Cleaver, Angela Davis, and other visible figures from the militant 1960s are pointedly lampooned.

In 1976, Reed published what Henry Louis Gates, Jr., has called "perhaps Reed's most 'intelligent' novel," *Flight to Canada* (*Flight* 80). Like *Mumbo Jumbo*, it received overwhelming praise and solidified Reed's reputation as an innovative and accomplished novelist. Included in this collection are reviews by Joe David Bellamy, Edmund White, Greil Marcus, and Gates. Bellamy defines *Flight* as an "ebullient, comic novel" which shoots "straight from the hip" (148-149). It derives its "pleasures" from "its feats of association, improvisation, and wit" (149). White's review describes *Flight* as "a brilliant montage of scenes, potent with feeling and thought" (247). White refers to Reed's previous novel as "careless, sexist [and] didactic" (247) and describes his earlier fiction as focused too exclusively on African HooDoo, intuition, and problems within the women's movement. He argues that *Flight to Canada* includes the "finest character Reed has ever created" in "the hair-raising Mammy Barracuda" (248). White compares Reed's novel to Balzac's work, "not for its style but for its remarkable drive" (249). He concludes by calling *Flight to Canada* "the best work of black fiction since *Invisible Man*" (249).

In his review for the *Village Voice*, Greil Marcus argues that Reed is "perhaps our most adventurous novelist, black or white" (47) and a writer who is unafraid to proclaim the "role of blacks as creators of American culture" (47). Reed's fiction often causes "a certain amount of confusion" (49), as Marcus summarizes the misstatements concerning key players and ideas in *Flight*:

> One reviewer got Raven mixed up with Swille . . . More than one writer has called the novel "the rock version" of the Civil War, which is as close to being meaningless as any statement about the book could be. (49)

While Marcus claims that Reed can be insensitive--"Reed's misogyny is as rampant as ever" (49)--he also finds the novel "outrageously funny," a trait which most reviewers (except Howe) have recognized in all of Reed's novels, no matter how much they might suspect his motives. Evaluating Reed's work with "spurious profundities" (49), Marcus concludes, will only diminish the impact of this "style" and "force."

In his review, Gates criticizes other scholars for classifying Reed almost solely "under the vague, dubious, and often derogatory euphemism of 'satirist'-- as if that form of writing relegated his stature as an artist to some nebulous corner of the absurd or else, as with so many labels, allowed him to be dismissed summarily" (*Flight* 79). *Flight* is satire, but it is also an "attack on naturalism" (79) and complements Reed's other novels, which "are almost essays on the art of black fiction-making" (79). Declaring *Flight* to be a "major work" (80), Gates agrees with Derek Walcott's "assessment" that Reed "alters our notion of what is possible. His importance to our use and understanding of language will not be obvious for many years" (81).

Janet Beck's previously unpublished essay on *Flight* explains how "Reed is both intrigued by the slave narrative tradition and cognizant of its limitations." She opens her essay with the question, "Why would Reed, a rollicking literary libertarian of 20th century style and sensibility, choose to write a novel in the most restrictive of genres?" The answer, she suggests, lies partly in Reed's "assertion" that not much has changed for African American authors in the past century and a half, "since the ante-bellum slave narratives were appropriated by white abolitionist editors and audiences." Reed, in the role of "literary abolitionist," redefines the genre by "exuberantly misappl[ying] a variety of 20th century technologies to 19th century events." He also structurally "dismantles" the formulaic narrative by incorporating both poetry and prose. For Beck, Reed "has become, in effect, a cultural underground railroad, a literary North Star providing direction for writers who would reclaim the [slave narrative] tradition as their own."

In "Heading Them Off at the Pass," Peter Nazareth uses an innovative critical approach which mirrors Reed's own fiction. A scholar who has written an important book based partly on Reed's role as an American trickster, Nazareth focuses primarily on *Flight to Canada* and *Yellow Back Radio Broke-Down*--quintessential Reed novels operating on many different levels.[3] Like *Mumbo Jumbo* and *Louisiana Red*, these books challenge and frustrate narrow-minded critics. "The difficulty for a critter--excuse me, critic," Nazareth interjects, "--is that Reed has a hundred things going on at the same time while the critic goes in a straight line, pursuing one lead" (6). Such a "linear reading" (6) restricts Reed's landscape to a convention he has challenged since his earliest publications.

1980s

Compared to his other fiction, Reed's three novels from the 1980s have received the least critical attention. Even at the time of their release, they garnered mixed reviews and contributed significantly to Reed's literary estrangement from a large segment of the reading public. This response is reflected partly in what some critics consider the esoteric style and subject matter of *The Terrible Twos* and *The Terrible Threes* as well as the controversial stand Reed takes against some white and black feminists in *Reckless Eyeballing*. Some reviewers complained that Reed was merely reworking the technique that had won him so much critical support a decade earlier. In "Kinships and Aginships," a review on *The Terrible Twos*, Stanley Crouch wrote: "The trouble with *The Terrible Twos* is that [Reed has] said it all before and said it much better" (618). Published in the *Nation*, Crouch's piece provides a brief overview of Reed's career as a concerned artist at "war with what he considers ethnic and academic provincialism" (617). It also summarizes Reed's involvement in publishing African American, Asian American, and Hispanic American writers, which helped originate "the idea of multi-cultural art and the formation of a literary army which Reed hopes will grow until academic and publishing forces have to acknowledge its place in American literature, its definitions of the American experience" (617). But for Crouch, Reed's sixth novel appropriates the same

> self-obsessed harpies, the mission Indians, the black hero who takes over the white form . . . the dumb black street hustlers who get into a game too complicated for them to understand, the corruption of Christianity.... (618)

A review by Henry Louis Gates, Jr., also included in this collection, balances Crouch's perspective and describes Reed's novel as "a tale that is humorous, riveting and moralistic in much the same curious way that ancient parables and allegories are written" ("Call Him Ishmael" 16). After comparing Reed to Richard Pryor, another artist with "a prophetic gift of vision," and after identifying the novel as "Reed's first attempt at a satirical analysis of the nature and function of the current American political and economic system," Gates writes:

> Reed's stature as one of our most inventive, daring and prolific writers lends credence and force to the strength of his satires. He may well emerge as one of the black community's most salient, if subtle, voices in our struggle to criticize the pernicious forms of racism-cum-capitalism. (16)

A review by Peter Nazareth, also included in this collection, complements Gates's piece and concludes: *The Terrible Twos* "proves that Reed is one of the most inventive American novelists" (*Twos* 458).

In "Ishmael Reed's Multicultural Aesthetic," Jerome Klinkowitz offers one of the few essays on *The Terrible Twos*. Klinkowitz argues that, since the beginning of his career, Reed has conflated history and imagination (fusing non-fiction essays with fiction) as a way of characterizing twentieth-century America. He argues that *Twos* should be read alongside *God Made Alaska for the Indians*, a collection of essays Reed also published in 1982. In both books Reed celebrates a multi-cultural America and condemns the "exclusionary and one-sided . . . standards of cultural authority" (23) represented by Euro-American whites. For Klinkowitz, Reed "gives language free play to project itself into previously unexplored corners of public experience, lighting up some truths which those afflicted with cultural tunnel vision might otherwise never see" (32).

Nazareth's comments on *The Terrible Threes*, the sequel to *Twos* and the second installment of an intended *Terribles* trilogy, are also included in this collection. While he laughs "less at Reed's new novels than at such earlier ones as *Flight to Canada*," Nazareth states that Reed "is as inventive as ever and continues" his trademark style of "signifying on everything and everyone" (*Threes* 310). Like his other novels, *Threes* is characterized by quick and simultaneous action, a de-emphasis of character, and a conflation of past and present. Nazareth suggests that critics have been unfairly "dumping" on Reed and that even his "least powerful works are worth reading" (311). Writing for the *New York Times*, Gerald Early disagreed, arguing that the "essences of the Reed narrative making, the pulling together of discrete, seemingly unconnected shreds of culture into complex secret conspiracies and patterns of knowledge, become the elements of his undoing here" (34). According to Early, Reed has "finally reached the impasse of actually writing a novel that truly does not make sense" (34).

One of the best critical overviews of Reed's *Terribles* series is in Darryl Dickson-Carr's previously unpublished article, "The Next Round: Ishmael Reed's Battles in the 1980s and 1990s." Dickson-Carr argues that Reed's last four novels are "direct reflections of the changing faces of African American and general American politics" during the last twenty years, and that Reed consistently seeks to expose neo-conservative "mean-spiritedness that has overtaken the American social and political landscape." Although he acknowledges negative remarks leveled at *The Terribles*, Dickson-Carr also points out that many of Reed's "predictions of the arc of American politics" in *Twos* and *Threes* "came true." Moreover, he argues that "Reed is at his best attacking buffoonery at every level of society."

Published in 1986 four years after *Twos* and before *Threes*, *Reckless Eyeballing* is Reed's albatross and a book that still haunts him twelve years after its publication. The criticism surrounding it has caused many to overlook Reed's best fiction. Generally considered a response to what Reed felt were distorted, negative portrayals of black men in Alice Walker's novel *The Color Purple* (1983), *Eyeballing* was panned by most readers and considered by many a vindictive, reactionary book out of step with contemporary gender politics. Reviewing the novel for the *New York Times*, Michiko Kakutani argued that Reed "goes so far as to imply that black men are currently being stereotyped and maligned in much the same way the Nazis once treated the Jews" (12). The book is full of "ugly talk" which does everything but "jar the reader into some new perceptions about bigotry" (12). The "sexist banter of men" in the novel "tends to come off as sort of 'boys will be boys' silliness," Kakutani writes, "whereas feminist criticism of men assumes decidedly more sinister proportions" (12). The stance Reed takes in *Reckless Eyeballing* is a "paranoid position with disturbing implications," Kakutani concludes, "and it does a disservice to Mr. Reed's own notable career" (12).

Michele Wallace notes that some critics and scholars in the 1980s began to react to Reed's writing with silence--that is, in order to quiet what they felt were unruly and unnecessary tirades against political and social forces active in the United States, they dismissed Reed's novels and other writings by refusing to review his work. Wallace disagreed with this approach, especially considering Reed's already established reputation. In "Female Troubles: Ishmael Reed's Tunnel Vision," she discusses what she feels are the general faults with Reed's outlook in *Reckless Eyeballing*. "The problem appears to be that Reed doesn't relish the idea of black women making public judgments about black men," Wallace writes, "although black men in the know, from the ubiquitous Dr. Poussaint (psych consultant for the Cosby show) to Reed himself, insist on their right to define and describe black women" (9). For Wallace, Ian Ball, the protagonist of the novel, "doesn't know his ass from his elbow when it comes to American feminism . . . Reed's determination to see feminism as a historical error reduces his black feminist characters to hand puppets mouthing his inane views" (11). Wallace recognizes the benefit of Reed's Neo-HooDoo vision, especially in its "intellectual alternative" to "passive assimilation" (9), but she believes *Reckless Eyeballing*, like some of Reed's other novels, blames women for the world's wrongs.

Daniel Punday's article, "Ishmael Reed's Rhetorical Turn: Uses of 'Signifying' in *Reckless Eyeballing*," argues that reviewers and critics have been misreading the controversial novel all along. According to Punday, Reed is quite conscious of how his audience "will read and even misread" (446) his work, and purposely baits them by signifying on the established African American literary tradition. Playing to his critics by attacking feminism, Reed tricks "his readers into reading the novel in a way meant to reveal their own cultural assumptions about the African-American tradition" (454). Punday argues that Reed's complex use(s) of signifying focuses on "the reaction of an audience only problematically conscious of" (458) the African American literary tradition. Punday writes:

> Many reviewers took Reed's attack on feminism...as [the] content of the work. Yet...the 'content' of the work is much more the responses that this attack elicits. [Reed] structures the novel to reflect back on his readers' expectations and ways of reading and uses such controversial material as a way to involve them and strongly elicit their reactions. (460)

In his response to Reed's later fiction, Dickson-Carr also argues that the "uproar and backlash" attributed to *Eyeballing* "is not entirely deserved." If feminists and feminism are issues in Reed's novels, so too are "the materialism of the Black middle class" and "the overwhelmingly materialistic 1980s that indirectly causes Black art and culture to suffer." Reed's focus then is as much on his characters trying "to assimilate and achieve bourgeois status" as it is on trying to criticize or push a specific political agenda.

1990s

Four years passed before Reed published *Japanese by Spring* (1993), his latest published work of fiction. Considered by some his most accessible novel, it is, in the words of Dickson-Carr, "largely a revision of *Reckless Eyeballing* as far as the structure of its plot" and "updates the problems of academic racism and intellectual cooptation for the cultural warriors of the 1990s." Writing for the *Christian Science Monitor*, Merle Rubin wonders if Reed's advocacy of cultural diversity as an "internationalist antidote to any one culture's attempt to dominate others" (14) might not lead to another form of replacement and control. Rubin asks: "Is everyone who favors teaching Western Civilization merely, as this novel seems to suggest, a racist in disguise? Is 'cultural diversity' a panacea for nationalism or a potential hothouse for new outgrowths of ethnic chauvinism?" (14). While Rubin recognizes Reed's gift of humor and ability to instruct through satire, Rubin also questions "Reed's seeming inability to comprehend the pervasive oppression of women in almost every culture" (14).

In his review, also included in this collection, Peter Nazareth points out that, once again, Reed is unafraid to "plunge into the maelstrom" and targets a number of people and issues plaguing academia and "the American consciousness" (*Japanese* 610), including Rodney King, Anita Hill and Clarence Thomas, the war in Iraq, General Colin Powell, Dinesh D'Souza, current modes of literary criticism, and right-wing conservative think tanks.

The articles by Leon Lewis and Mark Vogel are previously unpublished essays that provide valuable insight into the gamut of characters Reed parades through the novel and the misconceptions many readers have about *Japanese by Spring*. Lewis argues that Reed creates two basic groups of characters: those "competing academicians and administrators at Jack London College" who "are either diminished to puniness and pettiness by inherent hypocrisy or bloated to grotesquery by vicious immorality"; and those "powermongers" affiliated with the American university system who are "devoid of the slightest vestiges of consideration for anyone else in their lust to carry out agendas of personal aggrandizement." Reed depicts the first group "with some semblance of understanding," but he shows no mercy for the latter who are "versions of enemies who have plagued [Reed's] life for decades." Among them are D'Gun ga Dinza, an "assault" on the neo-conservative social critic Dinesh D'Souza, and April Jokujoku, a radical, black, lesbian, feminist poet and stand-in for some African American women writers Reed feels receive undue attention because of their political affiliations. Caught in the middle of these diverse characters is Chappie Puttbutt, the novel's wayward protagonist, and Reed himself, who, Lewis believes, functions not to manipulate "the reader's sympathy," as some readers have charged, but to negotiate "the gap between Puttbutt's limits and a positive vision of a cultural community of decency and justice." For Lewis, Ishmael Reed the character serves as a hopeful device which recognizes "that the richness of human experience depends on a blending of attributes and that no one individual has the best or only approach to anything."

In the beginning of his article, Vogel recognizes the reasons why some people find Reed's novel so distasteful, but he also contends Reed's "surrealistic collage contains shock tactics to get a reaction, to destroy the clichés so blithely pushed by editorials, by public officials, and much of the public." Like Lewis, Vogel also focuses on Ishmael Reed the character, pointing out that Reed's "hodge-podge of fact and fiction rearranges our notion of story." To support this rearrangement, Reed the author has Puttbutt learning Japanese from a book called *Japanese by Spring*. "Reed presents a novel within the novel," Vogel writes, "and little separation between the fictional and non-fictional world." Vogel also examines and emphasizes Reed's role as trickster figure; his reliance on naming, which "lets us know the figures to be respected and reviled" in the novel; and his position on multiculturalism, which is also articulated in *Airing Dirty Laundry*, the collection of essays Reed published alongside *Japanese by Spring*.

Finally, Reed responds to his own critics in "A Conversation with Ishmael Reed," a phone interview I conducted with Reed in August and September 1997. Reed talks candidly about his critics, including those he feels have unfairly attacked him or misrepresented his work, especially since the publication of *Reckless Eyeballing*. Reed is particularly hard on Henry Louis Gates, Jr., and seems to return to Gates no matter what question is asked. Reed prefers "the pre-1987, early Gates, the intellectual warrior and ass-kicker to the one we have now." "Skip Gates didn't discover me," Reed says about the favorable criticism Gates has written about him. And because so many other writers are "afraid to criticize" a man of Gates's power, Reed considers it his job "to keep the guy honest."

According to Reed, the charges of misogyny he continues to receive are primarily the reactions of white feminists, many of whom he argues have never even read his work. Reed says he gets along well with most African American women writers and argues that "when it comes to black men, feminists are engaged in hypocrisy and chicanery and obey a double standard." Reed also comments at length on many of the other critics and scholars included in this collection. He applauds those writers who research his work before reviewing it, including Robert Elliot Fox and Peter Nazareth, but condemns those critics that Reed feels turn out "hatchet jobs" on his writing, especially a newer generation headed by David Bradley, Darryl Pinckney, and Gerald Early. (Of Early's review of *The Terrible Threes*, Reed states: "If someone sent me a book to review and it didn't make sense to me"--as Early maintains in his review-- "I'd send it back so that another reviewer could review it.")

Toward the end of the interview, Reed discusses *The Terrible Fours* and *Making a Killing*, his forthcoming "O.J. Simpson novel" guaranteed to "raise some sand." Like *Mumbo Jumbo*, it will incorporate drawings and photographs, and, as in *Japanese by Spring,* include Ishmael Reed as a character. According to Reed "the case against O.J. was driven by public hysteria, whipped up by the press, especially that of white feminists who've lost their minds over black misogyny." Reed concludes the interview with a statement on his drama, an area he has been working on since the early 1960s when he wrote his first full length work, a play called *Ethan Booker*. Reed's remarks clarify and help balance some of the other critical statements collected in this volume. For Reed, controversy comes with the territory, and he seems determined to "expose the foibles" of even the most powerful interest groups in order to avoid compromising his art. While his attacks have often ostracized him from segments of the reading public (including many academics), his work has consistently been provocative. As many of the critics in this collection maintain, Reed's fiction ranks beside that of some of the most influential postmodern American writers and undoubtedly will continue to draw the critical attention it deserves.

This anthology represents a significant cross section of available scholarship on Reed, yet is obviously a very small part of the whole. I regret that I have had to omit several scholars associated with Reed criticism for a variety of reasons, including difficulties with reprint permissions. Occasionally I have included more than one article or book review by an individual author in order to show either some sense of consistency attributed to that critic or to suggest that his or her contributions provide significant and unique insight not available elsewhere. I have tried to include significant scholarship not represented here in the bibliography at the end of this book. Finally, this anthology is a corrected printing. Contaminated computer disks were mistakenly used during the first printing, generating misinformation and other defects. As editor, I sincerely apologize to all contributors and ask that *The Critical Response to Ishmael Reed* be judged by this corrected printing.

This collection would not have been possible without the help and support of many people. I am indebted foremost to Pavel Zemliansky, an Appalachian State University graduate student, who has provided valuable assistance from the start. His knowledge of computers helped with the editing of this text. I'd also like to thank Bill Pillow, another ASU student, for being there when I needed him. Shannon Winston provided valuable assistance in the early stages of this project, as did Gary Mitchell near the end. I am especially grateful to my colleagues, Mark Vogel and Leon Lewis, and to Amritjit Singh, Gabriella Motta-Passajou, Edelma Huntley, Tom McLaughlin, Tom McGowan, Daniel Hurley, Peter Nazareth, Robert Elliot Fox, Jerome Klinkowitz, Reginald Martin, Philippe Lamy, Susan Weinberg, and W. T. Lhamon, Jr., for valuable suggestions and help at various stages of the editorial work. I would also like to thank the ASU Graduate School for a grant to help pay for permission fees. Finally, I'd like to thank Ishmael Reed, who has patiently answered questions and facilitated the completion of this volume in many other ways.

NOTES:

1. Since the 1980s several books and chapters have appeared on Reed's writing, including *Conscientious Sorcerers: The Black Postmodernist Fiction of Leroi Jones/Amiri Baraka, Ishmael Reed, and Samuel R. Delany* by Robert Elliot Fox (1987); "'The Blackness of Blackness': A Critique on the Sign and the Signifying Monkey" (*Critical Inquiry* 1983) and "On 'The Blackness of Blackness': Ishmael Reed and a Critique of the Sign" (*The Signifying Monkey: A Theory of African American Literary Criticism* (1988) by Henry Louis Gates, Jr.; *Ishmael Reed and the New Black Aesthetic Critics* (1988) by Reginald Martin; *Ishmael Reed* (1993) by Jay Boyer; and *In the Trickster Tradition: The Novels of Andrew Salkey, Francis Ebejar, and Ishmael Reed* (1994) by Peter Nazareth. In 1995, Bruce Dick and Amritjit Singh co-edited *Conversations with Ishmael Reed*, a collection of thirty-one interviews covering Reed's career as a writer. Most recently, Patrick McGee published a book called *Ishmael Reed and the Ends of Race* (1997). In 1984, *The Review of Contemporary Fiction* devoted almost half an issue to critical articles on Reed's work.
2. A slightly revised version of "Blacking the Zero" appears as Chapter 3 in Fox's book *Masters of the Drum: Black Lit/Oratures Across the Continuum* (Greenwood, 1995).
3. This article appeared in a longer version in *The Review of Contemporary Fiction* 4.2 (1984): 208-225.

WORKS CITED

Beck, Janet Kemper. "I'll fly away": Ishmael Reed Refashions the Slave Narrative and Takes It on a *Flight to Canada*." Previously unpublished essay.

Bellamy, Joe David. "Ishmael Reed: *Flight to Canada*." Rev. of *Flight to Canada*, by Ishmael Reed. *Fiction International* 6/7 1976: 148-149.

Crouch, Stanley. "Interview with Ishmael Reed." 1976. *Conversations with Ishmael Reed*. Eds. Bruce Dick and Amritjit Singh. Jackson: University Press of Mississippi, 1995. 96-110.

---."Kinships and Aginships." Rev. of *The Terrible Twos*, by Ishmael Reed. *The Nation* 22 May 1982: 617-619.

Dick, Bruce, Amritjit Singh, Eds. *Conversations with Ishmael Reed.* Jackson: University Press of Mississippi, 1995.

Dickson-Carr, Darryl. "The Next Round: Ishmael Reed's Battles in the 1980s and 1990s." Previously unpublished essay.

Domini, John. "Ishmael Reed: A Conversation with John Domini." 1977. *Conversations with Ishmael Reed.* Eds. Bruce Dick and Amritjit Singh. Jackson: University Press of Mississippi, 1995. 128-143.

Early, Gerald. "Still Subverting the Culture." Rev. of *The Terrible Threes*, by Ishmael Reed. *New York Times* 7 May 1989:34.

Fabre, Michel. "Ishmael Reed's *The Free-Lance Pallbearers* or the Dialectics of Shit." *Obsidian* 3.3 Winter 1977: 5-19.

---."Postmodernist Rhetoric in Ishmael Reed's *Yellow Back Radio Broke-Down.*" *The Afro-American Novel Since 1960.* Bruck, Peter, Wolfgang Karrer, Eds. Amsterdam: B&R Guner Publishing Co., 1982, 167-189.

Fox, Robert Elliot. "Blacking the Zero: Toward a Semiotics of Neo-Hoodoo." *Black American Literature Forum*, 18.3 (Fall 1984): 95-99.

Friedman, Alan. "Part vision, part satire, part farce, part funferal." Rev. of *Mumbo Jumbo*, by Ishmael Reed. *New York Times Book Review* 6 August 1972: 1, 22.

Gates, Henry Louis Jr., "Call Him Ishmael--He's Still a Good Reed." Rev. of *The Terrible Twos*, by Ishmael Reed. *Black Enterprise* April 1983: 16.

---."*Flight to Canada*: Book Review." Rev. of *Flight to Canada,* by Ishmael Reed. *Journal of Negro History* Vol. 63 January 1978: 78-81.

Helm, Michael. "Ishmael Reed: An Interview." 1978. *Conversations with Ishmael Reed.* Eds. Bruce Dick and Amritjit Singh. Jackson: University Press of Mississippi, 1995. 144-160.

Howe, Irving. "Books: New Black Writers." Rev. of *The Free-Lance Pallbearers* and *Yellow Back Radio Broke-Down*, by Ishmael Reed. *Harpers* December 1969: 141.

Kakutani, Michiko. "Gallery of the Repellent." Rev. of *Reckless Eyeballing*, by Ishmael Reed. *New York Times* 5 April 1986: 12.

Katzman, Allan. "Books." Rev. of *The Free-Lance Pallbearers*, by Ishmael Reed. *East Village Other* 2.23 (15 Oct./1 Nov): 17.

Kinnamon, Keneth. "Book Reviews General: *The Free-Lance Pallbearers.*" Rev. of *The Free-Lance Pallbearers*, by Ishmael Reed. *Negro American Literature Forum* 1 Winter 1967: 18.

Klinkowitz, Jerome. "Ishmael Reed's Multicultural Aesthetic." *Literary Subversions: New American Fiction and the Practice of Criticism.* Carbondale, IL: Southern Illinois University Press, 1985.

Lewis, Leon. "The Resurrection of Olódùmarè: Ishmael Reed's Vision of Renewal in *Japanese by Spring*." Previously unpublished essay.

Marcus, Greil. "From the Shadows." Originally published as "Uncle Tom Redux." Rev. of *Flight to Canada*, by Ishmael Reed. *The Village Voice* 15 November 1976: 49-50.

Martin, Reginald. "The *Freelance Pallbearer* Confronts the *Terrible Threes*: Ishmael Reed and the New Black Aesthetic Critics." *MELUS* 14 (Summer 1987): 35-49.

Mercer, Joye. "The Improvisations of an 'Ethnic Gate-Crasher.'" *The Chronicle of Higher Education* 17 February 1993: A6-A7.

Nazareth, Peter. "Heading Them Off at the Pass." *Toronto South Asian Review*, Vol. 4, No. 3 (Spring 1986): 1-10.

---."*Japanese by Spring*." Rev. of *Japanese by Spring*, by Ishmael Reed. *World Literature Today* 67.3 1993: 610.

---."*The Terrible Twos*." Rev. of *The Terrible Twos*, by Ishmael Reed. *World Literature Today* 57.3 1983: 458.

---. "*The Terrible Threes*." Rev. of *The Terrible Threes*, by Ishmael Reed. *World Literature Today* 64.2 1990: 310-311.

Punday, Daniel. "Ishmael Reed's Rhetorical Turn: Uses of 'Signifying' in *Reckless Eyeballing*.'" *College English* 54.4 (April 1992): 446-461.

Reed, Ishmael. *Airing Dirty Laundry*. Reading: Addison-Wesley Publishing Company, 1993.

---."Books in Black." Letter. *Harpers* March 1970: 6-7.

---."The Writer as Seer: Ishmael Reed on Ishmael Reed." 1974. *Conversations with Ishmael Reed*. Eds. Bruce Dick and Amritjit Singh. Jackson: University Press of Mississippi, 1995. 59-73.

Rubin, Merle. "Clever Satire, Inspired Nonsense." Rev. of *Japanese by Spring,* by Ishmael Reed. *Christian Science Monitor* 9 March 1993: 14.

Schmitz, Neil. "Neo-HooDoo: The Experimental Fiction of Ishmael Reed." *Twentieth Century Literature* (April 1974): 126-140.

Settle, Elizabeth A., Thomas A. Settle. Eds. *Ishmael Reed: A Primary and Secondary Bibliography*. Boston: G. K. Hall & Co., 1982.

Shadle, Mark. "A Bird's-Eye View: Ishmael Reed's Unsettling of the Score by Munching and Mooching on the Mumbo Jumbo Work of History." *The North Dakota Quarterly* (Winter 1986): 18-29.

Shepperd, Walt. "When State Magicians Fail: An Interview with Ishmael Reed." 1968. *Conversations with Ishmael Reed*. Eds. Bruce Dick and Amritjit Singh. Jackson: University Press of Mississippi, 1995. 3-13.

Slappey, Lisa. "Nature as Sacred Text: An Ecocritical Reading of *Mumbo Jumbo*." Previously unpublished essay.

Smith, Barbara. "Recent Fiction: *The Last Days of Louisiana Red*." Rev. of *The Last Days of Louisiana Red*, by Ishmael Reed. *The New Republic* 23 Nov. 1974: 53-54.

Thomas, Lorenzo. "The Black roots are back." Rev. of *Mumbo Jumbo*, by Ishmael Reed. *The Village Voice*, 15 March 1973: 19+.

---."Two Crowns of Thoth: A Study of Ishmael Reed's *The Last Days of Louisiana Red*." *Obsidian* II.3 (1976): 5-25.

Vogel, Mark. "Post-Modern Realism: Ishmael Reed and *Japanese by Spring*." Previously unpublished essay.

Wallace, Michele. "Female Troubles: Ishmael Reed's Tunnel Vision." *The Village Voice Literary Supplement* No.51 December 1986: 9,11.

White, Edmund. "A Fantasia on Black Suffering." Rev. of *Flight to Canada*, by Ishmael Reed. *The Nation* 18 Sept. 1976: 247-249.

Young, Al. "Interview: Ishmael Reed." 1972. *Conversations with Ishmael Reed*. Eds. Bruce Dick and Amritjit Singh. Jackson: University Press of Mississippi, 1995. 41-51.

1960s

THE FREE-LANCE PALLBEARERS (1967)

Book Reviews General: *The Free-Lance Pallbearers*

Keneth Kinnamon/Review

Ishmael Reed is a man both amused and outraged by the absurdities and obscenities of the state of the nation as the last third of the century begins. In his first novel, *The Free-Lance Pallbearers,* an extravagantly satirical allegory of the journey of Bukka Doopeyduk from innocence to experience in a mad, mad, mad, mad, mad country, called Harry Sam, Mr.Reed is more successful in conveying his amusement than his outrage.

Dropping out of college, where he had aspired to become the first bacteriological warfare expert of the colored race, Bukka marries a sloppy shrew named Fannie Mae, moves into a housing project in Soulsville (Harlem), and works as a hospital orderly efficiently enough to be awarded a golden bedpan engraved with his initials. Originally right thinking, anti-subversive, and religiously orthodox, the protagonist is hoodooed and dehoodooed, henpecked and insulted, patronized and exploited, fired and humiliated, publicized and lionized, duped and deceived until dictator Sam, "a self-made Pole and former used-car salesman," appoints him to replace Eclair Porkchop as Nazarene Bishop of Soulsville; but the disillusioned Bukka recoils at last from his Tomism to lead an assault against Sam, part of an apocalyptic world revolution. He manages to do Sam in before meeting his own death at the hands of counterrevolutionaries.

In this kaleidoscopic narrative, Mr. Reed aims his satire at a bewildering variety of targets. Academicians, anti-busing racists, Uncle Toms, the anti-communist paranoia, white liberals and radicals, the Roman Catholic hierarchy, the Black Muslims, *Studies on the Left* and *The Village Voice,* medical ethics, Ralph Ellison, the W. E. B. Du Bois Clubs, Richard Nixon and Checkers, down-home types in New York, hippies, Cardinal Spellman, Edgar Allan Poe and T. S. Eliot, conservative civil rights leaders, organized labor, petition signers, veterans organizations, *Ebony* magazine, Jewish slumlords and their Negro flunkies, homosexuality, American judicial processes, black writers conferences, anti-Semitism, Bostonian gentility, happenings, the anti-poverty program, the East Village scene, the *Playboy* cult, J. Robert Oppenheimer, television interviews, the United Nations, militarism, Rutherford Birchard Hayes and Lyndon Baines Johnson--the list is by no means exhaustive. Mr. Reed's basic difficulty is simple enough. His scattergun technique disperses rather than concentrates his satiric energy. There is seldom an attempt at developing a satiric case, and when one occurs the development is horizontal rather than vertical, accretive rather than inclusive.

This is not to say that *The Free-Lance Pallbearers* totally lacks unity. Bukka's picaresque adventures provide an element of continuity. Characters appear and reappear, relating one episode to another. But the most pervasive unifying device is the central metaphor of shit, of which the novel is full. Sam, the ruler of Harry Sam, suffers from an illness, which has forced him onto a toilet throne to defecate for thirty years. The state symbol is thus the Great Commode. Naturally enough, a national emergency ensues when Sam's John becomes clogged. Mr. Reed's excremental vision encompassed virtually everyone and everything. U2-Polyglot, a dean at Harry Sam College, conducts research for a scholarly article entitled "The Egyptian Dung Beetle" in Kafka's *Metamorphosis* by rolling about a ball of manure with his nose. Bukka's father-in-law treasures in his old age the two distinctions of his life: "He had been president of the colored Elks in 1928 and once kissed Calvin Coolidge's ass." Bukka's position at the hospital teaches him "about the relationship between texture and color of feces and certain organic and/or psychological disturbances," and one of his duties in "the preparatory surgery division" is to remove hairs before hemorrhoidectomies. There is much more in the same vein. Clearly Mr. Reed gets to the bottom of things--and stays there.

The scatology of *The Free-Lance Pallbearers* fails to convey adequately its author's moral indignation. Too facilely clever, it entertains more than it nauseates the reader. But even the entertainment is shallow and contrived, for the novel seems too self-consciously determined to cash in on the vogue of black humor, of which Mr. Reed is a practitioner in a dual sense. Bukka and his playmates owe a great deal to Burroughs, Barth, Heller, Southern, and the rest, but perhaps they owe even more to the wisecrack-and-slapstick satire of *Mad* magazine. With his mastery of idiom, his bizarre imagination, and his sharp perceptions of the American madness, Mr. Reed has considerable satiric gifts. It is to be hoped that he utilizes them to better advantage in his second novel than he has in his first.

Negro American Literature Forum 1 (Winter 1967): 18.

Ishmael Reed's *The Free-Lance Pallbearers* or the Dialectics of Shit.

Michel Fabre/Article

In his first novel *The Free-Lance Pallbearers*, Ishmael Reed seems to shrink from breaking with literary tradition, as though for the purpose of satire fiction had to be shaped according to literary realism before language could generate fiction through the interplay of word patterns and scriptural systems. In this novel which teems with attacks on the sociopolitical scene in the United States, verbal invention is so apparent, however, that Reed at times appears reluctant to have to trust language so much, since it can be easily reclaimed by the same powers that transformed it into reassuring "toy talk" for the propaganda-fed masses. In this novel whose major ideological achievement is the denunciation of prostituted state-controlled communication and the unmasking of individual pretense under the citizen's fine words, the very status of the writer is questioned, since both fantasy which claims to be illusion and earnest discourse which pretends to be realistic can be suspect. Can the writer do more than let language generate fiction according to laws which guarantee its functioning freely, though not according to indeterminate and absurd patterning?

Satirizing processed and prostituted language represents one of the prime purposes of Reed in *The Free-Lance Pallbearers*. This may not be evident, though, if one considers only the more visible targets of his derision. These multiple targets are, in fact, the many facets of an enormous balloon he wants to deflate, some American King Ubu, alias Nixon-the-Awful who upholds a system rotten to the core. One of Reed's poems, contemporary with the final version of the novel since it was published in March 1966, beautifully summarizes the novelist's intentions. In "The Gangster's Death," the crumbling of U.S. power under the blows of international guerilla warfare occurs in the very terms used in the finale of *The Free-Lance Pallbearers* where the dramatic effects of Doopeyduk's odyssey somehow leave it in the background.

Just like Jarry's King Ubo, Reed's potentate, HARRY SAM, stands under the aegis of shit, under the sign of the turd. As a symbol he obviously refers to the figure of the ogre father, to cannibalistic consumption, to oral-anal phantasms more than to any other form of myth or sexuality. The opening quotations indicate this unambiguously. A sentence from Elias Canetti's *Crowds and Power* reads: "The excrement, which is what remains of all this, is loaded with our whole blood-guilt....It is the age-old seal of that power-process of digestion which is enacted in darkness and which, without this, would remain hidden forever." And Shirley Temple is quoted as declaring after seeing *Night Games:* "We felt so dirty after seeing it that...we ordered the spiciest food they had just to burn ourselves out, inside." The comparison between the workings of authoritarianism and of the digestive tract is clear.

Nothing surprising, therefore, if the opening section reveals that the dictator of HARRY SAM disappeared down the john thirty years before due to some mysterious and ravaging illness. The lavatory, located in the immense motel on top of Sam's Island at once becomes the fixed pole of the novel and its topography mirrors that of the human body, with "long twisting corridors and passageways descending to the very bowels of the earth" (p. 2). As could be expected, the outcome of monolithic personal power is comparable to a sewer discharge of half-digested matter:

> At the foot of the anfractuous path which leads to the summit of Sam's Island lies the incredible Black Bay. Couched in the embankment are the four statues of RUTHERFORD BIRCHARD HAYES. White papers, busted microphones and other wastes leak from the lips of this bearded bedrock and end up in the bay fouling it so that no swimmer has ever emerged from its waters alive. (pp. 2-3)

Excremental waste is in keeping here, and the indication that microphones and papers, coming from the statue's mouths are the agents of pollution is no coincidence. As everywhere else in the novel, the microphones are "busted," a sign of perturbed communication, while the "white papers" refer to government publications. Metaphorically, the mouth is equated with the anal passage and the linguistic process parallels the consumption-defecation process. The fourfold statue sends forth its foul gospel to the four points of the compass and, literally, the excrement of speech appears in order to stink and cry to high heaven. It is no coincidence either that "shit" designates this very type of perverted speech in Afro-American usage. The cannibalistic syndrome mirrors not only the exercise of political power, it also partakes of the obscene exercise of language.

With the help of this prevailing metaphor, which is woven through the narrative by innumerable motifs and terms, the symbols become readily decipherable: the mouth, both as the speech organ and the entrance for food, is linked with the anus (we are reminded, among others, of the Church of the Holy Mouth, or of Sam's mother dying of hoof-and-mouth disease). Smell and the nose are privileged to the detriment of hearing since the "high-pitched screams and cries going up-tempo" are muted through the good services of the national Ear Muffle Factory. The analysis of similar symbols could be pursued for pages, but only a few major directions will be hinted at here. Consider the prevalence of noses: the beaklike nose of the Jewish social worker; the noses of the dwarfs in the merry-go-round which adumbrate the monstrous appendage of Whimplewhopper, the midget judge; Trostky's nose which Mr. Nosetrouble carries devoutly in a leather suitcase. All such noses can inhale the awful stench everyone is supposed to keep silent about, especially if their owners wear the Great Commode Button. "Sam has body odor" is an utterance forbidden to loyal citizens, even though dissenters derisively recall: "Don't you know that HARRY SAM is full of shit?--Dat man do smell no matter which way you look at it" (p. 54). The country of

HARRY SAM is a contemporary stable of Augias, just like the Doopeyduks' refrigerator of the hospital where "Make-en-shit" Bukka studies the relationship between feces and certain organic and/or psychological disturbances" (p. 8). This is a viscous, gooey universe which Sam generates and befouls, as the novel proclaims through an insidious slip of the pronoun when the dictator argues about his foreign policy: "I read what you had to say about my foreign matters and you know what I think about it. It's shit. That's what it is" (p. 19).

Bag-of-shit Sam might be comparatively harmless, all things considered, if patriotism only meant kissing his ass or, as his favorites do, submitting to his homosexual whims. But he is addicted to two major perversions. One is the eating of little children, preferably black, whose tiny skulls are kept in the "classified" section of his library. Such is the logical outcome of mass consumption in a society whose symbol reads EATS EATS EATS on the motel roof. The second perversion is that of processing language into "toy talk," i.e. broadcast propaganda building up the image of the Great White Father on whose lap every citizen dreams of sitting one day. This propaganda speech is dangerous in its very appearance of naivety: "Slurp. Slurp. I'm not gonna get all flowery like the fella who preceded me quotin' all them fellas that wore laurels and nightgowns. I'm gonna give you people the straight dope" (p. 19) says Sam demagogically in anti-egghead stance. The workers, instead of following their leader's policy of activism, also want him to deal in "Toy Talk/Jing-a-ling dipsy noodle/N.B.C. and Cock-a-doodle," that is, the reassuring trash of telecast programs. Telephone employees can thus be said to "negociate toy talk for a living."

Through historical time, language can become degraded into byproducts that rob it of its relevance. At best, it dessicates instead of fermenting. This is the case of the old newsreels which the veterans in Franz Joseph Park kiss endlessly. Their souvenirs consist of "carts filled with artifacts and relics...some parched manuscripts belonging to Wilfred Owen, stacks of broken violin scrolls, some twisted marble toilet bases and a big rock, the only remnant of Hadrian's wall" (p. 57). Such fragments shored up against modernity are garbage as dead as the patriotic tradition they represent. Kissing the newsreels connotes obscenity because the act of kissing, as performed in the novel by Sam's favorites or by Fanny Mae's father in order to honor the president's or Calvin Coolidge's buttocks, has become a perversion of the mouth.

One encounters speechifying at all levels in *The Free-Lance Pallbearers* and Bukka always distrusts speech whenever it becomes sclerosed and inhibits intellectual nimbleness or shackles the creative imagination. Bukka's wife wastes her days in front of their television set or reading movie magazines; his neighbor devours King Kong comic strips. Himself a devout apprentice of the Nazarene faith, the hero pores over his textbook and, when he attempts to continue his training, he studies tricky problems of dogma concerning the shape and color of Sam's commode. Yet, "reading the Nazarene manual for loopholes and making notes.../ didn't even want to get into the subject of tissues; that one stumped the best scholars in the movement" (p. 74). By falling into the technological trap, he is afraid of being guilty of the same sin he often denounces.

Technological or academic discourse in fact grievously contributes to the perversion of language. The sure proof is that dictator Sam not only tolerates the specific activity of the intellectual caste but generally uses their criticism as part of the power game, provided it is performed according to certain rules. Sam tells Bukka:

> You got to watch these eggheads....The only thing they're good for is for handing honorary degrees to my generals and my Screws....One of them guys is pushing a ball of shit all over the world by the tip of his nose....They push them little mega-morphosis all over the world for me and I give them peanuts and then they start signing petitions and debatin' the white papers what me and the boys hustle up once in a while to keep peace and harmony down there and cut out all the yakkity-yak. (p. 97)

Political power does not dislike poets, especially when they are white and dead. They can become part of the Great Tradition updated. At Sam's big party, one can hear the poems of Emerson, Longfellow and Thoreau, "all white men with three names-dead many years," and such folk songs as "Your cock was nevah so good but when I laid yuh in the calabash field" resound with authority all over the Black Bay. SAM even admires intellectuals whose linguistic sophistication impresses him: because he masters words such as "quibbicale," Aboreal Hairyman gets appointed as an ambassador. Yet the dictator is quick to condemn what passes his understanding: when a party of academics come and sing "Gaudeamus Igitur" in the presidential motel, Sam believes that "They had the noive to get up there in their hats and gowns singin' Blow, he ain't much eager to," and he resents this supposed hint at his (deviant) sexual impotence.

The system decidedly prefers to use academics for its own ends. Thus U2 Polyglot, the dean of the university Bukka once attended, a congenial looking little fellow, is one of Sam's spies in the cultural war. In him, the metaphors of the nose, of speech and of shit perfectly coalesce since he goes around the world pushing a ball of manure with the tip of his nose in order to prepare a paper on "The Egyptian dungbeetle in Kafka's *Metamorphosis*" (which Sam called "mega-morphosis" in a previous quotation). Bukka is confronted with the dean at crucial stages in his career and when saboteurs plug up the presidential toilet with bantam feathers, Polyglot displays "officious-looking papers bearing the greenish-brown seal of HARRY SAM" (p. 39) to prevent the police from arresting them.

After Bukka's death, The Freelance Pallbearers who come, according to the legend, in order to lay his body to rest, cannot get through because of Polyglot's scholastic achievement:

> There was this great ball of manure suspended above Klang-a-Lang a-Dong-Dong. Held down by spikes and rope it stank to high heaven....U2 Polyglot [was] making his way to a mailbox...His arm was in a sling. He had been winged while U-twoing through Indochina but nothing can stand in the way of scholarship. So he dropped his greenish-brown envelope containing the manuscript into the mail. He sat down to contemplate his next paper. (p. 116)

The novel thus ends with the apotheosis of the ball of shit, whose academic perfection not only pollutes the universe but, weighing down fiction under the dead mass of erudition, eclipses what should have been the protagonist's passion. Ironically, the only change brought about by Bukka's rebellion and Sam's death occurs along linguistic lines, since Chinese characters are now used to transcribe the nation's motto EATS EATS EATS when the new president takes over. Metaphorically, individual creation and fictional fantasy are defeated by political permanence and fossilized language.

Ishmael Reed nevertheless propounds a valid antithesis to the greenish-brown seal and the Dean's ball of manure; it is the bright ball which a white seal balances on the tip of his nose at the entrance to the tribunal where judge Whimplewhopper sits. Here, the performing seal heralds the coming into action of the dynamic, alive, ever-present, inventive performance of the creative artist. This theme will become a major one in *Mumbo Jumbo* where the tradition of the dancing God Orisis is re-established against the death-like legacy of Seth. In both novels, creation in the becoming is opposed to the fixed and obscene artifact; fluidity offsets solidity; life-giving change negates petrifying order. Without going into details, it is easy to see that Sam is obscene, not because he defecates, but because his defecation is protracted and abnormal. Whether he has been spending thirty years in the john owing to unceasing diarrhea/logorrhea or because he is grievously constipated is an interesting question for Nazarene theologians to resolve; yet, there is no doubt that Ishmael Reed, on the level of speech, opts for fluidity against solidity.

The Free-Lance Pallbearers thus represents an attempt to debunk myths not only because they may be ideologically harmful, but because they set up impoverished aspects of reality as enduring monuments. Reed's later novels, such as *Yellow Back Radio Broke-Down,* in which he demystifies the whole American tradition, and *Mumbo Jumbo* in which he attempts to create a counter-tradition, take the question further and, significantly, in *Mumbo Jumbo,* the cultural legends propounded remain a series of avatars and metamorphoses and do not constitute a fixed mythology. In *The Free-Lance Pallbearers*, it is important that Sam's library, where skulls are filed behind rows of leather bindings is a real morgue. It is equally important that the patriotic litanies recited by the veterans finally prove to be no more than the results of horse races. Any book, any type of fixed discourse can be reduced to appearances and thus easily subverted.

On the contrary, performance, defined as a show implying audience participation or as any type of artistic creation achieving reciprocal communication, tends to invade the strongholds of the novel in order to proclaim a viable alternative to the obscene production and consumption of speech. One could even say that Reed's fiction is structured between the negative pole of clogged discourse, which rots and stinks, and the positive pole of self-generating dialogue or continually expanding narrative.

The circus metaphor[1] serves precisely to state and illustrate this viable alternative and to reestablish some kind of linguistic and aesthetic balance in the novel. It appears most convincingly in the hilarious episode where Bukka is summoned before Whimplewhopper because his wife wants a divorce. Bukka tries to recite all the events that culminated into his present confusion, starting with Fanny Mae's grandmother's attempt to put the voodoo on him. His telling is so complete and complex, while he tries to account chronologically for simultaneous events, that the concatenation of his report is broken. Not only does his telling run wild but so does the narrative, according to a trajectory which accurately illustrates how fiction can be generated within Reed's favorite fictional/textual field.

Here the narrator begins with mixing up elements of coherent speech which soon function illogically. When he tries to rectify the judge's summation of his story, Bukka soon ends up saying:

> "With all due respect, your honor, you got it all wrong. It's Dr. Christian who pushes the ball all day through areas where nuns are raping the buns and my father-in-law kisses Versailles 1919....I mean," fumbling and stammering, "no, it goes this way...a...a" (p. 66)

At once two members of the audience intervene and compound the confusion by supplying details pertaining to former episodes but never given by Bukka in the courtroom. Whimplewhopper's next intervention thus has no bearing on Bukka's actual declaration. Echoing the sentence, "You left out the old woman who kidnapped Checkers," the judge asks "If SAM has taken Checkers, then who is in the john?," but this alludes to a part of the novel which only the narrator and the reader are supposed to know about since it is the contents of Bukka's former dream. In this instance the narrative jumps abruptly from the coherent "reality" of the episode to a pseudo-coherent discourse referring to a fictional dream, thus eliciting reactions which defy the logic of fiction that can be expected from characters traditionally limited to what they have supposedly experienced.

Thus it is not surprising if, at this stage, another member of the audience turns the judge's question into the refrain for a conga which the whole courtroom starts chanting and dancing: "If SAM has kidnapped Checkers, then who is in the john? a-one, a-two, a-three, kick." This is the world of the Marx Brothers or *Hellzapoppin*, and the text at once conjures up a whole orchestra in tuxedos, still dripping wet because, in Bukka's dream, a few chapters before, they were part of the mad chase started by the old woman who had kidnapped Nixon's spaniel on board an ocean liner. Here, language properly resuscitates characters and generates fiction. The dream episode is picked up again because a few words and audience participation call it forth from the limbo of potentiality where the orchestra was waiting.

Several critics have characterized this aspect of Reed's creation as "crazy," "incoherent," or "freewheeling." One should note, however, that it is consistently structured. Moreover, the author here attempts to bring this de-railing of fiction to an end through the narrator's remark: "I went apeshit. 'WHAT DO YOU THINK THIS IS, SOME KINDA JOKE OR SUMTHIN? STOP THIS MONKEY BUSINESS. RIGHT NOW!² YOU KNOW THIS PLACE NOWHERE, NOTHIN BUT KLANG-A-KANG-A-DING-DONG-A-RAZZ-A-MATAZ'" (p. 66). Of course, this utterance sounds ironical since the terms supposed to denote an actual geographical place only refer to a sort of nonsense erected in a fictional reality. Yet, the protagonist calls for meaning and the judge quickly follows suit: "STOP IT! STOP IT! He took out a whistle, puffed his jaws and blew. DO YOU THINK AMERICAN JUSTICE IS SOME KINDA WEIRD CIRCUS? SOME FREAKISH SIDESHOW? A CARNIVAL ROUTINE? Everybody hurried back to their seats and the orchestra rushed from the courtroom" (p. 66). The words used by the judge to designate what the courtroom normally is not, metaphorically characterize what it has momentarily become and what has been revealed of the essence of justice. The trouble stemmed from the metaphor being taken literally. This confusion appears again when the judge duplicates Bukka's syntactic and syntagmatic mistake, as he exclaims: "I'm not going to have my circus...turned into a courtroom...dog bite it" (p. 67). He corrects himself, Bukka apologizes, and the fiction seems to get back on the right track, but the circus metaphor has been activated and it creates fiction in its turn: sure enough, when Bukka turns around to leave, we see him "almost bumping into the next case which was the bearded lady and the fat woman who had brought the juggler into court for hitting them over the head with the liontamer's stool" (p. 67). Fictional reality now has caught up with metaphoric fancy; it has given birth to more fiction, as if to justify the apparent running wild of language.

Throughout the novel, fancy, the circus, the show, the performance prove to be the only mode of action capable of generating a counter-discourse which will melt and push back the pollution of powerful static systems, be they political or linguistic. One of the most frequent and the most efficient mechanisms of Reed's comic and verbal creation is at work here.

Metaphorically, the hero, the poet, the creator, is thus valued in opposition to the academic, the potentate, the technician of grammar or mass media jargon. He is *the one who can play,* to the full extent of the term. The courtroom scene sheds a farcical light upon the narrative, but it also logically leads to the protagonist's finding a Monopoly card in his pocket and his going to Entropy Productions to collect 200 dollars. Fired from the hospital, he is hired as the main actor in a "becoming," managed by the astute Cipher X, a manipulator who reveals his conception of all things as theatre and the world as a stage. The ritual happening in which Bukka participates is an unrehearsed, spontaneous performance on his part;

in the stocks, he is hit by a ball-throwing robot while a recording predicts racial retaliation to the predominantly white audience. From dramatic interview to dazzling TV show, the image of Bukka is blown up into that of a dangerous revolutionary and his power increased accordingly. He finally explodes, denouncing the inequities of the system--without condemning Sam, however--and as a result he is invited to the presidential motel. Thus, he has been used and manipulated as an actor or public performer, yet performance has transformed him from a small-size man-in-the-street into a debunker of myths, finally able to see through the camouflage of masks and to vent forth grassroots anger against exploitation by the state.

One should note at this point that *The Free-Lance Pallbearers* recalls, in more ways than one, Ralph Ellison's *Invisible Man* whose naive narrator also related the steps in his initiation to the ways of the world. In both novels, comparable elements recur: college life or individual study, the Brotherhood or trade-unionism, the veterans at the Golden Day or those in Franz Joseph Park, white radicals vs. black nationalists in Harlem or Soulsville, Cipher X or Brother Jack, Rinehart or Elijah Raven, etc. The attitude of the protagonists, who are more victimized than heroic, towards language, power, the dynamics and fluidity of shapes and form are comparable, conditioned as they have been by their gullibility; their roads take them from innocence to an underground hole or to butchers' hooks after failing to perform any kind of revolution. A detailed study might show how adroitly Reed has assimilated Ellison's essential teachings which however detracts nothing from his profound originality.

Reed's first novel is especially new on the level of linguistic creation, due not so much to lexical coinage as to a deliberate refusal of neo-realism. He liberates the creative potential of language. A brief analysis of the courtroom scene was enough to show how his use of words could spontaneously generate fiction, how a character's imaginings acquired the same degree of existence as the events supposedly shared by several characters.   Similar instances are frequent, where the linguistic "starter" consists of a mere verbal possibility. For example, when Bukka meditates on Nazarene casuistry, "he is afraid of using dialect for fear the academicians would circulate a petition." He goes so far as thinking out loud the wording of the petition: "We refuse to sit on our RANDS and listen to the steady erosion of the English language. Not since Craxton has there been such a crisis in letters" (p. 74). As a logical result, a few pages further, the Vice-Dean of the University of Buffalo, who is the type Bukka thought might initiate such a petition, comes to life as a full-size character and plays his part until the end in the novel with all his faculty and students instead of disappearing again like the wet orchestra. Such parallel sub-sequences, unessential to the plot, are born and thrive for the fun of it, as though the narrative were a tapestry of sequences in which one thread is toyed with for a while and then forsaken to be picked up again or not, as though creative speech were not responsible for the survival of those few elements, among its innumerable semantic or representational potentialities, which now and then come to be actualized. As a consequence of the equality of opportunities granted to each element, Reed's fiction seems to discard the very notion of hierarchy, through both aesthetic and political choice. No character, no episode, no detail is more important than another and the dream or the potentiality are just as "real" and valid as the fictional event. This is reflected in the titles chosen for the different chapters: one of them is called "An Old Woman Kidnaps Checkers" after a comparatively minor dream sequence which is only echoed again in the courtroom scene. Simply because the courtroom is adorned with frescoes depicting the deeds of the nineteenth president of the United States, such as his denigrating everything Chinese and celebrating stupid American customs, the corresponding chapter is entitled "Rutherford Birchard Hayes is Thrown from a Horse" although the president's opening the Wichita Pickle Fair on October 22, 1864, after having been kicked in the head by a horse, is by no means part of the plot.

The reviews of *The Free-Lance Pallbearers* justifiably praised Reed's linguistic invention, although coinage already current in Afro-Americanese was sometimes attributed to him. At his best, he plays with words and makes puns in the style of ghetto rapping (when evoking "an old spindly woman with two bricks for breasts" or "a scourge of a scrounge") or in the fashion of the Marx Brothers ("Have a Bromo-Seltzer...the dumpy man fizzed"). This is all good and funny. His so-called nonsense words raise disturbing questions, however, about the very nature of language. When he describes the country of HARRY SAM as a "not-to-be-believed out-of-sight, sometimes referred to as O-BOPSHE-BANG or KLANG-A-LANG-A-DING-DONG" (p. 1) the very sounds locate the fictitious place in unreality. Yet, with the help of repetition, these phonemes applied to NOWHERE and NOTHING, assume existence and definition to such an extent that Bukka's later calling the place a WAY-OUT BRING-DOWN entails a revolution. Or when NOWHERE becomes NOW-HERE, when Sam says "I look through my binoculars and see everything flying in NOTHING which is ME. NOTHING escapes my eyes" (p. 95) or again "As long as I am dictator of ME...I'll do my best to improve NOTHING" (p. 98) the semantic implications are disturbing because opposite meanings coexist. Very possibly, the apparent carelessness of Fanny Mae's grandmother who calls Bukka "Dippidick," "Daffydink," "Dankeydim," "Doopeydank or whatever your name is" in the course of a short telephone conversation, is not simply ludicrous but symptomatic of the dangerous interchangeability of words and of the questionable identity of things and people. Such interchangeability seems accidental and abnormal in everyday intercourse, yet Reed's resorting to it thus poses anguishing questions about self-identity, about the mechanisms of meaning and about the nature of language and communication. Interpolated substantives at first generate comedy as a sound reaction against the static forms of fixed speech, yet they also hint at the absence of relevant rules. The reader is not confronted with a record needle stuck in a groove but with a talking machine that garbles messages. The burden of a World War I song turns into disquieting strains when it becomes: "Roger Young was the glory and the story of the everlasting tires of the infantry who died for you and me young Roger Young of the story and the everlasting wires of the infant free lies the story and the glory of you and me" (p. 60). Homophonic elements dislocate and soon crumble into a reiteration of phonemes which is the more threatening as it is only half-senseless; the listener loses his grip upon reality as language apparently loses its grip upon meaning.

Halfway, then, between the stinking rigidity of power or congealed speech and the formless diarrhea-like fluidity of nonsense the exultation of mastering language stands metaphorically in Reed's first novel. It is also the exultation of being able to control one's destiny. Significantly, when Bukka reaches the apex of his career in society, when he is appointed a Nazarene Bishop and dreams of fulfillment in Soulsville, he walks up the path towards the motel "exultant, rehearsing the phonemes of UNNERSTAND and INNERSTEAD" (p. 11). Admittedly, the circumstances are ambiguous because Bukka, combing his hair "with a two foot comb," is in danger of becoming a replica of effeminate, arrogant judge Whimplewhopper. He is rehearsing phonemes (sounds without meaning) which he will use in an awe-inspiring piece of toy-talk. Yet Bukka's (or any characters') ability to control language often appears in the novel as a proof of his superiority, especially according to the rules of the ghetto where playing the dozens is a means to self-assertion. Brought before Whimplewhopper, Joel, the white activist properly defeats the judge at that game when he exclaims: "Your mama must have humped a whole bunch of anteaters for you to have a snout like that" (p. 62). The joke costs him up to thirty years in jail but victory is his.

As a rule, in the novel, one of the endearing characteristics of the common man lies in his distrust of grammar and four-syllable jawbreakers. Fanny Mae speaks of "mega-morphosis" just like Sam, and the upstart barn-burner become president describes the octopuslike Black Bay monsters as "Latin roots, the terrible man-eating plants" (p. 105). We all laugh with the janitor in his exchange with the Nazarene social worker:

> "Kulchur 'prived children? What's dat, Yo Excellency?" "Oh, that means they can't go to the Lincoln Center and devour Lily Pons." "Wait a minute, suh. Now I'm jess a poor Screw who is a traitor and the abomination of my peoples but even I know dat Lily Pons ain't gone hep dese kids. Dey need someting stantial in their stomicks, like roast pork or steak. Lily Pons! Why dat's food fishes eat, ain't it?" (p.15)

Yet the man-in-the-street remains a dupe of power through his gullibility and inability to understand what is really going on. On that level, mastery of language constitutes a strong ideological weapon. The Word is all-powerful, especially when its meaning has been redefined along other than preestablished lines. Thus Mr. Nosetrouble explains the importance of Trostsky who:

> In a speech before the cemetery of Prague said "Blimp Blank Polooka Dookey,"
> and standing in a threadbare coat, shaking his fist in the rain for hours said "Blank
> Palooka Dookey Blimp," and who on more than one occasion warned the ruling
> circles "Dookey Palooka Blank Blimp." (p. 27)

The power of the word consists in establishing, not some sort of meaning, but some meaningful relationship, as Cipher X cryptically explains to Bukka: "You are interested in loopholes, I'm interested in hooplahoops--they both have diphthongs. I can't see why we can't collaborate" (p. 81).

Contrary to his intentions in *Yellow Back Radio Broke-Down,* Reed is not interested in pulling apart traditional genres in *The Free-Lance Pallbearers.* Starting with the prophecy which justifies the novel's title ("Legend has it that when the fateful swimmer makes it from Sam's Island to HARRY SAM...the Freelance Pallbearers will take SAM," p.3) the narrative begins like a fairy tale, complete with dwarfs, ogre, old witch, magic phial and hero battling with monsters. Yet the tale soon turns into parody and it calls forth satire through many-sided allusions to the American classics, literary or otherwise: to Hemingway's novels which Sam reads on his stool, to popular magazines and comic strips, to the good old movies with ubiquitous Betty Grable and Roy Rogers, etc. Some parodic reminiscences of Edgar Allan Poe sound even more spoofy. Bukka remembers:

> "At three oclock in the morning there came a tap-dap-rapping at my door, a
> tit-tat-klocking on my hollow door." (p. 26)

It is only a woman in black looking for her lost children, yet the ominous bird is not far behind in the shape of Reverent Elijah Raven and Lenore soon appears as the Harvard fiancee of Alfred, an avatar of the Salem witches sentenced by Whimplewhopper to cook for Sam's cannibalistic feasts. Even the backdrop for "the fall of the house of Sam" derides Poe's suspense:

> The door slowly opened, its rusty hinges squeaking. Before me were concrete
> steps that disappeared into the hollow of an abysmal throat. The moans were
> definitely coming from the oval-shaped darkness. Putting my fingers on the
> trigger of the turkey-musket I started down the endless steps. Through the soles of
> my shoes I could feel the concrete; the slime of tiny animals squashed underfoot
> and rats dashed across my shoe-strings. Wispy spider webs brushed against my
> face as I pushed on--my ankles moving through sludge--until I came to the gasps
> and snorts echoing through the dank ol' house steeped in mildew. When I came to
> the middle landing an awful stench attacked my brain that smelled of the very
> putrescence of mass graves. I took a handkerchief and held it to my nose as I ran
> through the passageways and past propped-up human skeletons in cabins. (pp.
> 101-102)

What is the function of literary allusion, if not to allow Reed's narrative to carry such dead pieces and fragments and dispose of them through laughter? As well as political myths and patriotic litter, worn-out literary codes and forms as thus exploded through parody. Just as Reed denounces the dictatorship of the static word and offers performance as its antithesis, he plays with the usual notions of realism. In spite of appearances, he also manhandles the customary notion of fictional time since only at the end does the reader discover that it is a dead narrator who has been telling the story. In a significant and belated effort to answer Rapunzel's question about the "Nazarene thing [he] kept yapping about," Bukka stammers and finds his death:

> "You see, there was this thing stuck in my trig and it asked could I arrange an appointment for it with Sam.... O, no, that's not the way. What's the use?" I said, giving up the ghost as the little man removed his derby... (p. 115)

At that point, the omniscient narrator should logically pursue but Bukka does not give up his tale with his ghost. When the pallbearers finally arrive, he indulges in a bad joke on their delay before acknowledging they have come to cut him down. Only then does he dissolve into a kind of indefinite persona who remarks how little political change has been achieved, thus justifying a posteriori the use of a continuous present tense in the opening section: revolution amounts to simply going round in circles; history, or fiction, is a closed world which seems to repeat itself. At the very end, the narrator and the author seem subtly to coincide through typographical arrangement. Just as the final lines of the narrative are in capitals, so are the place and time indications pertaining to the writing of the novel. Again, the categories of fiction and reality are proclaimed as interchangeable.

When he challenged the state of things in HARRY SAM, Bukka once threatened to mix NOWHERE and the U.S.A., fiction and reality:

> "If you keep on talking of places like Bronxville that don't even exist, the place will be turned out. Pure and simple. Every damned cobweb will be ripped to shreds." (p. 86)

This is precisely what Ishmael Reed attempts and achieves in *The Free-Lance Pallbearers*. Having questioned the function of language in a repressive sociopolitical system through the metaphor of shit, he sets up the dynamics of linguistic performance as a viable alternative. Meanwhile he rips to shreds the fine web of traditional American belles-lettres, with its respected classics and established genres and conventions. He thus proclaims that fiction is generated primarily through an act of language, at what might be called the third, synthetic stage of the dialectics of "shit."

All page references are to the Bantam Book edition (New York, 1969) of *The Free-Lance Pallbearers.*

NOTES

1. Although close to the merry-go-round, the circus metaphor has positive connotations because it relates to open, creative action while the recurrent, circular movement of the merry-go-round is a closed and repetitive circuit. In the novel, the merry-go-round and the dwarfs have been subverted by Sam and they function as bait for the imaginative children who want to be carried across the Bay.
2. The reference to "Monkey Business" is only a hint at the use Reed adapts from the Marx Brothers' technique of slapstick dialogue and the fashion in which mere words generate situations in their films. In *Yellow Back Radio Broke-Down,* active punning on "mouse" and "moose" seems to be derived from "Animal Crackers." Reed's indebtedness to the Marx Brothers certainly deserves to be studied in detail.

Obsidian 3.3 (Winter 1977): 5-19.

YELLOW BACK RADIO BROKE-DOWN (1969)

From: Books: New Black Writers

Irving Howe/Review

And last of all Ishmael Reed, who writes "movie books" irresistibly recalling humor columns in high-school papers. *The Free-Lance Pallbearers* features a young gentleman named Bukka Doopeyduck who wanders through a constipated country called Harry Sam; *Yellow Back Radio Broke-Down,* set in the Wild Old West, stars the Loop Garoo Kid, a black cowboy, and Drag Gibson, a bad cattleman. Testimonials from weighty sources declare Mr. Reed a comic master; he himself announces his style to be "literary neo-hoodooism"; and I can only crustily say that I read him without a guffaw, without a laugh, without a chuckle, without the shade of a smile. Packed with *Mad* magazine silliness though his work is, Mr. Reed has one saving virtue: he is hopelessly good-natured. He may intend his books as a black variation of Jonathan Swift, but they emerge closer to the commercial cooings of Captain Kagaroo.

Harper's (December 1969): 141.

From: Books in Black

Ishmael Reed/Letter to Editor

I found Irving Howe's comment ["Books: New Black Writers," December], "their appearance causes conflict, since it threatens entrenched cultural interests and styles," the most honest and truthful statement in a long "book review" in which Black writers of diverse aesthetics were lumped together in a cultural slave quarters....Mr. Howe's critical approach demonstrates that he hasn't read with comprehension the newest White writers, let alone Black.

"He may intend his books as a black variation of Jonathan Swift," Howe writes of my novels in typical White chauvinistic manner. Perhaps I intended the books to be a variation of Afro-American novelists Wallace Thurman and George Schuyler but it seems that Howe is illiterate of Afro-American literature written prior to 1938; a fact which raises serious doubts about his ability to intelligently evaluate this novelistic tradition which dates back to 1854.

Incidentally the "review" of my work was a lazily assembled patchwork of reviews which have appeared elsewhere. Perhaps Mr. Howe can do for some of that "hard work" and "discipline" he so patronizingly counsels Hal Bennett to cultivate.

I would propose that the author of *A Treasury of Yiddish Poetry* and editor of *Dissent* is a delegate for these "entrenched cultural interests and styles" threatened by what is probably the most exciting upsurge in American writing history. With his flippant, nasty, arrogant comments--a phrase used by John Williams is termed "fatuous"--Mr. Howe has, under the guise of criticism, performed as a cop for these dying interests...Thirty years ago during Mr. Howe's heyday this would have worked for Afro-American artists who naively believed that White criticism arose from the loftiest motives instead of serving as a subterfuge for certain political, cultural and sexual interests....

A dying culture will always call up its intellectual warhorses, no matter how senile they may be, when pagans are breaking down the gates. Mr. Howe's hysteria--LeRoi Jones is called an "anti-Semitic Bulgarian"--proves that we have drawn blood and we will now do what pagans have always done when confronted with a racist, imperialist, tyrannical system.

We will move in for the kill, and this is what the Seventies will be all about.

Harper's March 1970: 6-7.

Irving Howe Replies

Irving Howe/Letter to Editor

The one possibility that Mr. Reed seems unable to consider is that--unlike other young black novelists whose work I did praise--he has not yet written a book worth taking seriously.

Harper's March 1970: 7.

Postmodernist Rhetoric in Ishmael Reed's *Yellow Back Radio Broke-Down*

Michel Fabre/Article

Whereas the fantasy of Ishmael Reed's first novel, *The Free-Lance Pallbearers* (1967) was carried along, rather than structured, by the sprawling form of the *Bildungsroman,* the framework of *Yellow Back Radio Broke-Down* (1969), his second novel, is a multidimensional Western, re-enacting the ancient struggle of conflicting world views. Here, Reed strikes at the heart of American history's most mythical dimension--the winning of a continent. Frontier life and the conquest of the open lands, wagon trains, powerful owners and boisterous cowboys, cattle migrating along the Chrisholm Trail, shotgun towns complete with outlaws and their saloon and main street battling places--all are described colorfully. The expected cliches accompany the myth of Eldorado and the Rocky Candy Mountains (the seven cities of Cibola), while ghost towns evoke encounters between legendary heroes like Billy the Kid or Kit Carson. He casts as villains not only land capitalist Drag Gibson and his gang of thugs and cowpokes but also all the powers that be, whether state or federal, religious or military. He sets up as hero a black super cowboy, Loop Garoo Kid, who can wield curses as efficiently as he can the bullwhip, being an inventive Voodoo *houngan* as well as a somewhat apocryphal twin of Christ. Loop busies himself avenging a group of circus performers and "flower power" children who have been butchered by the villains on their way to the techno-anarchical paradise of Cibola. Chief Showcase, the good redskin, comes to the rescue of the hero who is also seconded by the eternal feminine, diversely embodied by voodoo priestess Marie Laveau alias Zozo Labrique, by Haitian *loa* Erzulie/Yemaja, or by the Virgin Mary alias Black Diane. The bad guys are legion: a couple of Negro Judases with Greek names; outlaw and killer John Wesley Hardin, summoned for the occasion; Bo Shmo, chief of the neo-realist gang; masochist Reverend Boyd; several doubledealing prostitutes and a dozen disreputable historical characters handed down to posterity as Founding Fathers or brave explorers by primary school textbooks; not to mention Royal Flush Gooseman, the unscrupulous fur trapper, and Mighty Dyke, the bulldyker octoroon. Since none of them prove able to beat Loop, Pope Innocent himself is sent for to help Drag restore law and order, but he only manages to compromise with the black cowboy for whom God the Father has a strong liking and the Blessed Mary a definite crush.

The myriad episodes in this comic strip struggle are truly hilarious, but they also function quite logically according to the genre of the Western, with its set antagonistic parties and its stereotypical roles, out of which Loop's creative spiritual technology--namely hoodoo--emerges triumphantly.

The widening of the space and time categories in *Yellow Back Radio,* which greatly expands the scope of the plot as cosmic drama, closely corresponds to the development of the part played by voodoo. In the first novel, Booka Doopeyduck had been turned into a werewolf through the spells cast by his wife's grandmother while Lenore, convicted of witchcraft by the court, was a reincarnation of beneficent occult powers. In the second novel, Loop Garoo (i.e., werewolf, from the French *loup garou*) is endowed with superhuman stature because he is a *houngan*, while New Orleans voodoo priestess Marie (whichever alias she may assume) also plays a major part.

Although the links between the parodic strategies of *The Free-Lance Pallbearers* and *Yellow Back Radio* are patent, the second novel represents a significant departure front Reed's *Bildungsroman* whose anti-hero failed to debunk an obscene, Nixon-like potentate. *Yellow Back Radio* ranges over at least three telescoping centuries and the whole of the North American scene, even drawing upon ancient European and African religions in order to portray this local conflict as the mere avatar of long-standing cultural warfare.

As for power, here defined as the power of private property dictating governmental and papal policies, it remains akin to the dictatorship of Harry Sam, whom Drag embodies in new ways. Like Sam, Drag is characterized by lust, violence, greed and treachery; like Sam, he is surrounded by a team of ruthless, sycophantic and uncivilized ruffians. Sam was literally a heap of constipated "shit"; in spite of his deodorant, Drag also stinks, if only of formal dehyde, offending even his own cowpoke's noses. Like Sam, he is a hopeless homosexual who marries only in the hope of bequeathing his noxious genes to his scions. Although he is introduced at first as a "ladykiller" and brags about his sexual appetites, he is only a murderer of women: like Bluebeard, he has done away with six wives and will dispose of the seventh in the course of the novel. His sexual games remain largely verbal or oral: he is mostly seen French-kissing his green horse (which the mares avoid, thinking that "Since green he was a queer horse.") (p. 19), or reading the life story of Catherine the Great on a velvet sofa in his negligee, or else "sticking a pudgy hand in the pocket of his monogramed silkrobe" (p. 44), when not spreading mascara on his eyelashes to pose as a Mexican dancer. He explains that "Drag is not only the name for the horseman who rides to the rear of the cattle but...also the shorthand for something scaly, slimy and huge with dirt" (p. 47). Since Gibson etymologically means the offspring of a gelded cat, the man is a contradiction in terms.

It is significant that two other embodiments of power in the novel, military chief Theda Doompussy Blackwell and politician Pete the Peke, should also be notorious "fairies." Aristocratic Theda, as his name suggests, finds satisfaction in the hands of his black masseur in a late eighteenth century club which strongly evokes a male harem. The fact that he is a white field marshall implies no small criticism of American army brass and of the so-called master race. As a result, power and abnormal sexuality are pictured as equivalent in obscenity. It is significant, not only of the literary genre chosen but also of Reed's own aims and prepossessions, that sexuality and culture should be so tightly linked. Three main stereotypes are thus defined and exploited: the female, the homosexual and the supermale. Next to the prostitutes and Hurdy Gurdy girls in Big Lizzie's Rabid Cougar Saloon, Drag's bride, Mustache Sal, is an interesting representative of the liberated woman who selects her partners and uses them for her own enjoyment and profit. The homosexual ranchman allows her to indulge in frenzied nymphomania with his employees and guests, but contemporary society begrudges her orgastic gratification, especially when she breaks racial taboos by trying Chief Showcase's "little-man-in-the-canoe" erotic technique.

Such triumphant, if overriding, female sexuality contributes to Reed's definition of a heroic protagonist, even though, later in the novel, the cult of the female initiated by the Blessed Mary is satirized as a Women's Lib fad. In contradistinction, as we have seen, the villains are pictured as "fairies." To the ridiculous figure of the white pseudo-male, Reed contrasts that of the somewhat stereotyped phallic man of color, under the dual guise of the Black and the Red.

Although he appears first as a dandy and a bizarre "paraphysical" neo-surrealist, Chief Showcase (Cochise) soon develops into a fundamental embodiment of a positive cultural essence. Through allusion to Sitting Bull and nineteenth century battles, Reed starts with the traditional, derisive image of the Indian massacred in the name of religion and dispossessed for economic purposes: children dress as Indians, cowboys exhibit their scalps, tourists weep over a bygone past, the head of an Indian appears on the nickel, and his artifacts are embalmed in the Smithsonian Institute or the Metropolitan Museum. From genocide to ethnocide, Indian culture barely survives on reservations, exemplified by Showcase's teepee. Himself a "showcase" for the bland display of picturesque ethnicity, the New Indian is doomed to read militant poetry for the entertainment of people whose forebears were responsible for the massacre of his ancestors. Thus, Showcase performs as a buffoon to Drag and his henchmen. However, he soon appears to be outwitting his more powerful adversary: Showcase's flattery is steeped in irony, when he emphasizes white honesty concerning Indian treaties, for instance. Showcase thus performs as the mythological trickster through his use of double entendre. He dissembles and plays several parts, employing language as a tool against white power. His elegant Beau Brummel accoutrement is contrasted with the raggedy appearance of his white "superiors." The Indian is also cast as the superior technologist, the inventor of a flying craft which the white man has appropriated, a wielder of words whose phrases survive in American usage. He is an embodiment of the Promethean spirit and also of Apollinian forces, a harmonious blend of mind and body, superior even to the black superlover.

Loop is something of a braggart, yet the passion which the Virgin Mary feels for him and his irresistible attraction for Sal are evident proofs of his abilities as a lover. It is even doubtful that Reed is deriding the myth of the black supermale, among others, when he makes Showcase the outright winner in the field of dalliance, since he never divorces manliness from manhood or even machismo. Although male chauvinism triumphs, it appears that the novel mostly advocates naturally free and uninhibited sex, which admits of license but not of deviation from "healthy" heterosexuality.

However, Loop is less a sexual superman than a spiritual high priest, and it is significant that he should resort to a black mass instead of a shootout in the streets of Yellow Back Radio or Video Junction in order to achieve his ends as an avenger. Thanks to magic spells and the supernatural help of the African python-god, Loop triumphs over the hydralike embodiments of white greed and racism. This role of the hero as *houngan* is remarkable in two ways: first, it establishes voodoo as a viable countertradition to the officially recognized beliefs of the Judeo-Christian faith; second, it defines the artist as a maker of spells ("ouangas" or "wangols"). This is reiterated in the lines of Reed's poem "catechism":

> D YR ART D WAY U WANT
> ANY WAY YOU WANT
> ANY WANGOL U WANT

and in his definition of the Afro-American artist as a "conjurer who works Juju upon his oppressors; a witch doctor who frees his fellow victims from the psychic attack launched by demons."[1]

Critics have occasionally found that the Pope's long lectures about Christianity and voodoo were a disservice to the book, turning it into a book about hoodoo instead of a hoodoo novel. [2] It is true that they slow down the narrative considerably, but they perform the important function of helping the average American reader to acquaint himself not only with voodoo as a syncretic religion but also with the cultural/ideological warfare which has been waged for centuries in the name of religion. Above all, they allow Reed to bring together Christianity and voodoo in a larger spiritual framework in which Innocent and Loop are not only intimates, rivals and friends but also equivalents: the leader of the Catholic Church supports the institution's ensuring white supremacy while his black counterpart undermines them. In that respect, one of Loop's accusations is illuminating: "You and your crowd are the devils. The way you massacred the Gnostics, not to mention the Bogomils, Albigenses and Waldenses!" On the contrary, the principle he represents has "always been harmless" and such popular rituals as Christmas were destined to make him appear "foolish, the scapegoat of all history" (p. 165).

More interesting than Loop's claim that he is a twin brother of Jesus or that Mary (or Black Diane) fell in love with him the day after Jesus was crucified and is eager to make up their quarrel is the reinsertion of the Judeo-Christian tradition into the wider context of earth goddess cults, depicting Christianity as an outgrowth, or pseudo-rationalization, of authentic primeval faiths. This was to be more elaborately developed by Reed in *Mumbo Jumbo* (1972), a novel in which the white Cartesian tradition of the Atonists is challenged by Egyptian lore of the partisans of Osiris, Dionysian champions of "soul," physical exhilaration, vitality and creative impulses.

For the traditional opposition of races, an opposition of cultures is substituted, the sophisticated civilization of the Reds and the vital force of the Blacks being vindicated against the violent acquisitiveness of the Whites. The three major protagonists, Chief Showcase (the red Indian), Drag Gibson (the white lord of the land) and Loop Garoo Kid (the black cowboy), and the lesser characters who side with each of them, all can be analyzed as embodiments of opposed or complementary principles in this "chrestomachy" which, as the narrative develops, can be read as a triumph of "soul" (black) over materialism (white) which had overpowered the spirit (red). Thus, when Pope Innocent defines voodoo as an American version of the Ju-Ju religion that originated in Africa--you know, that strange continent which serves as the subconscious of our planet--where we've found the earliest remains of man (p. 152), not only does he imply the anteriority of the African "soul" principle but also its deeper roots in man's original being.

Loop's own brand of voodoo is defined as a "syncretistic American version" with potentially revolutionary undertones, hence the danger he represents for the supporters of Western culture. What is more, the neo-hoodoo artist (whom Reed portrayed at a greater length as a "necromancer" in his introduction to the anthology, *19 Necromancers from Now* (1970)) is said to be:

> scatting arbitrarily, using forms of this and adding his own. He's blowing like that celebrated musician Charles Yardbird Parker improvising as he goes along. He's throwing clusters of demon chords at you and you don't know the changes. (p. 154)

The artist, here the black American novelist-cum-wizard innovates only within the ancient but vital cultural tradition of voodoo, projected as a liberating consciousness which whites find hard to share. The structuring of the novel, both on the spatial/temporal and the metaphysical levels (a kind of "before and beyond" which explains and inspires Loop's behavior), represents a major innovation from *The Free-Lance Pallbearers* which was only a satire on Nowhere, i.e. Now/here, the American *hic et nunc*. *Yellow Back Radio* is to be decoded simultaneously on several wavelengths which range from B.C. to the present and pertain to a variety of modes, from carnival to morality play. This qualitative jump reflects a definite improvement which could be illustrated by a comparable development in textual and linguistic achievement. In the first novel, for instance, Bukka says of Sam's mother, "Dead as a doornail, she died, mean and hard" (p.1) the idiom being made only slightly more striking through alliteration. In the second novel, a cowboy exclaims, "Bingo, poor, and my man is in doornail country." We could say that the same qualitative gap exists between the two novels as that between the metaphoric connotations of "doornail country" and the cliché "dead as a doornail."

Reed has said in an interview that he was extremely aware of form when he wrote *Yellow Back Radio,* and that he tended to consider the Western genre as an example of fiction legitimately getting the better of reality:

> Yellow Back writers were really dudes from the East like me. The cowboys would read their books and begin to ape the exaggerations of themselves they read. A case of life imitating art.[3]

These "Yellow Backs" were popular Western novels, a genre which confers some stature to John Wesley Hardin, the killer hired by Gibson--"the famous gunslinger I've read in da lurid yellow kivered books" (p. 128). Another reference to "Yellow Back" could be found on the shelves of Drag's library: "The shelves were full of yellow kivered books and volumes on the life of the benevolent despotess Catherine the Great" (p. 114). The "Radio" element in the title and in the name of the city of Yellow Back Radio, which is located about fifty miles from Video Junction, is surprising; although this reference to the mass media seems satisfying, as Loop Garoo's magic could be understood to account for the breakdown in the station. In the interview quoted above Reed brings all these elements together in his explanation of the title's meaning:

> The title ... was based upon a poem by Lorenzo Thomas called Modern Plumbing Illustrated ... I based the book on old radio scripts in which the listener constructed the sets with his imagination; that's why "radio"; also because it's an oral book, a talking book ... There's more dialogue than scenery or description. "Yellow back" because that's what they used to call Old West books about cowboy heroes, they were "yellow covered books and were usually lurid and sensation," so the lurid scenes are in the book because that is what the form calls for. They're not in there to shock. "Broke-down" is a take off on Lorenzo Thomas's "Illustrated." When people say "Break it down," they mean to strip something down to its basic components. So *Yellow Back Radio Broke-Down* is the dismantling of a genre done in an oral way like radio.[4]

This last remark points to the novelty of Reed's attempt in his second novel. Fiction, stripped of its defenses, with its back to the wall, is thus dismantled, reduced from a complex whole to the sum total of its discrete elements. In *The Free-Lance Pallbearers* Reed's narrative was essentially exuberant, full of proliferations and excrescences, or whirling upon linguistic merry-go-rounds whose spirals were hard to arrest. Here, Reed himself undertakes to break things down, to slow the narrative movement in order to designate its processes and to catalogue the elements and conventions of which he makes use not without derision. From paranoid, Reed's style becomes schizoid in the disjunctive mode of Nathanael West whom he admires. *Yellow Back Radio* thus owes much to comic strips, not only because each sequence can work forward and backward in time and space but also because even the typographical arrangement juxtaposes description and dialogue in blocks (units might be a better term) separated by wide blanks. *Yellow Back Radio* is visually characterized by its discontinuity, the basic elements being rather long sentences, remarkable for their lack of relief. Similarly, each character speaks his (or her) lines, then is silent, seldom angry or excited enough to shout in capitals. Each narrative block seems to repudiate narration in order to become a set of stage directions rather than a description. In brief, the novel assumes the function of a film script.

Stripped down to such minimalness, fiction is offered almost defenseless to the reader's manipulating appetites. He can slow down or speed up its course, which implies an increased participation on his part. This is a characteristic of what Reed calls "an oral book, a talking book. People say they read it aloud: that is, it speaks through them, which makes it a *loa*."[5] For Reed, the spirit which moves the participant in a voodoo ceremony is synonymous with inspiration, and he speaks of his works as being dictated to him by the *loas*. Here, voice alone can animate what would otherwise remain a flat comic strip. The narrator's status is affected by this; at the opening, he is an omniscient author/raconteur:

> Folks. This here is the story of the Loop Garoo Kid. A cowboy so bad he made a working posse of spells phone in sick. A bullwhacker so unfeeling he left the print of winged mice on the hides of crawling women. A desperado so ornery he made the Pope cry and the most powerful of cattlemen shed his head to the Executioner swine. (p. 1)

We thus launch right into a "tall tale" with its unbelievable hyperboles. The first stage in a rhetorical strategy aimed at creating the mythical character of Loop also presents a rather accurate summary of the plot; it is programmatic and invites the reader to leave things in the narrator's hands, or rather in his mouth. When read aloud, the narrative is sustained and given credibility by the narrator/reader, whose audience is much wider than the part of himself which listens to him reading. The reader thus becomes actor/narrator while remaining necessarily part of the audience.

As an accomplice vindicating the "tall tale" and a "do-it-yourself" maker of fiction from the separate parts of the "broke-down" fictional kit, the reader refers to the directions for use provided by the author and adopts the latter's perspectives concerning genre and form, even when disagreeing with his ideological outlook. In *Yellow Back Radio* more than in any other novel Reed alludes to texts and books, developing a network of intertextuality in order to confront his aesthetics with conflicting stance and to clearly differentiate himself from other schools. All of this takes place within the very genre of the comic strip Western which sets up character, background and scene according to their appropriate canonic function and status.

First of all, Reed aims at repudiating the sort of mimetic fiction which has been revered by "the great tradition"; this is expressed by the cultural revolution of the Flower Power children who have driven the adults out of town:

> For three hours a day we went to school to hear teachers praise the old. Made
> us learn facts by rote. Lies really bent upon making us behave. *We decided to*
> *create our own fiction.* (p. 10; emphasis mine)

As the circus for whom Loop is employed arrives, what assuages the children's
suspicion (together with the traveller's costumes) is Jack the Barker's allusion to
the Seven Cities of Cibola, which significantly symbolize, not an Eldorado of
wealth, but a "magnificent legendary American paradise where...man could be
free to dream" (p. 24). When the surviving children participate in the "jigsaw of
a last minute rescue" in the final chapter (here fiction is explicitly called a
"puzzle," i.e. a playful putting together of irregular, imbricating parts), they have
actually discovered Cibola and it is, as could be expected, "a really garish super
schmaltzy super technological anarcho-paradise" (p. 170), which smacks of
Marcusian utopia. Moreover, at the last moment, the children leave Loop alone
on stage, forsaking the "broke-down" to turn to a different performance, this
time an audio-visual one: "Let's go, the late late show is about to begin on the
boob toob and we can watch eating Pooped Out Soggies" (p. 173).

In his vignette-like advertisement for the circus, Jack comments:

> Stupid historians who are hired by cattlemen to promote reason, law and order -
> toad men who adore facts - say that such an anarchotechnological paradise...is
> as real as a green horse's nightmare. Shucks, I've always been a fool, eros
> appeals to me more than logos. I'm just silly enough to strike out for it
> tomorrow...(p. 25)

As should be expected, the narrative will apply itself to realizing the prophecy
thus evoked. Jake is, in fact, the mouthpiece of Loop, who represents the Artist
(he later defines himself as "the comic jester"), and Reed himself is his twin,
born, like Jake, in Tennessee.

In Chapter Two, the writer is defined *a contrario*, in a dazzling exchange
between Loop and Bo Shmo. The latter, whose only talent was playing
Hoagland Howard Carmichael's "Buttermilk" backwards in the 1930s, has
acquired the reputation of being a charismatic leader among fellow citizens who
yearn to be duped. He is at the head of the socio-realist gang and declares, "All
art must be for the end of liberating the masses. A landscape is good only when
it sees the oppressor hanging from a tree" (p. 37). This pronouncement of the
part time autocrat monarchist and guru does not apply exclusively to a CP
commissar, but satirizes whoever would dictate what the writer ought to write,
including black nationalist critics.[6] In fact, Bo's literary specialty is "those
suffering books I wrote about my old neighborhood and how hard it was."
Ideological rivalry as well as fear of economic competition lead Bo's men to
hasten the death which awaits Loop in the desert:

> If he makes it across the desert he might land a typewriter and do a book on his trials. He'll corner the misery market and pound out one of those Christian confessionals to which we are so much endeared. (p. 26)

Lacking originality, as might be expected, the socio-realists thus bury Loop up to his neck in the sand and smear his face with jam.

The criticism leveled at Loop by Bo interestingly recalls that heaped on Reed's first fictional attempt by a number of American critics: Loop is "an alienated individualist," making "deliberate attempts at being obscure," a "buffoon, an outsider and frequenter of sideshows." Bo ends up calling him:

> Crazy dada nigger that's what you are. You are given to fantasy and are off in matters of detail. Far out esoteric bullshit is where you're at. In those suffering books that I write...every gundrop machine is in place while your work is a blur and a doodle. I bet you can't create the difference between a German and a Redskin. (pp. 35-36).

One can note in passing the allusion to Amiri Baraka's "black dada nihilismus," with which Reed did side, and the definition of his own fiction as "a blur and a doodle," but one should emphasize Loop's statement of his novelistic aims: "What if I write circuses. No one says a novel has to be one thing. It can be anything it wants to be, a vaudeville show, the six oclock news, the mumblings of wild men saddled by demons" (p. 36). All those are fair descriptions of Reed's fiction, and the novel's declaration of independence vis-a-vis its author is even more striking: the novel is said to become anything *it* wants to (not anything its author wants it to), as if it were gifted with a sort of autonomy. This is a distinctly post-modernistic position.

Endowed as it is with the power of generating itself, and with its tendency to give precedence to comedy and dreams, it is logical that such fiction should take off on the least suggestion or challenge from pseudo-realism. A fine example of this is to be found in Chapter Three, entitled "Loop Garoo Comes Back Mad." Pages 59-65 are devoted to Loop's elaborate do-it-yourself voodoo ceremony aimed at providing the Avenger with a panoply of spells to be unleashed against the villains. The following episode begins, as could be expected, with a violent outbreak against the cattlemen:

> The Germans attacked the next day. There had always been skirmishes to the north between these dauntless, hearty warriors and the cattlemen who taxed them heavily, rode off with their women, rustled their cattle, stole their best grazing areas and burned their corn.
> A warrior blew a signal from the top of Blackfoot Mountain. (p. 66)

Caught up in a whirlwind of battle axes, naked bodies and horned helmets, the reader, as accustomed as he is to repeated skirmishes against Red Indians and to Reed's frequent puns and surface games, first believes that there is an error in the text, if he has not actually misread "Indian" for "German." Yet, "German" is repeated, and one realizes that Germans and Indians have the same battle tactics. Is Reed confused? Certainly not. Only then does the attentive reader remember that, on page 36, Bo Shmo had told Loop, "I bet you can't create the difference between a German and a Redskin..." At that time, the phrase was supposed a gratuitous insult, yet it acted as a challenge which the fiction has later taken up. Although the present passage seems to vindicate Bo Shmo's accusation, subtle differences in detail do appear (between horned helmets and feather headgear, or tomahawks and battleaxes, for instance); even if, referentially, there is indeed little difference between "Germans" and "Redskins" as far as warfare is concerned.

The fictional challenge becomes compounded as violence increases and one fears that all the villains, Drag included, will be slain, bringing the novel to a premature end. Indeed, the battle scene (which is printed in italics) stops abruptly by being defined as a story within the story, the significance of which appears to lie less in the tale itself than in its telling:

> *The warriors obediently walked over to the horse's stall and were about to chop off its head* when it awoke--wringing wet and snorting from the effects of its recurrent nightmare. (p. 68)

The episode now defines itself as a dream; fiction thus explicitly appears to be the narration of tales, which repudiates the claim for its truth or verisimilitude made by socio- or neo-realism. This fictional episode clearly picks up the gauntlet thrown by Bo Shmo but it also disproves the contention of the "rationalists and law givers" who, earlier in the book, asserted that the anarcho-technological paradise Cibola was "no more real than a green horse's nightmare" (p. 25). From a current metaphor, here taken literally, a fictional episode has sprung whole. One could even say that Drag Gibson's green horse has a nightmare in the novel *because* a linguistic expression had challenged the possibility of such an occurrence. Likewise, the German (and not the Indian) raid on Drag's farm occurs because Bo Shmo, some forty pages earlier, had accused Loop in an aesthetic exchange of being unable to create the difference between the two. At the same time, the reality of fiction as such (not as a reflection, or mimesis, of any referential world) is vindicated, since there does indeed exist little discernible difference between the two groups in the attack episode and since the attack itself has just as much reality as the ugly dream of a fictional green horse, although this nightmare has been motivated in the plot by Loop's casting spells upon the ranch.

In this perspective, the reader must always be ready to consider that any potentiality enunciated in the narrative, be it on a trite linguistic or purely metaphoric level, can be realized later in the novel. For instance, when we hear that Drag Gibson keeps Chief Showcase around "in case the Pope wants to visit or something" (p. 126), this is not just a figure of speech; sure enough, the Pope will actually (and we might say, because of the phrase) pay a visit to Drag. This does not mean that anything can happen: rather, an eventuality evoked by the narrative can only become actualized according to certain rules (even if these are opposed to traditional novelistic processes) which contain the genre of the "broke down."

References to other literary or narrative genres are quite frequent in the book. Probably with the aim of emphasizing less the fictive character of artistic expression than the fact that it should not attempt reflection or mimesis, the narrator comments in the desert episode:

> Loop Garoo had to shoot his hoss...You ever see a horse shot in the movies? So that gives you an idea of the fluke of luck Loop was reeling in on this queer fish of a day. (p. 34)

Each character knows the limits of his role and the rules of the genre, with the result that telescoping narrative codes not only produces comedy but questions the rules which have heretofore prevailed. When left alone, a character acts and thinks according to the requirements of his role or of the given situation according to the genre. Thus Drag ponders upon his marital problems, "alone with his thoughts which is a spooky situation since Drag ...is also shorthand for something scaly, slimy and huge with dirt" (p. 47). He is contemplating getting rid of his wife when she appears:

> It was like a monster flickah drammer--the confrontation. Horrible Hybrid meets Spooky Situation. Horrible Hybrid was dripping wet...In a quivering voice the Various Arrangement of Dead Parts said: What happened Drag dear husband you were supposed to bring me a towel? (p. 49)

Or, upon hearing Showcase's helicopter in the desert, Bo Shmo exclaims: "Gads! the arch-nemesis of villains like me. The Flying Brush Beeve Monster. Let's get out of here" (p. 37). Here, the character (as opposed to the protagonist) remains a prisoner of the definition imposed upon him by fiction and of the part he is cast in: the villain, the monster perform accordingly, just as the Sheriff, the Banker, and the Reverend fulfill their social roles in Yellow Back Radio City. Horrible Hybrid herself, who is a symbol of the "broke down" since she is a "Various Arrangement of DeadParts," can only literally fall to pieces when she dies. Conversely, the good guys, the positive protagonists, are defined by their capacity for change, for conceiving other shapes and assuming several roles. Crossing the boundaries and limits of genre, Loop finds no difficulty in turning to another narrative type in order to describe his situation: "Not only would he be desert carrion but now something right out of Science Fiction was descending upon him from the heavens Loop thought" (p. 37). As a consequence, the character/role tends to be petrified in stereotyped discourse whereas the protagonist/author generates dynamic and eclectic fiction. Drag fears Loop's revenge because it is made inevitable by the literature he is found in: "He'll come after me...You know the revenge motif" (p. 48). Similarly, the Sheriff believes he can escape by taking shelter behind the clichés of the genre--"Now Kid, the Marshall will, what is a Western without tall tales and gaudy romance. Have a drink!" (p. 101)--when Loop arrives, Zoro-like, with whip in hand. Of course, this is not enough to save the Sheriff. As Loop later tells Drag: "No amount of romantic dosage is going to save your neck, dead man, Heroes given to hyperbole--I even chased the Marshall out of town!" (p. 117).

Intelligence versus violence, imagination versus rhetoric, fantasy versus sentimentalism, such is Reed's aesthetic, forcibly outlined by Chief Showcase as he swoops down in his helicopter to rescue Loop from Bo Shmo:

> Those mediocre bandits...Deserts are for visions not for materialists. Read any American narrative about crossing-apparitions, ravens walking about as tall as men, the whole golden phantasmagoria...I'm a kind of patarealist Indian going around inventing do dads. This machine comes in better than nags and creaky stagecoaches. Stupid shmucks and books around here think it's some kind of flying ghost cow...Bo Shmo and the cattlemen are in the same routine. Afraid of anything that can get off the ground, materialists that they are--anything capable of groovy up up and aways strikes terror in their hearts. (p. 38)

Along these lines, the narrative continually opposes conflicting aesthetics. For Showcase, functionalism and fun are more important than harmony and beauty. He reminisces:

> The Indian names Toohoolhoolzote, Looking Glass and Alan-Afraid-Of-His-Horse which opened up new possibilities of being named after phobias, objects and even words which didn't mean anything but sounded like music...Chief Showcase is a kind of letdown. I assure you it works though. You see I'm Chief Cochise's cousin which makes me Chief Showcase. Yuk, yuk,yuk,yuk. (p.41)

Even between well-intentioned cowboys, the so-called logic of grammatical rules easily leads to joking:

> You mean moose, don't you bartender? the Marshal asked.
> No Marshal meese. Goose is to geese what moose is to meese. I know we're out in the old frontier but everything can't be in a state of anarchy, I mean how will we communicate?
> You got a point there, Skinny added, but we cowpokes make up language as we go along. Compare our names for landscape, towns, industry, with those of tenderfoots back East--Syracuse, Troy, Ithaca...Seem to worship Europe. Why there's a whole school in New York of poets writing like Frenchmen. But when you get out here, except for those names given by injuns and Spaniards, cowpoke genius takes over--Milk River, Hangtown, Poker Flats, Tombstone, Boot Hill. (pp. 53-54)

Similarly, every speechmaker or poet in the book has an original style, perceived differently by others. The tortured lyricism of the masochist Reverend who declares, "Stomp me o lord!!/ I am the theoretical mother of all insects!!/ mash my 21 or so body segments!!" (p. 101), is applauded by the cowboys as "poetic allegory." The vengeful lyrics of Chief Showcase hurling maledictions at his people's tyrants in "Wolf Ticket" meet with the approval of a lone hurdy-gurdy girl ("What bitter and tortured Americana. Hey Indjun come over here and loop up my dress" (p. 79)), while an obscure academic, "a Japanese semanticist" out of the curtains, is dissatisfied with the ethnic tendency of the "child of nature" to overuse the word "like." Last but not least, Loop's wild lyricism lends scope to his voodoo invocation which culminates in:

> *O Black Hawk American Indian houngan of Hoo-Doo please do open up some*
> *of these prissy orthodox minds so that they will no longer call Black People's*
> *American experience "corrupt" "perverse" and "decadent"... Teach them that*
> *anywhere people go they have experience and that all experience is art.* (p. 64)

And the two black traitors, Alcibiades and Jeff, who listen to him are only able to laugh and remark that "with gossip columnists invading our skulls you should not be surprised that we should ridicule anything we can't understand" (p. 65).

There could be no better plea for cultural tolerance.[7] In fact, an open-minded approach is rare indeed for, to the average character, a stroke of originality is worse than the plague. As soon as he leaves his prescribed role, he loses his head, and he is quick to notice that he is literally out of character. For instance, when Reverend Boyd, having drunk himself to a state of delirium tremens, says "something about a Gila monster who was God," Drag retorts, "Those Protestants, so lazy with allegory." The cowpokes immediately react with, "What did you say, boss?" And Drag is forced to apologize, "Nothing boys, just a blue streak inflaming my mind. It'll go away" (p. 46). A far-fetched aesthetic comparison made by Skinny, the uncultured overseer, brings about a similar self-correction:

> This place is really getting eerie...there's a disproportionate amount of shadows
> in reference to the sun we get--it's like a pen and ink drawing by Edward
> Munch or some of them Expressionist fellows.
> Huh?
> See, got me talking out of my noodle. (p. 97)

Fiction cannot treat a specific character worse than by putting in his mouth someone else's text, a text he is not supposed to generate according to the rules of realism. When he discovers he can utter such discourse, he has to admit he is mad.

Is the point, then, just to achieve striking effects, clever staging and theatricality, when, for example, John Wesley Hardin, the gunman, finds good excuses to appear too late on stage ("Sorry I missed your cue, Drag, but I was looking for your copy of the good book?" (p. 115)). Maybe, but there exists a fundamental difference between traditional forms and Reed's innovations: traditional aesthetics are expressed in the grand show of Crucifixion which, Loop believes, exploited gaudy effects like striking *deus ex machina*, lightning and thunder techniques on Golgotha. When he envisions his capture and possible martyrdom, Loop does not want to "set up his own happening," as Pope Innocent accuses, but to emphasize through parody the emptiness of Christian ritual. Loop's strength consists in never taking anything too seriously, including himself. He thus defines himself as "the cosmic jester" (p. 165), more harmless than any kind of sacrificial scapegoat in the tragic mode. He stakes his claim for a type of aesthetics characterized, through laughter, as "monkey business":

> What's your point? Horse opera. Clever, don't you think? And the Hoo-Doo cult of North America. A much richer art form than preaching to fishermen and riding into a town on the back of an ass. (p. 163)

As a result, when the black cowboy on Drag's green horse crashes in upon the scene of his second wedding, Drag accurately defines him as a "BLACK MAGICIAN TO END THEM ALL PSYCHING UP A BAD LOONED SPEECH OF GRAFFITI THAT WOULD ESTRANGE POPEYE" (p. 81). As an avant-garde artist who seriously works to liberate language without mistaking his role as a writer for a mission, Loop remains conscious of the critical establishment he derides. Chief Showcase also admits of taking his audience into consideration:

> I don't even want to get into how Moses sneaked around the Pharaoh's court abusing his hospitality by swiping all the magic he could get his clutches around. If I run down that shit, Loop, the book won't be reviewed in Manhattan. (p. 39)

Loop retorts, "If I ever sell this mind sauna to Hollywood I'll give you all of Gene Autry's bicycles" (p. 43).

This fictional type, which had initially been defined as a "brokedown," is finally that of the "horse opera" taken to its (il)logical extremes. It abolished space and time conventions as well as linguistic ones, mocking in turn each of its successive avatars. Reed never apologizes and hardly explains his aim when he mixes centuries or superimposed settings; thus, gigantic prehistoric sloths coexist with futuristic technology, Germans with Red Indians, Revolutionary War generals with late nineteenth-century cowboys, fiery dragons with the Pope; and Loop can be rescued by a group of Amazons from being beheaded on the day when the annexation of Texas is decreed, with the Seven Cities of Cibola looming on the horizon. All the elements of this gigantic jigsaw puzzle already existed or, when need be, are invented on the spot. As a result, anachronism becomes impossible, and character can allude simultaneously to the guillotine as a device from the "recent" (1789) French Revolution and to the crosses marking American graves at Omaha Beach. Like time, space is distorted and becomes distended; the American East and West coalesce in the same quest for power. Fiction itself can jump unexpectedly ahead, reverse and backtrack in low gear, or take off for the heavens like Showcase's Brush Beeve Monster or the Pope's ship.

Linguistic dexterity, linked with a coherent, if often far-fetched, use of lexical resources, gives Reed's fiction the impulse necessary to bring the pieces of the puzzle together nicely in the end. Meaning is impacted from one term to another, from one episode to the next like a ball in a pinball machine, ringing bells, lighting markers, bumping back and forth and ascoring again and again. As in *The Free-Lance Pallbearers,* Reed's language is characterized by the blending of many styles and levels to which an often near-phonetic transcription gives a degree of homogeneity. But syntax and use are less strictly Afro-American than in the earlier novel, and hardly realistic; rather than ethnic speech, they reconstruct the parlance of the media as befits the genre. The vocabulary ranges from pseudoscientific terms like "oviposit" to words disfigured by common usage like "stiffificate." There is definitely more invention through semantic combination than through word coinage; however, Reed resurrects a number of obsolete terms, particularly black slang of the 1920s and specific agricultural vocabulary. An example of this is "woodshed" (an improvised solo in jazz circles), which is superbly fitted to Loop's Improvisation of a voodoo ritual in his cave. Another is "mitt man," which seems to spring from some Teutonic dream and has a touch of the pimp as Sal Mustache ecstatically applies it to Loop. The term takes on its full meaning when it is applied to a religious charlatan by association with Christ: it seems to be a Reedian transcription of "myth man" though it was coined half a century ago.

The abundant similes are just as hilarious as they are appropriate. Drag, for instance, has "an ego as wide as the Grand Canyon"; the guillotine invented by the French is "a device said to be as rational as their recent revolution." An utterance may even lose track of itself, as when Drag says, "I'm a big man in these parts, fish fill my fill I mean full fish my swim" (p. 74); and stops short without even bothering to correct his sentence, yet gets an appropriate response from Sal. Or noises simply become language, such as Showcase's "yuk, yuk, yuk" or the Marshal's "her, her her," not to mention the "va-va-voom" of engines and other sounds which belong to comic strip captions.

Comedy often arises simply from the accumulation, or agglomeration, of terms, as in the sentence, "We've braved alkali, coyotes, wolves, rattlesnakes, catamounts, hunters" (p. 115). Sometimes, this is coupled with grotesque descriptions:

> The street was a dumpheap of Brueghel faces, of Hogarth faces, of Coney
> Island hotdog kissers, ugly pusses and sinking mugs, whole precincts of flat

peepers and silly lookers. The sun's wise broad lips smiled making the goats
horny with cosmic seed as monstrous shapes who could never unbend their
hands all looked as the Marshal ripped off his badge, boarded his horse and
rode out of town. (p. 104)

Here accumulation is less important than the juxtaposition of connotations
hinting at widely different fields of reference (lurid "cultured" caricature;
popular imagery; mythological pan-eroticism), all in the context of stereotyped
behavior, and surface baroque becomes the mark of surrealism. In fact, if one
compares the triumphant parade of Eclair Porkshop in Soulsville (in *The Free-
Lance Pallbearers*) with Pope Innocent's ride into Yellow Back Radio on a bull,
one quickly perceives that, although they are picturesque and pertinent in both
cases, the symbols refer mostly to an invented, synthetic system in the first case
and mostly to a corpus of beliefs rooted in Western ideological tradition in the
latter. The brief apparition of Reverend Boyd as a winged and electrified imp
(whom a papal squirt incapacitates at once) is a response to Drag's mockery of
Protestants for their lack of an allegorical sense. Yet, on the semantic level, this
apparition serves to turn the scene into an extended metaphor or to locate the
discourse on the level of a "morality play"--which actually happens in the final
dialogue between Pope Innocent and the Loop Garoo Kid.

   Without this opposition and mythical complementarity in which the conflict
between diverse avatars of the static and the dynamic, of good and evil,
functions, the whole narrative would be reduced to a comic strip, a cleverly
structured but one-dimensional series of syntagmatic sequences proliferating in
all spatiotemporal directions but devoid of paradigmatic depth. In fact, above the
appropriate creation of a "broke down" technique, the success of *Yellow Back
Radio* is due to the ability of Reed's fiction to reach beyond thematic
developments and manicheistic chrestomachy, not so much in the direction of
parallel fantasies as towards the deeper areas of our subconscious imagination,
to fly "up up and aways" in order to reconcile our dreams and our beliefs.

   In later novels, such as *Mumbo Jumbo* and *Flight to Canada* (1976), Reed
makes more refined use, respectively, of the clash between antithetic cultures as
expressed in gang warfare and of the interplay between history and fiction in the
South and the continuing racial and Civil War. In those two novels he exploits
each direction more fully and, possibly, more artistically than he did in *Yellow
Back Radio*. However, the balanced blend of challenging thematic development
and "reconstructed" form is unique here; possibly making his second novel his
richest attempt to date at exploring new verbal techniques as well as at reflecting
critically upon the possibilities of fiction in the post-modern age.

NOTES

1. "Introduction," *19 Necromancers from Now,* New York: Doubleday, 1970, p.
xvii.

2. See, for instance, Neil Schmitz in "Neo-HooDoo: The Experimental Fiction of Ishmael Reed," *Twentieth Century Literature*, 20 (April 1974), 135.

3. "Ishmael Reed: A Self-Interview," *Black World*, June 1974, p.25.

4. *Ibidem*.

5. *Ibidem*, p. 24.

6. One may wonder whether this plea does not reflect, culturally speaking, a return to traditional stances, such as art vs. commitment. Reed's position, however, has to be judged globally and his activities in the publishing field provide enough evidence of his effort to serve the needs of cultural minorities by providing alternate outlets to the monopoly of New York publishing houses.

7. Most Black Aestheticians either overlooked Reed's writings or else did not know how to deal with them. In *The Way of the New World* (1975), Addison Gayle acknowledges Reed's definition of the novel as "anything it wants to be" yet only mentions him as a superior satirist whose novels verge on the surrealistic. *In Black World* (June 1975), Houston Baker is rather severe in his review of *The Last Days of Louisiana Red* because of its satire of Blacks. *Negro Digest / Black World,* however, devoted much space to reviews of Reed's books and articles by him.

The Afro-American Novel Since 1960, Eds. Peter Bruck and Wolfgang Karrer, B&R Guner Publishing, 1982: 167-189.

1970s

MUMBO JUMBO (1972)

Part vision, part satire, part farce, part funferal

Alan Friedman/Review

The Norton Anthology of Poetry spans the centuries from Chaucer to Reed. Whether he likes it or not, Ishmael Reed has for some time now occupied a black outpost in a white landscape. To judge from his new book, he doesn't like it much. His latest work, written with *black* humor, is a satire on the unfinished race between the races in America and throughout history. It is a book of deliberate unruliness and sophisticated incongruity, a dazzling maze of black-and-white history and fantasy, in-jokes and outrage, erudition and superstition. Not only to white readers like myself will the way into and out of this maze be puzzling. For though it's a novel, the author's method is not novelistic. Wholly original, his book is an unholy cross between the craft of fiction and witchcraft.

I don't mean merely that *Mumbo Jumbo* is about HooDoo or VooDoo. "Black Herman walks to the bed, picks up her scarf, and casts it to the floor where it becomes a snake." I mean that it attempts, through its deadpan phantasmagoria of a plot, and through the black art of the Magus as storyteller, to achieve the kind of hold on the reader's mind that from ancient times and in primitive contexts has always been associated with the secret Word, the sacred Text.

The plot of *Mumbo Jumbo* is mind-boggling. In the 1920s an epidemic called Jes Grew begins to infect the United States, especially its black citizens. Topsy said he "jes' grew," but Reed traces the origins of the Jes Grew infection back to the Egyptian god Osiris. As the plague spreads in the 1920s, a worldwide conspiracy, the "*Mu'tafikah*(!)," begins to seize African, Oriental, and native American art treasures from white museums (Centers of Art Detention) in order to return them to the peoples who created them. Locked in deadly combat with this "Black Tide of Mud" are "an ancient society known as the Atonist Path" (Aton, the Sun God), "its military arm the Wallflower Order," and the medieval Knights Templars. As someone in the book notices, "It has been an interesting 2000 years."

But just what is this potent infection the author calls Jes Grew? "Ask Louis Armstrong, Bessie Smith, your poets, your painters, ask them how to catch it. Ask those people who be shaking their tambourines impervious of the ridicule they receive from Black and White Atonists, Europe the ghost rattling its chains down the deserted halls of their brains. Ask those little colored urchins who 'make up' those new dance steps and the Black cook who wrote the last lines of the 'Ballad of Jesse James.' Ask the man who, deprived of an electronic guitar, picked up a washboard and started to play it. The Rhyming fool who sits in Re'-mote Mississippi and talks 'crazy' for hours. The dazzling paradizing punning mischievous pre-Joycean style-play for Cakewalking, your Calinda, your Minstrelsy give-and-take of the ultra-absurd. Ask the people who put wax paper over combs and blow through them. In other words, Nathan, I am saying Open-Up-To-Right-Here."

The book is like that, frankly and consummately freewheeling, part historical funferal, here a highbrow satire, here a low-key farce, even *roman a clef*. The villain of the piece is a controversial book publisher named Hinckle Von Vampton who wears "a black patch on his eye from an old war wound." But Hinckle Von Vampton also turns out to be a thousand-year-old Crusader who had learned to cheat death through a secret diet. Reed loves to mix his elements: spiritualists with cops and robbers, literary criticism with caricature, "a little bit of jive talk and a little bit of North Africa," romance and necromancy, Egyptology, etymology, bibliography, hagiography, politics, Teutonic knights, and marvelously bizarre headline--"MUSCLE-WHITE BAGS COON."

Through all this, though he tells a fast-paced story, the author plays fast and loose with the conventions of storytelling. For example, in the very midst of a kidnapping, the tension is interrupted to provide--as a motive for the kidnapping itself--a long myth of Osiris, Moses and Jethro. Readers will find the experience rough, unless they are willing to put aside the usual expectations about what a novel is supposed to be, and the satisfaction it is rumored to provide. Ishmael Reed is unique and he has other things to offer. If one stays with *Mumbo Jumbo*, uncannily, the book begins to establish its very own life, on its very own terms.

The terms are demanding. Reed wants to convince, not persuade. When William Golding unfolds his fable in *Lord of the Flies*, when Kurt Vonnegut spins his satire in *Cat's Cradle,* we are led to believe in the fantasy by a persuasive context: by tone, detail, characters, timing and drama. Disbelief is in fact easy to suspend because belief is what the audience craves and the storyteller loves to create. But Ishmael Reed, in the manner of William Burroughs, avoids persuasion, he invites disbelief. Our very refusal (inability) to lend credence to the lurid anti-logic of *Naked Lunch* leaves us reeling--and then, if we can still turn pages at all, mesmerized by the novel's inner vision. Still, Burroughs deals in junk nightmares, Reed in black ritual. "I . . . I don't want to be difficult with you, Hierothant 1 says pressing the button so that 3 weird looking dudes in 3d Man Theme trenches enter through the doors leading to the round room. One carrys the ritual dagger on a pillow."

Reed's tone here and elsewhere is curiously flat, opaque, hypnotic and carefully chosen. Earlier, in *The Free-Lance Pallbearers*, he displayed a prose style of considerable transparency and brilliance. That first novel was a satire, too. A tale of slapstick and martyrdom; persuasive, but not convincing. His second novel, *Yellow Back Radio Broke-Down*, was a Gnostic Western, a bizarre epic of cowpunching, hexing, execution and papal intervention. So wild that there the question of belief could hardly arise. "Drag bent over and french kissed the animal between his teeth, licking the slaver from around the horse's gums." "A novel," the hero asserted after shooting his horse, "can be anything it wants to be, a vaudeville show, the six o'clock news, the mumbling of wild men saddled by demons."

Mumbo Jumbo is all of these, but it is also sterner stuff than anything in his earlier books. The author is after bigger game now, and he has taken a risk. His terms in *Mumbo Jumbo* go beyond those of fiction. Beneath the passions of individual characters, beneath the conflict of blacks and whites, beneath every plague and blessing in the book, lies an opposition between the gods, between Osiris and Aton (compare Dionysos and Apollo). There is a precedent, a novel at once satiric and holy: "The Golden Ass" of Apuleius written for the ancient sect of Isis. But that was long ago. And Reed sees the problem:

"A sacred Black Work, if it came along today would be left unpublished." It would be "the essential Pan-Africanism . . . artists relating across continents their craft, drumbeats from the aeons, sounds that are still with us." However, since the ancient Text is still missing, "we will make our own future text."

So I suspect that for Ishmael Reed *Mumbo Jumbo* is something a good deal more than a novel. Through all the wild gyrations of its black comedy, he casts a nonfiction spell, he weaves an incantation with footnotes, he endows his Text with power. And if one reads it through, one risks succumbing to the text . . . or as Reed once put it in a poem, disappearing into it.

the hunger of this poem
  is legendary
it has taken in
  many victims.

From *The New York Times Book Review* 6 August 1972, pp. 1, 22. Copyright © 1972 by The New York Times Co. Reprinted by permission.

The Black roots are back

Lorenzo Thomas/Review

Back in the early '60s, Ed Sanders promised the arts would soon provide a total assault on the culture. By culture, he meant the madness that informs Ted Agnew and Archie Bunker, which is satire without purpose. But then what can you expect from corporate t.v.? The serious artists of our moment are fulfilling Sanders's prophesy--if that is, indeed, what it was. Total assault. Sanders and Manson take care of the sacred cows, the New York poets melt the golden calf into junk jewelry. Bijou. And the Black writers tell it as it is. Whatever "it" may be pretending to be.

Mumbo Jumbo is another further; it goes beyond assault to re-definition. Ishmael Reed is one of the people who are defending the culture that is replacing the madness called culture we are suffering now. He is one of the original members of the Black Arts movement but his concern covers the entire spectrum of our condition. He was one of the founders of the East Village Other/underground press phenomenon and did Ramparts-style investigative reporting for a Black newspaper in Buffalo when today's bright stars were still running to the deli for coffee.

As with Lennox Raphael's play *Che!*, all Ishmael Reed's works begin with a willing disruption of belief in the imitation society of America. His first novel, *The Free-Lance Pallbearers*, showed the multiple fallacies of the so-called Black ghetto, and *Yellow Back Radio Broke-Down* showed a kinship to underground comix and completely dissected the American myth of the open road. Reed's current book, *Mumbo Jumbo*, deals with a more accessible reality (i.e., more demonstrably historical) than his previous novels did, but the incisive method is the same. *Mumbo Jumbo* is funny, if you can stand satire that talks about *you*.

The book is, on the simplest level, a detective story concerning stolen documents and international "terrorism." Classic. Of course, all of this is semantically and politically determined. Everything is subjective. Like the Munich Olympic games. Or the Pentagon papers. You understand? These are very satirical portraits of Carl Van Vechten, Noble Drew Ali, George Schuyler, Nat Hentoff, and Hugh M. Hefner. Roman à clef? More like the dirty dozens.

Foolishly, someone will ask what *Mumbo Jumbo* is all about. What?! Josephine Baker on the cover. And a rose. C'est la vie. The 1920s the "jass" Age and something called Jes Grew (Black Art/nigger cult-ure) is sweeping . . . that's right SWEEPING . . . the USA with or without Chevvies (sorry, Wordsworth). The entrenched witchcraft is fighting back. Plots. Violence. Thought. Sell-outs (both kinds). The Harlem Renaissance. The stock market disaster. Lawd! Proof of the assassination of Warren Gamaliel Harding, the first Negro President. . .

In fact, it's a disservice to attempt to summarize the plot because *Mumbo Jumbo* is not only a novel--it is a history book dealing with the prolific realities that Mr. Toynbee managed to overlook. It is also a spell said by a very efficient houn'gan (which Doctor?) who, as Ishmael Reed allows himself to be identified as a novelist. What we have here is also a HooDoo narrative but Reed beat the ethnologists in the race to the printer's. The most useful thing I could do is tell what to expect from *Mumbo Jumbo*. Expect a complete turn around to the madness that currently reigns. Expect a madness that saves. Reed writes: ". . . life will never end; there is really no end to life; if anything it will be death." Sure you're right, Ishmael Reed! Expect nouvelle vague smack up against penny dreadful. Expect a mystery story with footnotes and bibliography containing 104 entries including Sam Charters, Gibbon, the Koran, and Stefan Zweig. And expect to be cussed out if you condone Nixon's nonsense.

Ishmael Reed offers an impolite explanation of what is happening in this country, why the logical elite of America (bright young people, Black and White) walk around looking like tramps. The fact is they have no other lifestyle to turn to unless the society is willing to recognize its Black roots. See, the peroxide played out with Jean Harlow's death and was only temporarily resurrected in Norma Jean. And she, sadly, is gone too. So the Black roots are back, America. You have to get right! And Reed's *Mumbo Jumbo* will show you how all the celebration of Life you think is your own is growing from those degraded and despised Black roots. Reed's historical focus on the Twenties is a ploy to convince you once and for all that peroxide America is through.

Check it out. At the very beginning W. E. B. Du Bois announced that the problem of the 20th century is the problem of the color line. He was right. Reed begins with that truth and proceeds armed with the cultural insights announced by Reuel Denney and Kees & Ruesch. What one does not notice clearly in oneself is what is truly personal. And real. Stuff folks will fight over. McLuhan deals with this. African peoples call it "possession." Makes sense, too. Zora Neale Hurston ran it all down. And on a lower level (the McLuhan level), these are the cultural influences in our lives that become so imperative we sometimes think they are natural. Thank you Robert Ardrey ha ha.

And this is what *Mumbo Jumbo* is really about, the crisis of a culture that refuses to acknowledge itself. Narcissus fleeing from the riverside. It eventually comes down to the personal horror of our daily and ignorant lives where we have all been swept up in the hell-bound train of America.

Consider the cultural realities through the medium of Ishmael Reed's fantasy. Begin with an understanding of the dilemma the White Cultural Imperative (as Harold Cruse calls it) has put all of us in. I call it madness, but there's more to it than that. The characters in Reed's evocation of the Harlem "Renaissance" are embroiled in the problem, but not in dull sociological terms. Reed deals on the level of Mythology, our ancient and futuristic Black Science. Sound science. Bebop. Reed's *Mumbo Jumbo* is in the African and Afro-

American tradition without compromise to Europeanism. He practices sound science.

Understand this. If the Black (i.e., African anywhere) literary tradition is really an "oral tradition," what we mean by that phrase is that Thought is simultaneous with Sound. Just like jazz. Or lies. Or the Truth. Did you ever hear Booker Little? Step out of a "dream." Know what Steve Cannon said about Babs Gonzalez? Did you ever sit in a cell down Catwalk Alley and shout stories to the brothers on down the line? It's magic. The opposite thing is the European mode of plotting, "characterization," "exposition." A system of exploitative development. In other words, the synchronization of several untruths which they call Fiction and teach in their schools. And their schools are geared to deal with Reed's *Mumbo Jumbo* in the same manner his book could be compared to Ellison's *Invisible Man* as a further extension of surrealist social comment; but *Mumbo Jumbo* is most nearly like Robert Deane Pharr's *The Book of Numbers* as a work of historical revision, an illuminating book. Or anything by J.A. Rogers.

Reed's revelations about America and the fading of beauty are not to be confused with Richard Brautigan's wistful ecological longings for the pristine vistas of Merriwether Lewis and whoever Clark. Perhaps not personally, but culturally, Brautigan's stance is the petulance of the disinherited; the fuming of the fence who has been taught to desire the ecstasies of a thief. Sartre, Levi-Strauss, and Barthes vis-à-vis Genet and Burroughs. Burroughs (whose writing Reed's sometimes resembles), of course, has it both ways: he is, in all reality, Baudelaire's "la plaie et le couteau." None of that here; and unlike Brautigan, what there is of Reed's anger comes from elsewhere. He is not one of the spiritual ecologists. The ecologists fear that, unlike Lewis and Clark, they will inherit an America with nothing left to steal and/or despoil. Ah, our cultural dilemma again!

I am not putting Brautigan down to build up Ishmael Reed the way *Time* magazine used *Mumbo Jumbo* to. In fact I dig Richard Brautigan for expressing a certain reality. But Ishmael Reed is coming from somewhere else. He is probably the best Black writer in America today, culturally Black--not just on the dust-jacket. For example, Brautigan's "woman in red" in *Trout Fishing in America* is out of the European tradition. She is la belle dame sans merci, the betrayer of John Dillinger (hero of all Caucasian have-nots in America one way or another). But Reed's "woman with the red dress on" is something else. Somebody. Beloved by Ray Charles and the Saints. The Lady. Even if she act crazy. She don't betray a man who loves her. She is the mother. Protection and riches. The Star. The water. Outpouring. The Star. An oath or vow. That's love. Revenge; when the chickens flutter to roost. And the United States is today, as Malcolm X perceived, a chicken's Capistrano. Check it out.

This is all reality on one level or many, if culture is real. And it is fantasy or fiction or Thought in a book. Ishmael Reed has put all that and much more into

Mumbo Jumbo, for those who listen and understand. *Mumbo Jumbo* is pure inner attainment. Bebop. Sound science.

Read Ishmael Reed. Then you will understand where we are. Where we are going. And you will know what "possessions" you will need for the trip.

The Village Voice 15 March 1973: 19+.

Nature as Sacred Text: An Ecocritical Reading of *Mumbo Jumbo*

Lisa Slappey/Article

Our relationship to our environment reflects our relationship to other human beings; both depend heavily on our notions of what is sacred. By reading the natural world as the sacred text of *Mumbo Jumbo*, I intend to show that Ishmael Reed connects the suppression of indigenous nature-based religions, in particular Vodoun, with global colonialism and environmental abuse. Exposing the fallacies and limitations of the Western monotheistic tradition, *Mumbo Jumbo* explores as an alternative the liberatory possibilities of ancient pantheistic nature-based religions. In this polyvocal novel, the environment speaks through the mythic and contemporary figures of Osiris and PaPa LaBas, one a deity and the other a houngan, both of whom are affiliated closely with the natural world.

Reed sees affinities between African and Native American tribes in terms of both their systems of belief and their victimizations by European and American political, cultural, and religious imperialism. He asserts that tribal peoples could be mutually useful in mounting a counterattack on Western Civilization, particularly by empowering themselves through the ancient stories and practices. In *Mumbo Jumbo*, Reed uses the Osirian system of belief as the mytho-historical background to provide just such a counter-narrative of colonialism. The powerful Egyptian deity Osiris is a fertility god associated with both the Black Bull Apis and the Nile; he is also the embodiment of the dead and resurrected king.[1] Osiris's scribe and interpreter, Thoth, whose words have magical qualities, is credited with inventing writing and languages. *Mumbo Jumbo* casts the Book of Thoth as the written text of Osiris's Jes Grew dances; it is this missing sacred work for which PaPa LaBas, the voodoo detective, searches. In the contemporary world, however, the ancient nature-based religions have been either corrupted or supplanted by Western monotheism or forced underground, surviving, for instance, as Haitian Vodoun, or the American version, Hoodoo. Reed would argue that all religions have pagan roots, and that all tribes, including the Europeans, could free themselves from various forms of oppression if only they would acknowledge those roots. Instead, *Mumbo Jumbo* shows our world as one of degeneracy and violence resulting from Set's witchery. The Atonists, followers of Set and precursors of the Christians and

Masons, with their military branch, the Wallflower Order, defenders of "the cherished traditions of the West,"[2] have been in power for more than two millenia. The loas are in their Petro mode; they are malevolent. The earth's spirits are angry at us and are therefore out of harmony. How did this imbalance happen, and how can the loas be appeased so that they will once again be the benevolent Rada spirits?

In part, the conflict is between indigenous and invading peoples, and between indigenous and imposed systems of belief. In essence, this novel depicts an ongoing war for cultural identity. Through the ancient Egyptian story of Osiris and Set, Reed provides a mythic narrative to explain the imposition of Western Civilization as a monocultural socio-political construct designed to inhibit and invalidate multicultural reality. Historically, imperialists have of necessity viewed the earth not as a sacred, living being, but only as a resource to be conquered and exploited for political and economic purposes. This disrespect for the earth translates directly into a disregard for human life. In *Mumbo Jumbo*, the witchery begins with Set, Osiris's brother, enemy, and murderer. Whereas "Osiris had developed such a fondness and attachment for Nature that people couldn't tell them apart" (166), his brother Set is a cannibal who hates humanity and the rest of the natural world: "Set hated agriculture and nature which he saw as soiled dirty grimy etc. . . . People hated Set. He went down as the 1st man to shut nature out of himself. He called it discipline. He is also the deity of the modern clerk, always tabulating, and perhaps invented taxes" (162). He is a frustrated control freak who epitomizes the constraints of a civilization invested in promoting only a single vision.

Whereas Osiris's religion springs autochthonously from the soil, Set's is a corruption of the Osirian rites, rewritten and imposed on the Egyptian people. Portraying Set as an unwelcome outsider, H. Te Velde writes that, "On the mythological level Set is a disturber of the peace, on the cosmic level a thunder-god, on the geographical level a foreigner."[3] The vast majority of the followers of the Atonist Path are either whites or assimilated people of color. Functioning as black Osiris's white brother, Set brings an important, if stereotypical, racial element to the story. He is the white man who would enslave and dismember his black brother in order to usurp the power that has been denied him. He desires everything his brother has: the kingdom, the adoration of the people, marriage to their sister Isis, rhythm. Dancing is an integral part of Osiris's religion and the main symptom of Jes Grew. Because Set cannot dance the Osirian rites, he wants to ban others from doing so as well. The last line of the Atonist creed hearkens back to Set's immobility: *Lord, if I can't dance, No one shall* (65).

Like other imperialists, such as the Spanish conquistadors, who were followed closely by Roman Catholic priests, Set uses religion as a tool for subjugation. He turns his anger and jealousy against his brother and his people, establishing himself as the one god through Atonism, which Akhenaton later reified as Egypt's state religion and which Reed suggests gave rise to the Western monotheistic religions. Through this self-deification, Set intends to build an empire by obliterating all forms of alterity and plurality. As a warmonger, Set is infuriated to see the Egyptian people "Enjoying themselves when there was hard work to be done, countries to invade, populations to subjugate. Egypt was prospering under Osiris and there was peace" (163). To destroy Osiris's pantheistic nature religion, Set's legislators "went through the old texts and started rewriting things to make Set look good and Osiris look bad" (174). Not surprisingly, doctoring the texts creates disharmony; Set can practice only black magic. Under Set's leadership, witchery is unleashed and evil prospers.

Set's mission to disempower the gods and their followers requires a desacralization of the natural world, a denial of spirituality where once it abounded. Worldwide, however, the priests and missionaries who introduced monotheism to the tribes encountered difficulty in overcoming deeply ingrained systems of belief rooted in the cycles of the natural world. Set can never eradicate Jes Grew, which springs from the ancient agricultural rites celebrating life and fertility. Dancers, chief among them Osiris, honor and emulate the plants and animals, encouraging them to multiply. The rites emphasize performativity, singing, and dancing through "a theater of fecundation generation and proliferation" (161). The Book of Thoth records these sexualized ritual dances as the Text of Jes Grew. The ancient ritual continues through the practice of Vodoun and through jazz, which Reed interprets as metaphors for the writing process. Louis Armstrong and Charlie Parker are Hoodoo houngans who play the improv text of Jes Grew. Vodoun is an amalgamation of various African, Roman Catholic, and Haitian Indian traditions that came together in Haiti, then spread to New Orleans and Brazil and back to West Africa. Reed believes that Vodoun is the universal religion because of its pagan base and syncretic nature. In an interview with Peter Nazareth, Reed stated, "that's what Vodoun does: bring people from all different nations and backgrounds together."[4] As a figure of unity, Osiris symbolizes the syncretism of Vodoun, whereas Set foments the divisiveness that characterizes the exclusionary practices of monotheism.

The stories passed down through the oral tradition give the people a means of resistance against the Western imperative, a method of maintaining their cultural identity, and a measure of hope that contemporary evils are merely temporary aberrations. Therefore, the sacred text sought in this novel is essential to cultural survival, even if, as Abdul Hamid proclaims, "the words [a]re unprintable" (95). *Mumbo Jumbo*'s lost text is the ancient Book of Thoth, but it never appears in Reed's novel. Intended as a guide for the people, it is the written version of Osiris's dances, which "taught people to permit nature to speak and dance through them" (165). The main force of the novel, Jes Grew is an "anti-plague" that "enliven(s) the host" (6) sweeping the United States in the 1920s, snaking like Damballah with jazz from New Orleans to Chicago to New

York, where it senses, correctly, that its Text has been collected. PaPa LaBas explains that "Jes Grew is the lost liturgy seeking its litany" and warns that "If it could not find its text then it would be mistaken for entertainment" (211). Reed's implication that the Harlem Renaissance could have brought the people to consciousness, but instead was reduced to "entertainment" and co-opted by white society, challenges the reader to look beyond the marketplace manifestations and acknowledge the underlying significance of African-American cultural traditions.

Conflict over who has possession of or access to the sacred text reveals the extent of the cultural conflict that drives *Mumbo Jumbo*. Throughout the ages, people and factions have sought the Text of Jes Grew. From Moses and Hinckle Von Vampton to Abdul Hamid to PaPas LaBas and the Haitian Benoit Battraville, everyone in *Mumbo Jumbo* has an investment in recovering the text: to either eliminate Jes Grew or promote it. Possession of the text, however, does not imply possession by the text. Much as in cases of voodoo possession, in which the loas emerge through supplicants, dancers are possessed by Jes Grew. Satisfied loas provide physical benefits from the spiritual world, bringing prosperity and keeping away the duppies. The question of who has the text is related to that of who has access to or control over the natural world and its inhabitants. The Atonist thug Biff Musclewhite is described as a "World War 1 combat veteran and hero who once told Nature where to go" (124), while another Atonist takes delight in charting the extinctions of species. The Atonists believe that they can maintain power by keeping the text to themselves, because as Buddy Jackson proclaims, "the Masonic mysteries were of a Blacker origin than we thought . . . the reason they wanted us out of the mysteries was because they were our mysteries!" (194). Recovering the text would mean recovering an entire African tradition, much like liberating stolen artifacts from museums to return them to the "aesthetically victimized civilizations" (15) that produced them could "conjure a spiritual hurricane which would lift the debris of 2,000 years from its roots and fling it about" (88). In fact, *Mumbo Jumbo* asserts that all of Western Civilization is built on Moses' misreading of the Egyptian fertility dances described in the Book of Thoth, a work he acquires from Osiris's widow, Isis.

Those who can read the texts have certain insights when they get the message right. Misreading, however, can have disastrous consequences. Moses's inability to read the Book leads to the creation of the Western patriarchal religions, which Reed posits as a corruption that incorporated some aspects of Osiris's religion (for instance, Isis and Horus become Mary and Jesus) while condemning others (pantheism, dancing, fertility rites). Moses bases his religion on the sacred text he stole from Isis, and makes his own Faustian deal with Set to promote Atonism. Moses becomes a *bokor*, or charlatan, rather than a *houngan*, a true practitioner of what PaPa LaBas terms The Work. The Book is so powerful that Moses must hide it; the Knights

Templar who find and translate the Book misread it because it refuses to reveal its true meaning to them: "the Book was not going to be their whore any more and gave them the worst of itself. It was saving all its love and Rada for when it reunited with its dance and music" (188). Hinckle Von Vampton worships a black doll, but encounters only the Petro aspect of the loas. As a result of this misreading, the Knights Templar and their Atonist descendants, the Masons, practice with the Left Hand. Misreading/misusing the text leads to disharmony, disunity, oppression, hatred, warfare, and evil. Only Abdul Hamid, Reed's representative of the Nation of Islam, can read the original text. He translates the Book of Thoth from heiroglyphics, a skill he taught himself while imprisoned. In fact, the collage effect of Abdul Hamid's education and technique "the way I taught myself became my style, my art, my process" (38) mirrors Reed's own. He states, "I have an anthology that's really going to shake them up" (39), yet he is so shaken by its revelations that he burns the Book. Although Abdul Hamid, who predicts the coming of Malcolm X, is in general an admirable character, here Reed criticizes the Black Muslims for departing from what he considers the original African spirituality by submitting to yet another form of institutional monotheism, and as Black Herman warns, "That bigoted edge of it resembles fascism" (40).

Among so many bad readers in *Mumbo Jumbo*, the best reader is perhaps PaPa LaBas, the voodoo detective whose business is reading the signs and clues. PaPa is, of course, a Jes Grew Carrier. His spiritual work at the Mumbo Jumbo Kathedral is unrecognizable to the Atonists, who cannot see past their stereotypes:

> He is contemplative and relaxed, which Atonists confuse with laziness because he is not hard at work drilling, blocking the view of the ocean, destroying the oyster beds or releasing radioactive particles that will give unborn 3-year-olds leukemia and cancer. PaPa LaBas is a descendant from a long line of people who made their pact with nature long ago. (45)

The son of a New Orleans root dealer, PaPa LaBas is the Legba character from the African tradition, the trickster houngan who serves as intermediary between the spiritual and material worlds. Although these worlds are not distinct, we need people like PaPa LaBas because we most often are so focused on the material aspects that we fail to communicate with the spirits that inhabit the natural world. PaPa opens people up to the loas, healing them by allowing the spirits to work through them. To appease the loas, who are often associated with ancestors, Voodoo rituals require offerings of animals and plants. PaPa warns Charlotte against revealing even diluted versions of The Work to Atonists: "Upset a loa's Petro and you will be visited by troubles you never could have imagined" (52). Charlotte's murder by Biff Musclewhite comes as no surprise. Skilled in the technical aspects of Hoodoo, PaPa LaBas gains confidence after his meeting with the Haitian practitioner, Benoit Battraville, reveals that his detective work has been correct.

Spiritual forces need the text as a focus to keep them visible and strong, and as much as *Mumbo Jumbo* wants to become, on a metanarrative level, its own sacred text, the novel demonstrates that Jes Grew exists outside its own written text within the text that is the natural world. PaPa LaBas predicts that even without its text, Jes Grew will survive because future generations of artists will write new texts. These textual messages have always been there in the stars, and PaPa LaBas suggests that Jes Grew could even have caused the Big Bang. They are written in the rhythms of the seasons, of music, of blood. They exist in the consciousness of certain people, the carriers of Jes Grew, and in the unconscious of others, extending through the continuum from the ancient to the contemporary to the future world.

NOTES

1. See E.A. Wallis Budge, *Osiris: The Egyptian Religion of Resurrection* (New Hyde Park, NY: University Books, 1961).
2. See Robert Gover, "An Interview with Ishmael Reed," *Black American Literature Forum* , 12.1 (1978), in which Reed states, "If you scratch the Christian-Judaic culture, underneath you got a Pagan. And the thing that would unite all these tribes is the thing I call Hoodoo" (15).
3. H. Te Velde, *Seth, God of Confusion*, trans. G.E. van Baaren-Pape (Leiden, Netherlands: E.J. Brill, 1967), p. 118.
4. Peter Nazareth, "An Interview with Ishmael Reed" (1979), in *Conversations with Ishmael Reed*, Eds. Bruce Dick and Amritjit Singh (Jackson: University of Mississippi Press, 1995), p. 193.

Previously unpublished essay (1998). Printed with permission.

Blacking the Zero: Toward a Semiotics of Neo-Hoodoo

Robert Elliot Fox/Article

It is my intention to be able to confirm: to work towards an iconography that reflects the memories and prophecies of spirits, known and unknown. And in so doing, cause that energy ancient and precognitive, to be released.[1]

Quickskill thought of all the changes that would happen to make a "Thing" into an "I Am." Tons of paper. An Atlantic of blood. Repressed energy of anger that would form enough sun to light a solar system. A burnt-out black hole. A cosmic slave hole.[2]

That which we call "close reading," the Yoruba call *Òdá fá* ("reading the signs").[3]

A good deal (though hardly enough) has been expressed regarding the Afro-American *alchemie du verbe*, both spoken and written; in this essay, however, I propose to go beyond, or shall I say, *behind* the words to the signs and symbols which also speak across the African continuum. Specifically, I want to inquire into the plurasignification of a device used in the praxis of Neo-Hoodooism by Ishmael Reed, who has placed his discourse in several of his crucial texts[4] under the sign ● ○, which, in an earlier version of this study,[5] I called Reed's "ontological emblem," but which is more appropriately identified as a *vé vé* (or *verver)*, a design which represents a *loa,* traced on the ground in flour and ashes in Haitian voodoo[6] ceremonies. The *vé vé* has its counterpart in the *grafia dos Orixas* used in Afro-Brazilian religions such as Umbanda. According to one exegete, the point or period ● corresponds to the letters M or O, and the circle ○ corresponds to U or V. These and other fundamental geometrical figures which constitute the Adamic alphabet are employed in writing the names of the *orishas*[7]--as, for example, Xango (Shango):

SHA   N   G   O
CHA
XA

But, in ritual usage, it is written in this fashion[8]:

The particular *loa* invoked in this instance is Atibon-Legba, lord of the crossroads, the initiator, "opener of gates (opportunities),"[9] he who leads the way before--the perfect deity for guiding us into a text. The dual symbolism of black and white (the rooster sacrificed to Papa Legba must be a speckled black-and-white one[10]) is apt, for Legba is an intermediary between two different realities, just as a text is, among other things, an interface between imagination and action, creativity and (re)interpretation. Reed's PaPa LaBas the hoodoo detective, an American version of the Haitian Papa Legba, New World incarnation of the Fon divinity Legba, is, as Henry Louis Gates, Jr., correctly notes, synonymous with the Yoruba *orisha* Eshu (Exu in Brazil) a trickster figure who mediates between the human and divine realms. Eshu is "the-Black Interpreter, the Yoruba god of indeterminacy, the sheer plurality of meaning...."[11] He appears elsewhere in Reed's work as the Loop Garoo Kid and as Raven Quickskill, and is the informing principal behind Rinehartism in Ellison's *Invisible Man.* Indeed, Gates' brilliant exposition of "black mythology's archetypal signifier, the Signifying Monkey," demonstrates just how pervasive this figure is in Afro-American cultural discourse.[12]

The binary nature of the two terms *vé vé* we are investigating suggests a form of West African divination in which there are only two alternatives, right hand and left hand (yes and no). This is the divination system employing sixteen cowries, known in Dahomey (now the Republic Benin) as Legba-kika, and at Ife, in Nigeria, as Elegba, another name for Eshu (or Exu, as this type of divinatior is called in Brazil).[13] This divination system is simpler and held in less esteem in Nigeria than *Ifa,* but in the Americas it is more important because it is more widely known and practiced, partly due to the popularity of Shango, Oshu, and other *orishas* with whom it is associated, and also because it can be practiced by both men and women (women outnumber men in the *orisha* cults), whereas *Ifa* may only be practiced by men.[14] Corroboration of a very recent sort is offered by Toni Cade Bambara's novel *The Salt Eaters* from which I quote one brief, pertinent passage:

> MATRIARCHAL CURRENCY, the sign on the table had read. And she'd purchased the cowrie-shell bracelets for Palma less as a memento more as a criticism. Bought the cowrie shells to shame her, for she should've been on the march.... Divination tools...[15]

Black/white, right/left, yes/no: We are confronted here with a *coincidentia oppositorum,* or coincidence of opposite which, according to Mircea Eliade, is intended to produce a "rupture of plane" and end "in the rediscovery of the primordial spontaneity." It is, in fact, ultimately linked with a striving for "primordial completeness."[16] The aesthetic preoccupations of Neo-Hoodooism, Reed's rubric for his work and his methodology, adapted from the Afro-American occult/folkloric tradition and essentially describing a return to the magical possibilities of word and object,[17] likewise work toward a "rupture of plane," in the sense of exploding rigid, linear patterns of thought and creativity. Hans-Georg Gadamer's "hermeneutical impulse to reconstruct the 'question' to which a given literary text is the 'answer'"[18] and Derrida's project to shake the totality of the philosophic totalitarianism which he views structuralism as constituting[19] provide parallels to Reed's effort to deconstruct the cultural totalitarianism of Western civilization, which has not only equated itself with "universality," but has also within its own context, drastically defined the parameters of what it takes to be its authentic tradition by structures of exclusion that have historically kept out much that is valuable, the very "despised" elements Reed wishes to reinstate.[20] Reed wants to reassert the "questions" which the text of history has sidestepped. He is dealing not only with the *phenomenon* of possession (consciousness ridden by forces or concepts) and the *act* of possession (appropriation of ideas or artifacts) but also with re-possession--the reclamation of lost, scattered, or denied areas of experience and tradition(s). Reed, through a deliberate strategy of anachronism, multi-media devices, footnotes, bibliographies, and the like, opens up his texts, allowing dispossessed history to enter. If, as George Steiner has suggested, "the modernist movement can be seen as a strategy of permanent exile,"[21] then the post-modernist enterprise of Reed and other minority authors is decidedly post-exilic.

The concept of a coincidence of opposites is a very old one. It is an important feature of Quattrocento thought particularly among the Neo-Platonists; it was earlier espoused by the Orphic mystics and by Heraclitus,[22] among others. In Eastern philosophy and metaphysics, the idea is even more ancient. It is found as well in Africa, as can be seen in this description by Kofi Awoonor of the "mechanics" of African cosmology: "All extremes generate their opposites, and by containing conflict in a state of balance, rather than suppressing it, the generative forces are released."[23]

Marcel Griaule has a penetrating observation which again reinforces the African perspective. He writes that Dogon philosophy and religion express

> a haunting sense of the original loss of twinness. The heavenly Powers were dual, and in their earthly manifestations they constantly intervened in pairs.... It might even be supposed--though no Dogon has ever uttered such a blasphemy-- that the first misfortune in the universal course of things was the oneness of God.[24]

But not everyone shies away from such an utterance: Witness novelist/philosopher William Gass's remark that "The worship of the word must be pagan and polytheistic. It cannot endure one god"[25] --nor, Reed would argue, one monopolistic tradition. Reed inscribes his (re)visions and (re)interpretations in a manner that calls into question the tendency of literature to monumentalize one canonical form of discourse as *the* discourse which bespeaks tradition. He seeks to transform the monologue of such a discourse into a polylogue. Just as ● ○ may stand not only for textuality and orality respectively (print and the speaking wound, the mouth), but also for the dual Afro-American tradition of eloquence, *talking bad* and *talking sweet,* at the same time, as non-verbal signifier, it counters logocentricity, if only momentarily. Reed is demonstrating that the rhetoric of our cultural premises and prejudices extends beyond the verbal, and that its traces are embedded in other semiotic forms--in the very iconography of our society, the objective manifestations of our consciousness. You cannot discuss American history and culture without these signifiers: *black,* which subsumes the other shades (brown, red, yellow) of minority spectrum, and *white.* Yet anyone who reads the signs as emblems of ideological or racial closure is mistaken: their mutual gravity disrupts such definitive (and superficial) determinations.

In textual terms, the signifiers under discussion serve to remind us of the necessary interplay between black ink and white space. Whiteness is an erasure: the empty page, bleached consciousness. The imprinting of the self and impression of the text require an exercise of the black arts, to strike the proof of a meaning, an authenticity which *speaks for itself.* Reading a text, writes Derrida "we plunge into horizontality of a pure surface," into the depths "of the black sun, of the open ring, of the eluded center, of the elliptical return...."[26] The experience is a replication of the descent into what Wole Soyinka describes as "the deep black whirlpool of mythopoeic forces," in which the artist must immerse himself.[27]

The black disc is itself an ancient image, signifying womb of the Great Mother, the unconscious[28]; in other words, it is closely linked with imagination and creativity.[29] Indeed the dark or virtual, versus the sun, is one class conjunction of opposites. The black circle precedes the white one because darkness came before light. But there is another way in which to consider this. Quoting Soyinka again: "Only one who has himself undergone the experience of disintegration, whose spirit has been tested and whose psychic resources laid under stress by the forces most inimical to individual assertion, only he can understand and be the force of fusion between the two contradictions."[30] Soyinka is referring to the mythic significance of Ogun as a mediator between destructiveness and creativity, but his statement is also applicable to the historical situation of the black man, especially in the Diasporan matrix. If black leads in the signifier ● ○, it is because the knowledge of the victim is greater and more poignant than that of his persecutor, and only the oppressed can liberate the oppressor as well as himself through his more profound understanding. Blacking the zero, then, is not only an inking of the void, in the sense of writing or printing; it is a redressing of the balance which was long ago upset by the whiting out (or zeroing) of reality. The white silence--suppression of other realities--covered with evidence from history's buried or disparaged alternative traditions.

Once more I want to invoke Derrida. "What is metaphysics?" he asks, and proceeds to answer his own question:

> A white mythology which assembles and reflects Western culture: the white man takes his own mythology (that is, Indo/European mythology), his *logos*-- that is, the *mythos* of his idiom, for the universal form of that which it is still his inescapable desire to call Reason.[31]

This is ethnocentrism raised to a very abstract but crucial level: It provides an ontology, a "spiritual" schema, for a particular world view that sees itself as all-important. But this self-assurance hides a special form of blindness, of vacuity, as Derrida goes on to articulate:

> What is white mythology? It is metaphysics which has effaced in itself that fabulous scene which brought it into being, and which yet remains, active and stirring, inscribed in white ink, an invisible drawing covered over in the palimpsest.[32]

In other words, the Western, rational mode has lost conscious touch with its primal roots: The magical has given way to the mundane, creativity has become utility, spirit has been made subservient to matter.

This materialism is not incidental; it has embedded it in the very fabric of thought: "It is remarkable how insistently the metaphysical process is designated by paradigm of coinage, of metal," Derrida notes. "We have long known that value, gold, the eye, the sun and so on, belong to the development of the same trope." What is crucial is that "the obverse of the coin is effaced," and, along with it, a whole other aspect of consciousness.[33]

The two terms of our signifier ● O not only give us both faces of the metaphysical coin, but also the two "faces" of the cowries used in the form of divination previously referred to. Keeping in mind that poetic "statements" accompany the act of divination,[34] I want to juxtapose here two essential equivalent declarations--first, from the Dogon sage Ogotemmeli: "'To have cowries,' he said, 'is to have words'"[35]; second, from Zora Neale Hurston: "Language is like money."[36] In divination, the cowries "speak." Cowries also provided a common form of currency in precolonial Africa. Like money, words can be "spent," and in traditions of eloquence, they are often spent lavishly. There is also the aphorism that "Money talks." The trope of coinage Derrida has remarked on underlies all this. What Reed has done, however, is to forcibly remind us that just as a coin has two sides, so, too, every experience in America has at least two matrices: white, and non-white. The true meaning is to be found not only in the cleavage between these two realms of experience, but also in their contiguity. The cultural coin's two faces cannot be spent separately. If, historically, the "token" tended always to land white-face-up, it is clear that the odds were stacked, but the odds are changing. The population growth among minority groups in the United States compared with that of the white population suggests that a largely Euro-America is slowly being transformed into Meta-America.

Because there is always another side to the coin, there is always an alternative, a different story--e.g.,

Nonsense=MUMBO JUMBO=Neo-Hoodoo (positive magic)

The different "readings" in this instance are not racially determined; they are predicated upon consciousness. But from a black point of view, the transition from "nonsense" to a positive interpretation is one in which the slave becomes the master. Although the English language has basically equated the expression "mumbo jumbo" with gibberish," the etymology which Reed provides derives from a Mandingo term relating to a process which calms the troubled spirits of the ancestors.[37] Ironically, at the same time that the words lost their original meaning, they took on a meaning which troubled the spirits of whites, invoking the fearful, atavistic vision of the "dark continent" that Africa inspired in the West, which Vachel Lindsay summed up in his poem *The Congo* (1914):

"Mumbo-Jumbo will hoo-doo you." A derivation of "mumbo jumbo" from a Swahili expression suggested by Henry Louis Gates, Jr., and "loosely translated" as "What's happening?",[38] is also instructive, for the answer is supplied by various strategies of trickery and redress, of fending and proving. Western rationalism, having suppressed or distorted Afro-centric concepts, black source meanings, is countered by Neo-Hoodooism, which provides an old new twist to the braided strands of Western reality.

The "changes" which Legba has gone through provide a paradigm for the complex fate of African realities over time and across the continuum. In Dahomey, Legba "once loomed as the procreative and primal energy of all things," whereas "he appears in Haiti as suffering and aged....It is as if in coming westwards to the New World he lost the potential and the power of his own history."[39] In this wise he would appear to have experienced the same deprivation, suffered by the slaves who survived the Middle Passage (who were euphemistically referred to as "ebony wood" and "black coal," expressions revelatory to the *thing-ness* to which they had been reduced in white eyes). But Legba still stands "at the crossroads where spiritual and material realities intersect,[40] and his transition from Africa to the New World is sufficient testimony that treating the slaves, abjectly and as *objects* did not sever their vital connections with the metaphysical, nor did it totally strip them of their Africanness. Voodoo, too, made the crossing and assimilated much of Catholicism into its own rituals. The loa do not borrow the attributes and characters of the Catholic saints to whom they are supposed to correspond. Instead, the opposite is true. The saint, stripped of his own personality, takes on that of the loa. Although decayed in physical appearance, Legba's "psychic energies are still active," and his all-embracing knowledge exposes "all that is lacking in Western culture."[41] Reed's PaPa LaBas is able to "arrest" the Western whitewash of history precisely because he shares this knowledge. Like Eshu, like the Loop Garoo Kid, he is an "agent of discipline,"[42] helping the real world to work its way up, and get over.

In keeping with our conjunction of opposites, Legba, who reigns over the crossroads which is "the meeting point of opposites," is met there by his own opposite, Loko Carrefour, who represents youth, night, and the moon, just as Legba stands for age, day, and the sun. Loko and Legba "are the ones who can fathom the mirror, the field of the reflected image, that is symbolic of the entire world."[43] Opposition is associated with vitality. Unity created by removing conflicting or opposing elements is a hollow and meaningless unity; it is the unity of a component and not of the whole. It is analogous to Set's suppression of difference in Reed's reading of the Osiris myth. A complementary relationship of opposites is a requirement for the full realization of life; this is the meaning of the Tai-chi Tu, or Chinese diagram of the Supreme Ultimate:

Or to quote Ayi Kwei Armah: *"Receiving, giving, giving, receiving, all that lives is twin. Who would cast the spell of death, let him separate the two. Whatever cannot give. . . knowing only taking, that thing is past its own mere death. It is the carrier of death."* [44]

Apart from the Legbaran lineage, two additional metaphysical associations should be noted for our signifier. The black term, of course, suggests darkness, which is symbolized in Eastern mythology as *Naga,* the snake, who stands for "the pre-formal, the primordial sacred force," and is connected with "magic, yoga, the occult sciences."[45] The African linkage here is Damballah-Wedo, the Dahomean *loa* of fertility, who as *Da* is "the origin and essence of life," of rhythm.[46] Furthermore, the snake as a symbol of eternity is common in African art, and in one Dahomean myth coiled snake supports the Earth itself.[47] The white term, on the other hand, invokes the "white divinities" *(orish funfun)* such as--Orishala, "the God of Whiteness and the Creator of Mankind," in whose cults sixteen-cowrie divination is employed.[48]

Among the Bambara people of Mali, black symbolizes "Obscurity, Beginning, Secret Transformation, Original Word, Primordial Knowledge," while white symbolizes "Explication, Demonstration, Revelation, Truth, Spoken Word, Language, Work."[49] Black is the interior, the impalpable; white is exterior, visible. Spirit, preceding matter; subject before object; intuition versus logic; emotion versus reason--the latter terms have had the ascendancy in the Western framework and have recently been making inroads in the non-Western world; hence one wants to invoke the Old Man's cry in Wole Soyinka's play *Madmen and Specialists:* "Black that Zero!...Shut that gaping hole or we fall through it."[50]

But sometimes it is the black hole which one falls through.[51] In astrophysics, a black hole is the remnant of an exploded star which has collapsed into such instability that it generates gravitational forces so powerful that even light cannot escape. Furthermore, any object that falls into a black hole loses its separate identity. This concept is one which has recently exerted a powerful effect on the creative imagination, not only of astronomers and astrophysicists but also of speculative fiction writers.

The theory of black holes has given rise to a newer and even more intriguing postulate, the theory of white holes. Not unnaturally, astronomers and astrophysicists, once having admitted the probability of black holes, began to wonder what might be on the other side. The concept of a white hole--a black hole's obverse--came into being. One version of the theory holds that a white hole simply opens out into another universe; a second version speculates that it could open out at some other point in our own universe forming the opposite end of some incomprehensible tunnel in the fabric of space/time through which future astronauts might be able to instantaneously traverse the enormous distances between the stars. But the essential point for our purpose is that black holes and white holes seem to be mutually dependent: The existence of one implies--indeed creates--the other.[52] One supposition is that a white hole, conjured into being by the creation of a black hole through the further collapse of a neutron star, itself necessitates the existence of another black hole, and so on--a stupendous cosmic dance of alternating images. It is *yin* and *yang* on an Einsteinian plane.

Within each black hole is a singularity, a point at which all the known (or assumed) laws of physics break down; in other words, they contain within themselves unpredictability and uniqueness. The Uncertainty Principle, which has come to play an increasingly important role in threshold physics must operate paramountly in the unfathomable regions of black hole. A white hole, too, must possess a singularity and, considering the Janus-like intimacy between the two concepts, it is likely that a black hole/white hole pair may share the same singularity; it is the singularity itself which penetrates the fabric of space/time, opening up new dimensions.

The singularity which joins the black hole and the white hole is like the crossroads between two realities, over which Legba presides, where opposites meet and are no longer held to be contradictory. "Unpredictability" is a characteristic of the trickster, whose indeterminacy is surely a metaphysic version of the Uncertainty Principle; unpredictability, too, was one trait which made the slave so troublesome to his master, and it is the essence of Jes Grew, Reed's personification of black protean energy.

It is evident, in sum, that the signs of Neo-Hoodoo exhibit "a prodigious quantum of talismanic potency."[53] Reed has helped to reappropriate literature to the people by rooting novelistic language in popular speech and culture in a non-banal and non-condescending manner. Neo-Hoodoo is not in the manner of Blake or Yeats, a private symbology, but one employing folk roots: an aesthetic drawn, as it were from the public domain, though shaped and instigated by the individual artist/houngan. In the words of Henry Allen as quoted by Ishmael Reed, "Anywhere they go my people know the signs."[54]

One further suggestion: Reed's *vé vé* reminds me of the expression "one eyegonblack" from *Finnegans Wake,* which is not only a reference to James Joyce himself (he wore a black eyepatch) but also a pun on the German word *Augenblick,* meaning "moment." Darkness is associated with eternity, light with time. A literary work is itself a temporal construct with its own ebbs and flows; moving through it, as in moving through the world, we need to stop momentarily and see where we are at (what's happening?) This is the meaning of Reed's device on a purely typographical level: Pause and Reflect. There are possibilities other than those that immediately meet the eye/I.

NOTES

1. Sculptor Ed Love, quoted from the catalogue of a 1973 exhibition of his work, in Samella Lewis, *Art: African American* (New York: Harcourt Brace Jovanovich, 1978), p.180.
2. Ishmael Reed, *Flight to Canada* (New York: Random House, 1976), p.82.
3. Henry Louis Gates, Jr., "The 'Blackness of Blackness': A Critique of the Sign and the Signifying Monkey," *Critical Inquiry*, 9 (1983), 688.
4. Introduction to *19 Necromancers from Now*, the short fiction "Cab Calloway Stands In the Moon," and the novels *Yellow Back Radio Broke-Down* and *Mumbo Jumbo*.
5. Presented as a staff seminar at the University of Ife in 1979.
6. Voodoo derives from the Fon word *vodu*, meaning a god of gods. See P. Mercier, "The Fon of Dahomey," in *African Worlds: Studies in the Cosmological Ideas and Social Values of African Peoples*, ed. Daryll Forde (Oxford: Oxford University Press, 1954), p.215. The word *hoodoo* as a synonym of voodoo entered the English language at an undetermined moment, for although the supplement of the *Oxford English Dictionary* quotes an example from 1875 as the earliest known literary use in the United States, one assumes that the term was current in the spoken vernacular for some time prior to this date. The OED's first example of the word hoodooism (from *Harper's Magazine*, Apr, 1881) is prophetic for the present inquiry: "What is hoodooism, anyway?" The citation, however, is incomplete, and a *Dictionary of American English on Historical Principles* quotes the answer to the question: "It's de ole African religion, honey. It's jes like white folk's religion on'y it's heathenism, an'dey worships de debbil." One can agree with the first sentence of this "explanation" regarding hoodoo's African roots, but the second sentence is a value judgement embodying an ethnocentrism and ignorance that unfortunately is still evident.
7. The Yoruba word *òrisà* (spelled *orixa* in Brazil), as a generic term for the divinities, is cognate with the word *loa*. For the sake of convenience, except in direct quotations, I will dispense with Yoruba orthography and tone markings, and anglicize: e.g., *orisha,* Shango instead of *Sàngó* , Eshu rather than *Esù.*
8. W. W. da Matta e Silva, *Doutrina Secreta da Umbanda* (Rio de Janeiro: Livraria Freitas Bastos, 1967), pp. 118-19, 130.

In "Characteristics of Negro Expression," Zora Neale Hurston writes that the white man "thinks in the written language and the Negro thinks in hieroglyphics" (in *The Sanctified Church* [Berkeley, CA: Turtle Island, 1981], p.50). This sounds like a Negritude version of linguistics. Does anyone actually think in a "written" language? If one takes the whole business of literacy into account, it is true that people who have long possessed a literary tradition will indeed be more *textually* oriented than people from societies where literacy is more recent or problematic. But is this the same thing as *thinking* textually? It would probably be more accurate to say that literates think more abstractly, and people from primarily oral cultures more symbolically, but this is not a *racial* distinction.

9. Zora Neale Hurston, *Tell My Horse* (1938; rpt Berkeley, CA: Turtle Island, 1981), p.142.
10. Ibid., p.151.
11. "The 'Blackness of Blackness,'" p.688.
12. Ibid., p.687.
13. See William Bascom, *Sixteen Cowries: Yoruba Divination from Africa to the New World* (Bloomington: Indiana University Press, 1980), p.4.
14. Ibid., p.3.
15. (New York: Random House, 1980), p.36.
16. *Yoga: Immortality and Freedom* (Princeton, NJ: Princeton University Press, 1970), pp. 265, 271-272.
17. Samella Lewis notes that among the slave-craft items surviving from the colonial period are "numerous fetishes associated with voodoo or hoodoo." (*Art: African American*, p.9). These sacred ritual objects are three-dimensional analogues of the *vé vé*, although, since they are intended to manifest the spirit of the material plane, it would be more correct to speak of them as four-dimensional and three-dimensional, respectively. Consideration of these objects must enter into any profound discussion of black aesthetics.
18. See Terry Eagleton's "The Idealism of American Criticism," *New Left Review*, 127 (May-June 1981), 63.
19. See Alan Bass's "Translator's Introduction" to *Writing and Difference* by Jacques Derrida (Chicago: Universtiy of Chicago Press, 1978), p. xvi.
20. Derrida, speaking of Foucault's *Madness and Civilization*, talks of the possibility that "the structure of exclusion is the fundamental structure of historicity." (*Writing and Difference*, p.42). He notes, too, that Foucault does not establish "whether an event such as the creation of a house of internment is a sign among others." (Ibid, p.43). There are so many examples supporting the first supposition that it is scarcely necessary to begin making citations. As far as the second idea is concerned, Reed, in *Mumbo Jumbo*, posits a house of internment for *creativity* in his reference to the Art Detention wing of a New York museum, repository for the psyche of the "primitive" cultures enshrined in numerous stolen artifacts which demand liberation.
21. *Extraterritorial* (New York: Atheneum, 1971), p.17.
22. In his 27th fragment, Heraclitus declares that "without opposition all things will cease to exist." And in fragment 98: "Opposites cooperate. The most beautiful harmonies come from opposition..." (For a useful summary of this

topic, see C.J. Emlyn-Jones, "Heraclitus and the Identity of Opposites," *Phronesis*, 21, No.2 [1976], 89-114.)

23. *The Breast of the Earth* (Garden City, NY: Doubleday, 1976), p.72.

24. *Conversations with Ogotemelli* (Oxford: Oxford University Press, 1965), p.198.

25. *On Being Blue: A Philosophical Inquiry* (Boston: Godine, 1976), p. 20.

26. *Writing and Difference*, pp.288,289.

27. *Myth, Literature and the African World* (Cambridge: Cambridge University Press, 1976), pp. 153-154.

28. Compare Charles Frye's "The Psychology of the Black Experience: A Jungian Approach" in the Spring 1973 number of *Black Lines: A Journal of Black Studies*.

29. Compare these lines from a poem by Oswald Mouyiseni Mtshali in *Poems of Black Africa*, ed. Wole Soyinka [New York: Hill and Wang, 1975], p.293): *"Black is the hole of the poet,/a mole burrowing from no entrance to no exit."*

30. *Myth, Literature, and the African World*, p.150.

31. Jacques Derrida, "White Mythology: Metaphor in the Text of Philosophy," *New Literary History*, 6, No.1 (1974), 11.

32. Ibid

33. Ibid, pp. 14, 17.

34. It is significant that the *Odu,* the "readings" accompanying the divinatory act in both *Ifa* and sixteen cowrie-divination, are in verse and often highly metaphoric (as George Steiner notes, "Metaphor ignites a new arc of perceptive energy" [Extraterritorial, p.68], for in Yoruba aesthetics, art begins in the "clothing" of the naked Word, which embodying causative elements of creation--Ogbon (wisdom), *Imo* (knowledge), and *Oye* (understanding)--cannot be "seen" unclothed. (I am grateful to my friend Roland Abiodun, of the Department of Fine Arts, University of Ife, who is engaged in a detailed exposition of these matters, for enlightening me on this and related subjects.)

35. Marcel Griaule, *Conversations with Ogotemmeli*, p.202.

36. "Characteristics of Negro Expression," p.49

37. *Mumbo Jumbo* (Garden City, NY: Doubleday, 1972), p.10

38. "The 'Blackness of Blackness,'" p.703.

39. *A Rainbow for the Christian West*, by Rene Depestre, trans. With an intro by Joan Dayan (Amherst: University of Mass. Press, 1977), pp. 59-60.

40. Ibid., p.66.

41. Ibid., p.248, n.11, p.67.

42. 'Wande Abimbola, *Ifa: An Explosion of Ifa Literary Corpus* (Ibadan, Nigeria: Oxford University Press, 1976), p.51.

43. Introduction to *A Rainbow for the Christian West*, p.74

44. *Two Thousands Seasons* (Nairobi, Kenya: East African Publishing House, 1973), p.xi.

45. Eliade, *Yoga: Immortality and Freedom*, p.352.

46. Introduction to *A Rainbow for the Christian West*, pp. 60,63.
47. See Geoffrey Parrinder's *African Mythology* (London: Hamlyn, 1967), pp.38,42.
48. Bascom, *Sixteen Cowries*, pp.4, 9, 37.
49. Benjamin C. Ray, *African Religions: Symbol, Ritual, and Community* (Englewood Cliffs, NJ: Prentice Hall, 1976), p.94.
50. In *Collected Plays 2* (New York: Oxford University Press, 1974), p.275.
51. In *Stolen Lightning: The Social Theory of Magic* (New York: Vintage Books, 1983), Daniel Lawrence O'Keefe writes that "black holes have punctured our four-dimensional coordinate systems and a new world view threatens to emerge that might legitimize the magical sciences" (p.105). Ishmael Reed would zero in on "threatens" as a revealing word, for he recognizes that, as O'Keefe himself admits, "magical protest speaks both for the individual ego *and* for the marginal groups" (p.150), and that magic raids across the border that taboo guards (p.191). O'Keefe's humanistic logic sees magic as dangerous to the social order, whereas Reed views it as an aesthetic and cultural guerilla tactic, a counter-logic designed to hoodoo the Establishment. Moreover, he is unwilling to dismiss varieties of experience. To quote again from Toni Cade Bambara…"voodoo, thermodynamics, I Ching, astrology, numerology, alchemy, metaphysics, everybody's ancient myth--they were interchangeable, not at all separate much less conflicting. They were the same, to the extent that their origins survived detractors and perverters" (*The Salt Eaters*, p.210). All of these strands are woven in Neo-Hoodoo.
52. Such symmetry seems to be basic for the structure of matter itself. Elementary particles, such as the electron (-) and the proton (+) are balanced or mirrored by the positron (+) and the antiproton (-). Collisions between such particles (of ordinary matter on the one hand and anti-matter on the other) cause mutual annihilation which results in the creation of new positive and negative particles, neutrinos (uncharged particles), and energy in the form of gamma radiation (photons). Thus the symmetry is not static but dynamic: These transformations occur in extremely short spaces of time (microseconds) and offer an image of continuous creation/dissolution/recreation. The concept of an alternately expanding/contracting universe recapitulates this dialectic on a metacosmic level.
53. This phrase appears in quotation marks in my notebooks, but (alas!) without a reference.
54. *Yellow Back Radio Broke-Down* (Garden City, NY: Doubleday, 1969), p.5.

From *Black American Literature Forum* (*African American Review*) 18.3 Fall 1984: 95-99.

A Bird's Eye View: Ishmael Reed's Unsettling of the Score by Munching and Mooching on the Mumbo Jumbo Work of History

Mark Shadle /Article

Simply stated, it is my belief that some critic/scholars have read Ishmael Reed's work too literally, looking for a consensus of revisionist history,[1] while others have read him too figuratively, uncovering the illusions and allusions of his literary structures.[2] The problem with the former viewpoint is that it often ends in the confusion of attempting to apply or associate his work programmatically; this merely reverses the flow of uniformity Reed is trying to undo. Conversely, the difficulty of the second "inlook" is that it leaves his work brilliantly and busily impassive, a parody of duality so massive it cannot get beyond the acceleration of doubling and twinning.

Because I have found both approaches stimulating and helpful, but either alone limiting, I intend the following few pages as a meditation upon, and celebration of, multi-pli*city* in Reed's novel, *Mumbo Jumbo,* which is at the center of his work.[3] My emphasis is "triadic" and upon the number three as representative of what I will call a "multiverse" we try to share (as opposed to a "*universe*" we simultaneously "*duel*" over in an attempt to dominate). More suggestive than exhaustive, this "Bird's-eye" view is aimed towards the holistic criticism/scholarship Reed's work demands, and goes in through the music of "the old song and dance."

Early in the book we are given a clue and asked a crucial question: "So Jes Grew is seeking its words. Its text. *For what good is a liturgy without a text?*" (*MJ* 6; my italics). Jes Grew is the ancient wedding of song (as "his/her-story"), dance (as "my-story/stery") and their orchestration of word/deed in time/space.[4] All we need do to answer the question above is alter it. Jes Grew needs the plurality of a "multiverse": "liturgies" rather than "liturgy," "texts" rather than "Text." However, each liturgy and text must be a personal "recollection" and "re-enactment" within the tradition(s). The sum of Jes Grew's texts (traditions like jazz and Afro-American literature) is greater than its parts (individual music and texts) precisely because they are "parts"--the only way truths can struggle on. As Henry Louis Gates, Jr., says, "Reed's open-ended structure, and his stress on the indeterminancy of the text, demands that we, as critics, in the act of reading, *produce* a text's signifying structure."[5]

Yet Reed does not see this "indeterminancy" as the danger of "ambiguity," as do many other contemporary writers.[6] Instead, this openness is what Robert Fox has helpfully called "polyguity."[7] This is Reed's solution to the old philosophical riddle of "the one and the many"--the idea that individuals can work "in concert" in multi-cultural groups that use (rather than sacrifice) their individuality. This is Hinckle Von Vampton's constant worry; as he says: "Individuality. It couldn't be herded, rounded-up; it was like crystals of winter each different from one another but in a storm going down together. What would happen if they dispersed, showing up when you least expected them; what would happen if you couldn't predict their minds?" (*MJ* 160).

As Reed answers elsewhere: "The Afro-American's great asset may be his 'unpredictability,' an asset which may ultimately be proven to have a psychic connection" (*SO* 167). Co-operation among individuals is an imperfect process because we are, by nature, imperfect. Yet this leaves room for a beautiful process of struggle. The push toward oneness and doubleness in Reed's work is an indication of the frustration with this, our basic imperfection, part of which is an insatiable need for "form." But a plurality of forms celebrates and transforms this imperfection into possibilities.

The symbol for this limited multiverse of small groups (which together represent unlimited possibilities) is the number three. Against the continual stream of doublings and opposition (especially the war between the Antonists and Neo-HooDooists) beats this symbolic three, a stand-in for the multiplicity of "conversations" that can widen out of mere "debate." Thus the most powerful version of this number is a "triad" of threes, while doubling this (six-six-six is Noxon's number; *N* 303) goes back to the ugly uniformity of the crowd and war of two trios.

Reed even describes himself as an "old fashioned triadist" of body/mind/spirit (*SO* 3). Robert Fox lists some of these threes and their meanings below:

> *Mumbo Jumbo* is, to begin with, Reed's third novel; it was "finished" at 3 p.m. (*MJ*, 249). America, we are told, is "born" at 3:03 on July 4 (17). The Center of Art Detention houses 30,000 items (97). Berbeland and Thor are charged 3 cents for a cup of coffee (102), and Von Vampton gives W. W. Jefferson 3 cents to buy an "August Ham" (114). (In "Cab Calloway Stands In for the Moon," Papa LaBas has a dog named HooDoo 3 cents.) Ancient Egypt had 30 dynasties (204). Julian the Apostate was assassinated in 363 a.d. (195); and *there are numerous other examples...* Three is the first step beyond that binary sensibility which not only permeates our culture but is also the basis for cybernetics. (Man's machines are an extension of man's thinking.) Three symbolizes that thinking...which mystics would term cosmic consciousness, which Reed would call Neo-HooDoo.[8] [my italics]

In between the twin beginnings of Chapter One (with its two narrative voices, one in italics) and Chapter Two (with its single narrative voice) are the three epigraphs concerning Jes Grew which are mirrored by three dedications on the "opposite" page. *Mumbo Jumbo* is not only at the center of Reed's work, but written at the center of his life--he was thirty-three when writing it. Yet, in his poetry, Reed shows his oscillation between the "Petro" (often warlike) and "Rada" (gentler) aspects of the "Neo-HooDoo" of his life and work. In "Loup Garou Means Change Into," Reed salutes the latter when he says: "Folks say if you get to 30/ You can make it to 35 / The Only stipulation is you / Leave your

Beast outside" (*CHAT* 50). However, in "The Author Reflects on / His 35th Birthday," Reed says (perhaps with a mixture of seriousness and self-parody): "Make me hard as a rock / 35. . . / Meaner than mean." (*CHAT* 53). Thus, as Reed says elsewhere, "Jealousy and love are different perfumes from the same root" (*SO* 4).

The protagonists of Reed's books demonstrate a steady and inclusive shift in outlook from Petro to Rada rites of Voodoo. Bukka Doopeyduk is the lonely, involuntary victim of HooDoo curse in *The Free-Lance Pallbearers*. While Loop Garoo is helped by Chief Showcase, and is a conscious HooDoo avenger, he still invokes the Petro loa, Ogu (*YB* 75), and builds a fetish against Drag Gibson in Reed's second novel, *Yellow Back Radio Broke-Down* (*YB* 73). But in *Mumbo Jumbo* the single protagonist is split into a number of interlocking trios. Characters like Benoit Battraville, Buddy Jackson, and Ti Bouton carry on the Petro aspect against enemies like Hinckle Von Vampton, Safecracker Gould, and Biff Musclewhite.[9]

Papa LaBas, as loa Legba, "opens the gates" between characters, just as he does between real and spiritual/artistic worlds. Along with trickster figure, T Malice, and fellow "houngan" (or shaman), Black Herman, he is a healer in the Rada mysteries. After Bergelang leaves Mumbo Jumbo Kathedral, Papa LaBas triangulates with Earline and Charlotte. Bergelang is divided between his triangulation with Earline and Charlotte on the one hand, and Fuentes and Yellow Jack of the Mu'tafikah on the other. While Reed criticizes the Petro path (or at least the misuse of it) of Voodoo in *The Last Days of Louisiana Red*, both Rada and Petro are available in *Mumbo Jumbo*.

In fact, there are three main Voodoo rites--Rada, Petro, and Congo. Besides the triangulation of the "Luminous Delta," of the three spheres, and of song/music/dance, there are the three drums of each rite (except the Petro, which has two).[10] And if "twinning" is important in African mythologies, the third child (or "dossu"), born after twins, is sacred.

From my point of view, Neil Schmitz is wrong in saying, "the language of music is not the language of literature. The Black musician's access to Jes Grew is different."[11] I feel Reed's consciousness is most powerfully non-Western and related to "Third Worlds." His many "(sub-)plots" and "(inter-)texts" in *Mumbo Jumbo* suggest polyrhythmic African music--usually with seven to eleven separate lines and remind us that blues, ragtime, jazz, etc. do have African origins. The lack of resolutions, and/or multiple resolutions of these many story lines, which are also often imperfectly parallel, imply the polymetric qualities of African music, as well. This is an "additive" rather than "divisive" principle (and also applies to Egyptian mythology). As Gunther Schuller explains in the following statements: "When the European thinks of polyrhythm, he generally conceives of it as two or more rhythmic strands occurring simultaneously, retaining, however, vertical coincidence at phrase beginnings and endings, at bar lines, and at other focal points. The African, on the other hand, conceives his polyrhythms on a much more extended, more complex, poly-metrically organized basis, where phrases rarely, and sometimes never, coincide vertically. In fact, his overriding interest is in crossrhythms, the more subtle and more complex the better."[12]

Returning to our pun "multi/ecology"--we are able to understand how the etymology of both speech and music run back to "muse," "muthos/mythos" and, ultimately, to first utterance in place as "mouth/mu." As Jane Harrison says, "A myth becomes practically a story of magical intent and potency. Possibly the first *muthos* was simply the interjectional utterance *mu*, but it is easy to see how rapid the development would be from interjection to narrative."[13]

The title, "*Mumbo Jumbo,*" finally takes on a symphony of meanings. The common meaning of the phrase, "gibberish" (*MJ* 72), is overturned by another dictionary meaning: "magician who makes the troubled spirits of ancestors go away" (*MJ* 10). However, on a third level, these "troubled spirits" are appeased precisely by "re-enactment" of the first act(s) of language/music/dance. A purposeful sound is mother/ancestor of speech and music, but is also action ("dromenon"), since Jane Harrison also reminds us that "verse means to turn, as the [ancient] chorus did."[14]

These meanings are realized and symbolized in the title. The original voice, "mu" is re-done in mirror image of "stuttering meaninglessness," "um" ("*mubo jumbo*"). And lurking, anagrammatically, with "mu"/"um" is either "mojo"/ (or) "bomb" (as fetish power). The phrase begins with the palindrome ("mum") that shows first voice ("mu") leading back on itself ("m u m"), and to the pun of an oracular "great ma." "Umbo" is doubled ("mumbo jumbo") to show double meaning/act of "mu" in meaningless "um" as "navel" (or origin) and "boss" (knob on a shield).[15]

And just as "um" is "mu" re-versed, so is "ho" (as abbreviation for back order) re-versed to counterweight of "oh" (as in the obnoxious planet "Ob" of Noxon; *N* 295).[16] "Umbo" also suggests "umbra," which is complete shadow or hidden meanings in the book's title that celebrates the unexplored "first utterance/act" (which can be mistaken or go unnoticed as "no meaning").[17] And this reminds us that Reed was an important member of the Umbra poetry group early in his career (*SO* 6). "Umbo" also re-calls "(h)'umfo(r)," the place of sacred Voodoo rites, where those possessed speak the "meaningful" but sometimes "unintelligible" "Guinea" (language of Ife, the homeland of the African spirits.)

These clusters of multiplying meaning(s) in the groupings of words, characters, and narratives are less a "my-stery" and more the "mysteres" (loas/gods) of "my(-)story" as a reader of the novel if I think musically. Charlie ("Bird") Parker is the appropriate incarnation of Thoth (the ibis-headed "Birdman" and god of knowledge and the arts in ancient Egypt), for Parker was the prime mover of the "bebop" era of jazz. "Be-bop" (however unfortunate the phrase) resembles the phrase, "mumbo jumbo," in its surface meaninglessness.

Socially and musically, be-bop musicians distanced themselves as a dissonance. They were the little groups of idiosyncratically dressed musicians who "moonlighted" after-hours away from uniformed "big bands," and whose extended, improvised solos and chords in small clubs displaced the orchestrations of "bit parts" in large ballrooms. Altered chords (musical intervals like the fifth and ninth were raised or lowered a halfstep) created the "dissonance" for be-bop's first listeners, and superfast tempos often made the music seem undanceable. The "vocals" even became "instrumentals" as "scatting" (the "scat-singing" of nonsense syllables, like the word, be-bop) became common, and as vocalists imitated the musical lines of horns. Musically, then, be-boppers like Parker "signified" upon or mocked existing jazz tunes by transforming them (just as their predecessors had). They often did this by changing the title, speeding up the rhythm, providing a new melody, and either embellishing the existing chords (by extending them vertically as far as the interval of the thirteenth, or altering the given pitches) or making chord "substitutions." Parker played the crucial role in this latter area when he discovered that chords extended up to, say, the interval of the ninth, provided incredible freedom for improvisation because they offered the *feeling of playing in three keys at once.*[18]

Risking oversimplification, an example would be a C-major ninth chord (read vertically up the treble clef staff from middle C, as C-E-G-B-D)--offering a C-major triad (C-E-G), plus a major seventh (B) and a ninth (D) could simultaneously be read as an E-minor seventh chord (E-G-B-D) if read from the second note (E, or major third) of the original C chord, or a G-major chord (G-B-D) if read from the third note (G or perfect fifth) of the original C chord. While all three chords are at home in the key of C, they could be *substituted* for each other with interesting results. This development also gave "tonal" music (with one key center) the illusion or chance of being "atonal," and let jazz musicians think "enharmonically" about each chord.

Yet the word "atonal" is misleading for jazz since be-bop. Instead of being "atonal" or "tonal," such jazz is "polytonal"--a sense of simultaneous, multiple keys which parallel the multiple texts of Jes Grew. It is a harmony that embraces dissonance to overcome their duality. And this "anti-plague" re-verses "Aton" to "nota," the "mark, sign or letter" that parallels the hieroglyphics of the *Book of Thoth.*[19] "Note" also derives from "noscere," or "to know," which is appropriate, since Thoth is the god of knowledge. Written "notes" and musical "notes" are thus both "annotations" of history and mythology. Atonists, or "persons of note," are balanced by those "persons of notes" (or musicians) who carry Jes Grew. A "note" is even the "cry of a bird"--we know which one.[20]

Jes Grew, particularly be-bop jazz, stands for the diversity and musicality of language(s). Musically, it is the physiological "tone" that comes from speaking/singing/dancing, when possessed by the joyful "anti-plague" of Jes Grew *(MJ* 9). Charlie Parker used the appropriate scales to "horizontally" spread out the "vertical" chords (especially in their upper reaches) as arpeggios in his improvised sax solos. Reed explains this perfectly when he says Jes Grew "led Charlie Parker to scale the Everests of the Chord" (*MJ* 239, 241).

In this sense, be-bop is the ideal stand-in for Reed's Jes Grew, in its opposition to the Atonists. "Atony" is not only lack of physiological "tone" (especially in contractile organs), but a lack of accent or stress (read uniform, unmusical speech) in phonetics.[21] "Atonality" for the Atonists is not "playing in multiple keys simultaneously; rather, it is a disregard of all musical keys." The Wallflower Order puns upon the slang meaning of "wallflower," as someone never chosen to dance they have the repressive motto: "Lord, if I can't dance, no one shall" (*MJ* 74)--to mean a group unchosen in the history of the Teutonic knights. For them, "harmony" (musical and social) becomes mere conformity to "rules/rites."

In *Yellow Back Radio Broke-Down* we are told that "Loop *seems* to be scatting arbitrarily, using forms of this and adding his own. He's blowing like that celebrated musician Charles Yardbird Parker improvising as he goes along. He's throwing clusters of demon chords at you and you don't know the changes, do you, Mr. Drag?" (*YB* 184; my italics). If we "know the 'changes'" (jazz slang for chords), the chords are no longer "demons" and Loop and Parker are not speaking/singing/playing/dancing nonsensically (the "mumbo jumbo" of "scatting.") Instead, they are adding their own improvisations to/through the "laws" (from which the word for gods in Voodoun, "loas," derives)[22] of jazz. (Such a discrepancy in outlook exists between white settlers and Native Americans; apparently only the former saw America as a terrifying "wilderness"--a function of not knowing how to live in a different world.)

Reed is as interested in Parker as "worker" as he is in the legends that surround him; in his essay "Bird Lives!", Reed quotes Ross Russell: "He [Parker] had learned at first hand from the masters of his art, had listened to every important soloist in Kansas City. He was determined, dedicated, tireless, ambitious. Charlie had put no less than fifteen thousand hours in on an instrument toy by a conservative estimate" (*SO* 127).

These "laws" of jazz are multiple, eclectic, and syncretistic, ready to incorporate new systems of meanings. They demand that the "player" stand simultaneously open to past/present/future, and to multiple layers/levels of understanding.[23] Similarly, Reed says: "This is what my kind of writing is all about. It leads me to the places where I can see old cultures resurrected, and made contemporary. Time past is time present" (*SO* 3). In following the "story of jazz" from its blossoming in "Storyville" in New Orleans through its focal points in Chicago, New York, etc., Jes Grew demonstrates the "epidemic," traveling nature of jazz. Yet a truer history of jazz proves that such a mapping is stereotypical, that jazz is "pandemic."[24] Thus, when Benoit Battraville tells Nathan Brown how to "catch" Jes Grew, he recommends not only famous musicians like Louis Armstrong, but the obscure, dancing "urchins," lyric-writing cook, and the "Rhyming Fool who sits in Re-mote [sic] Mississippi [sic] and talks 'crazy' for hours" (*MJ* 174).

Against the participatory folk speech/music/dance of individuals who share traditions, we have Moses, the artist-guru trying to shape the traditions to himself. In the novel, Moses says, "I'm the 1. For once music wouldn't just be used as a background to dancing but he would be soloist and no 1 in the audience would be allowed to play" (*MJ* 209). In other words, if he is "no 1" (number one), anyone else is "no 1" (no one). Similarly, Minnie (as incarnation of Sophocles' Antigone) causes Chorus (who has become the individual carrying the burdens of the chorus as group) to im/ex-plode in *The Last Days of Louisiana Red*. And Papa LaBas explains the murder of Abdul Hamid (as the assembler of the solo "Text" of Jes Grew, the *Book of Thoth)* by saying, "This was just too much traffic for one man to handle" (*MJ* 233).

Black Herman answers Moses for Reed: "Charismatic leaders will become as outdated as the solo because people will realize that when the Headman dies the movement dies instead of becoming a permanent entity, perispirit, a protective covering for its essence" (*MJ* 45). Jazz musicians (particularly be-bop ones) have occasionally used the complexity of the music to "bar" some players, and do know that the music can be a "weapon."[25] But generally they have invited participation and "jamming"--a constant cross-fertilization that heals small groups through innovation.

Henry Gates, Jr., points to a difference between the two narratives of "truth" and "understanding"--the former in present tense, the latter free to roam in time/space. These "framings" (the second in italics in the novel) are "set" off by what he calls a "bar" or "unbridgeable white space."[26] Yet poly-rhythmic/metric jazz helps us understand that this is literally another convention. The "white space" between words or notes in Western art may be likened to "the wolf," those incremental musical distances left out of, or hidden by, the "well-tempered" system.[27] A "wolf" is also musical slang for a "wrong note," but jazz musicians are magicians who find new ways of transforming/posing four notions of what is "wrong," just as they find notes which their instruments were not intended for (e.g., the quarter tones that may be produced by partially depressing the valves of a trumpet). *Mumbo Jumbo* develops our interest in the inclusiveness of "chromatics," whether of pitch, color, history, or mythology.[28]

So besides seeing these narratives of the novel separately (as "call and response"), we are asked to attend to them at once, continually cross-referencing new information in/to both. Reed's novel allows each reader to "re-sonate" "his/her-story" and "re-bind" the reverberations of the "texts." Musically, it is a "re-rec(h)ording."[29]

When "Papa LaBas steers the car over the bridge" at the end of the novel (*MJ* 249) and sees the lights of Manhattan, we know this bridge is an oxymoron of "individual synecdoche"; as Legba, LaBas is himself the bridging of real and spiritual worlds. Driving "at/on" multipli*city*, LaBas "re-collects" his improvisational lecture on the improvisations of HooDoo, jazz, and Jes Grew; in "the flights of fancy, the tangential excursions" (*MJ* 249), he has (in the slang of jazz) "taken a chorus" (or "played the bridge").[30] Both musical and land "bridges" are supported by "chords" that are "laid down" or "arpeggiated."

This bridge is symbol of individuality supporting multiplicity (and vice versa): its single span, from a vision of the singular architect (who is thinking of/for the many who will use the bridge), triumphs only because it is built by many workers in/to *crossing* of the river below; its approaches are each beginning/end, connecting the two land masses. "The bridge" in ancient Egypt was not only pose linking acrobatics and dance, but language itself (as hieroglyph).[31] The voice that spans from LaBas to Reed realizes from/as the bridge: "Time is a pendulum [like people moving back and forth across the bridge]. Not a river. More akin to what goes a round comes around" (*MJ* 249). The bridge is both suspension and clocking of time. Just as the same numbers come around on the clockface, but in a continuous stream of unique moments, similar decades are always a slightly different improvisation: "And the 20s were back again. Better" (*MJ* 249).

When we read: "Locomobile rear moving toward neoned Manhattan" (*MJ* 249), we can see this "carrier" ("a car designed to accommodate the philosophy 'small numbers make for distinctions, quantity destroys'"; *MJ* 54) of the "carrier" (LaBas) of Jes Grew moving at once forward and backward ("loco-mobile") into the future. The novel's end is at once commemorative, magical, and prospective. The fictive world is both real and fictional: "Skyscrapers gleam like magic trees" (*MJ* 249). The world of the novel may be a suspension of time when we are in it, but the novel is "suspended" the moment we turn from its reverberations: "Freeze frame" (*MJ* 249).

NOTES

1. An example would be Sondra A. O'Neale, "Ishmael Reed's Fitful Flight to Canada: Liberation for Some, Good Reading for All," *Callaloo*, 1 (October 1978), 176+.

2. An example would be Henry Louis Gates, Jr., "The 'Blackness of Blackness': A Critique of the Sign and the Signifying Monkey," *Critical Inquiry*, No. 9 (June 1983),685-721 (hereafter cited as Gates, "The 'Blackness of Blackness'".)

3. Reed's *Mumbo Jumbo* (*MJ*) (1972); rpt. New York: Avon, 1978) is preceded by two novels and three collections of poetry; it is followed by three novels, two books of essays and another one of poetry. While Ishmael Reed will no doubt write many more books, it is hard to imagine *Mumbo Jumbo* not remaining near the center of his work, "philosophically" speaking. The following works by Reed will be referred to parenthetically in the text by the abbreviations following the titles (using the more available reprint editions whenever possible): *The Free-Lance Pallbearers* (*FP*) (1967; rpt. New York: Avon,

1977); *Yellow Back Radio Broke-Down* (*YB*) (1969; rpt. New York: Avon, 1977); *D Hexorcism of Noxon D Awful* (*N*) in *19 Necromancers from Now* (New York: Doubleday, 1970); *Chattanooga* (*CHAT*) (1966; rpt. New York: Random House, 1973); *Shrovetide in Old New Orleans* (*SO*) (1978; rpt. New York: Avon, 1979).

4. For a much more specific rendering and application of the puns of this approach, see my "Polythythms of Love and Violence in *No Bride Price*: Music of the African Spheres" in *African Writing Today*, ed. Peter Nazareth (New Zealand: Outrigger; a special issue of *Pacific Moana Quarterly,* 6, No. 3/4 [July/October 1981). And for more on everything in this article, see my Ph.D. dissertation, "Mumbo Jumbo Gumbo Works: The Kaleidoscopic Fiction of Ishmael Reed," Diss. The University of Iowa, 1984.

5. Gates, "The 'Blackness of Blackness,'" p. 722.

6. The bulging "correspondences" between Reed and writers like Thomas Pynchon need to be examined at length. Yet Reed's work is different in that his characters can "act" in the world. For a gloss on this, see Douglas Fowler, *A Reader's Guide to Gravity's Rainbow* (Ann Arbor, Michigan: Ardis, 1980), p. 33.

7. Robert Fox, "The Mirrors of Caliban: A Study of the Fiction of LeRoi Jones (Imamu Amiri Baraka), Ishmael Reed and Samuel Delany," Diss. The University of New York at Buffalo, 1976, pp. 169-70. Fox's thesis is an early landmark in Reed scholarship (hereafter cited as Fox, "Mirrors").

8. Fox, "Mirrors," pp. 169-70.

9. While we are told that "The rites, principally Rada and Petro, are not inherently good or evil; it depends upon how they are used" (*MJ* 243), Benoit Battraville says, "I occasionally practice the Petro loa" (*MJ* 154). And the flag on Benoit's ship, with the words "din Bain Ding" ("Blood, Pain, Excrement") (*MJ* 150), is from a "Red (or cannibalistic) Sect" of Voodoo according to Milo Riguad, *Secrets of Voodoo* (New York: Arco, 1969), p. 164 (hereafter cited as Riguad, *Secrets*). Worse yet is "the Antonist Path, those Left-Handed practitioners of the Petro Loa" (*MJ* 241).

10. Riguad, *Secrets*, pp. 112-21.

11. Neil Schmitz, "Neo-HooDoo: The Experimental Fiction of Ishmael Reed," *Twentieth Century Literature*, 20 (April 1974), 138.

12. Gunther Schuller, *Early Jazz: Its Roots and Musical Development* (New York: Oxford University Press, 1968), p. 11. Also relevant, here, is his comment that "it is common knowledge that African drumming was originally a form of sign language" (p. 5).

13. Jane Harrison, *Themis*, quoted in Charles Olson, *The Special View of History* (Berkeley: Oyez, 1970), p. 22 (hereafter cited as Harrison, *Special View*).

14. Harrison, *Special View,* p. 22.

15. *Webster's New World Dictionary*, College Edition, s.v. "umbo" (hereafter cited as *Webster's*).

16. *Webster's*, s.v. "bo."

17. *Webster's*, s.v. "umbra." Relevant, here, is the knowledge that master African drummers memorize complicated rhythms by "nonsense syllables."

18. To my knowledge, no decent musicology of the be-bop era has yet been written. For some literary, contradictory accounts of Parker's harmonic breakthroughs, see Nat Hentoff and Nat Shapiro, *Hear Me Talkin to Ya: The Story of Jazz by the Men Who Made It* (New York: Dover, 1955). Paul Oliver writes of African griots who play three things at once on a Kora in *Savannah Syncopators: African Retentions in the Blues* (New York: Stein & Day, 1970), p. 47. The late Roland Kirk kept alive the tradition of playing on several woodwinds at once, using circular breathing.

19. *Webster's*, s.v. "nota."

20. *Webster's*, s.v. "note."

21. *Webster's*, s.v. "atony."

22. Riguad, *Secrets*, p. 10.

23. Perhaps the difficulty and artistry of jazz is at last to be recognized. This year Wynton Marsalis won "Grammies" in both jazz and classical trumpet playing. He has repeatedly claimed it is harder to play jazz.

24. Contrast the cliches of Marshall Stearns' *The Story of Jazz* (Oxford, England: Oxford University Press, 1956) with his more detailed and better *Jazz Dance: The Story of American Vernacular Dance* (New York: Macmillan, 1968), or with James Lincoln Collier's excellent *The Making of Jazz: A Comprehensive History* (1978; rpt. New York: Delta, 1979).

25. Concerning jazz as "weapon," a fascinating comment by Ornette Coleman, on how he felt he could start fights as a diversion by playing a blues in the key of D-flat is to be found in A. B. Spellman, *Black Music: Four Lives* (1966; rpt. New York: Schocken Books, 1970). Students of Reed and his Loop Garoo will note that wolves often "sing/howl" in the same key. A straight connection of jazz and the music of wolves can be found in records by Paul Winter.

26. Gates, "The 'Blackness of Blackness,'" p. 717.

27. *Webster's New International Dictionary of the English Language*, 2nd edition unabridged, s.v. "wolf" (hereafter cited as *WNID*).

28. *WNID*, s.v. "chromatics." Both directly and as parody, the two books on "color" (vision) Reed lists in the "Partial Bibliography" of *MJ* (numbers 72 and 94) should be explored.

29. *WNID*, s.v. "resonate, rebind, reverberation, record."

30. The "chorus/bridge" of a jazz tune is where the "player" both states the most repetitious part of the "versifying" song (as "his/her-story") and then transforms it, when s/he dances the self (into "my-story/stery") as personalized improvising. Without this personal energy/attention we have merely the burden, of increasingly anachronistic liturgy; in musical terms this is a "vamp" (or standard chord progression), and further explains Hinckle Von "'Vamp'-ton." Papa LaBas is probably transforming the Brooklyn Bridge, which is the ideal

candidate. Its singleness of vision broke the heart of its musical architect, Roeblings, and the poet, Hart Crane, who poured America into it in his *The Bridge*; yet this "suspension" bridge supported the chord "suspensions" of Sonny Rollins' jazz saxophone as he played upon its towers during his self-imposed isolation. For more on this, see Alan Trachtenberg, *The Brooklyn Bridge: Fact & Symbol* (Chicago: University of Chicago Press, 1979).
31. Lillian Lawler, "The Dance in Ancient Greece" (Middletown, Connecticut: Wesleyan University Press, 1964), p. 15. This position is even described partly *as a single pose in a pantomimic expression of the wind swaying back the reeds of the Nile* (p. 15; my italics).

The North Dakota Quarterly (Winter 1986): 18-29.

Neo-HooDoo: The Experimental Fiction of Ishmael Reed

Neil Schmitz/Article

Neo-HooDoo believes that man is an artist and every artist
a priest. You can bring your own creative ideas to Neo-HooDoo.
Charlie "Yardbird" (Thoth) Parker is an example of the Neo
HooDoo artist as an innovator and improviser.

Neo-HooDoo borrows from Haiti, Africa and South America.
Neo-HooDoo comes in all styles and moods.
          "Neo-HooDoo Manifesto" in *Conjure*

In his first novel, *The Free-Lance Pallbearers* (1967), Ishmael Reed emphatically declares what he will not do as a Black writer. Bukka Doopeyduk's narrative retells the tale told by countless Black heroes in Afro-American literature of their journey into the heart of whiteness only to deride its formulary disclosures and protests. Yet in parodying this confessional mode (the denouement of Doopeyduk's tale is his own crucifixion), Reed also attacks those Black writers who adopt fashionable approaches to experimental writing, who strive to be "Now-here" in "Nowhere." To turn from the stiffening form of the traditional novel James Baldwin shares with John Updike only to fall into the linguistic despair of William Burroughs or the elaborate glosses of metafiction is an artistic fate Reed has taken great pains to avoid. And therein lies the problem that has informed his subsequent fiction, *Yellow Back Radio Broke-Down* (1969) and *Mumbo Jumbo* (1972). How does one comprehend the significance of Burroughs' narrative form, write in the parodic manner of Thomas Pynchon and Donald Barthelme, and at the same time hold an opposed view of history, an optative, almost Emersonian sense of the dawning day?

In his collection of poetry, *Conjure* (1972), Reed unequivocally asserts that Neo-HooDoo, this new direction in Afro-American literature, constitutes "Our

Turn," a radical severance of his destiny as a writer from the fate of his White contemporaries. Appropriately the final poem, "introducing a new Loa," transforms Burroughs' emblematic nova, the dying light of Western civilization, into a "swinging HooDoo cloud," the birth of a new Africanized universe of discourse. "I call it the invisible train," he writes, "for which this Work has been but a modest schedule."[1]

The course of Reed's experimentation with narrative has thus increasingly involved his conception of Neo-HooDoo as a literary mode. My purpose in this essay is simply to take him at his word--the considerable claim that he has found a way of writing fiction unlike those decreative and self-reflexive fictive modes in which his white contemporaries seem imprisoned. Reed is careful, of course, not to establish Neo-HooDoo as a school. It is rather a characteristic stance, a mythological provenance, a behavior, a complex of attitudes, the retrieval of an idiom, but however broadly defined, Neo-HooDoo does manifest one constant and unifying refrain: Reed's fiercely professed alienation from Anglo-American literature. Ultimately, then, Neo-HooDoo is political art, as responsible as Richard Wright's *Native Son*, but without Wright's grim realism or the polemical separatism that characterizes Imamu Baraka's work. For Reed the problem is to get outside the "Euro-Am meaning world" (Baraka's term) without getting caught as an artist in a contraposed system. Yet Baraka's initial thesis is passionately embraced. "We must. . . be estranged from the dominant culture," James T. Stewart declares in *Black Fire*, the pioneering anthology Baraka, then Leroi Jones, helped edit with Larry Neal. "This estrangement," Stewart continues, "must be nurtured in order to generate and energize our black artists. This means that he can not be 'successful' in any sense that has meaning in white critical evaluations. Nor can his work ever be called 'good' in any context or meaning that could make sense to that traditional critique."[2] In Reed's fiction, particularly the novels after *Pallbearers,* this rigorous denial of the "dominant culture" and its critical values has led to paradoxes and ambiguities that are exceptionally "good" in the terms of "that traditional critique." One can invent myths, invoke legends, change his name and dress, but he cannot will himself into another language. And it is specifically literary language with its seductive devices, its forms and rhetoric, that pulls the self-styled exile back into the consciousness he professes to despise. More than any other contemporary Black writer, Reed seems aware of this dilemma, the difficulty of fashioning an art form that will liberate him from the double consciousness signified by the hyphen between Afro and American. Yet this liberation is the objective of *Pallbearers*, the meaning of its negations, and the challenge of his later fiction.

As the narrator of *Pallbearers,* Doopeyduk speaks literally from the grave. The scat-singing voice that introduces the novel does not belong to the Doopeyduk who speaks within the narrative duration of *Pallbearers.* In killing off that latter Doopeyduk, Reed murders a style, the Black writer's appropriation of what D. H. Lawrence (in a different context) called "art-speech."

Doopeyduk's attempt to fashion his discourse in formal English only reveals his stupidity, an ignorance not of correct grammar or proper diction, but of his world. For the Language in which he invests his feelings and perceptions is a dead language. He speaks to his wife, the combustible Fannie Mae, as though he were translating a text, and her response is appropriately ribald. It is not, however, just the White man's "art-speech" in the Black man's voice that Reed burlesques. He attacks as well the conventions of Afro-American literature, its traditional modes of rendering and interpreting Black experience. The progress of Doopeyduk in the novel follows a familiar script. He is a Nazarene apprentice who believes in the Nazarene Manual, who seeks to make his straight fortune in the crooked Nazarene world of HARRY SAM. The structure on which Reed relies in this narrative, which he inflates and explodes, is the structure of Richard Wright's *Black Boy*, Ralph Ellison's *Invisible Man,* and the many subsequent books like them: *"read growing up in Soulsville first of three installments /or what it means to be a backstage darky."*[3] Reed delivers the obligatory scenes of such confessional fiction with studied vulgarity. When Doopeyduk is fired from the hospital where he works as an orderly: "I dropped to my knees and threw the kat all kinds of Al Jolson mammies, one after the other, but he wasn't impressed. 'O, don't,' I cried, tugging at his pants. 'Don't take the golden bedpan, don't take it, do anything but don't take the goldenbedpan'" (*PB*, p. 92). The notes of this native son are writ large. Doopeyduk begins his travail in a well-lit and clearly marked place. "I live in HARRY SAM," he declares. "HARRY SAM is something else. A big not-to-be-believed out-of-sight, sometimes referred to as O-BOP-SHE-BANG or KLANG-A-LANG-A-DING-DONG. SAM has not been seen since the day thirty years ago when he disappeared into the John with a weird ravaging illness" (*PB*, p. 1). The rites of passage established by Wright, Ellison, and Baldwin in their fiction are stripped of their dramatic force and reduced to the pratfalls of a burlesque routine. Doopeyduk's award for promising service is a bedpan, not a briefcase and a scholarship, and SAM, both as place and person, holds no mysteries.

Like Ellison's protagonist, Doopeyduk is doubly victimized in *Pallbearers,* sold the bill of goods in the Nazarene creed, and then ruthlessly betrayed by Blacks who already know the swindle and work for their own ends within the game. Reed's mockery of pyrotechnical Black militant prose and the sermonic indignance of the Black bourgeoisie cuts through its pose to reveal the personal ambition it guards. Everything is false in HARRY SAM. Everyone is on the make. For all its sophisticated contrivance, the avant-garde BECOMING in which Doopeyduk is persuaded to participate turns out to be nothing more than an elaborate replication of the carnival booth where baseballs were once thrown at living Black Aces. But here it is Cipher X who puts Doopeyduk into the stocks and bombards him while a tape recorder intones manifestos.

WHITEY YOU DIE TOMORROW RIGHT AFTER BREAKFAST AND IF
YOU DON'T DIE THEN CHOKING ON YOUR WAFFLES DON'T
BREATHE A SIGH OF RELIEF AND SAY THANK GOD FOR BUFFERIN
'CAUSE THAT WILL ONLY MEAN THAT YOU WILL MEET YOUR
MAKER COME THE VERY NEXT DAY. HEAH THAT. HEAH THAT,
WHITEY, ON THE NEXT SUNNY DAY YOU WILL MEET YOUR
DEMISE, YOU BEASTS CREATURES OF THE DEEP. 'CAUSE YOU
CAN'T HOLD UP A CANDLE TO US VIRILE BLACK PEOPLE. LOOK AT
THAT MUSCLE. COME ON UP HERE CHARLIE AND FEEL THAT
MUSCLE. IF YOU DON'T WATCH OUT WE WILL BREAK INTO THOM
MCAN'S AND STEAL ALL THE SHOES. HEAH THAT, ANIMALS. (*PB*,
pp. 102-103)

If the scene recalls the degradation of Todd Clifton in *Invisible Man*, there is in
Reed's version neither polished prose nor intricate metaphor--just spiteful
laughter. In Ellison's novel such scenes are rhetorical see-pieces; they bristle
with allegorical signs (the long sequence in the paint factory), but most of all
they explain Black experience. A secret existence is revealed, a breast bared:
what it means to be a backstage darky. And the writer's credentials as bona fide
explicator are manifest in the finish of his language, his mastery of the European
tradition. In HARRY SAM, simply put there are no mythic labyrinths for the
black hero to explore. With its slashes of boldface, exaggerated diction, and
crudely scrawled characters, Reed's style mimics the stark simplifying line of
the cartoon. There is no difficulty in decoding Aboreal Hairyman, Eliyah Raven,
Nancy Spellman, the Harry Sam Motel or the Seventeen Nation Disarmement
Conference Bar, where aged conferees, lost in fond reminiscences of former
wars, sit amiably drinking. Nor is there any confusion in his representation of
the Nazarene establishment or the due process of SAM's laws. Judge
Whimplewhopper's court in *Pallbearers* clearly reflect Pigmeat Markham
vaudeville bench (*Here come da judge*), that scandalous joke American
jurisprudence imitates in its criminal courts. Reed's parody of the "Neo-Slave
Narrative" thus opens into a comprehensive attack on the American society.
When Doopeyduk at last loses his innocence, the most important of his
recognitions is that he is part of HARRY SAM, not at all an interloper. Jews and
Christians, Black militants and White Marxists, academics and gangsters--each
has his pipeline to the Harry Sam Motel, his own private GOAT-SHE-ATE-
SHUNS with SAM who squats upon the Great Commode, his closets filled with
the mangled remains of children. In *Pallbearers* the "lower frequencies" of the
invisible man's representative voice into ribald italicized blare.

    That is the nightmare of *Pallbearers:* an uproar of simplicities. In his
derisive rendering of the traditional form of Black action and his ridicule of its
questing heroes, Reed in effect writes the "literature of self-parody" Richard
Poirier describes in *The Performing Self*, that action which "proposes not the
rewards so much as the limits of its own procedures . . . shapes itself around its
dissolvents . . . calls into question not any particular literary structure so much as

the enterprise, the activity itself of creating any literary form, of empowering an idea with a style."[4] Yet Reed, as I have suggested, is not primarily concerned with the insufficient of literary form or the intrinsic value of writing. It is the inappropriateness of Anglo-American forms and imitative Black writing that leads him to burlesque and parody, modes which enable him to exorcise "style" and "form" in order to clear a space for a new approach to fiction. In *Pallbearers* Reed consistently thrusts literary devices at the reader, demolishing interpretation. "A cloud moved above sagging with rain. It seemed as if it had eyes, nose, lips. It did, my eyes, nose, and lips. Get it? Clouds. Head in the clouds" (*PB*, p. 93). In his preface to *19 Necromancers from Now,* an anthology of current Afro-American writing, Reed tells an anecdote that clarifies this attitude. "I have a joke I tell friends about a young Black poet who relies upon other people's systems, and does not use his head. He wears sideburns and has seen every French film in New York. While dining at Schrafft's he chokes to death on nut-covered ice cream and dies. He approaches the river Styx and pleads with Charon to ferry him across: 'I don't care how often you've used me as a mythological allusion Charon says. You're still a nigger--swim!'"[5]

The narrative voice that governs *Pallbearers* is ostensibly revitalized, purged of the "art-speech" that beguiled the sideburned Black in New York. Yet it is also studied in its funkiness, reminiscent at times of talltalk, roughened discourse that often slips into the rhythms of Robert Service's verse: "SAM's mother was a lowdown, filthy hobo infected with hoof-and-mouth disease. A five-o'clock-shadowed junkie who died of diphtheria and an overdose of phenobarb" (*PB*, p. 1). At his best, describing the grotesque madhouse inside the Harry Sam Motel at the end of the novel, Reed achieves the surrealistic brilliance of Burroughs' skits in *Naked Lunch.* But between these extremes the prose often stalls in orthographical and grammatical posturin--misspelling for the hell of it. Finally, then, the problem with Doopeyduk's posthumous voice is that it is too obviously worked, too strained in its license. Burroughs' ability to transform street language, the idiom of the junkworld, into powerfully stated and precise metaphors, a figurative language as dense and complex as any other in literature, remains the modern epitome of an accomplished colloquial style, an excellence Reed fails to attain in *Pallbearers.* What he does achieve, however, is the elliptical flow and quick displacements of Burroughs' narrative, the cutting edge of Burroughs' cold understanding of modern reality. The Hobbesian question--"Wouldn't you?"--posed in *Naked Lunch* as the resolution to the Algebra of Need is rephrased throughout *Pallbearers.* In HARRY SAM everyone is high on power and driven by the hunger to get higher. Yet if Reed manages to erase the whiteness in his writing (the well-wrought form and rhetoric that won Baldwin so much critical praise) and breaks conclusively with the traditional novel, he does not emerge with a contrary Black style. The language of *Pallbearers* is an orchestration of idiolects, conflicting types of speech that caricature their speakers, but no single voice rules this contrived discordance. Brought back from the novelistic life he so badly lived, Doopeyduk retells that novel like a theatrical impressionist, a mimic skillfully doing all its characters.

Yellow Back Radio constitutes Reed's attempt to reconstruct a coherent perspective and viable form from the necessary wreckage of *Pallbearers*. Armed with supernatural "connaissance," the magic of poetry, the Loop Garoo Kid replaces Doopeyduk, the hapless victim, at the center of Reed's fiction. "One has to return," Reed writes in the introduction to *19 Necromancers,* "to what some writers would call 'dark heathenism' to find original tall tales, and yarns with the kind of originality that some modern writers use as found poetry--the enigmatic street rhymes of Ellison's minor characters, or the dozens. I call this neo-hoodooism; a spur to originality, which prompted Julia Jackson, a New Orleans soothsayer, when asked the origins of the amulets, talismans, charms, and potions in her workshops, to say: 'I make all my own stuff. It saves me money and it's as good. People who has to buy their stuff, ain't using their heads'" (*19N*, pp.xvii-xviii). In brief, this is the significance of Neo-Hoodoo as an experimental mode, the concept that informs *Yellow Back Radio*. "The Afro-American artist," Reed continues, "is similar to the Necromancer (a word whose etymology is relieving in itself!) He is a conjurer who works Juju upon its oppressors; a witch doctor who frees his fellow victims from the psychic attack launched by demons of the outer and inner world" (*19N*, p.xviii). Such an art is the art of *bricolage*. Improvisational, decentered, restricted to the materials at hand, Reed's Neo-HooDooist (the exemplary Julia Jackson) indeed resembles the native *bricoleur* whom Claude Levi-Strauss describes at length in *The Savage Mind.*[6] It is this fluent state of mind that enables the Loop Garoo Kid in *Yellow Back Radio* to confound so easily the snares set for him in Drag Gibson's American West. In its syncretistic composition, its diversity of gods and forms of worship, its avoidance of dogmatic structures, voodoo is Reed's reality model, the known world forever hidden from the gaze of Westerners. Within it Loop is unvulnerable; sheltered by ritual, aided by the endless resources of Nature, and empowered by the full possession of his body.

In the "Neo-HooDoo Manifesto," which first appeared in the Los Angeles *Free Press* (September 18-24,1970), Reed devises a myth that divides history into a war between two churches, two communities of consciousness: the "Cop Religion" of Christianity and the transformed Osirian rite,Voodoo. Sounding at once like Burroughs and Davy Crockett he then declares the contest: "Neo-HooDoos are detectives of the metaphysical about to make a pinch. We have issued warrants for a god arrest" (C, p. 24). Loop is precisely that hero, the comic apostle of liberating heresies. The problem in *Yellow Back Radio* is to translate voodoo into a singular way of writing, to dislodge it from its status as a cultural myth and make it instead a state of consciousness. As we shall see, Reed does not write mythically--he writes about writing mythically.

If only in theory, then, Neo-HooDoo represents a new direction (so Reed argues) for the Black writer, an escape from the decadence of Anglo-American literature that reverses the path historically taken by Black writers and intellectuals in the United States. In *The Narrative of the Life of Frederick Douglass,* just before Douglass' epical fight with the "nigger-breaker," Edward Covey, another slave gives Douglass a "certain *root,* which if I would take some of it with me, *carrying it always on my right side,* would render it impossible for Mr. Covey, or any other white man, to whip me."[7] Douglass keeps this "*root*" italicized in his discussion of the event--it is Black magic--and what Douglass is striving to assert in his narrative is his possession of White magic, the word. Neo-HooDoo in effect stresses the power of that "*root*" and contends that the word is without value unless suffused and transformed by its occult force. It is this piece of Africa given to Douglass, and then forgotten by Douglass, that Reed strives to redeem.

But where are the "original folk tales" and native idioms in Reed's fiction? How far indeed does Neo-HooDoo (both as myth and mode) take him from established literary canons? His discourse in *Yellow Back Radio* and *Mumbo Jumbo* curves in and around colloquial Black English, which serves him as a stylistic device, not as a language. It is withal a learned and allusive discourse as mixed in its diction as Mark Twain's. His forms are not narrative legends taken from an oral tradition, but rather the popular forms of the Western and the Gangster Novel. As A. B. Spellman observes in *Black Fire*, this frustrated search for indigenous forms "is not the exclusive predicament of the Afro-American artist--the exponents of negritude in Africa and the Indies have spent years dealing with it. Novelist Edouard Glissant of Martinique had an extremely difficult time reorienting his style to develop a fictional form that conformed more to the oral folk tale than to the French novel. Glissant's compatriot, Aimé Césaire, feeling trapped in a European language, went back into Surrealism to find an anti-French, which would, in a sense, punish the colonialists for forcing him to write in a European language."[8] Césaire's fate, writing anti-French, resembles Reed's in *Yellow Back Radio* and *Mumbo Jumbo.* Reed is driven to Burroughs for an anti-English as Césaire was to André Breton. *Yellow Back Radio* is a Black version of the Western Burroughs has been writing in fragments and promising in full since the fifties. Not only is the content of the fiction eclectic in its composition, but Loop's performance as a houngan in it has a good deal of Burroughs' "Honest Bill." For the core of his narrative, Reed borrows almost intact the sociological drama Norman Mailer describes in *The White Negro*--that migration of White middle-class youth in revolt against the values of their own culture toward the counter-culture of Black America and then weaves into this phenomenon a barely disguised account of the student uprisings at Berkeley and other campuses. The shooting at Kent State comes after the publication of *Yellow Back Radio*, but it is accurately prefigured in the book.

In *Yellow Back Radio,* an unspecified town in the mythical West, the children, stoned on "pearl-shaped pills," have overthrown their elders and have begun to establish their own community. "Made us learn facts by rote," one bitterly complains. "Lies really bent upon making us behave. We decided to create our own fictions."[9] As the narrative begins, they are entertained by a visiting Black Circus that features Zozo Labrique, a hoo-doo *maman*, and the formidable Loop Garoo, an expert with the bullwhip. The festival, however, is short-lived. The subdued parents strike a deal with a tyrannical rancher, Drag Gibson, who then executes a bloody repression. There is a massacre, the town is recovered, and only a few children, along with Loop, survive. The children go off in search of Marcusian Utopia, the "Seven Cities of Cibola, magnificent legendary American paradise while tranquilised and smiling machines gladly did all of the work so that man could be free to dream" (*YB*, p.24). Only Loop is left to confront Gibson's brutally established imperium. The traditional forces of good and evil are thus quickly aligned in Reed's version of the Western, but in unlikely personages and without the typical resolution. From a cave in the hills, Loop fights Gibson's egomaniacal use of technology, his political and economic power, with spells and charms, with ecstasy and magic. There is no shoot-out in the streets. Loop will not fight on Gibson's terms and with Gibson's means. The phallic whip and his ruby-eyed snake are his weapons; he lurks in his cave-- insurgent libidinal force. The morality play of the conventional Western which pits the forces of law and order against the outlaw, the realm of the settled against the space of the nomadic, is thus subverted and transformed. The rancher (Gibson) and the outlaw (John Wesley Hardin) have finally one face, a single character: they are murderous racists. Their mythic struggle in the Western is a struggle for the booty, a quarrel among thieves, and not a grandiose opposition. It is rather the Black Circus, Loop's erotic laughter, that Reed sets against Gibson's villainy.

Into this revised Western, as I have indicated, Reed pours all the bitterness of present history. Certain Blacks betray Loop for the same dubious rewards that prompted Apache scouts to lead the cavalry to Geronimo. Official Washington is as blind and uncaring about the student massacre in the hinterland as it was during the Indian Wars of the 1880s. And like the Sioux after their crushing defeat at Wounded Knee, the victims of Gibson's peace (the students and Black militants of the sixties) dream apocalyptic dreams, create a drug culture (peyote/LSD), and retreat into themselves. So the narrative unfolds and draws to its necessary end. The only hold-out, the last authentic outlaw, is the artist, the worker of spells, Loop as necromancer. Yet in expanding the scope of the narrative in the final section to give Loop his mythopoeic due, Reed loses the bite of his allusive framework. The ending (Loop on a scaffold about to be hanged) presents a dazzling array of black-outs, bizarre Warholian bits, one-liners. But the laughter at the center of all this hilarity is so cold in its nihilism that it chills the book's critical perspectives. In *Pallbearers* Doopeyduk is finally crucified, having failed in his attempt to supplant SAM as a Black SAM, and life goes on. Loop, however, is a hero and presumptive victor, not another Black who gets it in the neck. But the history that gives Reed his narrative line in *Yellow Back Radio* runs out on him.

When the Pope arrives near the end of the narrative ostensibly to save Gibson from Loop's "connaissance," the book dissolves into lectures. His role is that of an interlocutor who makes intelligible to Gibson (and White readers) the occult nature of Loop's enduring power.

> Well anyway, the Pope continued, when African slaves were sent to Haiti, Santo Domingo and other Latin American countries, we Catholics attempted to change their pantheon, but the natives merely placed our art alongside theirs. Our insipid and uninspiring saints were no match for theirs: Damballah, Legba and other deities which are their Loa. This religion is so elastic that some of the women priests name Loa after their boyfriends. When Vodun arrived in America, the authorities became so paranoid they banned it for a dozen or so years, even to the extent of discontinuing the importation of slaves from Haiti and Santo Domingo. (*YB*, pp. 153-154)

The Pope has come, in any case, to renew an acquaintance, not to condemn Loop. They are intimates, the White Antichrist and the Black Antichrist, the former cynically supporting the institutions of civilization and the latter cheerfully undermining them. "That's me, the cosmic jester," Loop declares. "Matter of fact, I've always been harmless--St. Nick coming down the chimney, children leaving soup for me--always made to appear foolish, the scapegoat of all history. You and your crowd are the devils. The way you massacred the Gnostics, not to mention the Bogomils, Albigenses, and Walderses" (*YB*, p. 165). Gibson is lost in this shaming of myths. He becomes an ineffectual supernumerary in the vast drama Reed rolls down (again the painted vaudeville curtain) at the end of the narrative. Yet his transference of Loop from wicked necromancer to Black Eulenspiegel, while it frees Loop from the vicissitudes of American history, hardly opens "doors to the divine," the projected aim of Neo-HooDooism. If anything, it underlines the contradictions in *Yellow Back Radio*. In effect, the Pope's arrival restores the hyphenated consciousness Reed seeks to annul in his fiction. It is the Pope who fills us in, who makes the connections that enable us to see how and why Loop works as a character. *Yellow Back Radio* thus turns into a book *about* Neo-HooDooism. And every explanation, every concealed footnote, betrays the artifice of the myth. Reed's mythopoeic lore is as arcane as the cryptic references strewn about in Burroughs' fiction. And his art, it would seem, bears as much relation to James Brown doing the "Popcorn" or Jimi Hendrix stroking his guitars as does T. S. Eliot's, whom Reed consigns in his manifesto to the graveyard of Christian culture.

Mumbo Jumbo, Reed's most recent fiction, teems with citations. The recitative as a narrative form (*Yellow Back Radio* begins: "Folks. This here is the story of the Loop Garoo Kid.") is abandoned for a more sophisticated and complex mode, a composite narrative containing a variety of texts, the most important of which (the sacred text--the Book of Thoth) is never revealed. Indeed that is Reed's thesis in *Mumbo Jumbo*. *"So Jes Grew is seeking its words. Its text. For what good is a liturgy without a text?"*[10] Jes Grew is the Osirian/Dionisian phenomenon of the dance recurring in New Orleans around the 1890s. Reed takes the term from James Weldon Johnson's *The Book of American Negro Poetry*. "The earliest ragtime songs," Johnson wrote, "like Topsy, 'jes grew'" (*MJ*, p11). In his narrative Reed concentrates on the Harlem Renaissance of the twenties (Langston Hughes, Countee Cullen, et al), the first significant adaptation of the idiomatic energies present in Jes Grew by Black artists in the United States, and his fiction, except for the epilogue, is set in that period. The main dramatic action in *Mumbo Jumbo* revolves around the conspiratorial efforts of the Wallflower Order of the Knights Templar to adulterate Jes Grew, to bleach its blackness and neutralize its force. They are opposed by a number of Black figures in Harlem: the *Mu'tafikah* (a brotherhood of cultural subversives), Black gangsters led by Buddy Jackson, Black artists like Claude McKay, Abdul Hamid, a Garvey-like ideologue, and by PaPa LaBas, Reed's protagonist, an aging *houngan* who carries in his memory a long tradition of Jes Grew, who knows its mythic origin in the Osirian legend. *Mumbo Jumbo,* then, is primarily an historical narrative, a tragicomical review of what went wrong in the twenties, the failure of Jes Grew to retain its purity (secure its text). As such, the book is also an ingenious dissertation on the nature of Afro-American art, a dissertation with a program for the revival of that art.

By fracturing his narrative into a series of sub-texts (there is even a romance, Earline's love for Berbelang), Reed solves some of the problems that arise in *Yellow Back Radio*, notably the problem of introducing a great amount of mythological information. His spokesman, Papa LaBas, is a detached commentator who comes slowly to recognize that his practice of voodoo necromancy *per se* has cut him off from the larger movement of Jes Grew. The activities of Hinckle Von Vampton, the Templar assigned to suppress Jes Grew by diluting it with parasitic forms, brings LaBas (who recognized Von Vampton as the timeless agent of Seth, the arch-rival and assassin of Osiris) out of his parochialism into the multifarious fray of the book's numerous stories. Each story generates its own point of view, its own interpretation of Jes Grew, and gives Reed the ability to range widely over the dramatic possibilities within his myth. Similarly the diversity of these interpretations reflects the subtlety and complex nature of the Harlem Renaissance. Abdul Hamid, the puritanical Egyptologist who possesses the sacred text, the Book of Thoth, and then burns it, emerges as a cynical myth-maker with a narrow vision of the needs of Black people.

> These are modern times. These are the last days of your roots and your conjure and your gris-gris and your healing potions and love powder. I am building something that the people will understand. This country is eclectic. The

architecture, the people, the music, the writing. The thing that works here will have a little bit of jive talk and a little bit of North Africa, a fez-wearing mulatto in a pinstriped suit. A man who can say give me some skin as well as Asalamilakum. Haven't you heard? This is the country where something is successful in direct proportion to how it's put over; how it's gamed. *(MJ,* p. 38)

Rephrasing the beliefs of Papa LaBas, the Haitian, Benoit Battraville, later counters that argument with an eloquent appeal:

You see the Americans do not know the names of the long and tedious list of deities and rites as we know them. Shorthand is what they know so well. They know this process for they have synthesized the HooDoo of VooDoo. Its bleeblop essence; they've isolated the unknown factor which gives the loas their rise. [Battraville speaks here of the Afro-American practitioners of voodoo.] Ragtime. Jazz. Blues. The new thang. That talk you drum from your lips. Your style. What you have here is an experimental art form that all of us believe bears watching. So don't ask me how to catch Jes Grew. Ask Louis Armstrong, Bessie Smith, your poets, your painters, your musicians, ask them how to catch it.... Ask those little colored urchins who 'make up' those new dance steps and the loa of the Black cook who wrote the last lines of the 'Ballad of Jesse James.' Ask the man who, deprived of an electronic guitar, picked up a washboard and started to play it. (*MJ,* p. 152)

Battraville's address is directed at Nathan Brown, whom Reed castigates for his "literary" predilections. Readers unfamiliar with the leading figures and notable disputes of the Harlem Renaissance will have a difficult time with *Mumbo Jumbo.* Reed's text is even further complicated. Photographs and news clippings (with attendant commentary) are interspersed throughout *Mumbo Jumbo.* Warren G. Harding's supposed negritude is woven into Reed's maze of plots. The American occupation of Haiti is threaded into the central plot-- Haitian revolutionaries visit New York and negotiate with Papa LaBas. Unlike *Yellow Back Radio,* where Reed's focus often seems simplistic and his energies diffused, *Mumbo Jumbo* swirls with the taut intricacy of a Jacobean revenge play.

The missing text, the Book of Thoth which Papa LaBas and Hinckle Von Vampton strive to locate, is not only the nexus of all these diverse plot-lines; it is also the inadvertent symbol of the central paradox in Reed's Neo-HooDooism. The problem can be briefly stated. When an oral tradition is written down, it becomes inevitably literature. Yet the mystique of the oral tradition is compelling--particularly for Black writers. In Al Young's lovely first novel *Snakes* (1970), Champ succinctly states that knowledge when he reprimands some apprentice-musicians: "I don't care how good somethin' be soundin' on a record, it's always better when you can catch it in person."[11] When PaPa LaBas relates the history of NeoHooDoo art , he asserts the primacy of the text and the value of literature. Without words, without the permanence of language, without interpretation, Jes Grew is formless and random. In the Osirian legend the Dance at last gets out of control, and people, seized with its power, begin to neglect necessary tasks. An artist then approaches Osiris with an offer: "He called on Osiris 1 day and argued his theory that outbreaks occurred because the mysteries had no text to turn to. No litany to feed the spirits that were seizing the people, and that if Osiris would execute these dance steps for Thoth he would illustrate them and then Osirian priests could determine what god or spirit possessed them as well as learn how to make these gods and spirits depart" (*MJ,* p.164).

Reed does not investigate the ironies enmeshed in that event. By writing down the Osirian Dance, Thoth dispenses with its spontaneity. He creates, moreover, something that looks like the beginning of criticism. "Guides were initiated into the Book of Thoth, the 1st anthology written by the 1st choreographer" (*MJ,* p.164). Indeed, though Reed mercilessly attacks Eliot and Ezra Pound in *Conjure* as "Jeho-vah Revisionists," the archpriests of "atonist" literature, *Mumbo Jumbo* is as brocaded with mythic, literary, and historical allusions as either the *Wasteland* or the *Cantos.* "*Jes Grew is seeking its words*" (*MJ,* p. 6), Reed tells us at the start of the narrative, but by the end of the novel it seems rather that the text is searching for Jes Grew. "So don't ask me how to catch Jes Grew," Battraville advises Nathan Brown. "Ask Louis Armstrong, Bessie Smith, your poets, your painters, your musicians, ask them how to catch it. Ask those people who be shaking their tambourines impervious of the ridicule they receive from Black and White Atonists, Europe the ghost rattling its chains down the deserted halls of their brains"*(MJ,* p. 152). The point is stressed so often and at such length in *Mumbo Jumbo* that it becomes at last merely strident protest that is suspiciously excessive. What modern novelist perplexed by the decadence of his form would not dream of the fluent ease with which the folk artist performs or, for that matter, his copious store of material? Reed's image of the literary Neo-HooDooist is taken from that vision of writing as singing or playing. "Loop seems to be scatting arbitrarily, using forms of this and adding his own. He's blowing like that celebrated musician Charles Yardbird Parker-- improvising as he goes along" (*YB,* p. 154). In *Mumbo Jumbo* Brown is told to "Open-Up-To-Right-Here and then you will have something coming from your experiences that the whole world will admire and need" (*MJ,* p. 152). But, simply put, the language of music is not the language of literature. The Black musician's access to Jes Grew is different. Loop and Papa LaBas are more akin to Burroughs' wisecracking narrators than they are to Parker.

The conflict between the Atonists and the adherents of Jes Grew in *Mumbo Jumbo* thus dramatizes a fundamental tension in Reed's own art. His fiction has become increasingly complex, learned, and witty (*Mumbo Jumbo* has a bibliography that extends for five pages), and by that measure the figurative Book of Thoth, an Afro-American text written from within a coherent and unified hoodooed consciousness, seems proportionately distant. In a sense, the problem with *Mumbo Jumbo* is that it is not mumbo jumbo at all. Reed's uneasiness with his position in American literature, if not literature itself, is strikingly apparent in the introduction to *19 Necromancers* where, curiously enough, he begins by arguing the irrelevance of terms like "Black writing." Burroughs' "Argonauts Return" is cited as fiction that could have been written by a Black man. "The category of print," he concludes in that passage, "is not a racial or sexual category--and when one is reading print; decoding someone else's experience or non-experience, fairy tales, science fiction, fantasy, etc., the author may be a thousand miles away or dead" (*19N*, p.xiii). Yet it is "originality," the absolute otherness of Afro-American writing, that he zealously propounds in his theoretical expositions of Neo-HooDoo. The writings of Calvin Hernton, Cecil Brown, William Kelley (the Joycean Kelley of *Dunfords Travels Everywhere*), Lennox Raphael, and Al Young are "dazzling experiments in content and form . . . what these selections [in Reed's anthology] have in common is their originality--originality even within well-known literary modes" (*19N*, p. xxv). These are some of the writers who have presumably regained the virus of Jes Grew in the sixties--but where and how Cecil Brown's *The Life and Loves of Mr. Jiveass Nigger* (1969), for example, manifests the signs of Neo-HooDoo is not explained.

In fact, contemporary Afro-American writing is as diverse and generally parodic in its modes as contemporary Anglo-American writing--the milieu and idiom differs, not the fictional tactics. Reed's Neo-HooDooist moves finally along the same metafictive angle that Pynchon and Barthelme take in their fiction, probing folklore and myth with the same seriocomic intent, to wrench from them their own truths. What distinguishes Reed's Neo-HooDooist is his adamant optimism, his belief that "print and words are not dead at all" (*19N*, p. xxvii), the ringing note on which Reed ends his preface. "But Don Miguel," Robert Coover writes in his dedicatory prologue to Cervantes in *Pricksongs and Descants*, "the optimism, the innocence, the aura of possibility you experienced has been largely drained away, and the universe is closing in on us again. Like you, we, too, seem to be standing at the end of an age and on the threshold of another. We, too, have been brought into a blind alley by the critics and the analysts: we, too, suffer from a literature of exhaustion, though ironically our nonheroes are no longer tireless and tedious Amadises, but hopelessly defeated and bedridden Quixotes."[12] Reed shares Coover's apocalyptic view of modern literature, but only to the extent that the "blind alley" is Coover's fate, not his own. At the end of *Mumbo Jumbo* Papa LaBas asserts that the sensous humanism, the innocence and the aura of possibility that "jes grew" in the twenties will return. "Time is a pendulum," he declares. "Not a river. More akin to what goes around comes around" (*MJ*, p.218) Whether this time Jes Grew will flourish in Afro-American writing as well as in music, enabling the writer to create new and viable art forms, remains to be seen.

NOTES

1. Ishmael Reed, *Conjure, Selected Poems 1963-1970* (Amherst: University of Massachussetts Press, 1972), p.83. Subsequent references will be indicated *C* in the text.
2. James T. Stewart, "The Development of the Black Revolutionary Artist," in *Black Fire, an Anthology of Afro-American Writing,* ed. Leroi Jones and Larry Neal (New York, Morrow, 1968), p.6. Much of Reed's aesthetic theory parallels Stewart's argument in this essay.
3. Ishmael Reed. *The Free-Lance Pallbearers* (Garden City, New York: Doubleday, 1967), p.107. Subsequent references will be indicated *PB* in the text.
4. Richard Poirier, *The Performing Self* (New York, Oxford University Press, 1971), pp.27-28.
5. Ishmael Reed, *19 Necromancers from Now* (Garden City, NewYork: Doubleday, 1970), p. xvii. Subsequent references will be indicated *19N* in the text.
6. Claude Levi-Strauss, *The Savage Mind* (Chicago: University of Chicago Press, 1966), pp. 16-33. "One deprives oneself of all means of understanding magical thought," Strauss writes, "if one tries to reduce it to a moment or stage in technical and scientific evolution. Like a shadow moving ahead of its owner it is in a sense complete in itself, and is finished and coherent in its immateriality as the substantial being which it precedes. Magical thought is not to be regarded as a beginning, a rudiment, a sketch, a part of a whole which has not yet materialized. It forms a well-articulated system, and is in this respect independent of that other system which constitutes science, except for the purely formal analogy which brings them together and makes the former a sort of metaphorical expression of the latter" (p. 13).
7. *Narrative of the Life of Frederick Douglass* (Cambridge:Harvard University Press, 1971), p. 102.
8. A. B. Spellman, "Not Just Whistling Dixie," in *Black Fire,* p.164.
9. Ishmael Reed, *Yellow Back Radio Broke-Down* (Garden City, NewYork: Doubleday, 1969), p. 16. Subsequent references will be indicated *YB* in the text.
10. Ishmael Reed, *Mumbo Jumbo* (Garden City, New York:Doubleday, 1972), p. 6. Subsequent references will be indicated *MJ* in the text.
11. Al Young, *Snakes* (New York: Holt, Rinehart and Winston, 1970),p. 58.
12. Robert Coover, *Pricksongs & Descants* (New York, Toronto and London: New American Library, 1971), p. 78.

Twentieth Century Literature (April 1974): 126-140.

THE LAST DAYS OF LOUISIANA RED (1974)

Recent Fiction: *The Last Days of Louisiana Red*

Barbara Smith/Review

One of the many critical studies of Afro-American literature that needs to be written might be entitled "Irony and the Black Literary Tradition." Except for the serious odes of Phillis Wheatley, there is hardly a work by an Afro-American author that would not be illuminated by such an approach. On second thought, even Wheatley's poems embody the inherent irony of a black poetic spirit cramped into a white poetic mold. Irony is an essential element in black artistic expression because it is so integral a part of black life.

When this study is written the works of Ishmael Reed will have at least a chapter devoted to them. His new novel, *The Last Days of Louisiana Red*, might serve as a textbook on irony. In it he blends paradox, hyperbole, understatement and signifyin' so expertly that you can almost hear a droll black voice telling the tale as you read it.

One of Reed's best satiric methods is the interweaving of fantastic verbal absurdities with the familiar absurdities of everyday life. He compares the entrance of *Louisiana Red's* hero, Ed Yellings, into Berkeley, California to the entrance of Osiris into Egypt at a time when "cannibalism was in vogue."

> When Ed Yellings entered Berkeley "men were not eating men"; men were inflicting psychological stress on one another. Driving one another to strokes, high blood pressure, hardening of the arteries, which only made it worse since the stabbings, ravings, muggings went on as usual.

This is of course comic irony; in Reed's hands it is a mighty weapon.

The primary targets of Reed's wit are the black revolutionary organizations that sprang up in places like Berkeley in the 1960s. He condemns their use of revolutionary violence, which was at times indistinguishable from old-fashioned crime. The posturing, the rhetoric and the exploitation that sometimes characterized actual movements symbolize the forces of foolishness and evil in Reed's hoodoo drama.

Reed calls the members of the movement the Moochers, a term taken from a Cab Calloway song, and terms their mindlessly bloody tactics "Louisiana Red," which is also a kind of hot sauce. He explains:

> Moochers are people who, when they are to blame, say it's the other fellow's fault for bringing it up. Moochers don't return stuff they borrow. Moochers ask you to share when they have nothing to share...God, do they suffer...Though Moochers wrap themselves in the full T-shirt of ideology, their own ideology is Mooching.

The opposing forces of righteousness are led by Ed Yellings, founder of the Solid Gumbo Works and a discoverer of a cure for cancer. Actually, the Gumbo Works is a highly sophisticated voodoo operation, but Reed hilariously appropriates the slogans and symbols of capitalistic enterprise to describe its activities.

The plot of *Louisiana Red* is impossible to recount. Like Reed's last novel *Mumbo Jumbo,* it takes the form of a hoodoo detective thriller, features the master practitioner Papa LaBas, and generally focuses upon the struggle between the upright Gumbo Workers and the dangerous advocates of "Louisiana Red." For so many story lines and themes, however, a concept as linear as plot seems inadequate.

Consider, for example, that one of the characters is named Chorus, a performer supposedly in his 30s who has been out of work since people started writing plays like *Antigone.* Or that Reed draws constant parallels between the Antigone myth and his own tale. Or that contemporary versions of Kingfish, Amos and Andy appear. Or that a white teacher of Afro-American literature is undone by his study of Richard Wright's *Native Son* and is captured roaming the Berkeley Hills in a chauffeur's uniform, raving in black Mississippi-Chicago dialect of the 1940s. All of this is peculiar and improbable but somehow in the context Reed creates it fits together logically and even makes sense.

Reed can sometimes lapse into seriousness. He describes Moochism and similar phenomena as the legacy of slavery. Papa La Bas muses:

> Slavery. The experience of slavery. I'm afraid it's going to be a long time before we get over that nightmare which left such scars in our souls-scars that no amount of bandaids or sutures, no amount of stitches will heal.

Reed appears deeply concerned with the relationship between the sexes, but on this topic his perspective is frighteningly distorted. Throughout *Louisiana Red* there is joking contempt toward women, particularly black women. When he satirizes the women's movement his originality disappears and he falls back on the tired stereotype of feminists as man-hating dykes. The method for subduing these fierce, rough-looking women is attack and rape.

Reed's most astounding statements occur in a confrontation between Papa LaBas and Minnie, a Moocher leader. LaBas accuses Minnie and all black women as co-conspirators with white men in keeping black men in submission. LaBas intones: "Women use our children as hostages against us. . . The original blood-sucking vampire was a woman . . . I can't understand why you want to be liberated. Hell . . .you already liberated."

The violence and humorlessness of this diatribe, delivered by a character whom Reed respects, indicate that he wants his opinions to be taken straight. Reed's views on a difficult problem are antediluvian and for this reader they cloud the entire impact of his work. If he is so insensitive in this area, how can he be so incisive in others? (Can I laugh with a man who seems so hostile towards me?) As

a critic I found *The Last Days of Louisiana Red* brilliant. As a black woman I am
not nearly so enthusiastic.

New Republic (23 November 1974): 53-54.

Two Crowns of Thoth: A Study of Ishmael Reed's *The Last Days of Louisiana Red*

Lorenzo Thomas/Article

But after all
I did all in the world I can
But that little hoodoo girl
She's gonna hoodoo the hoodoo man
                    Lightnin' Slim

In 2750 we will have a new pole star. It is guaranteed by the white boy's system
of sidereal precession (stolen, like much of the West's star-knowledge from ancient
Africa's wisdom). Our present pole star, ridiculously known as Polaris, is located in
the tail of the constellation which is now called the "dipper" or "great bear" but was
anciently known as the "dog." The position of the star is symbolic, which is why
we look forward with joy to the new pole star. In that day coming, the tail shall no
longer wag the dog. If you know what I mean.

This is not an astrology lesson. We simply admit we're star gazers interested, as
Sun Ra puts it, in "the song of tomorrow's world." We are interested also in
understanding, as the Honorable Elijah Muhammad has urged us to do, "all truths
that were put in symbolic language." The stars transmit light, cryptic radio shows
and beautiful colors which are actually FORCE cast into visual form. The physical
appearance is symbolic of something more powerful. Take *red*, for example. *Red* is
just what you think it is. The symbolic associations of the color are Mars, blood,
fire, pepper. Red clay c/o Freddie Hubbard & Georgia, courtesy of the Creator.
Rednecks. Atheistic communism. Evil attitudes of ignorance, intoxication, and rage
. . . "Old Red Eye" and "seeing red" are the phrases in American culture. The
popular composer Randy Newman sings:[1]

    We're rednecks, we're rednecks
    Don't know our ass
    from a hole in the ground
    We're rednecks, we're rednecks
    keepin' the riggers down

All that's cool. But Ishmael Reed, a writer very much in contact with all of
America's spirits[2], is not concerned with rednecks; his interest is in Black people
and maroon aspects of red. Shimmy dresses and muggled eyes. It was genius Ray

Charles who sang, "See that girl with the red dress on / She can Birdland all night long!" Energy and joyful intensity. What the slang of the 30s called "a flame." Carrying a torch. But the Black aspect of red is not merely sexual nor is the violent side limited to the brutal North American ghetto/saint home. Reed's study of our situation reveals a spiritual strain of our maroon Africanness that forms the basis of a major motif in both our folk and "popular" arts. Geography does not limit it and certain social conditions in the world of oppressed peoples encourage it. In the West Indies, the Slickers sing:[3]

> Walking down the road with a ratchet in your waist
> Johnny you're too bad
> You're just robbing and stabbing and looting and shooting
> Now you're too bad

The symbolic expressions stretch from Toomer's "blood burning moon" shining down upon Stagolee and Billy DeLyons, to Wright's bad Nigger Bigger, back to Shango and West Africa's mystic fire. In his novel *The Last Days of Louisiana Red*, Reed attempts a broad-based investigation of the social and spiritual properties of the color symbol *red*.[4] The result is thought-provoking, militantly bourgeois and insanely funny.

The Last Days of Louisiana Red begins as the story of a Black family, the Yellings, tracing their exploits through two generations. The patriarch is the founder of Solid Gumbo Works, a hot bebop argot sauce factory whose chemists secretly discover a cure for cancer and an antidote to hard-drug addiction. The recipe is derived from ancient New Orleans voodoo mixtures similar to slavery days' *gombo*:[5]

> "Well, Ed being a botanist, and knowing something of pharmacology, synthesized the formulas left by Doc John into a pill--an aspirin-like white pill which he gave to his clients for what ailed them. He noticed that Doc John referred to certain human maladies in terms of astrology. One had a snake or a crab inside of one. It occurred to him one day that a crab meant cancer. Even the astrological sign for Cancer is a crab. Doc John cured cancer by using stale bread, ginger root soaked in sweet oil, blackberry tea and powdered cat's eyes and making a pill of these elements. You see, Gumbo was the process of getting to the pill--using many elements, plant, animal and otherwise.
> "Louisiana Red Corporation teamed through a spy who had access to Ed's papers . . . that he was on the brink of a cure for heroin addiction--a cure that would keep the victim off heroin forever. That's when they ordered their three spies to kill Ed."

Besides the murder, there are other problems. Two of Ed Yellings' children are spoiled and turn out bad, dragged down by the towering ignorance of urban Black society with all its frustrations, misinformation, and mistaken goals. They become dupes of various popular movements, which are vaguely "liberation" oriented but are rip-offs nevertheless. On another level, the book is a study of *malice* understood in the sense of harmful magic as well as everyday testiness.

On yet another level, *The Last Days of Louisiana Red* is a magical performance by Reed, again aimed at "ending 2000 years of bad news." And, though some critics call Reed's stuff nonsense, *this* spell was so seriously mistaken by the manufacturers of Tabasco sauce that they thought he was trying to put them "Out of Business" and sought an injunction on the sale of the book. But that's what you've got to expect from Louisiana Red.

In its strongest aspect, the whole book exists as an alternative recipe (Rx) or a musical ("poetic" in the Sophoclean sense) composition. The seemingly simple vernacular of Reed's language disguises a vast construct of artistic and psychic (i.e., symbolic) design. The freedom to mix genres, a direct literary analog to culinary gombo, was firmly established in Black literature by Jean Toomer and Reed makes good use of it here. Toomer's influence on Reed is not merely stylistic, however. It is quite clear that, like Toomer's Father John who critic Bernard W. Bell termed a "Black Nemesis," Reed's work since *The Free-Lance Pallbearers* chronicles an attempt to provide redress for wrongs committed when white people "made the Bible lie."[6] Some of Reed's ideas, derived from his study of Egyptian mythology and his understanding of C. G. Jung, closely relate to Jean Toomer's studies of Gurdieff and P. D. Ouspensky. Toomer's doppelganger constructions in the play *Balo* and in *Cane* (1923) come to mind when one considers Reed's concept of achronologically complementary worlds as expressed in the bold surrealistic time shifts of his novels.[7] Reed's approach is more sci-fi than sociological, but the main conceptual approach is reminiscent of Jean Toomer. His next book, *Flight to Canada,* based on fugitive slave narratives and concepts of discontinuous omnivalent time, comes even closer to the mix of prose and poetry that Toomer explored. Gombo. It's interesting to note that, while fugitive slaves in Spanish and English colonies were called *maroons*, the word for a runaway in French Louisiana was the Conglese *nkombo*. . . another indication of the complex associations that Reed veils and reveals in his simple style.

Other literary and extra-literary influences are revealed in this book. Reed's fondness for poet Bob Kaufman's work is evident in his definition of Moochers that recalls Kaufman's brilliant "Abomunist Manifesto":[8]

> Moochers stay in the bathtub a long time. Though Moochers wrap themselves
> in the full T-shirt of ideology, their only ideology is Mooching.

Elsewhere, he intercuts the Sophoclean riddling sphinx with a satirical take-off on confused Kafkaesque intellectualism. And, in his wittiest turn, the Kingfish choral interludes (written as screen dialogue) reveal a new aspect of Reed's comic abilities. For example, Kingfish and Andrew H. Brown are found on the campus of the University of California at Berkeley, standing near Sather Gate:[9]

[*Kinsfish:*] Remember the time we took over the Black Studies programs up here, Andy?
Andy: Yeah, I remembers. We bopped the bushwa nigger who was running it, and he had a big hickey on his head. Then we took over.
Kingfish: Those was the days, Andy, the sixties. They took us off television and the radio and gave us freedom to roam the world, unchecked, hustling like we never hustled before.

The dialogues between Kingfish and Andy also display Reed's application of media effects (television and film) to the novel form in an unexpectedly direct manner. He himself insists that he was first turned on to this area of attention by reading Ellison and Wright.

He has been working toward this for some time. "My narrative technique," he said in 1972, "involves having a kind of duo that one associates with the vaudeville stage. There's the straight man and the clown, the jokester. Like Laurel and Hardy. And there's a formula for it: one guy keeps breaking into dialect or slang, and slapstick or burlesque. That's what happens in *Free-Lance Pallbearers*. That's what I attempted to do. I was reading a lot of Mack Sennet and Bert Williams' scripts about that time, and burlesque, and listening to comedy routines."[10]

In this context, the use of Jean Toomer as a model is fortunate. Toomer's free forms, combined with Reed's own eclectic approach to mythology and so-called trivia, enable him to approach a mixed media form for the novel that promises more electric breakthroughs in the future. The technique shows that Reed is quite as aware of the past as he is of the present . . . and his idea of the past is continuous and unbounded. The mixed media concept brings him closer to the original artistry of the *griot*, the traditional African oral storyteller, who was and is the repository of the people's wisdom and who entertains at the same time he teaches. Speaking of his first novel, Reed stated:[11]

> . . . I wasn't really thinking about writing a novel; I was thinking about telling a story. Story-telling precedes the novel, which Frye and others say is a very recent and arbitrary form. I consider myself a fetish-maker. I see my books as amulets, and in ancient African cultures words were considered in this way.

The statement provides a clue both to the genius of Reed's work and to the greatest failure of *The Last Days of Louisiana Red*, which is too consciously written as "a novel," despite Reed's obvious attempt to escape that approach.

Let it be understood that questions of style and form in Reed's manner of doing art also involve message and social philosophy. In the same 1972 interview with John O'Brien, Reed said:[12]

> The ending of *Yellow Back Radio* was based on an introduction that Carl Jung wrote to *Paradise Lost* in which he traced the origin of Satan. What he claims is that the devil climbed out of art at a certain period along about the time of John Milton and that Milton was using an old gnostic idea of the devil as superman, a

man capable of all things. Jung contends that the devil became eminent in the world. In the ending of *Yellow Back*, which is kind of both a quasi-anarchistic and Tom Mix ending, the symbols of religion, the gods, return to art. They return to where they belong as something one contemplates but that doesn't participate in the world.

"Some people," he added, "interpreted it as Loop Garoo going back to Rome. But all the events that Pope Innocent VIII was talking about were taking place in art. And what happens is that people are on their own and Loop Garoo and the Pope return to art." We may note here that certain implications of such a trick ending for the real-life Vatican may not be quite as funny as Reed's irreverent wisecracks about the Pope seem to indicate. With the Amos & Andy characters in *Louisiana Red*, Reed gives the trick an interesting surface reversal. Kingfish and Andy, having escaped from popular art (due to NAACP protests in the late 1950s that the characters were derogatory stereotypes), have been wreaking their peculiar havoc on an unsuspecting world. Reed feels that we were all better off when their antics were confined to the TV screen and is determined to stuff them (and their attitudes) back into art via the pages of his novel.

Again, a larger problem is implied. "The poet," Jung wrote, "now and then catches sight of the figures that people the night-world--spirits, demons, and gods; he feels the secret quickening of human fate by suprahuman design, and has a presentiment of incomprehensible happenings in the pleroma. In short, he catches a glimpse of the psychic world...."[13] This idea is, essentially, the link that connects Reed's concepts to Jung's. And it is a fact that the poetic vision Jung speaks of cannot be transmitted except by extraordinary language and poetic structure. Art, because of its affective or suggestive dimension, is actually more than the sum of its parts which are tangible artifacts in any sense. The result is that the effective communication of literature more directly depends upon structure than on language. Structure in art becomes, at this level, the procession or play of symbols which Jung defines as "an intuitive idea that cannot yet be formulated in any other or better way."[14] And it is at this point that the question of social philosophy arises. We are all aware, particularly in terms of the almost suprahuman popular advertising media, of the ways by which a symbol or vision can be destroyed by means of inadequate structure. What is saddening is that we are not as familiar with the methods by which this is purposely done; though we should be by now, after the peculiar press agentry and media "support" that disrupted the Black movements of the 1960s.

Nor is the question of race the heart of the issue, despite the racist origins of Amos & Andy. The problem concerns the social role of the arts and the media in society, generally. William Burroughs bluntly outlined our problem. "Genet," he wrote, "says that a writer assumes the terrible burden of responsibility for the characters he creates. They are his creations and he is responsible for them. Journalists on the other hand have no responsibility whatever. Let them go out and hijack a plane, kill five women in Arizona, assassinate the President, and what happens to them after that? Who cares? A basic difference in attitude."[15] Of course, journalists cannot plot the destinies of their characters. Those who devise the fictional characters of the electronic media can, but choose to assume the journalistic non-responsibility that Burroughs describes. Similarly, the younger journalists who have been raised on these media fictions exhibit the same cavalier attitude to real people who are reduced to the stature of situation comedy characters on the electronic news. So Houston Baker is more than misguided when he bemoans Reed's decision "to drag out those poor, tattered creations of the white American psyche--Amos and Andy--my heavens, what dim corridor will next provide filler?"[16] The point that Reed understood is that after their creation of these characters, white radio artists Freeman Gosden and Charles Correll did not spend a day either tattered or poor. And they took no responsibility for the psychic effects of their creation, either. So Reed assumed the responsibility of symbolically eliminating their distorted symbols. You gonna kill him for that?

Reed's social philosophy is sound and his sense of what's happening actually and otherwise is better than most of his critics'. Yet there is a definite problem in this book. "A black writer sitting down doesn't have all of Europe looking over his shoulder," he has said.[17] But, in *The Last Days of Louisiana Red,* Reed allows the shadow of American Book-of-the-Month literature to reach his typewriter keys. As fast as he works (he can set a scene, make a scene & launch a polemic in a single sentence), it is a bit disturbing that he spends eleven chapters here (50 pages) setting up his story line. This may be a sign of an interest in "the novel" as a form, but it results in the book's being more interesting at the end than at the beginning, a fault not usually found in Reed's work. I consider this to be a structural flaw when the book is read, as I feel it should be read, as a movie or screenplay. In those terms (style, not morality, of the movies), the usual "novelistic" elements in the writing appear as irritating interruptions and weaken the construction of Reed's argument. And I mean *argument* in a traditional rhetorical or structural sense. Reed's audience expects him to know that his best effects are achieved without old-fashioned narrative editorial intrusion. His knack for building collages of insinuous detail, as in his description of Berkeley and Oakland (Chapter 23), is what we dote on. The man knows how to signify. If we wanted the other thing, we'd go elsewhere. Dickens or something.

Reed is best here as in *Mumbo Jumbo* (1972), when he concentrates on his spiritual matters. He has developed the ability to make visible the spiritual reality hidden in the everyday and, in doing this, his poetic structures reach a high point of compatibility with his content. He tries here, for example, to suggest the deeper reality of the lady in red, identified here as Minnie the Moocher. You remember the old Duke Ellington tune? You know her . . . the one that fingered Dillinger at the picture show, embarrassed her husband at the SCLC banquet, the one Richard Brautigan writes about, the one Michael McClure's Billy the Kid loves as Jean Harlow in *The Beard,* the one Baraka's Clay knows as Lula in *Dutchman* . . .

regardless of the color of she dress. Reed tries to tell us just how she got that way. La Belle Dame Sans Merci. Hard Momma. You know how she is.

Reed knows other aspects of her, too . . . some of them very particularized to Black people in this confused time and space. But then he always seems to understand many alternative visions.

Reed's approach to mythology is fascinating and grows more direct and intense in each work. Some of his ideas, such as the escaping of characters from myth into the real world, suggest a striking parallel to Robert Silverberg's fine short story "After the Myths Went Home."[18] Reed's social alertness far outstrips Silverberg's, however, and his axe is honed much more persistently. Reed's mythology is not only syncretic but synoptic. Collagistic. His Loop Garoo Kid in *Yellow Back Radio Broke-Down* (1969) can be read as the archetypal "American Negro" similar to Richard Wright's Bigger Thomas. Staggerlee bad nigger madman you can meet in any southern town today; the mad badman whose madness grotesquely metamorphoses into abject docility when the full light hits the sheriff's badge. On the other hand, Loop just might be a genuine Haitian voodoo werewulp. Naturally, in his treatment of the character, Reed consistently reverses all of the expected polarities.

He puts people off balance that way. Recently, I was amused to hear novelist Kristin Hunter refer to *Mumbo Jumbo*'s Papa LaBas as an heroic figure in pleasant contrast to the Biggers, crazy riggers, and other derogatory freaks of Black literature. In truth, Papa LaBas is the devil, as any West Indian knows . . . or any jazz buff who has heard Sonny Rollins' version of the old folk song "Fire Down Day" (re-christened "St. Thomas").[19] In Derek Walcott's play *Ti-Jean and His Brothers*, the character is portrayed as awful and exceeding strange and is addressed as Papa Le Bois, the cow-footed old man of the forest. No problem of identification there. In all ancient existential cultures Reed's Papa LaBas was well-known as the presiding spirit of choice, janitor of truth, god of the crossroads . . . Hermes, Elegbara, and Thoth, son of both Horus and Set. In Rome, equipped with the keys to the kingdom (Yakub's ladder), he appeared as St. Peter described as "the rock" (or herm).[20] So, in *The Last Days of Louisiana Red* as in *Mumbo Jumbo*, Papa LaBas is the stand-in for Eiegba or Exu, the first of the loa to be summoned in voodoo rites. The opener of the way. In ancient Egypt this role was given to Ptah, a name by which the figure became known in post-Egyptian Rome when the symbolic paraphernalia of Egyptian religion and mythology was taken over and mislabelled by the Church of Rome. In this sense LaBas, like all the other characters he uses, is not really a novelistic invention of Ishmael Reed's.

Similarly, "the lady in red" has a much deeper mythological identity than her appearances in popular culture and contemporary literature indicate. Minnie the Moocher (also Antigone) in *Louisiana Red* is closely patterned on the West African *orisha* Oya whose color in Africa, Puerto Rico and Cuba is maroon. Her emblems are fire and lightning; she is the *loa* of the cemetery and death. As the Niger River, Oya is angry Shango's favorite woman and, in the African system, personifies the

justice that Europeans revere as a woman with bandaged eyes. Well, they know
what they been doing! But, in the symbolic context of Reed's syncopated images,
justice is only blinded by congenital ignorance and rage. In other words, America
as we know it. The deterioration of the image from a woman with flashing eyes to a
blind one suggests the typical misuse of African mythology in the West. In ancient
Egypt, justice was the prototypical equal sign (=; in hieroglyphics ⊂), the twin
goddesses Mayet (Right & Truth). In the still-extant Spanish-language voodoo
system, Oya's prominence in the graveyard is a logical declension of the
duplication symbol that Mayet represented . . . the persistence of right and truth in
two worlds. As you sow, so shall you reap, etc. And you'd better believe that no
one except William Faulkner ever considered folks was sowing up there. The truth
extends into both life and death because the truth is, simply, what's true.[21]

Perhaps we are straying too far from the point, though we will return to this
concept of dual worlds again. The point is that *Louisiana Red* is an eponym, like
Jes Grew in *Mumbo Jumbo*, of a psychic level of feeling; in this case, alabaster
grimaces and red eyes. In this book, the quick-temper syndrome is raised to a
higher imagistic and symbolic dimension. Louisiana Red is at once pepper sauce,
an "evil" half-white octoroon woman steeped in HooDoo, and a psychic epidemic
of which all citizens are carriers. Just start some mess, you'll find out what it is.
This multi-level interlocking of images has been part of Reed's repertoire and
esthetics since his early days when he conceived of Martin Luther King's struggles
in terms of the metempsychosis of ancient slave revolutionists such as Denmark
Vesey.[21a]

The Last Days of Louisiana Red blends Reed's historical understanding of
corporate Christianity, voodoo, and the Black Power movement in all its
Californian extremity. The book also includes Reed's studies of politics, religion,
and mythology in ancient Egypt and Greece. *Antigone* in Reed's peevish redaction
becomes a comical tragedy (tragic because Antigone, the bad seed girl, emerges
victorious again) and we find the traditional Chorus "unemployed," absurdly
replaced by characters from Amos & Andy's Music Hall. Chorus, however, has his
splenetic say and Reed makes the most of it in some hilarious discontinuities:[22]

> Did Oedipus think that when he banished the Sphinx--in Africa a half-man,
> half-animal which became a grotesque female in Greece--did he think that when he
> banished this monster from Thebes, in thousands of years the Sphinx would
> reappear as his brother's niece, Antigone....

Antigone? Or does Reed's Chorus really mean militant feminist poets like Robin
Morgan? Chorus' chauvinism is, of course, based on the simple self-interest of
survival. After all, he's been unemployed ever since the turn in Sophocles'
Antigone! A walk-on in an Anouilh or Cocteau production barely keeps the Chorus
alive . . . not to mention government sociologists convincing folks that there's a
reason for this.

Of course, this is silly. Several critics have been irked by this type of foolishness. Yet--illogical, unorthodox, or not--Reed does manage to make a telling synthesis of Sophoclean poetics, the Antigone legend, and the Moynihahn-styled official analyses of our own day which effectively "explain' the disproportionate unemployment rate among Black males. Silly if one is trying to make masterpieces, but you damn bet you serious if you trying to make groceries. As Reed plays it, it's too uncentered to be propaganda and too loose to be "literary" protest; but I'm sure it connects synaptically with most of his readers who live in the reality that his fantasies are abstracted from. If he's a juggler, Reed is (like the hieroglyphic beetle Kepor-Ra parodied in *Free-Lance Pallbearers*) only juggling one ball of confusion: the world as it is now.

Reed delights in teasing his readers on all of the many levels of his work. For example, *Louisiana Red* itself is an exploration of several genres in the manner of Toomer's *Cane*, yet it seems most comfortably read as an undisguised "screen treatment". . . yet again, the Black pope cum HooDoo detective Papa LaBas reappears in this novel and Reed's oeuvre deliciously threatens to become a series a la Chester Himes. Modeled after New York spiritualist Professor Black Herman (who was actually a character in *Mumbo Jumbo*), LaBas also betrays Reed's share of vividly flickering memories of childhood's matinee Charlie Chan. This last observation may be offensive but it is demonstrably true. One of his reviewers unwittingly pounced on this; in the *New York Review of Books*, Roger Sale complains about the plotting of the story:[23]

> What Reed wants is to say that the best people are hard at work, not mooching; Ed Yellings's Gumbo works turns out to manufacture a cancer cure and an antidote to heroin. The trouble is that all this is just something LeBas [sic] says at the end as he plays Ellery Queen and solves the mystery of Ed's killing without even needing a clue.

Sale blunders because he neither understands the importance of Reed's HooDoo concept nor Reed's immersion in the popular media. The HooDoo detective is less interested in logical deduction than he would be in divination. He would value *connaissance* above clues. In fact, precisely because LaBas is not even remotely considering Ellery Queen or any other literary detective, the case is solved, not with a clue, but with information given LaBas by "the messenger" (read Isis) who stands "on the right side of Osiris" in the world beyond this world.[24] If there is anything of convention here, it is the fantastic apparitional continuity of the modern motion picture where things are known and unknown simultaneously and revealed without the deliberate "logical" progression of the written word. Beyond that, the narrative style of the entire book is much influenced by contemporary film-editing fashions, though always with a shrewd reservation for the dicta of Aristotelian poetics.

Hold it. All of that is fodder for formalists. The heart of the book is Reed's hearty denunciation of what he considers mistaken steps along the road to Black liberation. Eldridge Cleaver, the Panthers, Angela Davis, and the editors of *Black*

Scholar are all pointedly parodied. Strong comments are aimed at contemporary Black elected officials and at the so-called "new left" which Reed seems to think of as a collection of hippies who didn't have the guts to join the Weather-people and get their pictures on the FBI's late late show TV announcements. You know. VOICE OVER: "Bernadine Dohrn, dangerous fugitive" and high school yearbook photograph on screen. Parenthetically, one might recall that it was in *Yellow Back Radio Broke-Down* that Reed announced his awareness of America's intention of making criminals of its brightest and most conscious young people. Here, of course, Reed's purpose is lampooning the moochers and small fry who managed, through their own dullness and casual corruptibility, to slip through the honorable dragnet because of their cooperation with and cooptation by the system. Along the way of several head-shakingly funny bits of business, Reed manages to throw in teachings on the imagistic histories of voodoo in New Orleans, crime in Harlem, and provincialism in San Francisco, Henry George's hometowns. Besides all this, Reed delivers ventriloquilly (through the unemployed Chorus) a treatise on Sophocles' *Antigone* that may be spun of whole cloth but is, for our time (as we have tried to show), psychically and mythologically true. Why all this? Because Ishmael Reed finds all of these of crucial import and because these concerns, as various as they be, map out the shifting boundaries of his imaginative world.

His poem "Antigone, This Is It," was written while *Louisiana Red* was in progress and illuminates some of the concerns of the novel while indicating the wide range of the author's stylistic sources. In the poem, Reed accuses Antigone of crimes wrought by the *implication* of her acts:[25]

> You would gut a nursery
> To make the papers, like
> Medusa your Poster Queen
> You murder children
> With no father's consent

Her burial of her brother in defiance of Creon is seen here by Reed as a crime of disobedience that erases the merit of her obedience to her father. Creon as king rightfully succeeded Oedipus as Antigone's authority, in this view, because of his maleness and his sacred position. But from this somewhat perilous stand, Reed leaps into an insistence upon ritual orthodoxy that he casts in the language of voodoo:[26]

> Suppose everyone wanted it their
> Way, traffic would be bottled up
> The Horsemen couldn't con.
> There would be no beauty, no radio

He then accuses Antigone of failing to consider and, in that, reduplicating the transgressions of Oedipus:

No one could hear your monologues
Without drums or chorus
In which you are right
And others, shadows, snatching things
Fate, The Gods, A Jinx, The Ruling Class
Taboo, everything but you

Excuses, excuses . . . still she gets away with it. Reed gives us a fascinating cross-cut flash of the ridiculous trial of Angela Davis superimposed on the standard B-movie and cartoon book comedy of the unfair advantage women use against male eloquence and wisdom. It's a scene right out of Pigmeat Markham's notorious courtroom:[27]

All the while you so helpless
So charming so innocent
Crossed you; legs and the lawyer
Muttered, dropped your hankie
And all the judges stuttered

Nevertheless, the jury (*not* a presumptuously prejudicial Nixon) finds Antigone guilty and Reed sentences her to the tortures of the Egyptian underworld, Amen-Ta:

The jury finds you guilty
Antigone, may the Eater
Of the Dead savor your heart
You wrong girl, you wrong

Satirists are cold-blooded, but I do not think Reed disliked Angela Davis' cause, however misdirected that cause might have been, quite *that* much. Beyond that, Reed's relationship to the United States' racist authorities places him in much the same position as Sophocles' Antigone, continually facing the choice of conscience before "law" or "tradition" represented by our criminal ruling regime. That, if anyone doesn't recognize it, is what existentialism really is.

On the other hand, Reed identifies Greek mythology, in its deviation from the Egyptian original, as part and parcel of the anti-African forces he despises. To his credit, so different from certain come-lately 60s revolutionist writers, this attitude-- probably correct--has not prevented Reed from studying and commenting on the bastard Greek system and its many mysteries.

This poem, which also summarizes scenes from *The Last Days of Louisiana Red,* is an example of surface reversal. The trick done with mirrors that is so vital to the theatrical arts Reed examines, exercises, and exorcises in his writings. Surface reverse. Reed's total devotion to his HooDoo gods demands that he accept them as the only valid orthodoxy. Anything else is merely "mundane law." In other words, he outdoes Antigone and beats her at her own game. By doubling back.

What is most interesting, of course, is the engagingly disparate set of references Reed brings to the examination of any reality. The model, like a nuclear physicist's tinkertoy atoms, is Louisiana gombo, a culinary mix-up of whatever is at hand that Reed has raised to the level of a magical healing stew. Just like the physicist, neat in his white lab coat, punctual with his radiation-indicator clearance badge, preoccupied in his 2-year old station wagon (remember all those old science-fiction movies on TV?) . . . Ishmael Reed is a nice guy with a wife, teaches school, lives in a bungalow in California, has a little girl, plays with his cats. The difference is that Ishmael Reed's works are recipes for gombo remedies to end the madness of the ruling regime, to overthrow the whole evil psychic mess, including some people. You know who you are.

It is as if Reed's insistence that the world be a conjunction of spiritual forces leads him to examine the most mundane aspects of life in search of their spiritual content. To define their spiritual context. This was the brilliant breakthrough he made in his very first book, *The Free-Lance Pallbearers* (1967) when he unmasked the corporate structure of Christian theology through his examination of the follies of the Black proletariat. Besides that, Reed also maintains a deep enthusiasm for the artist's prophetic role. Enthusiasm, I said. Look it up.

Here, again, leave it to him to carry us into brilliantly intuitive conceptions beyond anything we might otherwise imagine. Armed with his Jungian studies, Reed finds more miraculous arms along his way. Explaining his method, he wrote: "HooDoo--or, as they say in Haiti and other places, 'VooDoo' or 'Vodun' [or vaudeville?]--was always open to the possibility of the real world and the psychic world intersecting. They have a principle for it: *LegBa* (in the U.S., 'LaBas')."[28] In old-timey minstrel shows, the idea resulted in the pseudo-planter figure Interlocutor and the result of the same idea applied to contemporary literature by Ishmael Reed is that "there were sections of *Mumbo Jumbo* which were written in what some people call 'automatic' writing, or the nearest thing to it."[29] But here we must be very careful.

Reed's version of automatic writing is closer to a surrender to the spirit Ahhhheeaiah ooo uh lord jedus huh than it is to André Breton's surrealist Hegelian concepts. Breton attempted to "present interior reality and exterior reality as two elements in process of unification...."[30] If anything, Reed would be concerned for such a *re*-unification featuring his oven militant version of the Holy Ghost or the descent of the *loa*. For him, a student of Jung rather than of Hegel, the unification of psychic and mundane realities is accomplished in the activated symbol of the crossroads. In *Louisiana Red* he writes:[31]

> [LaBas] relaxed in the Worker's garment worn only in privacy so as not to draw attention; B black blouse, black cotton pants. He was wearing the jet equilateral cross on a chain around his neck. The Watson cross.

and, again:

When the messenger entered the club, the few patrons who were there on this cool Berkeley night looked up. Even the bartender, suave Obie Emerson, a connoiseur, looked up. Every time she entered a place, people looked up. She was smiling, fresh from the crossroads. She was wearing a white cloche hat, white suit, white high heels, and white veil. She wore the cross made of jet; not the cross of anguish and suffering but the traditional cross of American Business people: the Watson cross.

One wonders if the Watson cross might be named for IBM's Thomas Watson (the book is, after all, about giving folks the business), if it is the plus sign (+) of corporate profit. Or *Louisiana Red,* and going back to the "lady in red" . . . is it the signature of the grave? It is definitely the sign of Hermes and Legba, the crossroads. And maybe, very likely, it is the Watson-Crick model of the DNA molecule: Life and individual personality resulting from one's genetic heritage. The "original" cross all tricked up in a tinkertoy model. The intersection at the crossroads. Elmore James used to sing all about that in a high and whining voice.

The intersection at that crossroads also is the tinkertoy model of the Blues. Anaphoric. Epistrophic. And still the intersection of the crossroads also plays a part as a location for the climactic vignette of Ishmael Reed's novel. After pleading for mercy for Minnie with the powers that be in the underworld, LaBas leaves in defeat:[32]

"Poor Minnie," LaBas said as he was about to enter the crossroads dividing two worlds. She was certainly in the hands of a primitive crew. They would eat her heart out.
Suddenly LaBas heard someone call behind him. It was Minnie.

Yes. And in her heart I know she was saying, well nigger who you think it was. Natural so.

The images can be found intact in the Egyptian *Book of the Dead.* The book of the Duat, the dualities. The scene at the crossroads is the ancient Egyptian judgment day in Amen-Ta, the hidden land where Thoth is the court reporter and here come the judge here come the judge Osiris is the judge. Your heart is weighed against the feather of Mayet, your deeds measured against justice. If you blow it, crocodile Sebek eats your heart out. . . at the same time documenting every move you make and crying crocodile tears. It can scare you more than the accented fulminations and warnings of the tent-show evangelists. You can break out in a cccold sweat at the library, reading the ancient Egyptian formulas and imagining impish Rodney Alan Rippys munching on sinners' bones and singing "Take life a little easier." Or, at least, more or less seriously. After all, it's your bones.

Reed, in the manner of any initiate or true believer, is aware that the intersection of realities, the unification (if it indeed occurs or exists) is not obvious to everyone.

On other levels and for other people, the two realities continue to be, as Andrè Breton stated: "In the present form of society, in contradiction."[33] Reed would surely agree that American society is jammed up with psychic contradictions, but his is basically a religious orientation (as exemplified in *Louisiana Red* by LaBas solving the case with information presented by the super natural "messenger") involved with "inspiration" to an extent that I would doubtlessly put off the surrealists. Automatic writing? One would suppose that Breton, as an empirical--if not imperialistic--romantic (awake or sleeping) would find Reed's position superstitious, though C. G. Jung maintained that superstition was a valid reaction to the awesome psychic world for primitive people. "It is only we," Jung wrote, "who have repudiated [the psychic world] because of our fear of superstition and metaphysics, building up in its place an apparently safer and more manageable world of consciousness in which natural law operates like human law in society."[34] Like tinkertoy models of fissionable molecules.

Breton would, naturally, have chosen the psychic path. But we must again caution the reader about careless application of European artistic ideas and concerns to the Black writers of the 1960s and 70s who are makers and students of an utterly unique consciousness. On the other hand, the Europeans are embarrassingly untrustworthy. As late as 1945, Breton (who must certainly have known Leon Dames' *Pigments* which appeared in 1937) could make the kind of automatic associations with the word *noir* that have justly (if sometimes stridently) been identified by contemporary Blacks with an offensive racist unconsciousness. Breton's concept of "intersection' is an insult. Paul C. Ray reports:[35]

> . . . a symbol of synthesis appears in *Arcane 17* in another quotation from Eliphas Levy, "Osiris is a black god" of which Breton says, "obscure words and more radiant than jet! It is they which, at the limit of human questioning, seem to me the richest, the most charged with meaning." The image of a black god from the Eleusinian mysteries supplied Breton with an exciting synthesis: to the traditional idea of god is added black, the color of the infernal powers. A black god is the synthesis of the divine and the demoniac, of the opposition between good and evil.

If that is the best insight automatism offered Breton, he would have done much better thinking on purpose! I suspect, however, that Ray is the culprit responsible for the idiotic notions just quoted.

Breton and the surrealists did make an effort to reject the acceptance of human law as natural law (the tinkertoy universe of the corporate scientists of death and greed) and attempted to open a way of communication with the psychic world. Others, as Jung pointed out, have not made the same choice or commitment. What the choice means to us today is well expressed by our writers. Amiri Baraka, in *Blues People* (1963), showed that the choice of mundane corruption is represented in 18th century history by the fact that "the North American settlements were *strictly* economic enterprises, with the possible exception of the Pilgrims.'"

"The straw that broke the camel's back," Baraka wrote, "and sent the American colonists scrambling headlong for independence from Great Britain was an excessive tax on dry goods. Instead of 'The Will of (our) God Must Be Done,' the rallying cry for a war could be 'No Taxation Without Representation.'"[36] In other words, justice is blind but everybody else knows which side their bread is buttered on.

Crazily and characteristically, Ishmael Reed goes deeper into the shadows of motives. Speaking of people with psychic abilities, he wrote:[37]

> It may be that a large percentage of Western people with such abilities were slaughtered (nine million people in two centuries) when the Catholic Church wiped out those who rivalled its authority as the supreme residue of Supernatural powers--you know, witches. Natural selection set in and most of the people who remain were benumbed.

The statement is made in Reed's usual cranky tone, but one need not retreat that far back into Western history to prove its essential validity. In 1935 the Pope of the Roman Catholic Church blessed the arms of Mussolini's legions before the invasion of Ethiopia and some American Blacks who followed the Catholic faith hold lifelong grudges. Coincidentally, Abyssinia's native Coptic Church (like the Eastern Orthodox Church) is a Christian denomination that antedates the Vatican organization. Plus, them niggers can prove it . . . even if it turns out in the end that Haile Selassie wasn't really related to Solomon and the comely Queen of Sheba. Heaven forbid! Still, the parameters of the struggle, as Ishmael Reed sees it, should be clear to all of us. There is even a hidden spiritual dimension in the news.

What André Breton called "exterior reality" is interpreted by critic Paul C. Ray (following Freud's concepts) as "material reality" in conflict with the unconscious. Jung, of course, rejected the dichotomy of the spiritual and the material with his rejection of Freud. Reed, in his distaste for Marxist-styled "social realism," would probably be able to identify the opposite of the psychic world as *materialist reality*; and Baraka's insight about the American revolution should illustrate the implications of that phrase. Baraka--we should note--has subsequently drawn conclusions, influenced by his political ideas, that are much closer to Breton's than to Reed's.

Reed's "automatic writing," then, involves actual visions (most often of words) brought to him from the psychic world. He enhances this communication through the study of the American adaptuitions of African spirit religions. He does not, in the French surrealist manner, open himself to his ignorances. This is not to deny the literary merit in the French mode, as demonstrated by Breton, Soupault, and Desnos. Not to mention Aime Césaire, the Antillean poet who taught them something . . . and who used voodoo, too.

Automatic writing or not, Reed's work does manage to escape premeditation. In *Louisiana Red,* one has the sense that the novel's ending astonished even the author. Reed, having convinced himself (and many readers) of the reality of

HooDoo, conceives of his writings as *wangas*, spells or "conjures" designed to
effect actual changes in the real world (i.e., the world that suffers from the false
materialistic definitions of several certain vested interests). Reed's works, of
course, provide corrective redefinitions of reality. They are also "readings" of
Ishmael Reed for the benefit of he himself and others. Houston A. Baker
acknowledged this, in a somewhat slighting tone, when he wrote: "I would like to
see *The Last Days of Louisiana Red* as a book that Ishmael Reed just had to get out
of his system."[38] But I can think of few writers today (after our experience of
Lowell, Kerouac, Ginsberg, and Baraka) who can actually avoid the sort of
"personalism" that Baker objects to in Reed. Poet Lewis MacAdams pointed out to
me that our literature is tending toward a fusion of fiction, poetry, and non-fiction
that requires a new basis for evaluation. This tendency is not new, it's as old as
Whitman, but it has lately acquired new force. While Kerouac in *The Dharma
Bums* (1958) still pretended to *roman à clef*, Steve Cannon pointed out the new
boldness when he included a real-life actual Nelson Rockefeller among the
characters of *Groove, Bang, and Jive Around* (1969). Similarly, it is hard to accept
Charles Wright's novels as merely fiction. Perhaps we are simply returning to the
original truth that the artist first struggles with his own soul and his world . . . that
anything he creates as "art" is the fruit of that struggle and must speak of it.

In *The Last Days of Louisiana Red* we can read of Ishmael Reed's struggle to
"do away" with intra-racial malice and violence. Yet, on another level, Reed's own
frustrations and heritage, his own sentimental attachment to the female, finally
betray him to passion. To his credit, and due to his calculatingly theoretical mind,
the weak aspect of this position is fictionally divided in the book between the
characters Papa LaBas and his informant, the baboon Hamadryas (read the ancient
Egyptian god of wisdom, Thoth). In the delicious pulp of the last pages, both
characters show symptoms of possession by Louisiana Red. LaBas thinks he
overcomes this seizure through an act of lenience and civil charity but the
implication of this act only serves to betray him into the hands of the deadly
Antigone, which is itself an epidemic presence similar to Louisiana Red. The
difference is Antigone is sex-linked. Militantly feminist dreadful Antigone
(orientalists can read Kali) is spontaneously reincarnated in Essencely fashionable
Ms. Betterweather, executive secretary at the Solid Gumbo Works, who uses her
casually feminine influence (all the wiles) upon LaBas so that he can spring the
awful and dangerous Minnie the Moocher from the lascivious male chauvinist
clutches of Hell. All them broads sticks together. At the very end, Papa LaBas
seems quite comfortably self-deluded. Until he hears the news.

Hamadryas, the wise mandrill, pushed to the end of his patience, physically
assaults his zoo keeper, and thus becomes a "horse" or vehicle for Louisiana Red
rather than the wise and gentle *loa* he and LaBas originally served.

There the book ends, striking a similar note to that sounded by *The Free-Lance
Pallbearers*. There is little else, short of the old bayou stories of haints and ghostes,
to compare it to. It leaves the same sense of foreboding that the end of Baraka's

Black Mass does. After all the struggle just depicted, we are told that the jihad begins now! Sure, we understand that this is just another expression of the storyteller's conventional art of surprise but it is effective and draws more moment from the dire political realities of our time. Reed's statement, like the cancer signal people's "A check-up and a check" is couched in much subtler terms than Baraka's inflammatory "These monsters are still at large."[39] But the message is the same. *The Free-Lance Pallbearers* told us "them spectres done got bolder" and the subsequent works of Ishamel Reed continue to inform us that our struggle is for sanity and that it grows deeper and more strenuous, always moving to a higher level . . . carrying us to a higher plane of our psychic and racial existence. Rocket number nine take off for the planet to the planet. Venus. And why not Pluto, too? Or the new boss star? Or Canada?

Yeah. Ishmael Reed is writing escapist literature all right. But it just might be the most significant escape of all time ...an escape from all the chains that bind us into the most dangerous unreality the planet has ever seen, a madness equipped with communications networks that depose and murder presidents of honest-to-goodness nations. And, let us make no mistake, such men are murdered for their goodness.

A book like *Louisiana Red* shows us that we are earthbound most of the time for reasons more profound than the domestic chaos Bukka Doopeyduk (the corporate zombie) went through in *Free-Lance Pallbearers*. Louisiana Red. But there is a distinctly merciful sense of hope here, too. Louisiana Red is, after all, only a thing. Ain't no big thing because Reed, our dutiful Public Health officer of the spirit world, makes us understand its sources and symptoms:[40]

> She was mad. Louisiana Red mad. Hot. You know how all those songs come out of Louisiana--those homicide songs, 'Frankie and Johnnie,' 'Betty and Dupre,' 'Stagalee.'

Notified again of our traditions, we make it what we want it and we put it where it is. "Cacophony!" Jass! We seek the true King on his righteous, rightful natural and embattled throne. We are, Reed's book reveals, still in search of the third and final crown: complete self-mastery. The Ph.D. the third degree, the 33 degree recast in our own greater dimension. That will be our real victory. The end (I mean STOP) of the tail wagging the dog anymore. You know what I mean. We will have Black people recognized in their genuine genius, their ancient and original spiritual power.

I walked into a cafe and met a young brother at the pool table. I asked what's happening. "I'm gonna make it," he said. And I said, "Get away." What he meant was that he was using all of his powers to live a natural gentle life well. And I meant to tell him to do that. I meant to tell him that that's what's happening now. We will be recognized as our own Black selves again . . . and then the onus is on us.

But that's alright. When it happens, the whole world will jump and shout. The King on his throne. At last, again. Wise and healing sergeants of mythology will no longer suffer disgrace, torment, and ungratefulness at the hands of women bruised by heels and stereophony ghetto "heroes" that Reed identifies as Moochers.

That is the dream and the goal, cast in the excessive rhetoric of Black imagism. At meetings on stumps couches crossroads street-corners, we demand action; but *The Last Days of Louisiana Red* is definitely not the triumphal New Year's march into Habana. Havana. The book is, rather, the journal of an intense but inadequate attempt to correct the total imbalance of the African peoples' lives in America. As such, it now becomes an instructional module. And it will prove to be a very effective one.

NOTES

1. Randy Newman, "Rednecks," *Good Ole Boys* (Warner Brothers MS 2193) 1974. Side 1, track 1. Lyrics by Randy Newman (c) 1974, Warner-Tameriane Publishing Corporation (BMI).
   The epigraph is taken from Lightnin' Slim, "Hoodoo Blues," *High and Low Down* (Excello EX-8018). Side 2, track 5. Lyrics by Otis Hicks (Lightnin'Slim) (c) Excellorec Music (BMI). Recorded in the early 1960s.
2. See Lorenzo Thornas, "NeoHooDoo: The Sound Science of Ishmael Reed," *University Review*, No. 29 (May 1973), 15-17, 28-30. Also, Thomas, "The Black Roots are Back," *Village Voice* (March 15, 1973), 19, 64.
3. The Slickers, "Johnny Too Bad," on Jimmy Cliff in *"The Harder They Come"* (Original Soundtrack) (Mango SMAS-7400), 1972. Side 2, track 1. Lyrics by The Slickers (c) Ackee Music Inc. (ASCAP). In the film, directed by Perry Henzell, the playing of the tune precedes a scene in which protagonist Jimmy Cliff knifes another man over ownership of a bicycle. But the film has established that the question is not exactly trivial.
4. Ishmael Reed, *The Last Days of Louisiana Red* (New York: Random House,1974). All quotations are from this edition.
5. Reed, p. 164.
6. Bernard W. Bell, "Jean Toomor's *Cane*," *Black World*, XXIII: 11 (September 1974), 96. See Jean Toomer, *Cane* (New York: Boni and Liveright, 1923),p. 237.
7. See Michael J. Krasny, "Design in Jean Toomer's *Balo*," *Negro American Literature Forum*, Vll: 3 (Fall 1973),103-104.
8. Reed, p. 17. See also Bob Kaufman, "Abomunist Manifesto," *Solitudes Crowded With Loneliness* (New York: New Directions, 1965), pp.77-87. The poems, signed "Bomkauf," were originally issued as a broadside NY City Lights Books in San Francisco in 1959. Ossie Davis and Ruby Dee produced an interesting dramatization of the works for National Educational Television.
9. Reed, p. 11B.

10. Ishmael Reed, see *Interviews with Black Writers,* ed. John O'Brien (New York: Liveright, 1973), p.178.

11. Ibid., p.172

12. Ibid., p. 180.

13. C.G. Jung, *The Spirit in Man, Art and Literature*, R. F. C. Hull, trans., Bollingen series XX (Princeton, New Jersey: Princeton University Press, 1966), pp. 95-96.

14. Jung, p. 70.

15. William Burroughs, "Time of the Assassins," *Crawdaddy* (September 1975).

16. Houston A. Baker, Jr., "The Last Days of Louisiana Red," *Black World* XXIV: 8 (June 1975), 52.

17. *Interviews with Black Writers*, p.181.

18. Robert Silverberg, "After the Myths Went Home," from *Noonjerks and Starsoups*. A recording of the story by Mike Hodel was produced at KPFA-FM. Berkeley, California. Pacifica Foundation archive No. BC 1942.

19. Sonny Rollins, "St. Thomas," *Saxophone Colossus and More* (Prestige P-24050), 1975. Side 2, track 1. Originally released on Rollins, *Saxophone Colossus* (Prestige 7079), 1956.

20. Norman O.Brown's *Hermes the Thief* (New York: Random House, 1969) provides an interesting study of the historical guises of this archetype.

21. Clues to the iconography of Oya'and Elegba can be found in Fernando Ortiz, *Los Negros Brulos* (Miami: Ediciones Universal, 1973), pp. 31-32, 38-40. The book originally appeared in Madrid in 1917 but was written in 1906 in Cuba.

Oya's character is well depicted in Pepe Carril, *Shango de Ima: A Yoruba Mystery Play* (Garden City, New York: Doubleday, 1970). The English adaptation is by poet Susan Sherman.

21a. Reed handles the continual shifts of characters in the "spirit world" with ease. His poem "Ghost in Birmingham," *Conjure: Selected Poems 1963-1970* (Amherst: University of Massachusetts Press, 1972) begins:

The only Holy Ghost in Birmingham
is Denmark Vesey's holy ghost

and goes on to draw satirical caricatures of M. L. King, Sheriff "Bull" Conner,and other figures of the Civil Rights struggle. The poem also includes a parody of Ezra Pound's "Hugh Selwyn Mauberly" (1920), lines 59-60. Pound's verses are themselves parodies of a line from Pindar. Reed's message seems to be that the modern world gets more and more ridiculous. His poem originally appeared in *Umbra* (1963).

22. Reed, *The Last Days of Louisiana Red*, p. 106. Reed's comic Antigone might have been suggested by Robin Morgan's *Monster* (New York: Random House, 1972), a collection of militantly feminist poems which appeared with a color

photograph of a snake-handling Cretan goddess figure on the cover. See note 25 below.

23. Roger Sale, "Winter's Tales," *The New York Review of Books*, XXI:20 (December 12,1974), 20.

24. *The Last Days of Louisiana Red*, p. 135ff.

25. Ishamel Reed, "Antigone, This Is It," *Chattanooga* (New York: Random House, 1973), pp. 29-30. The poem was originally published in *Black World* (1972).

26. The *loa* or *orisha* (gods) of the various voodoo cults are generally thought of as spirits who mount their "horses" (the ecstatic worshippers) during the course of the service. The Spanish term is "vehiculo." Fernando Ortiz, p. 83, writes that the worshipper "subirse el santo a la cabeza." Maya Deren described the Haitian *loa* as "the divine horsemen." It should also be noted that Haitian Creole *loa* is the equivalent of French *loi*, "law." The Spanish word Ori (Brazilian Portugese *orixa*) comes directly from Nigeria.

27. Cf. Pigmeat Markham, *The Trial* (Chess LPS 1451). Markham has performed this vaudeville routine for many years, making a subtle comment on ordinary American racism.

28. Ishmael Reed, "Ishmael Reed on Ishmael Reed," *Black World*, XXIII: 8 (June 1974), 23. This "self-interview" is described in an editorial footnote (p. 34) as Reed "talking to himself." Um hmmmm.

29. Ibid. p. 23.

30. André Breton quoted in Paul C. Ray, *The Surrealist Movement in England* (Ithaca, New York: Cornell University Press, 1971), p. 15. The quotation is from André Breton, *What is Surrealism?*, David Gascoyne, trans. (London: Faber and Faber, 1936), p. 49.

31. *The Last Days of Louisiana Red*, pp. 109,135.

32. Ibid., p. 169.

33. André Breton quoted in Ray, p. 15.

34. Jung, p. 95.

35. Ray. p. 54.

36. LeRoi Jones, *Blues People: Negro Music in White America* (New York: William Morrow and Company, 1963), pp. 5-6.

37. Reed, "Ishmael Reed on Ishmael Reed," p 23.

38. Baker, loc. cit.

39. Imamu Amiri Baraka; "A Black Mass," *Four Black Revolutionary Plays* (Indianapolis: Bobbs-Merrill Company, 1969) pp. 17-39 The script as originally published in *Liberator* (1966).

40. *The Last Days of Louisiana Red*, p.141.

Obsidian II.3 (1976): 5-25.

The *Freelance Pallbearer* Confronts the *Terrible Threes*: Ishmael Reed and the New Black Aesthetic Critics

Reginald Martin/Article

> *"The only really committed artist is he, who, without refusing to take part in the combat, at least refuses to join the regular armies and remains a freelance."*
>
> Albert Camus, *Neither Victims Nor Executioners (1945)*

> *"Today I feel bearish*
> *I've just climbed out of*
> *A stream with a jerking*
> *Trout in my paw*
> *Anyone who messes with*
> *Me today will be hugged*
> *And dispatched."*
>
> Ishmael Reed, Untitled, in
> *A Secretary to the Spirits (1976)*

Ishmael Reed's battle with the new black aesthetic critics began early in his career. From the very start, he has disliked being categorized and seems to find it impossible to play the literary game by the rules of others.

Clarence Major had said in his Walt Shepperd interview in 1969 that he was not sure if the novel form, as it was then commonly structured and marketed, was "worth saving," and that he wanted, in the ensuing ten years, to "do something new with the novel as form, and getting rid of that name would be the first step" *(Voices* 552). As early as 1969, then, Major had seen the need for newness and experimentation under the rubric of the new black aesthetic. Other critics were not to be so expansive and ecumenical.

Reed's first novel, *The Free-Lance Pallbearers,* did not exactly challenge the constitution of the novel form, itself, but the contemporary indices in the course of the novel certainly changed the reference points of American novels up to that time. Set in a city called HARRY SAM, which is also the name of the villain of the work, the action and plot of the novel rest on the broad concepts of human waste and corruption (Thomas Pynchon dealt with the concept of waste in the same year in *The Crying of Lot 49),* and is an extended satire on the state of the black artist in American Society circa 1966. HARRY SAM (Richard

Nixon?) represents all those things about the society which are crippling to individualistic yearnings different from his own; and the only things which interest HARRY are power and sitting on the toilet, through which he evacuated his waste to poison and stultify the city. Reed's "hero," Bukka Doopeyduk, wishes to become a "true believing Nazarene" (8), someone with power in the structure of HARRY SAM. When Doopeyduk achieves the mantle of Bishop of the Nazarenes, he is summarily crucified on meathooks and viewed by a television audience, including his mother and father.

But upon the death of Doopeyduk, there is no redemption for him or the other inhabitants of HARRY SAM; in fact, things carry on in a bit more depraved fashion than usual. This sort of satirical flippancy put Reed squarely against those who, as Reed said, wanted all work by black writers to "be one thing." In his satire of the Crucifixion and the Passion, Reed refutes this connection with the religious foundation of Western literary tradition. Secondly, although the book touches on issues serious to the black community (black mouth-pieces controlled by the white power structure, inadequate housing, the narcotic effect of Christianity on the poor) each issue is satirized. Polemics, so much a part of writing during this period of the new black aesthetic to this point, are gone; or at least, they are transfigured to be humorous as opposed to being only or purely instructional. Since this was his first widely distributed work, it seems to have escaped heated reviews from the new black aesthetic elite, but because Reed was to continue to develop his brand of satire, and because that development turned out to be popular, it was not long before his name began to be mentioned in the criticism of the major black aestheticians, such as Clarence Major in *Essence* (March 1971), Houston Baker in *Black World* (Dec. 1972) and Addison Gayle in *Contemporary Novelists* (1972).

In 1969, *Yellow Back Radio Broke-Down* met with good critical response, which laid the groundwork for numerous reviews of *Mumbo Jumbo* (1972); indeed, *Mumbo Jumbo* became a critical debating ground for the signs about the merits or faults of Reed's work. In general, the reviews of *Mumbo Jumbo* were positive; it was Reed's longest work to date, and also the text in which he made the switch from Egyptian symbols and myths to those of the Afro-American aesthetic or "Neo-Hoodoo" aesthetic. It is also his most sustained, illuminative satire, concretizing stand against things in Western culture which make it oppressive and dull.

One of the most positive reviews of *Mumbo Jumbo* came from Houston Baker. Writing in the December 1972 issue of *Black World,* Baker called *Mumbo Jumbo* "the first Black American novel of the last 10 years that gives one a sense of the broader vision and the careful, painful laborious 'fundamental brainwork' that are needed if we are to define eternal dilemma of the Black Arts and work fruitfully toward its melioration" (63). Adding that the novel has a few flaws, Baker ends his review of *Mumbo Jumbo* by saying that its "overall effect is that of amazing and flourishing genius . . ." (64). This review is typical of the way the black aestheticians initially regarded Reed. He comes out quite well mentioned in Gayle's *The Way of the New World* (1976). But between the *Black World* review of 1972 and the publication of Baker's review of *The Last Days of Louisiana Red,* published in numbers 3 and 4, 1975, the *Umnum Newsletter,* something has obviously happened to Baker's appreciation of Reed's literary talents. Perhaps the plot line of *Louisiana Red* in which the individualistic black, Ed Yellings, is the positive role model while "militants" and "moochers" (blacks who look to federal or other types of aid) are given extremely negative portrayals, was what offended Baker. He opens his review in this way:

> Ishmael Reed is at it again, wolfing, ranking, badmouthing, putting down those who stand in his way of love, harmony, common sense, and neo-hoodoo way. This time the target is close to home: the liberal struggle of the late sixties and early seventies. Reed gets behind the creative burners and begins to deal. He throws in three or four Black Militants to one portion of old-fashioned Uncle Tomism, adds a few liberated Black women, mixes in a little mafia and organized crime, stirs lightly and ends with a spicy dish. (6)

Later, Baker adds:

> The novel is too formulaic, relying heavily on the protagonist from *Mumbo Jumbo...* this is not to imply that Reed has nothing to say in his fourth novel. On the contrary, he has more than enough to say. This is the Swiftian opus, the one that clears out the system by putting down the folly of one's contemporaries and demonstrating how inane their most cherished enterprises are when exposed to the stinging barbs of satire.

Baker asserts that Reed saw in *Louisiana Red* a chance to "settle old scores." Here, Baker seems to indicate that Reed was angry at the small amount of commercial success his works had gained, and Reed is at this point, after the critical success of *Mumbo Jumbo,* criticizing all those whom he may have seen as having limited his stylistic and earning power. After destroying the culture the new black aesthetic critics were trying to help create, Reed, according to Baker, had "reduced its frantic and desperate activities to nonsense. The catharsis secured, he belches loudly, rubs his stomach, and turns to the next promising enterprise" (7). Baker accuses Reed of betraying the very movement which had brought attention to Reed's work. Without the new black aesthetic movement, Baker asserts, there would have been no Ishmael Reed. At the end of the review, Baker hopes that Reed will "turn again to serious satire, i.e., the exposure of the vileness and corruption at the root of the racialistic society" (7).

Reed's response was published in the same volume of the *Umnum Newsletter.* Under the title of "Hoodoo Manifesto #2 on Criticism: The Baker-Gayle Fallacy," Reed's kindest remark to Baker is that Baker's review is "unsubstantial." Reed accuses Baker of being an "educated native priest," such as those who helped Pizarro destroy the folk art of the Incas. According to Reed,

Baker is in no way in touch with what "real black people" are in touch with, because he is Western-academy trained and more interested in fitting in than in correcting inequities. Reed writes:

> Mr. Baker wants to be "right on" even if it means defending any wretch, any lout, or tramp who preys upon Afro-Americans, the kind of uncritical indiscriminate thought which has left a segment of a generation in intellectual shambles. (8)

And later Reed says, "I dare Mr. Baker to enter the faculty lounge at the University of Pennsylvania and dismiss Yeats' mystical theories as 'spurious.'" (As Baker had called Reed's notion of using aspects of voodoo as parts of a literary method). But Reed reserves his strongest words for the new black aesthetic. He had earlier in his writing called it a "goon squad aesthetics." At the end of the response to Baker, Reed insists that the new black aesthetic critics be able to understand Afro-American artistic forms:

> This means that they will have to (go to the) [sic] woodshed. It means when they speak of an Afro-American writer's "technical flaws," they must discuss whose "technical" they mean. They will have to abandon those theories which were consciously and subliminally drilled into them or their attempts of creating a "Black Aesthetic" will continue to be beside the point, like someone building a magnificent black Winchester Mystery House with stairs leading to nowhere and doors behind them; and most pitiful of all, built on a great fault. (11)

Again, the aim here is against the limiting notions, the artistic boundaries of the new black aesthetic. Reed wants the literary artist, black or white, to be free to create with boundaries only of his or her creation. Then, if the work fails, the artist has only himself or herself or her own ability and standards to blame.

For Baker, the terms of the new black aesthetic were more theoretical and helpful than Reed saw them. By 1980, for Baker, the term "black aesthetic" had taken on more of an anthropological and linguistic/cultural bent. Baker wrote in *The Journey Back* (1980) that one must know well the particular society or culture being examined to understand adequately the manifestations of that society, such as literature. This understanding may start with literature, eventually moving to other aspects of the culture in question. And in his Jerry Ward interview, Baker adopts the formally dreaded term *universal* as an admissable label for ways in which human communities perceive. He says that insofar as the term is used in a non-pejorative sense to address the similar ways in which cultures develop, he has no objection to the term's usage. Baker goes on to say:

> And to the extent that there are these trans-regional essential similarities in our culture, in Afro-American culture, whatever serious inquiries aesthetics we

make are going to have similarities. That is, the inquiries in the aesthetics, the Afro-American aesthetics, of Mississippi are going to connect, in my mind, persuasively with the aesthetics of Afro-America growing out of Philadelphia. They're going to connect more closely than they would with, say, the aesthetics growing out of Aspen, Colorado, and a colony of white poets. So that's my assumption. But I believe that to the extent that black scholars are provocative, brilliant, successful in their analyses, their findings are going to be claimed as evidence of universals, proof that all "human" communities perceive in essentially the same ways. (57)

Baker had been of a double-mind about Reed before (he published another review of *Louisiana Red* in *Black World,* June 1975, which praised some parts of the work and which was certainly not as virulently against Reed as his earlier review had been.) Perhaps that is indicative of the way Reed initially struck the new black aesthetic critics--Reed leaves them not quite sure of what he is doing or where he stands. In any event Reed's insistence upon doing exactly what he wished to do would put him squarely against any sort of formalistic critical structure.

After calling Reed "perhaps the best black satirist since George Schyuler" in *The Way of the New World,* Addison Gayle turns upon him in the same year in a strongly-worded review of *Flight to Canada,* which had also been published in 1976. Gayle criticizes Reed severely for the structure of *Flight to Canada,* as well as his handling of black male-female relationships. Gayle cites a flippancy about serious gender relations, as well as a "ridiculous" notion of collusion between black women and white men against black men, as some of the reasons he is displeased with *Flight to Canada.* In the winter volume of *Black Books Bulletin* (1976), Gayle had written that Reed was an "anomaly, and if much of his fiction, *The Last Days of Louisiana Red, Flight to Canada,* proves anything, it is that Black women have no monopoly on demons, real or imaginative" (51). Gayle calls Reed the "victim of the myths of others," and, after posing the question of whether blacks should be compassionate enough to call back to the fold of black brotherhood writers such as Reed, Gayle ends his review with this peroration:

> This writer has no such compassion, will join in no appeals to lure the prodigals back to the fold. At this juncture of history the battle lines are being drawn, wherever Black people are, in Africa, the Caribbean, South America, the United States, and one must choose for himself which side of that line he stands on. No, my compassion is not to be wasted upon writers, who, after all, must take responsibility for what they write. (51)

Reed was quick to respond. 1978 saw the publication of essays and interviews, *Shrovetide in Old New Orleans,* in which Reed begins to call by name his staunchest critics and enumerate their criticism of him in their works. Reed writes that Gayle, in the pages of *Black World* had said that "there is too much hedonism going on," and that *"Black World* thought it a simple matter of white faces being white racists. It should be so easy. Like Pogo said: 'We have met the enemy and they is us'" ("Hate" 285). In the same essay, "You Can't Be a Literary Magazine and Hate Writers," Reed calls Houston Baker "a slithering critical mugger," who "based an entire review of my book *The Last Days of Louisiana Red* upon where he thought I lived in Berkeley. Not only was the review illiterate, but he was too lazy even to check the telephone directory" (284). It is also in this essay that Reed labels Gayle the "Witchfinder General," and in the text of the speech, "Harlem Renaissance Day," Reed says,

> Some sullen humorless critics of the Black Aesthetic movement seem to have long since abandoned rational argument and take their lead from Addison Gayle, Jr., who at the conclusion of his careless new book, *The Way* of *the New World,* recommends the machine-gunning of those who disagree with him, surely a sign of intellectual insecurity. (297)
> A literary Banana Republic approach to things by those who've forgotten that the mainstream aspiration of Afro-Americans is for more freedom, and not slavery--including freedom of artistic expression.
> Perhaps the civil rights movement lost its steam because people noticed that blacks weren't practicing civil rights among themselves. Apostles of the Black Aesthetic held "Writers' Conferences," which served as tribunals where those writers who didn't hew the line were ridiculed, scorned, mocked, and threatened. The ringleader, Addison Gayle, Jr., a professor at Bernard Baruch College, argues that the aim of black writing should be to make black men feel better, as if we didn't have enough Disneylands. (298)

And in three interviews published in 1978, Reed makes it clear that two of the main causes of his dissatisfaction with the literary world are Gayle and Baker. In his interview in *Conversations with Writers II,* Reed calls Gayle and Baker "black opportunists in the English departments" who had been set up by liberal critics to keep Afro-American writers in check by imposing rigid guidelines for what would be considered acceptable writing by blacks (219). In his interview with *The American Poetry Review* Reed says that the Manhattan literary and dramatic establishment has propped up and speaks through "tokens, like for example that old notion of the *one* black writer, the *one* black ideologist (who's usually a Communist), the *one* black poetess (who's usually a feminist lesbian)" (33). A third interview in *Black American Literature Forum* gives the other important bases, aside from the limiting critical boundaries, for Reed's disapproval of the black aesthetic critics as the critics' interest in "meally-mouthedness" and their attempts at making things seem orderly and "serene" when in fact they are not (16).

Amiri Baraka had already written in his essay "The Myth of a 'Negro Literature'" (1962) that "A Negro literature, to be a legitimate product of the Negro experience in America, must get at that experience in exactly the terms America has proposed for it in its most ruthless identity," and that the Negro, as an element of American culture, was "completely misunderstood by Americans" (196). Thus, his rigidity in the face of any novelistic method which did not coalesce with his notion of the "Negro experience" was already stated five years before Reed's first novel would see print. And another comment, which would put Baraka squarely against Reed, who was according to critics an advocate of the black middle class, was Baraka's own polemic against a black middle class. In discussing why, in his opinion, there was so little black literature of merit, Baraka said,

> . . . in most cases the Negroes who found themselves in a position to pursue some art, especially the art of literature, have been members of the Negro middle class, a group that has always gone out of its way to cultivate *any* mediocrity, as long as that mediocrity was guaranteed to prove to America, and recently to the world at large, that they were not really who they were, i.e., Negroes. (*Aesthetic* 191)

Baraka wrote that as long as the Negro writer was obsessed with being accepted, middle class, he would never be able to "tell it like it is," and, thus, would always be a failure, because America made room only for white obfuscators, not black ones.

After Baraka formally announced that he was a socialist, no longer a black nationalist, and with some different goals (1974), his guidelines for valid black writing changed, but his new requirements, though with a slightly different emphasis (liberation of all classes, races, genders) and a slightly different First Cause (Monopoly Capitalism), were as rigid as his prior requirements. Writing in his autobiography (1984) of his change from black nationalist to socialist, Baraka says:

> But we made the same errors Fanon and Cabral laid out, if we had but read them, understood them. Because the cultural nationalism, atavism, male chauvinism, bourgeois lies painted black, feudal dead things, blown up nigger balloons to toy around with. I would say the Nation of Islam and the Yoruba Temple were the heavist [sic] carriers of this, the petty bourgeois confusing fantasy again with reality. The old sickness of religion--all the traps we did not understand. Crying blackness and for all the strength and goodness of that, not understanding the normal contradictions and the specific foolishness of white-hating black nationalism. The solution is not to become the enemy in blackface, that's what one of the black intellectual's problems was in the first place. And even hating whites, being what the white-baiting black nationalist is, might seem justifiable but it is still a supremacy game. The *solution is revolution*. We thought it meant killing white folks. But it is a system that's got to be killed and it's even twisted some blacks. It's hurt all of us. (*Autobiography* 323)

Baraka, as did Gayle in *Wayward Child,* sees certain black writers as disrupting the essential and beautiful Black Arts Movement of the 1960s and early 1970s. Baraka calls these writers, as was said of Booker T. Washington, "capitulationists," and says their movement was simultaneous with and counter to the Black Arts Movement. Baraka feels that the simultaneity was no accident. In his long essay "Afro-American Literature and the Class Struggle," in *Black American Literature Forum* (1982), Baraka, for the first time, makes several strong, personal attacks on Reed, and also attacks other black writers whom he feels fit into the capitulationist mold. And, again, Baraka echoes Gayle in his belief that the ground-breakers in the Black Arts Movement (as regards the social values to be embodied in literature read, new black aesthetic) were doing something which was new, needed, useful, and black, and those who did not want to see such a flourishing of black expression appeared to damage the movement.

Naming Reed and Calvin Hernton as "conservative," Baraka writes:

> Yes, the tide was so strong that even some of the conservatives wrote work that took the people's side. (The metaphysical slide [sic] of the BAM, even allowed Reed to adopt a rebellious tone with his "Black power poem" and "sermonette" in *catechism of d neoamerican hoodoo church, 1970,* in which I saw the struggle of Blacks against national oppression as a struggle between two churches: e.g., "may the best church win. shake hands now and come out conjuring." But even during the heat and heart of the BAM, Reed would call that very upsurge and the BAM "a goon squad aesthetic" and say that the revolutionary writers were "fascists" or that the taking up African culture by Black artists indicated such artists were "tribalists.") (8)

Much of the labeling of Reed as a conservative and a "house nigger" begins with the publication of his 1974 novel *The Last Days of Louisiana Red* in which, as I briefly noted before, a group of people Reed labels as "moochers" loiter around Ed Yellings, a black small-business owner who is making active efforts to earn a living and who, through voodoo, finds cure for cancer in the process. Critics interpreted "the moochers" as being stipulative of some of the black aesthetic group. Reed, in the course of the novel, explains moochers this way:

> Moochers are people who, when they are to blame, say it's the other fellow's fault for bringing it up. Moochers don't return stuff they borrow. Moochers ask you to share when they have nothing to share. Moochers kill their enemies like the South American insect kills its foe by squirting it with its own blood. God, do they suffer. Look at all of the suffering I'm going through because of you. Moochers talk and don't do. You should hear them just the same. Moochers tell other people what to do. Men moochers blame everything on women. Women moochers blame everything on men. Old moochers say it's the young's fault; young Moochers say the old messed up the world they have to live in. Moochers play sick a lot. Moochers think it's real hip not to be able to read

and write. Like Joan of Arc, the archwitch, they boast of not knowing A from B. (20-21)

This passage was seen as callous and unfeeling toward the disadvantaged. Relatedly, *The Last Days of Louisiana Red* contains figures who do little more than emphasize Reed's definition of moochers, and who continually re-enact negative black stereotypes. Ed Yellings, the industrious black, is killed by moocher conspirators. Does this mean that blacks turn against what Reed believes to be the good in their own communities? Ed Yellings is a business owner, a property owner, and this station puts him in opposition to the platform of Baraka. Attacking both Ralph Ellison and Reed in the same section of the *Black American Literature Forum* article, Baraka quotes Ellison as saying:

> "After all I did see my grandaddy and he was no beaten-down 'Sambo.' Rather he *owned property* (Baraka's emphasis), engaged in Reconstruction politics of South Carolina, and who stood up to a mob after they had lynched his best friend . . . I also knew one of his friends who, after years of operating a printing business for a white man, came north and set up his own printing shop in Harlem."
>
> Does this mean that everybody who didn't own property or become a small politician was "a beaten clown Sambo"? Ishmael Reed and Stanley Crouch both make the same kind of rah-rah speeches for the Black middle class. Reed, in fact, says that those of us who uphold Black working people are backwards (see *Shrovetide in Old New Orleans,* pp. 136-37) or as he says, "the field nigger got all the play in the '60s." Focus on the middle class, the property owners and music teachers, not the black masses Ellison tells us. This is the *Roots* crowd giving us a history of the BLM [Black Liberation Movement] as a rags-to-riches, Horatio Alger tale in brownface, going off into the sunset and straight for Carter's cabinet or the National Book Award. No, slavery was not as bad for the house-Negroes, nor is national oppression as grim for the petty bourgeoisie--not bad at all for the tiny bribed element among us. But for most of us it is hell, and we want it destroyed! (10)

Baraka also sets up a dichotomy for a "white aesthetic" and a "black aesthetic," but while defining the two, one would assume toward the end of endorsing one or the other, Baraka shows only the failings of each and discusses his points of divergence from "the Black Aesthetic Crowd."

In Baraka's dichotomy, the "white aesthetic is bourgeois art--like the 'national interests' of the U.S. at this late date when the U.S. is an imperialistic superpower" (9). Immediately following this excerpt, Baraka seems to defend the black aesthetic group over Ellison's negative criticism of them. Baraka writes that Ellison says of the black aesthetic crowd that they "buy the idea of total cultural separation between blacks and whites, suggesting that we've been left out of the mainstream. But when we examine American music and literature in terms of its themes, symbolism, rhythms, tonalities, idioms, and images it is obvious that those rejected 'Negroes' have been a vital part of the mainstream and were from the beginning" (9). Baraka then writes, "We know we have been exploited, Mr. Ralph, sir; what we's arguing about is that we's been exploited! To *use* us is the term of stay in this joint . . ." (9). Baraka writes that he takes issue with the comfortable commentator used with his own permission who seeks "no connection with the mass pain except to get rich and famous off it" (9).

Baraka's point is that it makes no difference if the corrupt person's black; the issue is still corruption, and it is a double insult to the oppressed when that corrupt one turns out to be black. (Ironically, this is one of Reed's themes in *The Free-Lance Pallbearers.)* But it is at that point that Baraka separates himself from others in the new black aesthetic movement:

> Where I differ with the bourgeois nationalists who are identified with the "Black Aesthetic" is illuminated by a statement of Addison Gayle's: "An aesthetic based upon economic and class determinism is one which has minimal value for Black people. For Black writers and critics the starting point must be the proposition that the history of Black people in America is the history of the struggle against racism" ("Blueprint for Black Criticism" *First World,* [Jan-Feb 1977], 43). But what is the basis for racism; i.e. exploitation because of one's physical characteristics? Does it drop out of the sky? Is it, as Welsing and others suggest, some metaphysical racial archetype, the same way the white racists claim that "Black inferiority" is? Black people suffer from national oppression: We are an oppressed nation, a nation oppressed by U.S. imperialism. Racism is an even more demonic aspect of this national oppression, since the oppressed nationality is identifiable anywhere as that, regardless of class. (10)

Baraka reminds the reader that his disagreement with the new black aesthetic elite is not to say that there is no such thing as a black aesthetic but that his conception of a black aesthetic manifests itself in his definition of it differently than it does for others. For him it is "a nation within a nation" that was brought about by the "big bourgeoisie on Wall Street who after the Civil War completely dominated U.S. politics and economics, controlled the ex-planters, and turned them into their compradors" (10).

After explaining his important divergence from the black aesthetic elite, Baraka attacks Reed and the quality of his work. He calls Reed an "arsehole" and says that his comments are "straight out agentry," and significantly, he claims that Reed and those who agree with him have their own aesthetic, one of "capitulation" and "garbage." Baraka writes:

> Recently, the bourgeoisie has been pushing Ishmael Reed very hard, and to see why let's look at his most recent book, *Shrovetide in Old New Orleans.* In essay after essay Reed stumps for individualism, and asserts ubiquitously that the leadership of Black folks is the Black middle class, rather than the working class, . . . (11-12)

Baraka takes other writers to task whom he feels have made money and fame on the Black Arts Movement, but who have turned viciously on true meaning of that movement. Michael Harper is called "rhythmless." Michele Wallace gets things wrong about the Black Liberation Movement because she "wasn't there and doesn't know," and, thus, she "takes the side of our oppressors." Ntozake Shange "deals in effects but not causes," which results in "one-sidedness and lack of information." Correspondingly, there are writers whom Baraka feels uphold his aesthetic standards, such as Sonia Sanchez in *I Been a Woman,* and Henry Dumas in "Will the Circle Remain Unbroken," and Toni Morrison in *Sula* and *The Bluest Eye* (16).

Toward the end of his article, Baraka says that the "main line" of his argument has been that "class struggle is as much a part of the arts as it is any place else" (14). His pleas and support are reserved for those artists who are "struggle oriented," those who are trying to "get even clearer on the meaning of class stand, attitude, audience, and study, and their relationship to our work" (14). And, thus, Baraka's argument is epanaleptic, as it turns back upon the same core of arguments of the other black aestheticians he has said he is in disagreement with; those arguments forming a complete circle with Baraka's stated premise that black literature, black art must do something materially positive to help black people. Art must be socially functional.

Reed responded in letters to *Black American Literature Forum,* and in an interview conducted in 1983, Reed called Baraka's charges "irresponsible," "scurrilous," and "outrageous" (Martin 184). He asserts that Baraka is one of the "romantic" heroes of the left, and that the left supports him for that reason (1986). Further, Reed accuses the new black aesthetic critics of their own brand of capitulation; i.e., a division of labor and resultant capital from the tacit agreement not to infringe on each other's critical territory. Reed says:

> I think there was a nonaggression pact signed between the traditional liberal critics and the black aesthetic critics. They were brought into the publishing companies about the same time I was . . . But the black aesthetic crowd came in and writers were required to conform to their Marxist blueprints. But that's happened to Afro-American artists throughout history. (183)

And, of course, Reed continues to insist that he is not against a black aesthetic or a black way of doing things; it is simply that, the way he sees it, censorship cannot be a part of the black aesthetic, an aesthetic which is intrinsically against critical limitation and is by nature racially syncretic.

Thus, Reed will not admit to being an "anomaly," a "spurious writer," or a "capitulationist," in the terms of Gayle, Baker, or Baraka. In Reed's work, white villains and crimes against oppressed people are shown in just as poor a light as they are in the works of his severest critics. In *The Terrible Twos* (1982), white businessmen have called a meeting to discuss the danger to their Santa Claus

Plan. Big Business decides that they could corner the Christmas market if there were just one *official* Santa Claus. But before that scheme can be hatched, the upsurge of color peoples' independence must be taken care of (54). But it seems that even with a peace treaty signed between the major "white" countries, the darker peoples of the world still will not learn their place and are doing ridiculous things every day, such as demanding decent housing, free education for their children, and enough food to eat. This is Reed's jab at "monopoly capitalism." But unlike his critics, there is often a healthy dose of black villains in his work as well, such as the "talking Negro Android" in *Mumbo Jumbo,* and the Amos and Andy moochers of *Louisiana Red.*

As I have pointed out, the major points of disagreement between Reed and the key new black aesthetic critics are thematic, philosophical, and programmatic. Baker cannot condone Reed's use of negative black characters in *Louisiana Red* and *Flight to Canada.* The only truly negative black character to the aestheticians is the traitor to black causes; admitted causes whose validity is established by the aestheticians themselves. Gayle accuses Reed of constructing themes which are frivolous and backward, as in *Mumbo Jumbo,* or which substitute one harmful set of myths for another, as in *Flight to Canada.* To Baraka, Reed's approach to the serious problems which still face black Americans is flippant, traitorous, and his use of satire is an escape method for not naming the true cause of distress in the world: capitalist exploitation. And Baraka admits that there are those who would say that there may be errors in Baraka's judgments about Reed, since Baraka, himself, has said that he has been wrong before. To these critics, Baraka writes: "People always say, 'Well, what's Baraka doing now? he keep on changing.' I am a Marxist-Leninist because that is the most scientific approach to making revolution. But for a long time most of y'all knew I wanted to be a revolutionary. I'm still committed to change, complete social change. We just got to get back on it" ("Afro" 14).

Recently, Reed has tried to get away entirely from the notion "aesthetics." He calls the "black aesthetic thing . . . a northern urban academic movement-- that's why you have a fancy word like *aesthetic* which nobody figures out. When you come to talk about standards of taste, everyone differs" (Martin 187). Certainly, the major new black aestheticians never adapted their own critical boundaries enough to admit Reed into their circles of critical acceptance; and Reed shows no signs of reining in authorial methods which keep him on the outside of these boundaries. Yet, between these two opposites, one senses on the parts of both Reed and his critics, a lack of *intended* opposition and animosity, as though the two sides are being only what they intrinsically are, living out their artistic desires in the only ways they can, finding that, *a priori,* their methods for constructing a new black aesthetic cannot be fused together. On the part of the new black aestheticians, one senses that they saw their purposes as essential and higher than structural arguments may have led some to view their movement. It was a chance for black intellectuals to lay groundwork for a kind of literature and study of literature that had not before been done; a chance to influence a younger generation of writers--white as well as black--toward more than one standard. From all the heat and confusion, and genius, must have come some good. Perhaps Baraka sums up the idea best toward the end of his autobiography when he writes:

> But even in that tradition, that dumb thrall, we built some actual things, we laid out a process of learning. For the close readers. We did step through madness and bullshit. But we were not just full-of-shit-tourists. We did take the city away from the lowest level, and if the next level is sickening, the task is of a higher order, and its solution is the current day's work. Are we up to it, anyone, anywhere? Of course, is the roared refrain. (326)

WORKS CITED

Baker, Houston. "Books Noted." *Black World.* (December 1982): 63.

---."*The Last Days of Louisiana Red*--A Review." *Umnum Newsletter.* 4, 3-4 (1975): 6. *The Journey Back.* Chicago: U of Chicago P, 1980.

Baraka, Amiri. *Raise, Race, Rays, Rage: Essays Since 1965.* New York: Random, 1971. What the Arts Need Now. *Negro Digest.* (Winter 1967): 43.

---."Afro-American Literature and Class Struggle." *Black American Literature Forum.* 14,1 (1980): 37-43.

---. *The Autobiography.* New York: Freundlich, 1984.

Domini, John. "An Interview with Ishmael Reed." *The American Poetry Review,* 1977.

Gayle, Addison. *The Black Aesthetic.* New York: Doubleday, 1971.

---.*The Way of the New World: The Black Novel in America.* New York: Doubleday, 1976.

---."Black Women and Black Men: The Literature of Catharsis." *Black Books Bulletin.* 4 (1976): 48-52.

---.*Wayward Child: A Personal Odyssey.* New York: Doubleday, 1977.

Gover, Roger. "An Interview with Ishmael Reed." *Black American Literature Forum* (1978): 12-19.

Jones, Leroi. "The Myth of a 'Negro Literature.'" *Black Expression: Essays by and about Black Americans in the Creative Arts.* Ed. Addison Gayle. New York: Weybright and Talley, 1969.

Martin, Reginald. "An Interview with Ishmael Reed." *Review of Contemporary Fiction* (Summer 1984): 176-187.

Northouse, Cameron. "Ishmael Reed." *Conversations with Writers II.* Ed. Richard Layma, et al. New York: Gale Research Co., 1978.

O'Brien, John. "Ishmael Reed." *The New Fiction: Interviews with Innovative American Writers.* Ed. Joe David Bellamy. Chicago: U of Illinois P, 1975.

Reed, Ishmael. *The Free-Lance Pallbearers.* New York: Bard, 1967.

---. *Yellow Back Radio Broke-Down.* New York: Bantam, 1969.

---. *Mumbo Jumbo.* New York: Avon, 1972.

---. "Hoodoo Manifesto #2: The Baker-Gayle Fallacy." *Umnum Newsletter.* 4,
    (1975): 8.

---. *A Secretary of the Spirits.* London: BOK, 1976.

---. "You Can't Be A Literary Magazine and Hate Writers." *Shrovetide in Old
    New Orleans.* New York: Avon, 1978.

---. *The Terrible Twos.* New York: McGraw, 1982.

Shepperd, Walter. "An Interview with Clarence Major and Victor Hernandez
    Cruz." *Black Voices.* Ed. Abraham Chapman. New York: Mentor, 1972:54.

MELUS 14 (Summer 1987): 35-49.

FLIGHT TO CANADA (1976)

Ishmael Reed: *Flight to Canada*

Joe David Bellamy/Review

Though some of this ebullient, comic novel may come "straight from the pages
of history," as the jacket copy claims, most of it comes straight from the fevered
absurdist imagination of its author, and straight from the hip. It is vintage Reed, a
disarming satire and an outlandish spoof. On one level, it is the story of the demise
of a slavemaster Arthur Swille, a Civil-War-era villain, and the takeover of his
plantation by his clever black manservant, Uncle Robin, as written by the runaway
and returned ex-slave Raven Quickskill. Swille, the prototypical decadent
19th-century Southern aristocrat, lives in a castle that is a replica of King Arthur's,
where, we are told, he routinely imbibes two gallons of what he thinks is
slave-mother's milk for breakfast. Actually, his manservant--having tampered with
Swille's will--has been slowly poisoning the evil fellow with Coffee Mate. Swille is
inadvertently burned to death at the hand of his own wife before the poison takes
effect, however.

While one strand of the narrative covers these cheerful events down on the
plantation in Virginia, the other follows Raven Quickskill during his flight to
Canada. Imagined as an Eden for runaway slaves, Canada turns out to be a big
disappointment for Raven since, with its neon signs and used car lots, "it could
have been downtown San Mateo." In a comic reversal of the
you-can't-go-home-again theme, Raven returns to the South--a new South--Swille
has died and Uncle Robin has taken over.

Reed's fictional world in *Flight to Canada* is set up to allow maximum scope
for wild inventions and the unleashing of a passel of demons. Its pleasures are
derived less from its deliberately cavalier view of history than from its feats of
association, improvisation, and wit. While tsk-tsking in admiration at Reed's
flights, one is occasionally reminded of that Ellison character, Peter Wheatstraw,

from *Invisible Man,* who quips: "All it takes to get along in this here man's town is a little shit, grit, and mother-wit. And, man, I was bawn with all three."

Fiction International 6/7 (1976): 148-149.

Flight to Canada

Henry Louis Gates, Jr./Review

Literate and not-so-literate early Americans chose *Pilgrim's Progress* as a perennial favorite. *Pilgrim's Progress*, that most graphic and edifying charting of a peculiarly singular spiritual pilgrimage, only consummated the eighteenth century's fascination with autobiography, a narrative tradition which made fellow travelers of such unlikely pilgrims as Nell Gwyn and Madame Pompadour, Fanny Hill and the Cardinal de Ree, the Prince of Conde and the Quaker, George Fox. Their mystical and often nefarious deliverances enchanted readers of French and English and made the journey "from blindness to insight" at least a reasonable expectation of their public. It should not surprise us then that the narratives of the escaped slaves, which consciously utilized these conventions as well as those of the sentimental novel, became during the three decades previous to the Civil War the most popular body of written discourse in intellectually awkward antebellum America.

Gustavus Vassa's *Interesting Narrative*, published in 1789, went to an eighth edition by 1794; Douglass's *Narrative,* an unprecedented commercial success, sold an unheard of thirty thousand copies by 1850, not including its French editions. In this period, only five per cent of the books published in England sold more than five hundred copies. But according to the *British Catalogue of Books*, no less than ten of these were slave narratives. One imagines that the advocates of slavery shared the frustration and distress of the author of a review of this subject that *Graham's Magazine* printed in 1853. What is civilization coming to, he asked none too rhetorically, in a nation which virtually inhales these "literary nigritudes [sic] whose editions run to hundreds of thousands."

These slave narratives, written as much to provide badly needed fodder in abolitionist cannon as to posit with the utmost finality the identity of the chattel become human being, continue to enchant not only the academic specialist but the general reader as well. For in their deceptively simple structure we are still able to discern that theme which Whitman and Melville and the great American symbolists made the crux of their works: the voyage of the human soul as a process of becoming; the exploration of symbolic geography as a mode of existence. Moreover for us, the black living, there remains the same enchantment with the word that became so early the recurring motif--if not indeed the mythical matrix--of the written testimony the slave made for all who would dare to listen.

What concerns the student of Afro-American literature is the kinship in narrative structure between the slave narratives and black fiction. The political use to which the abolitionists put black literacy demanded a painstaking verisimilitude--a concern with even the most minute concrete detail. At least to the publication in 1911 of Du Bois's *Quest of the Silver Fleece,* black writers felt compelled to vouchsafe the veracity even of their fictions, as Du Bois's prefaced "Note" makes evident: "In no fact or picture have I consciously set down ought the counterpart of which," he attests, "I have not seen or known." His was in part the legacy of slave testimony, where dogged realism proved the ultimate appeal to authority, and where the extended citation of detail and historical event aimed at making "fact" of fiction. It does not seem odd then that William Wells Brown's *Clotel,* our first black novel published in 1853, remains a curiously uneasy blend of sentiment and melodrama whose introductory, "Memoir of the Author" is none other than Mr. Brown's slave narrative itself.

This concern with realism, known as naturalism in fiction, characterized nearly the whole of black fiction until Ralph Ellison published *Invisible Man,* a novel descended directly from Herman Melville's *Confidence Man.* Indeed it remains the *sine qua non* of the literary heirs of Richard Wright, specifically for those whose works which assume as their silent second text Wright's *Native Son.* Of Ellison's direct descendants, including Leon Forrest, James Allan McPherson, Toni Morrison, and Gayl Jones, perhaps no one has mounted as concerted an attack on naturalism as has Ellison's mischievous step-child, Ishmael Reed.

Ishmael Reed is probably the most widely reviewed Afro-American author since Ellison--and also the most widely misunderstood. Reed's reputation most often is subsumed under the vague, dubious, and often derogatory euphemism of "satirist"--as if that form of writing relegated his stature as an artist to some nebulous corner of the absurd or else, as with so many labels, allowed him to be dismissed summarily.

Yet Reed's novels consistently manage to consolidate disparate, seemingly unrelated characteristics of black written and unwritten formal expression, and thereby to redefine for us the very possibilities of the novel as a literary form. His novels are almost "essays" on the art of black fiction-making. His use of satire is no accident. Thematically, he seems concerned to force us to rediscover the still largely untold role of blacks as creators of America's culture, or as word-sorcerers who maintain a secret culture which, from time to time, pervades all of American life. Formally, by taking imaginative liberties not only with plot, structure, and point of view but also with Newtonian notions of time and space, he is as effective in drawing attention to the craft of writing as Richard Pryor's *Book of Wonder* parody is in outlining the formal patterns of the black sermon and as Wonder himself is in satirizing the vapidity of so much of "classical" Western music when he sets the words of *Village Ghetto Land* to the form of the Concerto. This sort of satire by Pryor, Wonder, and Reed, is the subtlest and most profound of all--the parody of forms. And uncannily it reveals perhaps more about the ordering of the myths we live by than does even the most painstakingly "exact" photographic reproduction. Theirs is an art based on the tension of dissonance--on the power of art to say more than it states--as opposed to any art where normative judgment turns on a likeness to the world we experience every day.

Flight to Canada is Uncle Robin's slave narrative, written by Raven Quickskill--"the first one of [Arthur] Swille's slaves to read, the first to write, and the first to run away." The novel turns on the relationship between the demonic and decadent slaveholder, Arthur Swille, and three or four absolute "types" of slaves which sociologists have invented for convenience's sake. In addition to Raven Quickskill, the popular slave poet, there is Cato the Graffado ("So loyal he volunteered for slavery.... The slaves voted him All-Slavery."); Stray Leechfield who exploits his exotic blackness to satisfy the fantasies of a repressed Calvinistic Culture; Mammy Baracuda, a parody of Henry Bibb's unfaithful wife; but most of all Uncle Robin who, unlike his amaneunsis, never left Swille's plantation: "Robin, what have you heard about this place up North," Arthur Swille asks his loyal servant. "I think they call it Canada?" "Canada," Uncle Robin replies, "I do admit I have heard about the place from time to time, Mr. Swille, but I loves it here so much that ... that I would never think of leaving here .... Most assuredly, Mr. Swille, this is my Canada. You'd better believe it."

Oddly enough, it is the relationship between slaveholder and his loyal slave which is drawn the most compellingly in Reed's novel. Though we are meant to laugh at Arthur Swille, there lurks in his character a masterful depiction not of mere evil but of the hubris demanded to defy the natural order. For Swille is a man deranged by his own, nether side. "Nigger fever," he had railed.

> "Niggers do something to you. I've seen white people act strange under their influence. First, you dream about niggers, little niggers mostly; little niggers, sitting, eating watermelons, grinning at you. Then you start dreaming about big niggers. Big, big niggers. Big, big niggers walking all over you, then you got niggers all over you, then they got you . . . As long as they're in this country, this country is under their spell."

But not only is Swille pursued by his own demonic nature, he seeks to merge with it, to consummate his reverence for it. As death approaches him in the form of the ghost of his dead sister, with whose corpse he had been engaged in a deeply satisfying necrophilic liaison, the nature of Swille's true evil becomes vividly clear: his is the transgression of human limits and the construction of a nightmare world to justify that transgression.

And Uncle Robin? What of Uncle Robin after the sudden and tragic demise of his beloved master Swille? Uncle Robin rewrites Swille's will and inherits the great Virginia mansion of his master. Moreover, he rejects Harriet Beecher Stowe's subsequent attempts to buy his story then sends to Canada for Raven

Quickskill.

For as much as about any good-evil dichotomy, Reed is writing about what Robert Burns Stepto has called "narrative control"--the possession of one's own story, be that our collective history or even one's very own autobiography. He is concerned to wrestle the text away from those who would control it--be they Harriet Stowe, the well-intentioned abolitionists who "authenticated" the slave narratives, or even Clio, the Muse of History. "Why isn't Edgar Allen Poe recognized as the principal biographer of that strange war?" asks the narrator. "Fiction, you say? Where does fact begin and fiction leave off? Why does the perfectly rational, in its own time, often sound like mumbo-jumbo?" Or: "Strange, history. Complicated. too. It will always be a mystery, history. New disclosures are as bizarre as the most bizarre history."

Flight to Canada is a major work, perhaps Reed's most "intelligent" novel. One senses here a sort of ending for this aspect of his earlier fiction: for the search for The Word, which Reed began in *Mumbo Jumbo*, has realized itself finally in the successful search for The Text; the text that at all points comments upon itself. As Arthur Swille says in a disarmingly perceptive aside on the uses of black literacy:

> Look, Lincoln, one of them kinks, 40s, wiped me out when he left here. That venerable mahogany took all my guns, slaughtered my livestock and shot the overseer right between the eyes. And the worst betrayal of all was Raven Quickskill, my trusted bookkeeper. Fooled around with my books, so that every time I'd buy a new slave he'd destroy the invoices and I'd have no record of purchase; he was also writing passes and forging freedom papers. We gave him literacy, the most powerful thing in the pre-technological pre-post-rational age--and what does he do with it? Uses it like that old Voodoo--that old stuff the slaves mumble about, Fetishism and grisly rites, only he doesn't need anything but a pen he had shaped out of cock feathers and chicken claws. Oh, they are bad sables, Mr. Lincoln. They are bad sables. Not one of them with the charm and good breeding of Ms. Phillis Wheatley, who wrote a poem for the beloved founder of this country, George Washington.

One must concur with Derek Walcott's assessment of Ishmael Reed. "He alters our notion of what is possible. His importance to our use and understanding of language will not be obvious for many years." We must counsel Reed to be patient.

The Journal of Negro History 63 (January 1978): 78-81.

A Fantasia on Black Suffering

Edmund White/Review

Flight to Canada is, of all things, a comic exploration of slavery by the best black writer around. The novel is genuinely funny; for Reed has not rendered faithfully the horrors of servitude but rather created a grotesque Civil War America out of scraps and snippets of the past, the present and the mythic. In the process he has put together a brilliant montage of scenes, potent with feeling and thought, designed to flash on the mind's eye with the brilliance of stained-glass windows in a dark interior. The book is memorable, original and wonderfully entertaining.

The main character, Raven Quickskill, is a slave who runs away from his master, Arthur Swille, hides out in Emancipation City and finally, after the war has ended, makes it over the border into Canada. Until his former owner is dead and buried, Quickskill must remain a fugitive, since Swille has resolved to capture him come what may. Throughout the tale the narration alternates between scenes back at the plantation in Virginia and scenes of Quickskill's precarious freedom.

Reed blends the attitudes and trappings of the past century with those of today. Escaped slaves travel courtesy of Greyhound or Air Canada. Swille's bondsmen loll on waterbeds and watch color television in the luxury of the Frederick Douglass Houses. When Lincoln is shot, the event is served up to viewers again and again through instant replay on television. Lincoln himself is a hypocritical and befuddled Nixon, a racist who thinks of emancipation as a ploy, and Swille is a power-mad Rockefeller whose son is killed by an alligator (or an avenging alligator deity) in Africa. This historical melange could easily have turned tediously allegorical, but Reed never allows the parallels between the past and the present to become complete, nor does he permit the contemporary references to sap the vitality of his story.

When the double perspective is used to look at slavery, the vision becomes rich and nuanced. In his earlier novel, the careless, sexist, didactic *The Last Days of Louisiana Red*, one character attributes the evils of modern black society to the ordeal of slavery: "I'm afraid it's going to be a long time before we get over that nightmare which left such scars in our soul, scars that no amount of bandaids or sutures, no amount of stitches will heal." But in *Flight to Canada* the nightmare is plumbed. Quickskill, invited to Lincoln's White House reception for artists and intellectuals after publishing a poem, becomes dizzy and rests in the Lincoln bedroom. There he perceives himself as truly a slave, as property, an inanimate thing: "It puts the glass back on the rosewood rococo-revival table. It is lying in the bed that matches the table. It feels better...." At another point two of Swille's agents attempt to recapture Quickskill. The language Reed introduces is that of modern commerce ("Put a claim check on me just like I was somebody's will-call or something"). As one of the agents tells Raven: "Your lease on yourself has come to an end. You are overdue."

Later, when Quickskill has become an antislavery lecturer, he is heckled by other former slaves: "Slaves held each other in bondage, a hostile stare from one slave criticizing the behavior of another slave could be just as painful as a spiked collar, a gesture as fettering as a cage." The funniest and most ghastly updating of slavery occurs when servitude is paired with sadomasochism. Gladstone, a whip fetishist, comes out in Parliament in favor of the Confederacy because he considers Virginia to be the "Canada" of beleaguered sadomasochists; one escaped slave, Leechfield, makes his living in the North by running ads as a hustler: "I'll Be Your Slave For One Day. Humiliate Me. Scorn Me." So dynamic is Reed's meditation on slavery that it extends even to Quickskill's musings about literature: "He was so much against slavery that he had begun to include prose and poetry in the same book, so that there would be no arbitrary boundaries between them."

The most vivacious scenes in the book take place on "Massa" Swille's plantation. Reed's wit rises to dazzling heights and outrageous depths as he shows us the confrontation between Swille and Abraham Lincoln. The President has come, hat in hand, to beg Swille for money with which to finance the Civil War. And in a fit of pique with Lee, Swille gives it to him, preserving as he does so his notion that his plantation is an independent duchy, not a part of either the Union or the Confederacy. But Swille does not oblige Lincoln until after he takes him to task for his shabby clothes and hickish personal style ("Go to the theatre. Get some culture.") Rising in defense of the Sable Genius of the South, Swille defends Jefferson Davis: "Davis' slaves are the only ones I know of who take mineral baths, and when hooped skirts became popular he gave some to the slave women, and when this made it awkward for them to move through the rows of cotton, he widened the rows." Swille gets in a few licks against Mrs. Lincoln as well: "She looks like a laundromat attendant. Old dowdy dough-faced thing. Queen's accent....And why does she send those midnight telegrams to the *Herald Tribune* after drinking God knows what?"

The finest character Reed has ever created is the hair-raising Mammy Barracuda. She has so thoroughly identified herself with the oppressors of her race that after the war she entertains reunions of Confederate soldiers with rousing renditions of Dixie. By catering to the depraved tastes of Massa Swille for drugs and violence, the Mammy has won herself a cabinet full of jewels from Cartier's. She is not above laying it on thick with Lincoln and grabbing him by the waist, waltzing him about and singing, "Hello, Abbbbbbe. Well, hello Abbbbbbe. It's so nice to have you here where you belong."

Barracuda becomes as intimidating a brute as Balzac's Asia when she takes Ms. Swille in hand (once again Reed has cleverly conflated periods by discovering "Ms," the modern feminist's word and a perfect phonetic rendering of the deferential Southern pronunciation of "Mrs."). The mistress of the plantation, after attending Radcliffe and immersing herself in Harriet Beecher Stowe's writings, goes on a hunger strike against her husband's tyranny; Barracuda insults and terrorizes the poor woman back into being a Southern belle. Barracuda's tirade is a masterpiece of invective: "tool: like shit. On strike.

I got your strike, you underbelly of a fifteen-pound gopher rat run ober by a car. Sleep with a dog, he let you. You goat-smelling virago, you gnawing piranha, worrying that man like that."

Reed is not caricaturing the South as it ever was but as it exists in the imagination of some Southern writers and most Northern intellectuals--a land infatuated with death, sadism, Tennyson and feudalism. In this home of putrescent flowers, languishing belles and blood-curdling screams, Reed's Barracuda and Uncle Robin (a supposed prototype of Uncle Tom) prevail. They end up inheriting most of the master's estate; as Uncle Robin observes in the closing pages: "Yeah, they get down on mean Tom. But who's the fool? Nat Turner or us? Nat said he was going to do this. Was going to do that. Said he had a mission. Said his destiny was a divine one.... Now Nat's dead and gone for these many years, and here I am master of a dead man's house. Which one is the fool?"

Mammy Barracuda and Uncle Robin have run away from Reed if not from Massa Swille. In his earlier works Reed has preached that American blacks should reject Christianity and rationalism and return to African hoodoo and intuition. He finds women's liberation disrespectful of the patriarchal dignity of African society. And he treats the antisocial behavior of some modern blacks as a remnant of slavery or as parasitism, "Moochism," as he calls it. This odd collection of ideas fortunately finds little expression in *Flight to Canada* save in the exchanges between Quickskill and his Indian lover, Princess Quaw Quaw Tralaralara, which are the weakest moments in the book.

The attention and affection Reed lavishes on the unregenerate Massa Swille and the reactionary Mammy and Uncle must have alarmed the author as much as they confound and disquiet the reader. The virtuous Raven pales beside the plantation grotesques. Clever as his dialogue is, it cannot match the verbal energy of Uncle Robin's testimonial to Virginia: "I loves it here. Good something to eat when you wonts it. Color TV. Milk pail fulla toddy. Some whiskey and a little nookie from time to time. We gets whipped with a velvet whip, and there's free dental care and always a fiddler case your feets get restless."

The acrid merriment that boils under the Southern scenes thrills and disturbs us. How can we like these monsters? What moral sense can we make of a novel in which a fugitive slave ends up a whore and an Uncle Tom inherits a fortune (even if he has to forge his master's will to do so)? Reed's fantasia on the classic themes of black suffering is a virtuoso performance. His endless list of names for blacks (cocoas, sables, kinks, mahoganies, spooks, shines, sleezers, smokes, picks) is as funny and intolerable as a minstrel show. What troubles me is that *Flight to Canada*, the best work of black fiction since *Invisible Man*, both invites and outrages moral interpretation.

I'm not saying that Reed is endorsing inhumanity simply by portraying it; his views are not to be confused with those of his characters. No, the sin and the glory of this book is far more subtle. What Reed has done is to assign to his vicious characters, and to them alone, his own creative vitality--the very same "mistake" Balzac made, the titan whose novels Reed's book brings to mind, not for its style but for its remarkable drive. As someone once pointed out, Balzac's characters were not representative of humanity in general because he made them all geniuses in his own image; Reed has done the same thing with his terrifying Mammy Barracuda.

Quibbles aside, *Flight to Canada* must be hailed as an irrepressibly funny and mordant meditation on the eternal presence of slavery in America. The book, however, functions not only as a distorting mirror held up to the continuing history of servitude but also as the record of a single consciousness attempting to kill off the slave within--an heroic project that Chekhov once commended to us all.

The Nation (18 September 1976): 247-249. Reprinted with permission from *The Nation* magazine © The Nation Company, L.P.

From the Shadows

Greil Marcus/Review

History, as Ishmael Reed offers it in *Flight to Canada*: It is many years after Appomattox, and in the great Virginia castle of his late master, Arthur Swille, the black poet Raven Quickskill ponders the life of Uncle Robin, formerly Swille's quiet house slave. In the days before emancipation, Raven had run away to Canada, leaving rat poison in the master's Old Crow (and possibly sneaking back just in time to shatter the bottle with a bullet as Swille was about to pour Abraham Lincoln a drink--Lincoln being down at Swillle's to borrow gold to keep the Union solvent). Uncle Robin, though, had stayed behind.

> "Robin, what have you heard about this place up North, I think they call it Canada?" Swille says, eyeing Robin slyly.
> "Canada. I do admit I have heard about the place from time to time, Mr. Swille, but I loves it here so much that ... that I would never think of leaving here....Most assuredly, Mr. Swille, this is my Canada. You'd better believe it."

Uncle Robin never made a move--until, with the war over, he fixed Swille's will and inherited his property: his homes, his lands, his whips, and his collection of *Mandingo*-style porno movies. Harriet Beecher Stowe wanted the rights to Uncle Robin's surprising story (back in the 50s, she had considered him as a model for *Uncle Tom's Cabin* but thought better of it). Uncle Robin insisted the story was Raven's to write. After all, he was part of it. Raven muses over the war, that incredible event. "It affected us all, one way or the other." Uncle Robin had seen all around it. How, though? From over Raven's shoulder Ishmael Reed supplies a hint of an answer, disarming, ominous. "Uncle Robin knows his place," he says. "His place is in the shadows."

From the grave, Swille would understand that. A man who lived on the two gallons of slave mothers' milk delivered to him every day by Uncle Robin, and a decadent cousin to the demonic Colonel Sutpen who cut a swath through Faulkner's *Absalom, Absalom!* Swille was a monster--but he was no fool. Even after the success of his conspiracy to murder Lincoln, Swille realized his fate might well be out of his hands. He had railed:

> "Nigger fever. Niggers do something to you. I've seen white people act strange under their influence. First, you dream about niggers, little niggers mostly: little niggers, sitting, eating watermelons, grinning at you. Then you start dreaming about big niggers. Big, big niggers. Big, big niggers walking all over you; then you got niggers all over you, then they got you. Now they got white men fighting over land taken away from Indians--Rappahannock, Chattanooga. It's spooky. As long as they're in this country, this country is under their spell."

With Swille dead, the future would seem to belong to his bondsmen, and it would belong to them, except that Swille, too, casts a spell. His slaves had cursed him and won, but Swille had cursed the land itself. With Swille's property in his hands, Uncle Robin feels that curse:

> The devil's country home. That's what the South is. It's where the devil goes to rest after he's been about the world, wearying the hunted and the haunted. This is where he comes. The devil sits on the porch of his plantation. He's dressed up like a gentleman and sitting on a white porch between some columns. All the tormented are out in the fields picking cotton and tobacco and looking after his swine, who have human heads and scales on their pig legs and make pitiful cries when they are whipped.
>
> And the devil just grins, sitting there on his devil's porch. Rocking. Rocking like the devil rocks. And that old wicked...overseer, with his blazing Simon Legree blue eyes, is whipping a malnutritioned woman for the devil's entertainment. And the devil laughs his ungodly laugh....And there's blood coming from her mouth. This is the devil's vacation spot, where he personally takes care of all the reservations and arranges for the tour buses to reach various parts of Virginia Hell. Immoral is too polite a word. Devildom. Virginia is where the devil reigns. Can we save Virginia?

From his place in the shadows Uncle Robin had lived up to his master's fears; his secret song, if he had one, would be "The Blue-Tail Fly," sometimes called "Jimmy Crack Corn." It describes a slave whose job it is to keep the flies off his master's horse, and who one day simply lets the flies have their way. "The pony jump, he toss, he pitch/ He threw my master in the ditch/ He died and the jury wondered why/ The verdict was the blue-tail fly."

But it wasn't quite a slave song. When race is involved, the American muse rarely keeps to one side of the fence. "The Blue-Tail Fly" seems to have been written by a white abolitionist who based it on slave music. The tune was often performed by black-face minstrels: It was a favorite of Lincoln's. After the war, freedmen, who would not have dared to sing the song as slaves, took it back as their own.

In just such a way *Flight to Canada* and its hero, Uncle Robin, constitute Ishmael Reed's bid to take back the story of Uncle Tom from Harriet Beecher Stowe--probably because Reed thinks it too valuable to leave to a white writer.

Reed is perhaps our most adventurous novelist, black or white. The untold role of blacks as creators of American culture--or as keepers of a secret culture which at appropriate moments invades the mainstream--has been a dominant theme in his fiction, particularly in his great 1972 novel *Mumbo Jumbo*. Here, to start things off, Reed tells us that *Uncle Tom's Cabin* was a black man's testament to begin with, based on the brief published autobiography of Josiah Henson--a former slave and founder of the Dawn settlement in Canada. Mrs. Stowe's brother Edward, an abolitionist minister in Boston, had brought the two writers together; Mrs. Stowe liked to say that God had done the rest.

Reed ignores Mrs. Stowe's plot (though, for what it's worth, one of the two slaves who escapes with Raven is named Leechfield, and Mrs. Stowe was born in Litchfield, Connecticut). What's at stake is not a story line but crucial personalities of American whites and blacks--of Swille, Uncle Robin, Raven, and even Lincoln (to Reed, "Abe the Player," as in hustler). A good part of the novel is taken up by Raven's adventures on his way to sanctuary, north of the border, but they aren't nearly so compelling as Swille's evildoings or Uncle Robin's sleight-of-hand subversions.

Raven, on the run, is a bewildered man, unsure of his role in history or of his place in the half-world of fugitives, copperheads, slave-catchers, freebooters, abolitionist groupies, and Confederate spies. But there is something flat about this side of the story, as if the fact that Raven has cut his roots makes it impossible for Reed to focus either his sorrow or his wit. When Raven finally makes it to Canada, Reed surrenders the tale to an actual quote from a man who ferried escaped slaves from Buffalo to Ontario. His description of what he saw when his passengers reached the other side is so shattering--"They seemed to be transformed; a new light shone in their eyes, their tongues were loosed, they laughed and cried, prayed and sang praises, fell upon the ground and kissed it, hugged and kissed each other, crying Bless de Lord! Oh! I'se free before I die!"--that it lifts a reader right out of the novel, almost trivializing Raven's story, capsizing it.

Swille and Uncle Robin give the book its life, and Reed can shape them with a line when he wants to. "People don't know when the Swilles came to Virginia, and the Swilles ain't talkin'," suggests as much about the diabolical nature of Swille's hold on his possessions as a list of his perversions. Uncle Robin's response to the torments of Cato, Swille's white bondsman ("So loyal he volunteered for slavery....The slaves voted him All-Slavery"), brings us closer to the kind of image Reed wants to fix in our minds than any of Raven's perils:

> "And don't get smart either, just because Harriet Beecher Stowe came down and taped you. Ha! Ha! She didn't even use your interview. Used Tom, over at the Legree plantation. What did she give you?"
>
> "She just gave me a flat-out fee. I bought a pig, a dog, and a goose with it."
>
> "Ha! Ha! Eeeee. Ha! Ha!" Cato stands in the hall and slaps his head. "One of the bestsellers of all time and you only receive pig money. You are stupid, just like they say, you black infidel."
>
> "Yessir, Mr.Cato."
>
> Cato, whistling, skips down the hall to the kitchen. Uncle Robin stares after him. A stare that could draw out the dust in a brick.

Flight to Canada can be crude (Reed's misogyny is as rampant as ever--and as incomprehensible, at least to me); it can be outrageously funny (as in a hilarious confrontation between Swille's declining wife and the apparition of her dead son, all of it stage-managed by Uncle Robin). But I am drawn more to the book's darker side. Reed is no more merely tossing off words when he tells us Swille's origins are unknown than is Uncle Robin when he speaks of the devil in his rocking chair. Reed calls Edgar Allen Poe "the principal biographer" of the Civil War and, while he sometimes only plays with the idea (Swille keeps the poet on retainer as an expert on torture) his rendering of Swille's death provokes a sense of absolute and pervasive morbidity not very different from that of "The Fall of the House of Usher."

For all his odiousness, Swille appears more as a buffoon than anything else. But fighting off death--which appears in the form of the ghost of his dead sister, with whose corpse he has been carrying on a deeply satisfying necrophiliac relationship--Swille's evil, his refusal of all human limits, suddenly becomes real. It is a great moment in the novel--perhaps the best. It is certainly the scariest.

Reed shifts rough farce into precise nightmare; he sets off an eruption of the deepest feeling into a casual scene that was not built to hold it. He mixes artifacts of the present into the past (along with Mrs. Stowe's tape recorder, Swille's porno movies, and scores of other transpositions, Lincoln is shot on live TV). He ignores historical chronology; when it's convenient, he gives his characters knowledge of the future. The result, finally, is a broadly, bitterly comic work, defined by just those qualities identified by Constance Rourke, in 1931 in *American Humor*, when she wrote of the entrance of slave culture into the American mainstream--an event that took place in the 1840s and 1850s, in the form of minstrel songs and narratives performed by whites:

> The note of triumph, dominant in all early American humor, appeared in these reflected creations of the negro, but not as triumph over circumstances. Rather, this was an unreasonable headlong triumph, launching into the realm of the preposterous. It could be heard in the careless phrasing of the songs, in the

swift pulsations of their rhythms. Yet defeat was also clear. Slavery was constantly imaged in brief phrases or, in simple situations. Fragments of cryptic work-songs were heard--"Sheep shell oats, ole Tucker shell de corn." Echoes sounded of forbidden devil songs--"Oh, I'se sorry I sold my soul to the debbil." Defeat was hinted in the occasional minor key and in the smothered sidelong satire. In American humor the sudden extreme of nonsense was new, and the tragic undertone was new.

Uncle Robin triumphs over Swille and finds himself ruling over a land poisoned by crime; Raven keeps his soul, but Leechfield, his fellow fugitive, sinks to making sex movies with white abolitionists and, in the end, hires himself out to Notherners as a "Slave for a Day." But if the hint of defeat is almost never absent from *Flight to Canada*, it is that note of triumph--of revenge, of glee, of breaking loose--that stays with a reader. Uncle Robin and Raven are out to save Virginia, not to bury it.

Flight to Canada plays fast and loose with plot no less than history, and it has already caused a certain amount of confusion. One reviewer got Raven mixed up with Swille. Another placed Emancipation City, where Raven hides while awaiting the money that will get him to Canada, in Canada. More than one writer has called the novel "the rock version" of the Civil War, which is as close to being meaningless as any statement about the book could be. Though Reed's four previous novels have yet to gain him a very wide readership, this time around critics are treating him more favorably than ever--even if they still have trouble taking, or identifying, his writing for what it is. They have been too quick to tell us that when Reed writes of magic spells hanging over the land, he is engaging "metaphor" or "irony"--to tell us, in other words, that Reed is only kidding--or to pry acceptable messages from Reed's work. One approving reviewer has claimed, rather muddily, that Reed's interpolation of 20th-century objects into a 19th-century setting means that like the slaves, we are, all of us, enslaved by conventions and things. (So much for the terrors of real slavery.) "It isn't simple fun," the reviewer concluded, "backdrops for a minstrel show."

But it seems to me this is exactly what it is. *Flight to Canada* does come at us like a minstrel show--with Mrs. Stowe's tape recorder as a sight gag there to keep the story jumping. Reed derives much of his style, and his work much of its force, from old popular culture--from ancient superstitions, back-country hexes, narrative folklore, and minstrelsy--and there's no need to elevate his work with spurious profundities. If we do, both Reed's style and his force will elude us.

It was *Uncle Tom's Cabin*, after all, which, after the Civil War, became the most popular minstrel play. Reed notes early in *Flight to Canada* that black minstrel shows about Mrs. Stowe--and the money she made from *Uncle Tom's Cabin*--were not uncommon. The minstrel plays and "theatricals," put on all over the country by troupes of wandering actors, were written about everything from John Brown's execution to local scandals, and they were often written on the run. Travelers on the Mississippi told of seeing skits rehearsed at night on drifting flatboats; black preachers' sermons, animal fables, songs, Shakespearean fragments, tall tales, racial satire, and patriotic legends were set forth in barns, clearings, and graveyards, sometimes by candlelight and sometimes even in the dark, by moonlight.

This was the common coin of American culture in the days of which Reed writes--an improvised art, a very special, slightly surreal version of the American language. Reed has caught its spirit: the rough, overplayed humor and absurd coincidences; the frantic blackout plots with actors trundling on and off the stage, with perhaps three performers covering a dozen roles; the one-night theatricals stripped to action, interlocutor, and a final stirring speech guaranteed to bring down the house; heroes and villains, and the odd, ambiguous character playing from the side.

Constance Rourke's judgment on the minstrels tells us a good deal about Reed's achievement: "If they had failed to exhibit subtlety, fineness, balance, they created laughter and had served the ends of communication among a people unacquainted with themselves, strange to the land, unshaped as a nation; they had produced a shadowy social coherence."

And shadowy remains the word: We are still unacquainted and unshaped. If Reed's ambitions in *Mumbo Jumbo* and *Flight to Canada* are to exorcise the demons in our history while rescuing or reinventing those parts of our history that have been forgotten or ignored, his work is just beginning. In America, black history and white history have long since intermingled; we, each of us, carry a mystery of connections inside ourselves. As I read *Flight to Canada,* listening, in the kind of moment I wish I could invent at will, to my six-year-old daughter sing "The Blue-Tail Fly'' ("Where did you learn that song?'' I asked; "I just know it," she said), it seemed to me that Reed had drawn those connections out, made them visible, rendered their mystery tangible, and, thus, raised the possibility that one might yet solve it.

But that is only how it seemed. The mystery of what it means for a young white child to sing "The Blue Tail Fly" is surely beyond the ability of the singer to comprehend: it might also be beyond the power of the song--or of *Flight to Canada*, the story the song orchestrates--to reveal.

Jimmy crack corn and I don't care
Jimmy crack corn and I don't care
Jimmy crack corn and I don't care
My master's gone away.

The Village Voice. Originally published as "Uncle Tom Redux," 15 November 1976: 49-50.

**I'll fly away: Ishmael Reed Refashions the Slave Narrative
and Takes It on a *Flight to Canada***

Janet Kemper Beck

In 1852 Frederick Douglass was asked to address the citizens of Rochester, New York on the significance of the 4th of July for the Negro. He began with a wry question, "[P]ardon me, and allow me to ask, why am I called upon to speak here to-day? What have I, or those I represent, to do with your national independence?" (115). A similar question might be posed concerning Ishmael Reed and his neo-slave narrative, *Flight to Canada.* Why would Reed, a rollicking literary libertarian of 20th century style and sensibility, choose to write a novel in the most restrictive of genres, the largely formulaic 19th century slave narrative? The answer lies, partly, in Reed's assertion that not much has changed for the African American author in the hundred and fifty odd years since the ante-bellum slave narratives were appropriated by white abolitionist editors and audiences. He sees, what is to him, an obvious correlation between the 20th century black American writer and his 19th century counterpart. To develop this parallel, Reed creates a 19th century narrative in theme and plot and overlays it with a 20th century cornucopia of in-your-face ridicule, rebuke and sarcasm. Through his self-proclaimed neo-hoodoo aesthetic incorporating anachronistic flights of time and place; his calculated use of avian imagery reminiscent of the slave's obsession with flight; the dark humor and darker satire surrounding the wildly eccentric, yet often stereotypic characterizations and situations; and the stylistic incorporation of both poetry and prose in a genre generally considered formulaic, Reed has, in effect, liberated the slave narrative. In so doing, he has reclaimed the slave narrative tradition for the African American writer, creating what Douglass, in his Rochester address, would call "the storm, the whirlwind, and the earthquake" (118).

When Douglass delivered his 1852 speech on the evils of slavery, he was one of a group of slave authors highly cultivated by white abolitionist editors and audiences. With fiery rhetoric, he called for "scorching irony" and added "had I the ability, and could reach the nation's ear, I would, to-day, pour out a fiery stream of biting ridicule, blasting reproach, withering sarcasm, and stern rebuke" (118). The fact that he could not write as he spoke, however, had little to do with ability or accessibility, and everything to do with the restrictive nature of the slave narrative genre itself. For while not "only the anti-slavery public, but the whole world it seems, was eager to hear the life story of any Negro who had escaped from slavery or who had done anything else extraordinary" (Loggins 15), it was the white abolitionist editors and audiences whose expectations for the narratives dictated not only their form, but also, in part, their content. Ever conscious of the audience, the abolitionists "encouraged formula expressions of stereotypical persons who often did not correspond to what the narrator felt himself to be," with the primary focus of the narratives being denunciation of the slave system (Foster 60).

To ensure a market for these works and to perfect the tales as they would later be written, a host of slave narrators, Douglass among them, were encouraged to join the abolitionist lecture circuit. This exposure gave the ex-slaves "an opportunity to structure, to embellish, and above all to polish an oral version of their tale--and to do so before the very audiences who would soon purchase hundreds, if not thousands, of copies of the written account" (Stepto 9). In fact, many times when a slave gave a talk, he or she patterned it for effective presentation before ever committing it to writing. Thus, the audience of the oral version (often the same audience who would later read the written work) had ample opportunity to directly influence the composition of the story.

It is not surprising, given the abolitionist involvement, that the slave narratives closely correspond to a formula. Even a cursory reading of the narratives reveal striking similarities in style. The abolitionists "had certain clear expectations, well understood by themselves and well understood by the ex-slave too, about the proper content to be observed, the proper theme to be developed and the proper form to be followed" (Olney 158). The narratives, in fact, correspond so clearly to a formula that scholar James Olney has created what he calls a "Master Plan for Slave Narratives (the irony of the phrasing being neither unintentional or insignificant)" (153). Within this "Master Plan," the narrative often begins, "I was born . . ."; continues with a sketchy description of parentage; depicts a cruel slave master and a hard-working yet mistreated slave; describes a successful escape, and concludes with reflections on slavery (153).

Not only were the slaves encouraged to write in a uniform style that was easily palatable for the largely uneducated mass audience, but a concern for what would sell is evident in the sensational content of many of the narratives as well. In fact, the ante-bellum accounts often resemble a catalog of slavery's ills, replete with graphic depictions of violence (Mullane and Wilson 1). Also prevalent were instances of sexual assaults on black slaves by white lascivious masters, so much so, in fact, that the tales are described as "salacious by 19th century standards" (Blassingame xxviii). Further contributing to the sensationalism of these tales was the depiction of the mulatto, an obvious symbol of slavery's sins and one calculated to strike an emotional chord in the Northern audience. The narratives have such a disproportionate number of these characters, that many reading the narratives believed that southern blacks were "predominantly mulatto" (Foster 128-9).

The slave authors, while recounting the horrors of slavery, had a difficult task. They had to contradict the master's view of slavery while presenting their own, and do so for an audience that had more in common with the masters than with the slaves (Foster 14). As a result, the ultimate irony of the slave narratives is that once the slaves had escaped the literal bondage of slavery, they found themselves entrapped in a literary enslavement. Caught between audience expectations and abolitionist interference (albeit well-intentioned but nonetheless self-serving), the slave narrators were rarely completely free to tell their stories as they saw them.

Reed is both intrigued with the slave narrative tradition and cognizant of its limitations. In a 1968 interview with Walt Shepperd, he describes these works as "written by the common people" and feels they may ultimately "turn out to be the American art form . . . more than the novel" (12). He elaborates in a 1977 interview with John Domini, stating that all the "best examples of what it means to live free are in those slave narratives" and citing Henry Bibb, Solomon Northrup, William Wells Brown, [and] Frederick Douglass" specifically. Reed not only respects these writers but relates to them as well: "A lot of the problems I have, they had" (140). It is this bond, the inability of the African American writer to tell his or her own story that draws Reed to the slave narrative tradition. For Reed correctly views the 20th century publishing industry as overwhelmingly dominated by white males, "the managers, [and] the salesmen, they head the book reviews which support the works of other white males" (Domini 135-6). In a 1971 interview with John O'Brien, Reed states, "I'm getting more and more interested in slavery as a metaphor for how blacks are treated in this civilization. . . . The Irving Howe crowd and the liberals in New York are the abolitionists" (O'Brien 20). By adapting the slave narrative genre, strongly associated with both black freedom and white domination, he returns to what Ashraf Rushdy calls the "first form of black representation and resistance and the first literary instance of white appropriation of black texts and voices" (116). Reed is, in fact, ardent in his desire to escape white and black critics alike who dictate that "novels about African Americans should be about pain," wryly adding that he doesn't "think pain is all that great" (Ewing 120). His assertion that "we are going to get to our aesthetic Canada, no matter how many dogs they send after us" (O'Brien 20-21) reinforces his contention that the role of the 19th century abolitionist editors has been replaced with equally intrusive 20th century literary critics who continue attempts to influence what and how African Americans write. Specifically, Reed has commented that "...when a black man tries to be a satirist, tries to look at the whole universe, *The New York Review of Books*, Jason Epstein, *The New York Times*, all these cats get uptight" (Shepperd 9). Ultimately Reed's refusal to be a "slave to his narrative" is a result of his belief that "forms of slavery still exist in modern America" (Walsh 62-63).

Reed is acutely aware of the appropriations of the former slaves' stories. Early in the novel, the poet and ex-slave, Raven Quickskill, comments that human hosts "walk the streets of the cities, their eyes hollow, the spirit gone out of them. Somebody has taken their story" (Reed 8). Lest his point be lost, Reed cites the most well-known theft of a slave's story, Harriet Beecher Stowe's adaptation of Josiah Henson's story in *Uncle Tom's Cabin*. Part One of *Flight to Canada* is entitled "Naughty Harriet," an obvious reference to Stowe, and it is in this section that Raven comments, "When you take a man's story, a story that doesn't belong to you, that story will get you" (9). His sarcasm is scathing and leveled at Stowe, "that fanatical Beecher woman" (21). What particularly incenses Reed is the "cultural oppression, the exclusion not just of Josiah Henson from his story, but of his way of telling it" (Walsh 67).

Enter "writin' is fightin'" Ishmael Reed, literary abolitionist, with a plan to free the slave narrative that would confound not only the most racist Nebraska Tracker but also the most fervent abolitionist. Drawing a literary Mason-Dixon line in the sand, Reed refuses to allow the story of the house slave and Uncle Tom of the novel, Uncle Robin, to be appropriated. Quickskill will "write Uncle Robin's story in such a way that, using a process the old curers used, to lay hands on the story would be lethal to the thief" (11). This way, Uncle Robin will "have the protection that Uncle Tom (Josiah Henson) didn't" (11). Reed makes it clear that Quickskill will protect Robin's story in the same way that he himself will protect Quickskill's in spite of the fact that "the critics are going to give me some kind of white master. A white man. They'll say he gave me the inspiration and that I modeled it after him" (121). Quickskill, however, establishes whose story the poem, and by extension, the novel's, really is. He gives credit to William Wells Brown, saying, "I had you in mind..." (121). Reed acknowledges his own debt to Brown, stating "...Brown used newspaper clippings, interviews, travelogue material, autobiography, fiction, all in the same book . . . like a painter's form" (Nazareth 183). It is ironic that Reed sees in Brown's style a precursor of his own, for while Brown's slave narrative incorporates both newspaper clippings and poetry, it is in his fiction that Brown attains the greatest degree of artistic freedom.

That Reed completes the liberation of the slave narrative begun by Douglass, Brown, and others, is due in part to his absolute refusal to respect the conventions of the genre. He dismantles the form by incorporating poetry, prose, and drama in his work, and the content by parodying many of the typical situations found in the narratives. One technique he uses to accomplish both is his self-described neo-hoodoo aesthetic, which includes the free-flowing movement of time and place in the novel. That the reader is to be taken on an anachronistic roller coaster is apparent from the book's opening lines, as Raven Quickskill, the slave, writes, "Ain't no use your Slave / Catchers waitin on me / At Trailways / I won't be there / I flew in non-stop / Jumbo jet this A.M." (3).

The novel exuberantly and intentionally misapplies a myriad of 20th century technologies to 19th century events. The most frequently cited of these anachronisms occurs in the description of Abraham Lincoln's assassination as the "cameras were focused upon the President's box. Lincoln lay slumped to his left side, his arm dangling" (103). Reed continues, "They replay the actual act . . . . They promise to play it again on the Late News. When the cameras swing back . . . Miss Laura Keene . . . is at Lincoln's side live.' Her gown is spattered with brain tissue" (103). A reporter thrusts a microphone in Mrs. Lincoln's face, asking, "[H]ow do you feel having just watched your husband's brains blown out before your eyes?" (103). The intrusion of twentieth century electronics; the obvious comparison of Keene's gown and Jackie Kennedy's blood spattered clothing; the wickedly humorous description of an inhumane press; and the insertion of lines from the 19th century drama, *Our American Cousins*, all serve to reinforce the notion, never far beneath the surface, that not much has changed in the last 100 years (Harris 122; Walsh 59-60).

Another device Reed appropriates to further the connection to the 19th century narrative is flight. Noting that slave narratives contain "much avian imagery . . . [and] poetry about dreams and flight" (Reed 88), Reed ingenuously integrates the concept of flight throughout the novel. The choice of the fugitive slave's name, Raven, is a clever one. At once, the image of the black bird becomes synonymous with the slave's flight (Fox 69). Further, raven, meaning to devour or seize, is an apt description of what Reed has done in his reclamation of the slave narrative. Reed himself writes, Raven's "poem flew just as his name had flown. Raven. A scavenger to some, a bringer of new light to others" (13). A further analogy can be drawn with Poe's raven, a bird with mystical properties whose protestation "nevermore" echoes through the imagination (Fox 69), a declaration that could just as easily be Quickskill's as he protects Robin's story from abolitionist interlopers. Further drawing on this theme, Robin, the house slave, takes flights buying supplies for the plantation while Swille, the plantation master, often flies to Richmond to check on his investments. The literal flights of the characters echo the flights in imagination that Raven, and by extension, Reed, must make in their efforts toward liberation, the ultimate flight, to Canada. Reed, ever the trickster, is not content to simply bring to mind the flying African so prevalent in the slave folk tale tradition. Rather, in an ironic twist, he subverts the image so that, at least at one point, it represents the opposite of freedom, death for an entire people. Quickskill says, "people of my class . . . become like mythical Goofus birds, invented by lumbermen . . . who fly backwards and build their nests upside down. We get smashed and our endings are swift" (12).

Reed delights in appropriating stereotypic characterizations from the 19th century narratives and refashioning them with his sardonic humor. His description of the mulatto, Cato the Graffado, as a "butterscotched version" of Swille, the plantation master, with "sandy hair, freckles, aquiline nose'" (51) is a parody of the mulatto so frequently depicted in, and so essential to, the original narratives. Raven Quickskill, unlike Douglass, has numerous problems on the slave lecture circuit. Not only do things keep "going wrong with the microphone" (143), but some of the "people in the front row began to snore, and the black help from the kitchen [were] . . . making comments, talking loud and staring at him evilly" (144). In a 1993 interview, Reed admits that while "satire is one of the styles and techniques that I use," he prefers to think of his "stuff as comic" (Dick 349). More specifically, when asked whether "writin' is fightin'" is an appropriate metaphor for his work, Reed responds that his writing is a form of "comic aggression," a term appropriated from Charles Fanning's description of l9th century Irish American literature. When people do not have "power with technology they [use] their wit" (352-3). Clearly, comic aggression is an integral tool through which Reed refashions the genre, as he satirizes both the literary establishment and the culture which supports it.

In addition to content considerations, Reed literally dismantles the slave narrative structurally in his quest to free it. His novel incorporates poetry, prose and drama in an attempt to defy the narrow formational constraints placed upon its l9th century counterpart. The book actually begins with the poem, "Flight to Canada," about which Raven comments, "Little did I know when I wrote the poem, 'Flight to Canada' that there were so many secrets locked inside its world" (7). The poem, indeed, is both harbinger and microcosm of the novel. From its opening line "Dear Massa Swille: / What it was? / I have done my Liza Leap / & am safe in the arms of Canada" (3), to its closing "That was rat poison I left / In your Old Crow" (5), the poem encapsulates the novel's plot at the same time it becomes a metaphor for the slave's condition. Swille's observation that the poem has trapped him once and it'll trap him again is astute. Not only does the poem provide a literal clue to the slave's whereabouts, but Raven's writing, like that of his l9th century predecessors, becomes another form of entrapment, one Reed is determined to break (Rushdy 121).

A second poem, "The Saga of Third World Belle," appears in the section entitled "Lincoln the Player." In it, Quickskill explains to his "Indian Princess" that "Your favorite pirate uses / Your Dad's great-chief's skull / As an ashtray / And sold your Mom's hand-knitted / Robes to Buffalo Bill's / Wild West Show" (123). The reference to the pirate refers to Quaw Quaw's suitor, Yankee Jack, a "distributor" who decides what "books, films, even what kind of cheese, no less, will reach the market" (146). It is an angry Quickskill who comments, "we fuges know we're slaves, constantly hunted, but you enslave everybody" (146). While the poem serves once again to fracture the novel's form, it also reinforces the theme that white America will indiscriminately appropriate cultures, unabashedly making money in the process.

From his anachronistic flights in time and fancy to his structural dismantling of the formulaic l9th century narrative, Reed has become, in effect, a cultural underground railroad, a literary North Star providing direction for other writers who would reclaim the tradition as their own. Over one hundred years would pass between the 19th century narratives and Reed's novel, years in which there continued to be "something 'fugitive' about black writing and black experience" (Fox 68). Douglass, who transcended the l9th century slave narrative even as he was constrained by it, felt compelled to observe, "The truth was, I felt myself a slave, and the idea of speaking to white people weighed me down" (*Narrative* 120). It was, however, in "pleading the cause of my brethren" (120) that

Douglass ultimately discovered his voice as an anti-slavery lecturer. Quickskill, the fictional slave, found both literal and cultural emancipation through his poetry: "it was his writing that got him to Canada . . . for him, freedom was his writing" (Reed 89). But it is Reed, the novelist, who ultimately finishes what Douglass and Brown began. Unlike the movement in the earlier narratives, which is, by necessity, from south to north, slavery to freedom, Reed begins his novel with Raven "safe in the arms of Canada" (3) and ends with his return to the plantation. With this event, Reed has brought the slave and his narrative, literally and figuratively, home. With *Flight to Canada*, a tale which allows us to laugh at the monstrous evil called slavery, Reed has freed the 20th century African American writer to tell a story uniquely his or her own, while at the same time liberating an audience enslaved in its expectations of what a black writer should be. In so doing, Reed has taken us all on a *Flight to Canada*-- round trip--and brought the slave narrative home, where it should have been all along.

WORKS CITED

Blassingame, John W. Introduction. *Slave Testimony: Two Centuries of Letters, Speeches, Interviews and Autobiographies*. Ed. Blassingame. Baton Rouge: Louisiana State University Press, 1977. xvii-ixv.

Dick, Bruce. "Ishmael Reed: An Interview." 1993. *Conversations with Ishmael Reed*. Eds. Bruce Dick and Amritjit Singh. Jackson: University Press of Mississippi, 1995. 334-356.

Domini, John. "Ishmael Reed: A Conversation with John Domini." 1978. *Conversations with Ishmael Reed*. Eds. Bruce Dick and Amritjit Singh. Jackson: University Press of Mississippi, 1995. 128-143.

Douglass, Frederick. *Narrative of the Life of Frederick Douglass, an American Slave, Written by Himself.* 1845. *Frederick Douglass: The Narrative and Selected Writings*. Ed. Michael Meyer. New York: The Modern Library, 1984. 3-120.

---."What to the Slave is the Fourth of July?" 1852. *The Oxford Frederick Douglass Reader*. Ed. William L. Andrews: New York: Oxford University Press, 1996. 108-130.

Ewing, Jon. "The Great Tenure Battle of 1977." 1978. *Conversations with Ishmael Reed*. Eds. Bruce Dick and Amritjit Singh. Jackson: University Press of Mississippi, 1995. 111-127.

Foster, Frances Smith. *Witnessing Slavery: The Development of the Ante-Bellum Slave Narratives*. 2nd ed. Madison: The University of Wisconsin Press, 1979.

Fox, Robert Elliot. "Ishmael Reed: Gathering the Limbs of Osiris." *Conscientious Sorcerers: The Black Postmodernist Fiction of LeRoi Jones/Amiri Baraka, Ishmael Reed, and Samuel Delany*. New York:

Greenwood Press, 1987. 39-92.

Harris, Norman. "The Black Universe in Contemporary Afro-American Fiction." *CLAJ* 30.1 (1986): 1-13.

Loggins, Vernon. "Biography, Poetry, and Miscellaneous Writings, 1840-1865." *The Negro Author: His Development in America to 1900*. 1931. 224-32. Rpt. In *Nineteenth-Century Literature Criticism*. Vol. 20. Detroit: Gale Research, Inc. 1989. 15-20.

Mullane, Janet and Robert Thomas Wilson. Introduction. *Nineteenth-Century Literature Criticism*. Eds. Mullane and Wilson. Vol. 20. Detroit: Gale Research, Inc. 1989. 1-2.

Nazareth, Peter. "An Interview with Ishmael Reed." 1982. *Conversations with Ishmael Reed*. Eds. Bruce Dick and Amritjit Singh. Jackson: University Press of Mississippi, 1995. 181-195.

O'Brien, John. "Ishmael Reed." 1974. *Conversations with Ishmael Reed*. Eds. Bruce Dick and Amritjit Singh. Jackson: University Press of Mississippi, 1995.

Reed, Ishmael. *Flight to Canada*. New York: Atheneum, 1976.

Rusdy, Ashraf H. A. "Ishmael Reed's Neo-Hoodoo Slave Narrative." *Narrative* 2.2 (1994): 112-39.

Shepperd, Walt. "When State Magicians Fail: An Interview with Ishmael Reed." 1968. *Conversations with Ishmael Reed*. Eds. Bruce Dick and Amritjit Singh. Jackson: University Press of Mississippi, 1995. 3-13.

Stepto, Robert B. "I Rose and Found My Voice: Narration, Authentication, and Authorial Control in Four Slave Narratives." *From Behind the Veil: A Study of Afro-American Narrative*. 2nd ed. Urbana: University of Illinois Press, 1991. 3-31.

Walsh, Richard. "'A Man's Story is His Gris-Gris': Cultural Slavery, Literary Emancipation and Ishmael Reed's *Flight to Canada*." *Journal of American Studies* 27.1 (1993): 57-71.

Previously unpublished essay (1998). Reprinted by permission.

Heading Them Off at the Pass

Peter Nazareth/Article

The western stagecoach is being pursued by a posse of cowboys. No, the pursuers are wolves. The driver's assistant and some of the passengers throw bones of various sizes and shapes. The real loot is hidden. The leading wolves see these bones and stop to eat them, giving up the chase. Several wolves trip over these leaders. The dog in them leads others to fight for the bones. Not one

Wolf, however; he sidesteps the bones and the mess. He decided to run off in an oblique direction and head the stagecoach off at the pass.

Just watch the Loop Garoo Kid in *Yellow Back Radio Broke-Down,* Ishmael Reed's second novel, a Western. Loop Garoo is a black cowboy, like the famous Lash Larue of the fifties wearing black and using whips. First appearing as Loop Garoo in Reed's quintessential poem, "I Am a Cowboy in the Boat of Ra," he means wolf. Chapter 20 of Reed's *Flight to Canada* is prefaced by a poem by Raven Quickskill which ends, "Just like a coyote casetting amorous / Howls / in sugar Blues / I airmail them to you / In packages of Hopi Dolls / Ah ouooooooo! Ah ouooooooo!" The coyote is a small prairie wolf, the poem ends as a blues, and the howl comes from Howlin' Wolf, the famous bluesman. We were prepared for this wolf howl because we have heard the low moan of a solitary wolf at critical points throughout the novel. The son of Ed Yellings who is taking care of business in *The Last Days of Louisiana Red* is named Wolf. When the President gets to the presidents' hell in *The Terrible Twos,* "an animal in a white smock" dashes by which appears to be "a wolf or coyote."

The novel which gives me the best entry into Reed's path is *Flight to Canada.* Three slaves have escaped Arthur Swille, the slaveowner/ multinational, and are trying to get to Canada, to freedom. But when Raven Quickskill finally gets to Niagara, Canada, he meets Carpenter, beaten up by racists in Toronto, who tells him that Canada belongs to the Swilles, they just let the Canadians run it. Raven is deeply disillusioned and decides to return to the U.S. When I was in East Africa, Goans, my race, were always planning to fly to Canada. In 1975, my wife and I bumped into a Goan couple in Montreal who had left Uganda in 1970. The man hadn't found his Canada in Montreal and was thinking of looking for it in Toronto. We met other Goans who had not found their Canada in Toronto. When I chaired a panel on Goan literature at Madison, Wisconsin, a few years ago, Dr. John Hobgood presented a paper on Francisco Luis Gomes of the nineteenth century, from which I learned that Goans had been looking to Canada as the promised land a hundred years ago. Time was collapsed: past and present became the same. Yet I had not understood the Goan obsession with Canada until I read *Flight to Canada*: it is the flight from a long colonial oppression, the ravenous hunger for freedom, which is in the blood.

Getting to Canada is not simple. So Reed operates on multiple levels. The novel begins with a poem entitled "Flight to Canada," written by Raven to taunt his erstwhile master. The poet says, "That was rat poison I left / In your Old Crow." The crow is a sort of raven, which brings to mind "The Raven" by Edgar Allan Poe, which brings to mind "The Fall of the House of Usher," which brings to mind an implied incestuous relationship in a southern mansion, the underpinning of the novel that follows. The poem is a work of art. The blurb to Reed's first novel, *The Free-Lance Pallbearers,* indicates that this fiction is stylized.

It is the artistic imagination that has to recover the lost story. Raven speculates on Harriet Beecher Stowe, who took the story of *Uncle Tom's Cabin* from Josiah Henson. He made no money, his settlement going bankrupt while others got fabulously rich from a musical version of the novel. "Is there no sympathy in Nature?" Raven wonders. Then there should be sympathy in art: Reed puts her into an updated story of Uncle Tom, exposes her, and prevents her from doing it again. Reed demythifies history: she wrote the novel not because she wanted to undermine slave ownership or the aristocracy but because she wanted to buy a new dress. Uncle Robin is careful with his story, which he knows: he commissions Raven to tell the story. Uncle Robin played at faithfulness. Trusting Robin, Swille gets him to write out his will ("Massa's will") because he suffered from dyslexia. Robin consulted his own gods, who told him that he did not have to obey the laws of people who did not respect him as a human being. He doctored the will and ended up owning the estate. By remaining in the shadows and "tomming" when necessary, Robin lives up to his name and flies to freedom. He too could have fled, for he often flew on business for Swille. But he knows what Raven discovers: that the Master owns it all, he owns Canada. Robin uses his new ownership to free others such as Stray Leechfield. Swille did not accept the money Leechfield sent in: he wanted his property. Leechfield does not realize that one needs more than one wing to fly. Robin also gives Raven the freedom to work his art without fear of pursuit. Raven's speculations at the beginning are the means by which the work takes off.

So you want your own history, huh? Here it is. You can have your history. That is all you can have: gnaw on it. "'Get back to your language,' they say," says Adil Jussawalla in *Missing Person*. Reed ridicules this kind of obsession with one's own history in an exchange between Raven and Mel Leer, an immigrant Russian Jew:

> "Nobody has suffered as much as my people," says Quicksill calmly.
> The immigrant Mel Leer rises. "Don't tell me that lie."
> The whole café turns to the scene.
> "Our people have suffered the most."
> "My people."
> "My people."
> "My people."
> "My people."
> "We suffered under the hateful Czar Nicholas!"
> "We suffered under Swille and Legree, the most notorious masters in the annals of slavery." (p68)

Blowing up the balloon, Reed lets it burst. He shows that the oppression of people, which has actually happened, can be turned into what Derek Walcott calls a career (*Dream on Monkey Mountain and Other Plays*). This is the accusation by the actress playing Desdemona to the West Indian actor playing

Othello in Murray Carlin's play, *Not Now, Sweet Desdemona*. "We have suffered," she jeers. "We know what suffering is. We are all refugees, so will you pay my hotel bill.... Othello the Moor--and what is he? Another bloody self-pitying, posturing, speechifying Chairman of the Afro-Asian Delegation!" This is the danger of exploiting your people's exploitation. Princess Quaw Quaw Tralaralara enjoys the fame that comes from ethnic dances on college campuses. (Her name suggests squaw, a raven's cry, and flightiness .)

She is therefore hypocritical when she accuses Raven of being too obsessed by race--this is his reality. But real racism can make the recipient so touchy that he reacts to racism where it does not exist. Pirate Jack, a sophisticated middleman controlling the market and mass taste behind the scenes, is helping Raven get to Canada on his pirate boat. There is the following exchange:

> "You think that's manly. Huh? You think that's manly. One day I outwitted thirteen bloodhounds."
> "Preposterous."
> "I did. Thirteen bloodhounds. They had me up a tree."
> "That can't be. I've studied the history of bloodhounds since the age of William the Conqueror, and that's just a niggardly lie."
> "What did you say?"
> "I said it's just a niggardly lie."
> "Why you--"Quickskill rushes around the desk and nabs the pirate, lifting him up. (p. 151)

We know what Raven thinks. But the dictionary shows that the word comes from niggard, probably originally the Middle English negarde, meaning "stingy" or "miserly." Treating the subject on a comic level, Reed makes a serious point: he shows that the colonized has been programmed to destroy himself if he is not cunning, knowledgeable and self-aware. Pirate Jack was helping Raven elude Swille's men: his touchiness jeopardises the plan.

It is difficult for people in the belly of the whale to know what is going on and where the whale is going. Reed gives these invisible forces concrete names so we can deal with them. Louisiana Red is a hot sauce manufactured by a corporation:

> Louisiana Red was the way they related to one another, oppressed one another, maimed and murdered one another, carving one another while above their heads, fifty thousand feet, billionaires flew in custom-made jet planes equipped with saunas tennis courts swimming pools discotheques and meeting rooms decorated like a Merv Griffin Show set. (p. 7)

The reference to the Merv Griffin Show set both undermines the whole description through pathos and makes us understand the thing in an instant because we watch television. Reed identifies a category manipulable by Louisiana Red, finding a clue in Cab Calloway's hit song of the thirties:

Moochers ask you to share when they have nothing to share.... Men Moochers blame everything on women. Women Moochers blame everything on men. Old Moochers say it's the young's fault; young Moochers say the old messed up the world they have to live in. Moochers play sick a lot. Moochers think it's real hip not to be able to read and write. (p. 1 7)

Reed finds clues to make his psychic arrests all over the place. Why was Mammy so outspoken in *Gone With the Wind*, this precursor to the soap opera? There must be a meaning there, and Reed finds it in the hidden relationship between Mammy and the owner of the estate. Barracuda is not in charge of the plantation/multinational corporation but she has power within the household. She does not know her history and culture, she is not playing a game to win freedom. Note the looping relationship to the movie: Reed sees Mammy, reinterprets her in his novel of the civil war, and makes us see her differently when we see the movie again. Reed was conscious of the movie for the white woman acting as Minnie's nanny says "I have to shuffle about like Hattie McDaniel," who played Mammy in the movie. And *Vivian* Leigh was the Southern belle in the movie, while *Vivian* has this function in Reed's novel.

The ending of oppression must incorporate the restoration of manhood to the male. Fannie Mae, Mammy Barracuda, Ruby and Minnie do not recognize this, but Zozo Labrique, Joan, Aunt Judy, Bangalang, Esther and Erline work with the men to obtain freedom.

So you want black manhood? Here is a man! See him on tv. Read the papers! But Reed is already there. See, Reed says, Louisiana Red at work. Street Yellings: a selfish, greedy, vicious, mean thug, a murderer sprung from jail to be used against black people. Street had his consciousness raised in jail, and then spent several years having a good time in a radical North African country. There was a famous Street-type black leader of the sixties who killed a woman for the same reason as Street roughed up Ms. Better Weather a few years earlier: "Do you know who I am? Don't you recognize my picture? Haven't you seen my picture all over?" (p. 95) Real manhood does not need to "bully the blacks, to bully the women," as Vixen thinks in *The Terrible Twos*. It may work behind the scene because of the power of the bosses.

The flamboyant Leechfield thinks he can buy his freedom with money made from posing for pornographic photos and other schemes with Mel Leer. But Raven realizes what Robin already knows: that Swille's ruling philosophy is the love of property. Swille does not need money: he controls the source and supply of money. Since love of property may be too abstract an idea to grasp, the Western capitalist's love of property is concretized in *Yellow Back Radio Broke-Down:*

> Three horsemen--the Banker, the Marshal and the Doctor--decided to pay a little visit to Drag Gibson's ranch. They had to wait because Drag was at his usual hobby, embracing his property.
>
> A green mustang had been led out of its stall. It served as a symbol for his streams of fish, his herds,his fruit so large they weighed down the mountains, black gold and diamonds which lay in untapped fields, and his barnyard overflowing with robust and erotic fowl.
>
> Holding their stetsons in their hands the delegation looked on as Drag prepared to kiss his holdings. The ranch hands dragged the animal from his compartment towards the front of the Big Black House where Drag bent over and french kissed the animal between his teeth, licking the slaver from around the horse's gums....
>
> This was one lonely horse. The male horses avoided him because they thought him stuck up and the females because they thought that since green he was a queer horse. See, he had turned green from nightmares. After the ceremony the unfortunate critter was led back to his stall, a hoof covering his eye. (pp. 21-22)

The difficulty for a critter--excuse me, critic--is that Reed has a hundred things going on at the same time while the critic goes in a straight line, pursuing one lead. Reed warns us against this kind of linear reading: on page 183 of *Mumbo Jumbo* (New York: Avon, 1978, first published in 1973), one has to turn the book in circles to read what is being said. The love of property is imprinted on our cowboy-loving minds: the cowboy loves his horse more than anything else. This is a horse that has turned green from its nightmares. Nightmare--horse: the connection is that of the stand-up comic who, in this heterogeneous America, finds all words funny, like Groucho Marx's "Why a duck?" The horse is green, as in "greenhorn," from yellowback novels. The horse is led away, covering his eye with a hoof: this is out of movie cartoons. Lest we dismiss the whole thing as "unreal," we know from the very beginning that the story is stylized: it is a tall tale, a tradition as old as America: "Folks. This here is the story of the Loop Garoo Kid. A cowboy so bad he made a working posse of spells phone in sick. A bullwhacker so unfeeling he left the print of winged mice on hides of crawling women...." In its recurrent nightmare, the horse is about to be killed by Germans. The big American problem, says Reed, is that Drag, Swille and other American capitalists live in America but have their hearts in Europe. Arthur Swille is named after the Arthur of the mythic Camelot but he is actually no better than food for pigs, which is the fate of Drag, who is eaten by his hogs. The German chieftain hates green and wants his men to chop off the horse's head: the horse always wakes up just before they are about to do so. In the horse's nightmare, "The Germans burned down Yellow Back Radio in a matter of seconds--about the amount of time it takes for a station break" (p. 78).

Yellow Back Radio Broke-Down is a title that tells several stories. The "yellow back" is a wild-West novel. It refers to the young people who have taken over the town because they do not have "yellow fever": the fever for gold like many European adventurers and the paranoia against the Chinese and Japanese. They are not afraid: they are not "yellow." The word radio tells us that we are reading a radio script, that we are to hear the words that follow as we would a radio. The word radio also brings to mind Reed's quintessential poem, "I Am a Cowboy in the Boat of Ra." The poem connects up Ra, the Egyptian sun god, with "RAdio," suggesting that there is a world beyond one's perceptions from which, if one is tuned in, one can receive messages; conversely, one can tune out bad messages. Broke-Down suggests both that the whole system has broken down and that the radio has been "exploded" so that we can understand it. (The radio connection is extended to tv by the neighboring town being named Video Junction.) Yellow Back has yet another meaning, mentioned in *Mumbo Jumbo*. Beloit Battraville from Haiti, which is fighting an invasion by white American soldiers, says to the black Americans, "I know this is a strange request but if you will just 1 by 1 approach the Dictaphone, tell just how Hinckle Von Vampton propositioned you, the circumstances and the proposals he made to you, we will record this and then feed it to our loa. This particular loa has a Yellow Back to symbolize its electric circuitry. We are always careful not to come too close to it. It is a very mean high-powered loa" (pp. 172-173). The word electric is a clue that "to loop" is to join so as to complete circuitry. Thus although it would make no difference on radio, the difference in the spelling of Loup Garoo in the poem is significant. A loop is a sharp bend in a mountain road which almost comes back on itself like a snake. (So Loop fights Drag with a white python, Damballah.) In physics, a loop is an antinode, the node being the point, line or surface of a vibrating object free from vibration. To knock for a loop is to throw into confusion. A loop antenna is used in direction-finding equipment and in radio receivers. Once you get to the multiple meanings, you, the reader, begin to loop. Garoo, according to Toma Longinovic, a Yugoslav writer, means "essence." Reed's novel gets to the essence, doing more in 200-odd pages than a 600-page novel, and Loop practices HooDoo, which is the essence of VooDoo. Reed wants us to short-circuit the whole show, to break it down.

In *Mumbo Jumbo*, a multicultural group goes round reclaiming its stolen art from Western museums. Berbelang takes a great risk in including in the group a white man, Thor Wintergreen, because, the repentant son of a rich man, he wants to end exploitation. Berbelang sees the white man's history in terms of the myth of Faust, usually interpreted as the willingness to sell one's soul for power through knowledge, but which he interprets differently: he sees Faust as a charlatan, a thief magician who one day finds to his surprise that something seems to be working. Perhaps deep down, Berbelang speculates, Western man knows that he has been stealing the art and creativeness of non-Western man and knows he is a fake. If so, will the fear of exposure make him continue to keep non-Western people down? "I'm just 1 man," says Thor Wintergreen. "Not

Faust nor the Kaiser nor the Ku Klux Klan. I am an individual, not a whole tribe or nation." "That's what I'm counting on," replies Berbelang. "But if there is such a thing as a racial soul, a piece of Faust the mountebank residing in a corner of the White man's mind, then we are doomed" (p. 130). In the event, Thor is weakened by an appeal to his race by a descendent of the lower class of Europe, protecting white civilization and waiting for his chance to take over. "Son," says the tied Biff Musclewhite, "this is a nigger closing in on our mysteries and soon he will be asking our civilization to 'come quietly'" (p. 130). Thor tearfully unties Musclewhite, who proceeds to kill Berbelang, Charlotte and Thor. The media calls it suicide in two cases and justifiable homicide in the third.

Loop Garoo fights Drag with HooDoo, spells, thought control, psychic force. The problem gets serious enough for the Pope to appear in the West. He knows how to fight Loop since they are ancient enemies. The Pope wins a round but no fight: he really wants Loop to rejoin Christianity and bring his strengths in. He wants hegemony. It is an old fight: Christianity designated all the African gods as the devil. Yet the West needs the energy of the black world. This is the same fight in *Mumbo Jumbo, The Last Days of Louisiana Red* as in the James Bond movie of the same time, *Live and Let Die*. In the movie, the action alternates between New Orleans and a Caribbean island. There is a white woman possessed by a loa who loses her power after being seduced by Bond, then becoming a white virgin to be sacrificed by black Voodooists. At the end, there is a diversion: the conflict is presented as one between the forces of good (the West) and black drug dealers. But Baron Samedi survives at the end with his Geoffrey Holder laugh. We can see why Reed takes movies seriously but uses them in his own way. He has his own detectives, opposed to the Bonds, like Papa La Bas (really LegBa, the Yoruba god of communications) and Nance Saturday, out to make psychic arrests.

The anthropologist son of Swille sent to Congo to find energy sources for his father (missionaries now being too obvious) is thrown to the crocodiles. He comes back to haunt his father's mansion. Vivian, with whom Arthur commits necrophilious incest, haunts him to death. There are ghosts in the White House. President Dean Clift in *The Terrible Twos* is taken by Saint Nick to the presidents' hell, where he sees past presidents and would be presidents chained to their crimes against nature: Eisenhower (Lumumba), Truman (Hiroshima) and Rockefeller (Attica). Reed's fiction haunts. Is the American Indian really seeking revenge against the white man by introducing him to smoking tobacco so that he will die of lung cancer? Well...we know that smoking causes cancer.... Uncle Robin has been poisoning Swille with Coffeemate while Swille thought he was drinking slave-mothers' milk which would keep him young; will the F.D.A. announce that Coffeemate causes cancer? Just look at those nasty ingredients listed on page 174. Reed plants things in the mind and thereby changes the past. "No one says a novel has to be one thing," says Loop to Bo

Shmo. "It can be anything it wants to be, a vaudeville show, the six o'clock news, the mumblings of wild men saddled by demons" (p. 40). Reed presented a vaudeville show in 1970 of forthcoming attractions in his novels entitled, "D Hexorcism of Noxon D Awful," which introduces almost the whole cast of his characters in order to get a psychic fix and put a "Nix on Noxon."

When Professor Hobgood spoke at Madison, he produced a volume of Gomes's selected writings with the stamp of the Entebbe Goan Institute, of which I had been president three times and my father before me five times--and yet I had never noticed the volume. Suddenly all the layers of time were conjured up before me--by the introduction of a material medium of communication. This is what Reed does when he introduces the tv or radio into what we might think is the past. Lincoln is assassinated with the tv cameras on him, there is instant replay and an interview with his wife. What presidential assassination is this? Is the multinational involved? Reed would not call it anachronism. Reed's writing is like an electronic series. And through the constant tv, radio, video and electronic references, Reed is asking his people to acquire literacy as well as to leap to video and electronics or else they will be left far behind, as when they were denied literacy. Swille spells it out to Lincoln: "We gave him *Literacy, the most powerful thing in the pre-technological prepost-rational age*--and what does he do with it? Use it like that old voodoo" (pp. 35-36, my italics).

Raven Quickskill acquires reading and this makes him flee the condition of slavery outward. Robin, who is put in charge because of the flight of Raven, also acquires reading and uses it to move inward. The two need each other's skills: Robin gets Raven to write his story, which is also Raven's story. Raven comes from a Southwest American Indian curing story, he is a healer through words, as is the coyote: Reed learned about these stories from Leslie Marmon Silko of the Laguna Pueblo (see Reed's *Shrovetide in Old New Orleans*, New York: Doubleday, 1978; see also Silko's *Ceremony,* a novel, New York: Viking, 1977).

The original spelling of Loop Garoo's name in "I Am a Cowboy in the Boat of Ra" is Loup Garou, a wolf, actually a werewolf. The man who changes into a wolf does so to try to rescue the earth from the mess men of power have made in their blindness, greed and alienation from nature. The wolf also seeks to rescue those men of power who would be rescued. Thus in *The Terrible Twos,* Black Peter, Santa Claus and Saint Nick save Zumwalt and the President. Even the President who was elected in 1980, setting off a scrooge-like meanness in the spirit and a cold wave in nature, is not doomed because he did once take part in a movie in which he represented the plight of the oppressed. But some cannot be saved. The Christmas tree that an old Indian chief had tried to protect from the white man's bulldozers on the grounds that it was alive gets its revenge: when the President's wife turns the Christmas treelights on, she is electrocuted and burned to a crisp. The switch let the current pass. The Yellow Back loa is mean.

There is sympathy in Nature, LOUP GAROU, but it needs help from Art, LOOP GAROO, to close in on the western stage. Reed.

Toronto South Asian Review 4.3 (Spring 1986): 1-10.

1980s

THE TERRIBLE TWOS (1982)

The Terrible Twos

Peter Nazareth/Review

The Terrible Twos, Ishmael Reed's sixth novel, begins in the 1980s, just as Reagan is coming into office. Dislocation in the political order is reflected in the natural world: "By Christmas, 1980, the earth had had enough and was beginning to send out hints. Volcanoes roared. Fish drank nitrates and sulphur." This is the beginning of a mean, Scrooge-like mentality sweeping the nation, as Santa Claus says when he makes a speech in Times Square ten years later, calling on the people to boycott the corporations that have messed up the environment: "Two years old, that's what we are emotionally--America, always wanting someone to hand us some ice cream, always complaining, Santa didn't bring me this and why didn't Santa bring me that."

Reed used to play the trombone, and his writing is like jazz: he starts with a theme and lets it go where it will, playing infinite variations on that theme. Incorporating Dickens's *Christmas Carol*, but also taking in myriad other elements that have entered the consciousness, Reed situates the body of his story in 1990 and tries to set things right through the fictional re-creation of one of the country's central myths, that of Santa Claus. One of the corporations has bought the exclusive rights to Santa Claus and is building a Santa rival to Disneyland in the North. The poor have, therefore, lost their last, mythic helper.

But strange things begin to happen. As the criminologist Nance Saturday discovers, there is a version of Santa Claus in which he has a black helper, Black Peter, with some ambiguity as to who controls whom. The Nicolaites are a cult led by Boy Bishop, a rebel priest disowned by the Catholic Church who has taken a black ventriloquist off the streets of Harlem. The ventriloquist becomes Black Peter to a Santa "doll," really the body of a man who had been sent to kill them but whom they have killed instead. The Santa "doll" replaces the soap-opera actor hired to play Santa, kidnapped by the cult. (It is this Santa "doll" who delivers the radical speech to the people on Times Square: Black Peter has found a way, using the tears of a St. Nick statue, to keep "reviving" the dead man.) Later a split develops in the Nicolaites as "Black Peter" begins to convert Santa Claus into a more recent legend, Ras Tafari, since legend and history are quite different. The split ends in a shoot-out.

Unknown to most of these figures, but called up psychically by Black Peter, the "real" Saint Nick is going round saving key people in power from their inner alienation so that they do not have to wait until they are dead to become legends: they can take legendary, humanizing actions while alive. One of these is the President, Dean Clift, a former male model. As Clift is grieving over his wife's coffin (she is electrocuted while lighting the White House Christmas Tree), Saint Nick takes him to Presidents' Hell, where past presidents are chained to their crimes for not having the courage to act in terms of humanity: Eisenhower (Lumumba), Truman (the H-bomb) and would-be president Nelson Rockefeller (Attica). Clift comes back to life and, in a speech on television, blows the lid off the nastiness that has come over the land. He also reveals Operation Two Birds: a plan to drop a bomb on New York, blame Nigeria and then bomb Nigeria, all to kill off "the surplus people." (Yes, in 1990 Nigeria has the bomb, America is an ally of the Soviet Union and Hitler is posthumously declared an Amerian hero.) Then Clift plants a tree, calling the baby spruce a symbol of a new America, an America purged of its settler past: "You could tell a civilized nation by the way it treated the poor, the sick, the old, and the jailed, and...by every yardstick the country had failed in these areas." Clift is declared insane and thrown into an asylum by the Colorado gang's representatives.

The Terrible Twos does functionally what Saint Nick is attempting to do: combat the cold wave of the spirit, which is rooted in historical and economic problems. The work proves that Reed is one of the most inventive American novelists.

World Literature Today 57.3 (Summer 1983): 458.

Call Him Ishmael--He's Still a Good Reed

Henry Louis Gates, Jr./Review

By simply naming the deeper structures, myths and presuppositions of contemporary American society, Ishmael Reed's *The Terrible Twos* tells a tale that is humorous, riveting and moralistic in much the same curious way that ancient parables and allegories are written.

If I had to compare Ishmael Reed to another artist of another genre, I would choose Richard Pryor. Like any great orator or preacher, Pryor names things for us. He fingers, out loud, those private emotions--as well as those economic and racial relations by which society seeks to regulate our lives--the invisible network by which we are bound, which few even admit exists. Like Richard Pryor, Ishmael Reed has a prophetic gift of vision, that special insight Stevie Wonder calls "innervision." And, like Pryor and Wonder, Reed tells us not only who we are and where we are as a people, but why.

The Terrible Twos is Ishmael Reed's first attempt at a satirical analysis of the nature and function of the current American political and economic system. It is also the first novel in an apocalyptic trilogy. And before one thinks that *The Terrible Twos* reads like *Das Kapital,* let me quickly add that Ishmael Reed always makes his readers laugh even while he renders judgment.

To date, Ishmael Reed has written five novels, four books of poetry, two books of essays and two plays. Not bad for a black writer under 40. To top it off, he is the only writer ever to be nominated in the same year for a National Book Award in poetry and prose. His book of poems *Conjure* was also nominated for a Pulitzer Prize in 1973. Reed's stature as one of our most inventive, daring and prolific writers lends credence and force to the strength of his satires. He may well emerge as one of the black community's most salient, if subtle, voices in our struggle to criticize the pernicious forms of racism-cum-capitalism.

The book's title, *The Terrible Twos,* stands for the voodoo number for devilment and is the common American phrase used to describe the psychological state of two-year-old toddlers. Reed uses this as a metaphor for a two-century-old America and describes this state through the words of a mock Santa Claus character:

> Two years old, that's what we are, emotionally--America always wanting someone to hand us some ice cream, always complaining....Nobody can reason with us. Nobody can tell us anything.

He creates a fictional USA sometime between 1980 and 1990, when a small nouveau riche California elite (inextricably tied to oil money) runs the White House. There's President Dean Clift, a former model; Nance Saturday, a black and sexy sleuth on the trail of the real Santa Claus; and Jamaica Queens, a sensuous reporter who penetrates the inner sanctum of the Nicolaites (they who would restore St. Nicholas to the Church) only to discover Black Peter, everyone's favorite hoodooman and wizard.

> Ebenezer Scrooge towers above the Washington skyline, rubbing his hands and greedily peering over his spectacles. He shows up at the inaugural in charcoal-gray stroller, dove-gray vest, gray-striped trousers, a pleated-front skirt, and four-in-hand tie. Hail First Actor, and Ms. Actorperson on your throne-like blue winged chairs, and your opulent Republican dinners, and your tailors, and your fashion designers flown in from Paris and Beverly Hills and New York, and your full-page color coverage in *Women's Wear Daily.*
>
> How did *The Buffalo Evening News* put it? "The Wild West Is Back in the Saddle Again." In the west, he campaigned as a cowboy; in the south, the crowd wept and rebel-yelled at the sight of First Actor in a Confederate uniform. Miss Nancy's beautiful white people, in the Red Room, darkies in tails passing out sour mash left and right. Thank you, Miss Nancy, said Charlie Pride.

If all this sounds perilously familiar, it is supposed to. Fusing together ingredients as in a good chicken gumbo--Macy's Thanksgiving Day parade, Saint Nicholas, Rastafarian-Vodoun symbolism, the novels of social realism, Dickens' *A Christmas Carol* and Dante's *Inferno*--Ishmael Reed has written a novel about tiny groups of people who seek to turn a profit at the expense of blacks, Indians and the vast poor. What would be more appropriate reading for a corporate executive who still manages to laugh at the ironies of the system?

Black Enterprise April (1983): 16.

Kinships and Aginships

Stanley Crouch/Review

Ishmael Reed's obsessions center around the definitions of quality in American art and the literary politics that go into establishing one work as more valuable than another. At war with what he considers ethnic and academic provincialism, for the last ten years he has been using the term "multi-cultural art" to describe sources of artistic inspiration that lie outside European models. The only problem is that what Reed is talking about here is little more than an outdated spinoff of modernism. In fact, his position that the use of techniques and forms from so-called Third World esthetics is somehow revolutionary comes long after Picasso turned the art world on its ear by ringing his own changes on the inspiration provided by African masks; and in his experimentation with popular genres, Reed follows modern masters as diverse as James Joyce and Alain Robbe-Grillet.

But what is interesting about Reed is the tireless campaign he has waged against convention and orthodoxy within the worlds of black art and radical politics. He has long been opposed to the tar-brush racism of black nationalists and the pretentious communalism of ethnic nationalists; he has also been throwing Negro napalm--a mixture of syrup, potash and lye--at the barricades of simplistic feminism. In short, for all the problems and confusions of Reed's ideas, he has refused to submit either to ideologues or to the opportunists of the marketplace.

At the same time, however, Reed is prone to jump on other sorts of bandwagons. If he becomes angry at one writer, he will suddenly champion another he has previously denounced, especially if the latter assists him in the assault on the first. The literary magazines he helped bring into existence--*Yardbird*, *Y'Bird* and *Quilt*--have all reflected Reed's kinships and aginships. But they have also brought out a body of work that begins to suggest more the potential than the realization of America's immense cultural diversity--work by Negroes, Caucasians, Asians, Hispanics and Native Americans.

When Reed left New York for the West Coast in 1968, he initially promoted writers who were black but who were opposed to the agitprop howlings of LeRoi Jones and his imitators. After a few years, Frank Chin informed Reed that the entire Asian-American experience had been ignored by both the small and large press establishments. As a result, Reed began to seek out work by a wide range of ethnic writers. Hence the idea of multi-cultural art and the formation of a literary army which Reed hopes will grow until academic and publishing forces have to acknowledge its place in American literature, its definitions of the American experience.

To that end, Reed has developed a number of publishing ventures for other people's work; he has published novels, plays, poetry and fantasies, and seems to reserve the most uneven stuff for his periodicals and anthologies. He has championed this literature on speaking tours and on panels about little magazines. He recently said of it:

> What is new today is the use of avant-garde techniques for the expression of the
> ethnic point of view, taking what Europeans and white Americans have put out
> there and changing it the same ways jazz musicians changed Tin Pan Alley
> tunes to fit their experience and the world they know about. So when people
> accuse ethnic writers of imitating white writers, they usually mean the
> techniques, not what's being said.

This observation is significant in its recognition that innovations can be redefined rather than ignored--a healthy corrective for what ailed almost all militant black writing in the nationalist days: its anti-white rhetoric was asinine; its art, often out of ignorance, was a poor imitation of the Euro-American avant-garde.

Though none of the writers Reed has published have become successful through his efforts, his own penchant for satire and battle has earned him some devoted followers, the majority of whom swear most loudly by *Mumbo Jumbo*, his third novel and his most elaborate development of the themes that dominate the bulk of his fiction. His use of totemic characters in *Flight to Canada* led to the Tlingit Indians inviting him to Alaska, while his historical allusions inspired Leo Litwak to bring Reed to Los Angeles in 1981 to respond to papers on Frederick Douglass and Lester Young at a meeting of the American Historical Society. There, as in his recent book, *The Terrible Twos*, Reed opposes glamorizing street thugs and warns against demagogues, Marxists and the threat of "cultural imperialism." He describes monotheism as a metaphor for the kind of unilateral thought that dismisses Third World values and creativity, and he believes that combining the popular and the ancient is the key to contemporary vitality. In the wake of redneck racism he thinks he has discovered what Joseph Skvorecky once called "the censors of an entirely different dictatorship"; he identifies them as certain obnoxious black women and powerful white men who act in collusion. Reed lampoons this conspiracy--a relationship he believes has a history that stretches from the plantation to the hallowed halls of white-collar crime. He also sees it manifested in the world of publishing and criticism. "They accuse me of misogyny," he says, "but no one addresses the images and the monstrous actions of black males in the novels of Toni Morrison, Alice Walker and Toni Cade Bambara. I guess these white males and gullible feminists are too in love with their literary mammies to do that."

The trouble with *The Terrible Twos* is that he's said it all before and said it much better. This time out, he's picked another genre to tear apart with his imposition of varied forms and combinations of perspective. Just as he used Antigone in *The Last Days of Louisiana Red* to create a brilliant satire that collapsed under the strain of its near-misogyny, and just as he used the western for *Yellow Back Radio Broke-Down*, the detective story for *Mumbo Jumbo*, the slave narrative and *Uncle Tom's Cabin* for *Flight to Canada*, Reed weaves Rastafarianism and a reverse of the Todd Clifton dummy sequence from *Invisible Man* together with Dickens's *A Christmas Carol* in *The Terrible Twos*. Again we get the self-obsessed harpies, the mission Indians, the black hero who takes over the white form (unlike Todd Clifton, Black Peter is not controlled by whites who speak through his mouth--he speaks through theirs), the dumb black street hustlers who get into a game too complicated for them to understand, the corruption of Christianity, the secret society of powerful white bosses, the argument that preliterate custom and belief are just as good as modern civilization (if not better) and the beleaguered black hero who has woman problems (Reed touches on the sexual provincialism of black women, which didn't begin to change until the late 1960s when they had to compete with liberated and liberal white women for the affections of black men, but he doesn't do anything with that proverbial hot potato).

I'm not saying that Reed should abandon his concerns, but I am saying that for all the literary appropriations of *The Terrible Twos*, it hasn't the level of invention that made his best work succeed. There is too much predictability, too much dependence on revelation through conversation and interior monologue. Most of the mysteries must be explained by the characters, and what we do discover through their narratives isn't very interesting. When the President, for instance, is taken into hell, what he sees are the ghosts of presidents and vice presidents past, and there follow heavy-handed scenes of contrition and retribution--Truman grieving over the atom bomb, Rockefeller chained to the corpses of the Attica victims, etc. When Santa Claus and the President get their chance to speak out against the commercialization of Christmas on the one hand and the manipulation of the country by industrialists on the other, the cliches resound. But since Reed considers this novel a surrealist variation on the social realist novel of economic complaint, maybe he thought he should pop the corn rather than serve it in hard kernels. There are some funny passages along the way, however. There is even an attempt to infuse his surreal puppet show with realistic relationships, especially on an erotic level, and this brings what freshness there is to the novel. It also suggests that Reed may soon examine the range of sexual and social attractions that a multiracial society makes so possible, especially since the passage from Europe to the Third World can sometimes take place within only a few city blocks. If that is what he intends for his sequels--*The Terrible Threes* and *The Terrible Fours*--then the world he has developed, one quilted with endless allusions, mythology, improvisation and concentric circles of time and culture, could give birth to the potential so basic to the social contract and to the diversity of this country--Ishmael Reed's *All-American Novel*. *The Terrible Twos*, unfortunately, is mostly a shadow of his former work, and a shadow that tells us little we don't already know.

Reprinted with permission from *The Nation* magazine. (May 22, 1982): 617-619. © The Nation Company, L.P.

Ishmael Reed's Multicultural Aesthetic

Jerome Klinkowitz/Article

Those dour guardians of official culture Ishmael Reed calls "high-ass Anglo critics" have always had trouble with his work, especially when they try to segregate facts from fiction. Even his partisans have rough going from time to time as they try to pigeonhole this writer who's built much of his career on the flamboyant eclipsing of stereotypes. Take a friend who's been wondering if he should zap poor Ishmael for being a "grant-hoarder" (the term is Reed's and he isn't one). This investigator's crowning argument is that among the contributors' notes to *Yardbird Lives*! (coedited with Al Young for Grove Press in 1978), Reed simply lists himself as "a businessman," as if admitting he's in league with the folks who run America's acronymic corporations and grants establishments.

"Hey wait," I beg my friend and cite Reed's disclaimer from the first page of his funniest novel *The Last Days of Louisiana Red* (Random House, 1974), a note that warns that "in order to avoid detection by powerful enemies and industrial spies, nineteenth century HooDoo people referred to their work as 'The Business.'" The insipid grant-getting hustle my friend rightly condemns is hardly The Business our novelist describes, for if you read into *Louisiana Red* you'll find the HooDoo's Businessmen have their own name for such shenanigans every decent person would deplore: Moochism, as in Cab Calloway's "Minnie the Moocher." But for the victims of a monocultural education, artists like Calloway don't exist.

Businessman, HooDoo, Mama's Boy, High-Ass Anglo Critic--these are just a few of the words Ishmael Reed uses in both his essays and his fiction to articulate that odd confusion of history and imagination which so uniquely characterizes our times. Seeing how well his novel, *The Terrible Twos* (New York: St. Martin's, 1982), and essays collected in *God Made Alaska for the Indians* (New York:

Garland, 1982) work together will help straighten out my grant-busting colleague, but it's worth remembering that Reed has been doing this for over two decades while the rest of us have been slowly catching up. Take the description of "Dualism" from his *Catechism of d Neoamerican Church* (London: Paul Berman, 1970), a carefully articulated program of aesthetics masquerading as a book of poems:

> i am outside of
> history. i wish
> i had some peanuts, it
> looks hungry there in
> its cage
>
> i am inside of
> history. its
> hungrier that i
> thot

In *The Terrible Twos*, Reed is supposedly outside of history; he sets his story in 1990, when the President is a former male model, the economy is worse than ever, and all that's left to trickle down is Christmas, which a bunch of power-hungry goons who run the country successfully buy and sell. *God Made Alaska for the Indians*, on the other hand, assembles eight essays and an afterword of environmentalists, Native Americans, literary politicians, prize fight promotions, male sexuality, race relations, the troubles in Ulster as seen by Irish-Americans, and the problems of multicultural artists--all of which deal directly with the demoralizing state of events since 1976 when Reed's last collection was assembled. But with an author like Reed in control, there's no real difference in subject or in method, and the result is a penetrating vision which by now surely ranks as the new decade's most insightful literary critique of American morals and manners.

It's at this intersection that the battle over Reed's work is fought: can the identity of history and imagination, just because our age apparently confuses them, be a valid method for the critique itself? For years, Reed has been complaining about the intellectual colonialism which judges American literature by nineteenth century English and European standard--"all those books in rusty trunks," as he puts it, which, by contrast make his own writing seem "muddled, crazy, and incoherent." In his attack on these old-order standards, Reed does disrupt some emotionally held ideals, but his genius is to base his method solidly within the multicultural American lower-middle class, which he claims is more ready to allow "the techniques and forms painters, dancers, film makers, and musicians in the west have taken for granted for at least fifty years, and the artists of other cultures for thousands of years." Hence, you'll find Reed talking about (and writing like) Cab Calloway, who since 1928 has never lacked a low-brow audience, black or white, rather than the intellectually uptown musicians more conveniently taken as models. You can also find him listening to Native Americans describing their two-century battle against Russian and American white men, where he quickly notes their method:

> On the bombing of Angoon, another Tradition Bearer, George Davis, told me that in 1880 an American ship tried out a cannon-like gun and hit a whale. The whale leaped out of the ocean and "screamed like a wolf," he said as he told me a story part fiction, part autobiographical, part nonfiction (the new fiction is at least 20,000 years old). (p. 32)

Syncretism is one of the few formally abstract words in Reed's critical vocabulary, and he feels it is the key to a true national American literature reflecting the uniquely multicultural art which has evolved here. "Anglo" culture, as he calls it, then becomes one element among many, and the only loss is that of a dominant intellectual academy sworn to upholding the beliefs of a long-dead order. Gabriel Garcia Marquez says much the same about his own multicultural, coastal Caribbean background where, as opposed to the rigidly colonial Spanish culture of the highlands capital in Bogota, history and fiction were allowed to blend, making truth "one more illusion, just one more version of many possible vantage points" where "people change their reality by changing their perception of it." Within this aesthetic, fact and imagination become one. And as our present age has been shaped by this union, so Reed creates a common method for writing novels and essays by using the best of it while warning of its dangers when abused.

Both *The Terrible Twos* and *God Made Alaska for the Indians* are filled with Reed's customary mischief and fun. In the novel, President Dean Clift does things like help sell merchandising rights to Santa Claus and declaring Adolf Hitler a posthumous American citizen, but balks when his advisors plan nuclear war with Nigeria as a way of wiping out the economically "surplus people" on both sides. Meanwhile, back in the quotidian reality of *God Made Alaska*, Reed's research uncovers a "late nineteenth century American movement called Teutonism" in which a serious politician "proposed a way of ridding the land of both the unwelcome black and Irish: 'Let an Irishman kill a Negro and get hanged for it'" (p. 81). Both books are hilarious in their accounts of people being swallowed by their own cultural signs, but things get serious when Reed shows how dangerous a dead semiotics--a code of social behavior deriving from discredited cultural authority, such as monocultural white male dominance--can be. Mama's boys, Daddy's girls: both the real and fictional worlds suffer from them, and the biases of hot-sell TV and high-powered establishment educations only make things worse. There's a "scolding missionary tone" (p. 9) in the Sierra Club's attack on the Shcc Atika tribcs, and also a peculiar rhetoric to the presidential advice offered by *The Terrible Twos'* wealthy Colorado brewer who boasts that "my

family has been making beer since they came through the Cumberland Pass with
Dan Boone. They shot injuns alongside Mordecai Lincoln and joined old Andy
Jackson in his war against the Seminoles" (p. 102). Why should this self-styled
King of Beer worry about the Native Americans his commercial development,
Christmas Land, will drive from their Alaska homes? "Injuns come and injuns
go," he blathers, "but Regal beer is here for eternity" (p. 102). Is monocultural
America really this bad? Every paragraph in *God Made Alaska* makes it seem
worse, because Reed shows how it happens:

> Native-American historians accuse Arthur Schlesinger, Jr., of omitting any
> reference to the Trail of Tears of the Cherokee Nation in his Pulitzer Prize
> winning *The Age of Jackson*. Schlesinger, and others, prepare for leadership
> people like Reverend Billy Moyers, a former advisor to a President, who only
> recently found out that slavery wasn't merely the practice of some ignorant white
> trash overseers, but was endorsed by the judicial and legislative bodies of the
> time. His guest, A. Leon Higgenbottom, author of *In the Matter of Color*, was
> polite. He could have mentioned how American churches sold slaves to raise
> money to support their missionaries abroad, and how the American Government
> Sold Slaves to Raise Revenue!! (pp. 6-7)

In our time, history and imagination are confused because there's been a king-
hell conflict going on between two rival sign-making authorities, one authentic
(the multicultural and nativistically American lower-middle class, which has
invented jazz, blues, rock and roll, country swing, comic books, detective novels,
fast food, and other items native to our stores) and the other a carry-over from a
long-dead power (the European colonization, with its monocultural rhetoric and
monological dictates). What can Reed do in these circumstances: write a counter-
history of the Western world, as Khachig Tololyan says Thomas Pynchon has
done, exposing "the patriarchal and technological white West" while rallying for
the "imposed-upon" who've been "inscribed with other peoples' meanings"?
That's the negative side of his program, but our man Reed takes such positive joy
in the real American culture that now and then wins a fight that Pynchon's
solution seems fully unsatisfactory--there's too much joy to miss, both in exposing
the phonies and giving credit for the good stuff.

God Made Alaska for the Indians is a commentary about being a necessary
outsider to the monocultural elite. "Ishmael Reed?" some people will ask; "If he's
not on the inside of our academic and publishing establishments, who is?" As if to
answer, these eight essays range across contemporary America to indicate how
exclusionary and one-sided its standards of cultural authority still are. And not just
for black Americans. Reed's adversary vision is important because there is an
entire national culture being systematically outlawed by an educational and media
organization pledged to a set of ideals blind to what "nativistic" (meaning Afro-
American, Hispanic-American, Oriental-American, even lower-middle class
Polish American) literature is. "Here so long/We got spirit," Reed quotes the

Alaskan-American poet Andy Hope, who like Reed has to keep laying down the challenge for attention: "Look me in the eye when I talk and you'll remember what I say" (p. 34).

Despite the great social turnabout in the 1960s which helped get Reed and other necessary outsiders rolling, official American culture is still very much a closed code. Roland Barthes would call it petit-bourgeous thinking, a dullish inability to image anything other than itself, but the crying shame is that here in America it is not even our petit-bourgeous standard which is pulling down the blinds and locking the windows: it's a monocultural, monological, male-dominant and classical white European set of values which even as it died abroad took on an artificially new colonial life here. And despite all the radical social changes and curricular revisions, that attitude remains so strong as to be incessantly stifling, making contemporary studies a nuisance-ridden affair of having to continually struggle out from beneath the wet blanket of old, implacable cultural attitudes.

That's why Reed, whose "continuing autobiography of the mind" this collection is (following straight upon *Shrovetide in Old New Orleans* which was prefaced from the Alaska village where the new book's first essay begins), feels obliged to range from Sierra Club-Native American battles through the Ali-Spinks heavyweight championship bout and various linguistic, sexual, racial, and revolutionary topics to the book's impressive essay on the crazy spectacle of some displaced New York poets pumping Buddhist revival in woolly Colorado's Boulderado Hotel. Something, folks, is very wrong out there, and Ishmael Reed is the practising artist and cultural theorist who can tell us why.

My interest in Reed's work is personal, a concern absolutely central to his arguments in *God Made Alaska*. Anyone working on innovative American literature will inevitably confront the same problems he outlines here, and Reed's essays are helpful because they explain so much of what has been going haywire in our culture--for black writers, non-elitists, Native Americans, and whoever else can't fit the establishment's Aristotelian and colonial standards. And we are not talking about the trials of some foggy avant-garde. Closed attitudes precede naturalistically American work like bad news moving in advance of a known troublemaker. In 1981, the editor of an ongoing literary encyclopedia wrote me in desperation for a piece on Walter Abish, the novelist who'd caught academia off guard by winning the first PEN/Faulkner prize--it turned out his editor couldn't find a single scholar able "to comprehend Abish's work, let alone write about it." In 1982, the publisher of a supposedly on-the-ball San Francisco quarterly returned my essay on Richard Kostelanetz unread, saying he found it "impossible to deal with a writer whose values and methods" he couldn't understand. The pity is that this stuff has been going on, it seems, forever: way back in 1976, Reed's *Yardbird 5* reported my earlier report of walking into what I'd hoped would be a wide-ranging and open-minded literary gathering at San Francisco State University and being accosted by an old-style Americanist who answered my friendly "Hello, I am Jerry Klinkowitz" with a rather hysterical and fully unprovoked diatribe: "Ronald Sukenick! Ronald Sukenick! I can't read him! I just can't read him!" Close behind was the department's top graduate student, pledged to a thesis on the academically acceptable Thomas Pynchon (a fine Aristotelian decked out in classically European values), chattering "Monkey at typewriters! Monkeys at typewriters!" In this climate of self-professed illiteracy which characterizes so many English departments and publishing houses, there is not much one can answer back. Too often my own response has been to cash in my hand and call for pizza and beer. Reed, however, sticks around and fights, armed with a finely articulated brief against this claustrophobic set of cultural rules.

Reed's stature is, in part, measured by the greatness of his enemies, and in *God Made Alaska* he finds himself aligned against the entire Anglo establishment which disparages anything outside colonial culture, from the blues to cowboy novels (just two of the notable art forms unique to our shores). There is a very definite anti-American mindset to these constrictive attitudes; in one of the very first critical histories of our country's writing, *The Spirit of American Literature* (New York: Dodd, Mead and Co., 1911), Bostonian John Macy postulated that "in literature nationality is determined by literature, rather than by blood or geography" as a way of justifying his claim that "American literature is a branch of English literature, as truly as are English books written in Scotland and South Africa" (p. 3). Nobody would be so outrageous as to go on record with that specific claim today, but the spirit behind it sets the rules by which culture gets funded, published, and taught. Lower-middle-class Americans of all ethnic backgrounds are taxed to support a European-culture-oriented tradition of grand opera, symphony, and ballet they will never see or hear, even if they wanted to. When the environmentalists of the Sierra Club present their claims to Native American land, Reed notes that "they often used arguments which sounded similar to the Romanovs' appeal to divine rights. The rest of us lacked 'qualifications.' We didn't meet their "standards" (p. 4). The methods of "colonizing" them at the century's turn, or locking up their assets for "the national interest" now, Reed shows, are all based on the same monocultural arrogance that proclaims white male standards as the only ones with value.

By these same terms, a black heavyweight champion of the world becomes the unimaginable Other, the role Ken Norton was obliged to play in *Mandingo* and *Drum*: "The women want to ball him, and the men want to battle with him; some people want to do both" (p. 39). So much for official cultural standards, which an innovative champ like Muhamad Ali can subvert by going directly to the people whom the establishment has counted out more subtly but no less effectively: "He is more effective because he speaks to Americans in American images, images mostly derived from comic books, television, and folklore. To be a good black poet in the 60s meant capturing the rhythms of Ali and Malcolm X on the page... His prose is derived from the trickster world of Bugs Bunny and Mad Comics" (pp. 43-44). Reed identifies a further split between official and authentic culture in his challenge to Dick Cavett and John Simon on the issue of "Black English."

How can it be "eradicated," Cavett asks and Simon implores. "You'd have to eradicate the Black people" is the obvious linguistic answer, which Reed finds a "chilling thought, considering that there are historical precedents for people being exterminated because they didn't speak or write the way others thought they should" (p. 67). But more practically, Reed adds, there is a crucial difference between the received language of official culture (which is by definition drained of personal imagination for the purposes of "doing business" smoothly) and the way people within the culture actually think, speak and feel:

> You not gone make me give up Black English. When you ask me to give up my Black English you askin me to give up my soul. But for everyday reasons of commerce, transportation hassleless mobility in everyday life, I will talk to 411 in a language both the operator and I can understand. I will answer the highway patrolman who stops me, for having a broken rear light, in words he and I both know. The highway patrolman, who grew up on Elvis Presley, might speak Black English at home, because Black English has influenced not only blacks but whites too. (p. 68)

Right there is the issue: for mundane points of information, free of characterizing value, official language will have to do. But in terms of artistic expression and communication, where culture's lasting business takes place, there is another, nativistically American language which gets systematically discounted by the "King's English" crowd which insists that the discourse of novels, plays, and poems be conducted in the same tongue, now so stiffly formal because it represents a culture which died one hundred years ago on a land mass three thousand miles away. And because the real American culture is kept at home behind closed doors, the marketplace language is itself never transformed, and so through no free choice of their own white cops find themselves speaking to black citizens in an outmoded language formed by structures of colonial authority bearing small relation to the lives they personally lead. Richard Ohmann's *English in America* made this point nearly ten years ago, but Freshman Writing standards remain those of nineteenth century England because that's from where our official culture derives its values.

Stale images, such as the black-male-as-rapist, come from stale thinking, and Reed shows how there is easy money made from traffic in such worthless symbols. Meanwhile the real issue is deliberately ignored, for "the most lethal macho is white macho, since white men have extravagant means with which to express it. If the nuclear button is pushed, it will, no doubt, be pushed by a finger belonging to a white male. While black macho might be annoying, white male macho could be the death of us" (p. 73). But the official culture "reads white" having "more regard for whites in Europe than for non-whites in America" (p. 77) simply because the old standards of judgment point in that direction. When a culture is so isolated from its everyday personal language and values, it atrophies. Hence, Reed's well-meaning desire to "stir up some mischief" which at least

shakes open a few minds and closes a few mouths: "Ethnic purity. White
superiority. The Nazis were doing in the streets what some white Liberal Arts
departments preach elsewhere." Or even more tellingly, he suggests to an MLA
meeting "that certain characteristics of blacks in novels written by white liberal
intellectuals reminded me of the Nazi caricatures of their victims. A commotion
ensued. I thought I was going to have to slug my way out of the hall" (p. 79). But
as he learns from the Irish Republicans speaking at their own cultural center, "the
victors will not be those who inflict most, but those who endure the most" (p. 99).

At times in the past Reed's stridency has cost him part of his audience, but the
gentler fun of *Twos* and *Alaska* is calculated to open some minds even as it closes
some mouths. The egoless self-apparency of his method, based as it is on the
common language and sentiment of most Americans far away from intellectual
centers, virtually guarantees this; for when Reed simply "sits back and takes it all
in" as the monocultural aristocrats hang themselves with their own devoluted
chatter, how can you help but take his side? The emotional two-year-olds of his
novel are their own worst enemies; there's no need for the author to turn the knife
in them as he's been tempted to do in earlier novels. In Alaska's most conclusive
essay, "American Poetry: Is There a Center?", watch Reed stare in disbelief as
Michael Brownstein pumps him with the information that "the hottest scene in the
country was taking place in Boulder," which thanks to the Naropa Institute's
presence in the Colorado hills has made a place an "energy center." A few months
before, the smart boys had been telling Reed that all action was just north of San
Francisco Bay, but his checking reveals that their idea of the source, Bolinas, "was
a mere watering hole for international artists, intellectuals, and people who grew
up in households with five maids" (p. 105). So now he sits listening to this
academic enthusiast "who sometimes looks like a guy who wore a prep-school cap
and shorts at one time" claiming that Boulder's where it's at. Whose side are you
on through all this? Where do you think "the center of American poetry" might
really be? At the essay's end, far from the circus in Colorado (described with
merciless accuracy), Reed finds his answer: "In every poet's heart."

Monology works in curious ways, and Reed can speak his mind without
slandering Brownstein, who he quickly admits is a good and thoughtful poet. It's
the system, Reed advises, which makes this transplanted Tennessean sound so
bad: "People in centers see themselves as the center because they can't see the
whole scene with an eye for detail" (p. 120). Reed's idea, which is a lot closer to
the American reality which lies beyond the suffocating pale of Manhattan,
Boulder, and Bolinas, is one of multicultural syncretism--of a truly national
literature which can absorb radically different contributions and come stronger for
it. But the old system of "pledged allegiance to Anglo culture" still dominates the
news media, publishing, and education. Idi Amin is everyone's favorite black
ruler; alternatives to white culture in America are discussed by CBS on the level of
"tacos and watermelons," plus "there was that sad issue of *Partisan Review* (44,
no.2 [1977]) called 'New York and National Culture: an Exchange,' in which a

panel of New York intellectuals claimed to represent National Culture when in reality they sounded like village people whispering about haunted houses" (p. 114). Like the Romanovs, those who've assumed they hold divine rights do not change roles easily.

What Reed calls the Anglo establishment thrives on dead signs, cliches of a once-living culture which now misdirect and deplete our country's imaginative energy. Therefore, his first job is to expose this state of affairs and then to bring our language and its signs back to life as self-apparent realities. *God Made Alaska for the Indians* does this for the history we've shared since 1976, and *The Terrible Twos* takes further license to push the argument through fiction. All systems are fictions, our times have taught us, and fictions in turn create functional realities. Reed likes to demonstrate how the folks in control manipulate us--that's the wickedly funny part. Ishmael Reed triumphs as an American writer when he sizes the oppressor's tools and forges his own reality: a perception of disparate forces brought together in a single complex vision which is clearly superior, based as it is on a broader range of seeing and expressing. Consider what the media and the police made of Patty Hearst's kidnapping by the Symbionese Liberation Army, and how Reed's method pulls it all together:

> The security problem. From the early revolts there had always been the security problem. Even Gullah Jack couldn't protect Vesey from it. The American Secret Police has caused conflict between the Black Panthers and the United States; bugged Huey Newton's apartment; but the SLA brought out the Keystone in them. They flaunted their presence before the authorities, creating the arabesque American myth involving Patty Hearst and Cinque. Arabian nights of California, the rich white girl and her genie; the dragon has come. Visonary hostage-takers, Artaud's mad actors, burning up on television. Now the psychodramatic politician was on the scene. One man, no leaks, unless he's schizoid and rats on himself. The first time rebellion could achieve a force equal to the opponents of rebellion. Eight thousand tons of plutonium were missing. Who had them? Enough to make 80 A-bombs. (p. 90)

What a way to live, but that's what much of our culture has turned out to be, as rival sign-making systems fight it out in books and films and on records and TV. Like *God Made Alaska for the Indians*, *The Terrible Twos* is much more than a simple counter-history: quoting a penitent Nelson Rockefeller from the lowest circle of Hell and playing with some off-the-record apocrypha about his death from a group of corporate scoundrels, Reed can pull together the many different and contradictory levels of our contemporary American "truth" and give us a persuasive account of how we live today. Reed the novelist and essayist is a careful semiotic researcher who, once he's done the hard work of running up and down the stairs for facts, gives language free play to project itself into previously unexplored corners of public experience, lighting up some truths which those afflicted   with   cultural   tunnel   vision   might   otherwise   never   see.

Yet official standards remain belligerently exclusive and reductively stereotypical: "It's too bad that the different cultures which go to make up American civilization are communicating only on the tacos and watermelons level" (p. 125). Such prescriptions only weaken the parties who make them; for, as Reed argues, "the drive against integrating schools being waged by some oily politicians is regrettable since it's the white students who really need it if they are to survive in a complicated, multicultural world" (pp. 125-26). Who suffers most? "It is the white students who are being culturally suffocated because even black C students have it over them; they are bicultural, and the hispanic students are tricultural." But the ugliness and viciousness of an official culture, Aristotelian in its aesthetic and colonialistic in its ethic, for the most part prevails. "At this time in American history," Reed concludes, "we are like ghosts talking gibberish through different dimensions, and stupid men do not make good mediums" (p. 126).

From *Literary Subversions: New American Fiction and the Practice of Criticism.* Carbondale, IL: Southern Illinois University Press, 1985.

RECKLESS EYEBALLING (1986)

Gallery of the Repellent

Michiko Kakutani/Review

The way *Reckless Eyeballing* starts off reminds you of a seedy 1940's detective novel gussied up with some contemporary bigotry and anger: a large man, wearing sunglasses and a raincoat, has been assaulting prominent feminists. He ties them up, shaves off their hair, chastises them for giving black men a bad name, and leaves a chrysanthemum behind as his calling card. His explanation is that this is what the Resistance did to whores who collaborated with the Nazis, and that women today who help perpetuate ugly stereotypes about black men deserve a similar punishment for their sins.

This is Ishmael Reed's seventh novel and like much of his earlier fiction, it's a nasty, idiosyncratic blend of invective, satire and social criticism, served up with lots of narrative pratfalls and jokes. This time, he takes on what he sees as a cultural establishment bent on manufacturing and reinforcing racist cliches. And he goes so far as to imply that black men are currently being stereotyped and maligned in much the same way the Nazis once treated the Jews.

To make his points with full shock value, Mr. Reed himself employs stereotypes, creating a gallery of repellent characters, all painted in the flat, bright primary colors of farce. Detective Lawrence O'Reedy ("Loathesome Larry"), the cop who is pursuing "The Flower Phantom," is an Irish bully who combines the worst traits of Archie Bunker and Dirty Harry and is forever romanticizing "the old days" when "white men were in charge" and police brutality was never a community issue.

The Flower Phantom's first victim, Tremonisha Smarts, is a famous black female writer, whose hit play *Wrong-Headed Man* (which comes across as sort of a send-up of Alice Walker's *Color Purple*) features a lead villain who abused his children, "sodomized his missionary wife, put his mother-in-law in bondage, performed bestial acts with pets." Jack Brashford is a rich, black author who makes anti-Semitic remarks to explain his writing block--"the Jews have stolen all of the black material," he says, "so there's nothing for me to write about." And Becky French is a feminist producer who spends her time blacklisting--and blackballing--male writers who fail to adhere to the correct ideological line.

One of the fellows on that list is Ian Ball, an eager black playwright who's now willing to "adjust" his writing in order to win the feminists over. "I've written a play that's guaranteed to please them," he tells his mother. "The women get all of the good parts and the best speeches. I've taken all the criticism they made of "Suzanna" to heart." Whereas "Suzanna" depicted a whore, his latest offering *Reckless Eyeballing*, concerns a lynched black man, who's posthumously tried for "raping" a woman with his lecherous stares.

Told in overlapping takes with the story of the Flower Phantom, Ball's tale reads like the adventures of a warped *Candide*--set in the world of off-Broadway theater. Although Ball starts out thinking that success with *Reckless Eyeballing* is assured, things quickly begin to go awry: after the original director, Jim Minsk, is lynched by white Southerners, "Eyeballing" falls into the hands of the fearsome Tremonisha Smarts and Becky French, who quickly set about making "corrections" in the play.

By the time they've decided to pre-empt his play from the theater in favor of a feminist tract about Eva Braun--the show, which portrays Eva as a heroic victim, brings to mind *Springtime for Hitler* in *The Producers*--Ball finds himself feeling intermittent sympathy for the Flower Phantom. Which isn't so surprising, given his attitude toward women. After all, for all his willingness to pander to the feminists, Ball remains an unrequited chauvinist who likes to use certain four-letter words to refer to women and who is quick to assess any female in the room in lewd physical terms.

No doubt Mr. Reed's depiction of Ball, like his other characterizations is intended to gall many of his readers. In fact, by the end of the novel--by which time Ball has his theatrical hit, and has also managed to fulfill another menacing aspect of his destiny--both sexes, as well as practically every ethnic and religious group, have been eyeballed and lambasted. Characters have ranted and raved about "stupid" Irish, about "white women who are carrying on the attack against black men today, because they struck a deal with white men who run the country," and about Jews who "talk loud in restaurants and say crass and impolite things."

Yet if the motive behind all this ugly talk is to jar the reader into some new perceptions about bigotry, Mr. Reed does not appear to take an entirely even-handed stance. Some kinds of prejudice seem to concern him more than others. The Holocaust exists in this novel mainly as a point of comparison for contemporary prejudice against blacks. And the sexist banter of men tends to come off as sort of "boys will be boys" silliness, whereas feminist criticism of men assumes decidedly more sinister proportions.

What's more, Mr. Reed tends to stack the cards against certain characters by having them all too neatly recant at the end of the book: Tremonisha Smarts makes a lengthy confession, admitting that she's been used as a tool by white feminists, that she now intends to tend house, take care of her man and get pregnant; another black female writer makes a similar admission.

As for the New York arts world *Reckless Eyeballing* suggests that it's a closed shop, dominated by women and Jews, in which the only artists who get ahead are those willing to pander to them and adopt fashionable views. To say the least, it's a paranoid position with disturbing implications; and it does a disservice to Mr. Reed's own notable career.

From *The New York Times* 5 April 1986: 12. Copyright © 1986 by The New York Times Co. Reprinted by permission.

Ishmael Reed's Rhetorical Turn: Uses of "Signifying" in *Reckless Eyeballing*

Daniel Punday/Article

Critics have failed to account adequately for Ishmael Reed's recent fiction, and generally dismiss it as less interesting than his more controversial early writing. These recent novels seem more straightforward in their plots and messages, and much less experimental in method. I would like to suggest, however, that this apparent clarity is part of a complex and innovative style. We might characterize this style as "rhetorical" in the broadest and most pervasive sense--that is, its overall narrative strategies at the level of plot, theme and character are constructed primarily on the way the audience will read and even misread the novel. Reed broadens the definition of the rhetorical aspects of the literary text as part of a larger attempt to reformulate how his own works relate to the African-American tradition. Critics have noted that African-American writers often are particularly aware of their precursors and tradition. Reed, however, not only carefully situates himself in relation to tradition in the abstract, but also anticipates in the novel's plot and structure the reactions of actual readers who share that tradition only in a problematic way. Indeed, in Reed's recent fiction this problematic reception of the work becomes the primary "content" of the novel. The implications of this move force us to reconsider how we are to trace the African-American tradition and to what degree that tradition can remain independent of the readings given it by mainstream American literary culture. I would like to explore such rhetorical workings in one particular recent novel, *Reckless Eyeballing* (1986).

Critics and reviewers unanimously agree that Ishmael Reed is assaulting feminism in *Reckless Eyeballing*. His protagonist, Ian Ball, is called a "notorious sexist," and yet we are invited to suffer with Ball during his persecution at the hands of powerful women in the theater world. When Reed climactically summarizes Ball's victimization by revealing him as "two-headed," he seems to be using that common African-American trope of black "double-consciousness." This trope defines black consciousness as split into two identities, one acceptable to and partially created by the white hegemony, the other more authentic but disturbing to that same mainstream society. But if we simply read the trope conventionally, we stumble straight into Reed's trap, and this is what critics have done. Reed revises double-consciousness as "two-headedness"; Reed consequently uses this latter term to refer both to double-consciousness and to another kind of split consciousness that implicitly parodies double-consciousness. This kind of split consciousness (or "two-headedness") allows a person to respond to individuals as unique entities but also allows that person to make gross ethnic, racial, and sexual generalizations. With such two-headedness, we find it possible to like one Jew but believe anti-semitic slanders; or we can spout feminist hostilities about men, yet know individual men to whom they do not apply. I shall argue that understanding this second form of two-headedness permits us both to read the text much more effectively and to explain why it has so often been misinterpreted. Reed plays both forms of two-headedness off against each other, tricking us by giving us what we think we ought to be given. And just as Ball's struggles in New York are played out on the literary (and literal) stage, so too do the tensions between these two forms of two-headedness clearly reveal the politics of literary reception. Through this subtle metafiction, Reed indirectly comments or "signifies" on the readings and misreadings produced because of the reader's expectations. By anticipating and undermining such prejudiced interpretations of *Reckless Eyeballing*, Reed exposes the ethnic and sexual stereotypes that pervade mainstream literary reception.

1

On the most elementary level, *Reckless Eyeballing* tells the story of playwright Ian Ball's rise to stardom in New York. Reed focuses his novel, however, on the price Ball pays for his success, a price on which Reed insists even in the scene of his protagonist's triumph:

> Broadway. People in mink coats arriving from the suburbs. Chartered buses in
> front of the theater. Interviews. Women. Gol-lee, he said to himself. He was

becoming "bankable." Producers would be lining up. Three-hour lunches. Talk shows. *People* magazine. Parties. If only Chester Himes and Jake Brashford were less controversial, more amiable, more toned down. If only they had cooled it. They could have had all of this too. (116-17)

By assuming a second role at odds with his more genuine identity (by "cooling it"), Ball divides his sense of self in two. This type of split is the first and most obvious form of two-headedness. (For clarity and simplicity of exposition I will hereafter refer to this explicit, and as we will see, received form of two-headedness as "two-headedness (1)" and to the less obvious, revisional form as "two-headedness (2).")

This two-headedness (1) echos the traditional African-American theme of "double-consciousness." W.E.B. Du Bois describes this traditional trope, this figurative construct for representing black experience, in *The Souls of Black Folk:*

> After the Egyptian and the Indian, the Greek and Roman, The Teuton and Mongolian, the Negro is a sort of seventh son, born with a veil, and gifted with second-sight in this American world,--a world which yields him no true self-consciousness, but only lets him see himself through the revelation of the other world. It is a peculiar sensation this double-consciousness, this sense of always looking at one's self through the eyes of others, of measuring one's soul by the tape of a world that looks on in amused contempt and pity. One ever feels his two-ness, an American, a Negro; two souls, two thoughts, two unreconciled strivings; two warring ideals in one dark body, whose dogged strength alone keeps it from being torn asunder. (also qtd. in Gates 722-23)

The reconciling of these two "selves" is a key theme of the most common and traditional form of African-American writing, the autobiographical novel of entrance into white society. Reed makes clear throughout the novel that Ball is torn between just such irreconcilable drives--between a more basic or genuine but often controversial self and a politically smart identity. In the background of Ball's struggles in the New York literary scene is the mystery of the "Flower Phantom," who throughout the novel attacks prominent feminists and shaves their heads; the Flower Phantom turns out to be Ball's schizophrenic alternate self. Ball's conflicting responses to the Flower Phantom exemplify these irreconcilable drives: "Ian's head told him that this man was a lunatic who should be put away for a long time, but his gut was cheering the man on. His head was Dr. Jekyll, but his gut was Mr. Hyde" (51). When Reed finally introduces the actual figure of two-headedness (1) at the end of the novel, he climactically foregrounds the mental conflict on which he has more subtly insisted throughout. Before Ball was born, we discover, he had been hexed: in jealous anger, his father's first wife declared that Ball "would be born a two-head, of two minds, the one not knowing what the other was up to" (146).

This trope of split consciousness is not new in African-American literature; similarly, the characteristics and attitudes associated with Ball's two heads, his two drives, are very much in keeping with Reed's previous writing about the conflict of black and white cultures. Reed suggests something of this cultural opposition in his early essay "Neo-HooDoo": "A dangerous paranoid pain-in-the-neck a CopGod from the git-go, Jeho-vah was the successful law and order candidate in the mythological relay of the 4th Century A.D. Jeho-vah is the God of punishment. The H Bomb is a typical Jeho-vah 'miracle.' Jeho-vah is why we are in Vietnam. He told Moses to go out and 'subdue' the world" (42). The white, Judeo-Christian restraint and control asserted here and the implied contrasting black freedom are echoed in the two drives of two-headedness (1). Reed most clearly expresses the difference between the black and white selves when he contrasts Koffee's uncorrupted black, rum-like love-making and Ball's white, gin-influenced sex. Koffee's sex is pure pleasure: "Made you feel sweet and warm inside" (145). Ball's pleasure must come through restraint: "He wondered how it would be if he was holding her titties and giving it to her from behind, *maintaining his pleasure by concentrating on something dull"* (138, my emphasis).

What is important for our reexamination of *Reckless Eyeballing*, however, is not the cultural opposition two-headedness (1) suggests, but the conventionality of the form through which Reed asserts the opposition. Although the opposed characteristics associated with white and black cultures are consistent with his previous work, Reed's use of the trope of two-headedness (1) with its basis in the tradition of double-consciousness belies his characteristic rejection of "expected" forms of African-American literature. Loop Garoo, the central character of Reed's second novel, *Yellow Back Radio Broke-Down*, clearly addresses such expectations and asserts the individuality and freedom of artistic form:

> What's your beef with me Bo Shmo, what if I write circuses? No one says a novel has to be one thing. It can be anything it wants to be, a vaudeville show, the six o'clock news, the mumblings of wild men saddled by demons. (36)

Given that Reed rejects the expected and acceptable forms of minority writing, it would be surprising if his use of two-headedness were so decorous and conventional. Indeed, I am arguing that we have been over-eager to render Reed merely a traditional African-American novelist. Let us now look at the second kind of two-headedness, whose presence changes the meaning of the text.

Far from reinforcing the generalizations of race and gender evident in the two-headedness (1) discussed above, this other two-headedness (2) takes up the very issue of the application of generalizations to individuals. Shrank, the black doorman at Tremonisha's apartment who himself was once an important writer, displays this kind of two-headedness--he continually rails against Jews in general but drops everything to attend to the Epsteins when they enter the lobby.

While this conflict seems to echo Ball's split between a genuine black self and an inflicted white identity, there is nothing particularly "black" in Shrank's hatred of the Jews. Moreover, Shrank goes far beyond his duty and greets the Epsteins "gushingly," becoming angry when Mrs. Epstein congratulates Ball (57). Both aspects of Shrank's hypocrisy suggest not so much a split between black and white "selves" as a lack of mental connection between his hatred of the Jews and his eagerness for the Epsteins' approval. "Loathesome" Larry O'Reedy, a racist but troubled police officer, displays this two-headedness (2) in his attitude toward his own ethnic group: "What can you learn about Irishmen in a university that you can't learn down at the local gin mill?" (91). Although his son is right in suggesting that O'Reedy rejects his Irish ancestry because it reminds [him] of a world [he] want[s] to leave behind" (91), more important for our examination of the novel is the fact that O'Reedy does not seem to realize fully the connection between his generalization about the Irish and his own ancestry. O'Reedy two-headedly believes that he can distance himself from his own ethnicity and its more basic ties to his identity by perpetuating the stereotypes about the Irish. Ball too may display signs of this "other" two-headedness (2). His command to his driver in New Oyo, "Shut up, you black monkey" (132), suggests a split concsciousness; like O'Reedy, Ball does not include himself in his own implied ethnic generalization. Ball picks up and repeats generalizations about Jews from Jake Brashford, another once-important black writer who is now to some extent Ball's mentor: "Brashford said that the reason the Jews came up with monotheism is because they were too cheap to buy idols" (83). These generalizations are sufficiently out of keeping with Ball's friendship for the Jewish Jim Minsk to suggest that part of Ball's ongoing New York education is the development of such a split. It is Brashford, however, who most clearly expresses this "other" two-headedness (2): "[Ball] wanted to ask Brashford why he would praise Jim so when he knew that Jim was Jewish. How could Brashford have it both ways, put down Jews for an hour or so and then praise one?" (32). Later Brashford's wife Delilah explains the extremity of his split: "When he got to his studio he started to drink again and went into some anti-Semitic tirade, which is what always happens when he's drunk or feeling sorry [for] himself. It's crazy because I'm Jewish and he has a Jewish son. I think it's the play that's making him this way. He's trying to write a play of universal values, but everywhere he turns, he runs into ethnicity" (117). What we see here in Brashford we can discern in Shrank, O'Reedy and perhaps Ball as well--a split consciousness which recognizes unique individuals but is capable of the grossest ethnic generalizations.

Reed also offers an explanation for the cause of this individual/general split: generalizations develop from a loss of individual contact with the ethnic community and customs represented for Reed in ethnic literature. While Brashford's forsaking of ethnicity to write a "universal" play makes this fairly obvious, such a loss is also evident in Shrank: "Ball pushed him [Shrank] out of the way as the author [Shrank] of a collection of poems entitled *My Secret Enemy: Me* shouted at him, 'THE JEWS! THE JEWS!'"(67). The awkwardness of the phrasing of this passage suggests how hard Reed works to stress how Shrank's mode and subject of inquiry have changed. Shrank's self-scrutiny of the 60s, which produced the self-investigation of *My Secret Enemy* and consequently helped establish a black ethnic literature, becomes in the 80s of *Reckless Eyeballing* only a sterile and endless tirade in generalized terms about the Jews. Similarly Ball's developing aspiration to "politically" smart rather than self-expressive writing parallels his increasing tendency to repeat the generalizations which may be connected with Ball's development of two-headedness (2). O'Reedy's acceptance of his Irish roots, however, shows just the opposite--a growing if still half-hearted interest in the literature of his ethnic group:

> He looked at Sean. "I'm sorry about that...tell me about this guy James T. Farrell, you say he could write, huh."
> "The best. He wrote a novel about an Irish-American guy named Studs Lonigan. A real loser."
> "Kind of like me, huh. Studs Lonigan."
> "No, Dad. Studs was a victim of change." (124)

Learning about himself and his ethnic group through Studs Lonigan, O'Reedy shows us that the process of understanding ethnicity is intimately connected to the knowledge of the literature of that ethnic group. Moreover, understanding the place of the self within society proves impossible without some sense of that ethnic group's literature. Conversely, as Shrank's 60s writing shows, the process of self-investigation produces ethnic literature.

Understanding how stereotypes develop from a loss of roots enriches our sense of ethnic literature and its importance for Reed. Further, it will lead us to contextualize (though not dismiss) Reed's apparent sexism within his larger aesthetic and political goals. Ultimately, this contextualization of the sexual within the ethnic will lead us to understand how the two kinds of two-headedness interact in *Reckless Eyeballing*. American society demands assimilation and rejection of ethnicity as a prerequisite for success. Though sensitive to racial slights, Jim Minsk has clearly moved away from his ethnic group to become "one of the best directors on the New York scene" (46) and assimilated into mainstream American society: "He went about his house in a jumpsuit and ate 100 percent bran every morning. There were fern plants in his bathroom and health food store soaps" (15). Ball similarly discards ethnicity as he becomes a success in New York:

> "I'm too busy trying to...well...you know, go for it. His mother frowned.
> "He means, he wants to be a success," Johnnie Kranshaw explained.

"He speaks so much of that American language that he's forgotten the
Mother Tongue." (141)

Tremonisha, the feminist playwright who is one of Ball's principle antagonists
throughout the novel, more explicitly equates success with a lack of ethnicity in
her climactic and confessional letter to Ball. She says of her success in New
York, "I thought that by getting rid of the caftan and beard of my experience, the
people I admired would accept me. As a result, I became something I'm not"
(128).

This rejection of the ethnic derives from basic American assumptions about
the value of and need for assimilation both in day to day life and, particularly for
Reed, in art. Jim Minsk suggests this stigmatization of individual ethnic traits
and its relation to self-expression:

"It happens to old people. They get disoriented. You know. My uncle, his
younger brother, says that Pop always acted old. He'd go down to the deli or
the automat where some of these old-timers would read and discuss the
newspapers and talk about the old days in Russia. He'd spend hours there. Or
he'd have his head buried in some books. He wrote poetry in Yiddish. He clung
to the old ways while everybody else became assimilated, including my uncle,
who used to be a gangster." (15-16)

At the very heart of American society is the belief in the suppression of
difference and the art of "universal values." In this sense the "eyeball" of Reed's
title parodically echoes Emerson's "transparent eyeball" as an example of this
American devaluation of the ethnic and individual: "Standing on the bare
ground,--all mean egotism vanishes. I become a transparent eyeball; I am
nothing; I see all; the currents of the Universal Being circulate through me; I am
part of parcel of God" (24). For Reed, in contrast, it is the preservation of an
ethnic identity and contact with that group's literature that empowers the
translation of experience into writing. The pairing of ethnicity and self-
expression further suggests that the opposite of this preservation of heritage--the
assimilation and rejection of ethnic literature encouraged by American society--
carries with it the loss of such artistic power and encourages the development of
two-headedness (2).

The suppression of the ethnic by American society has, however, a far more
negative effect than this individual loss of ethnicity. By opposing the ethnic to
the "normal" and successful, American society has encouraged categorical and
simplistic ethnic generalizations. Shrank's change of subject matter noted
above--from himself to the Jews--usefully exemplifies this development of
generalizations. In his early self-investigation Shrank finds himself his own
"secret enemy," suggesting not the self-labeling of O'Reedy's "all Irishmen are
drunks" but a realization of the complexity of the self, a self which is "secret"
and thus hidden from inquiry by anyone but himself. As an examination of

"selves" from an exterior perspective, Shrank's discussion of the Jews shows just the opposite--an abundance of generalized and definite labels: "That's what all these Jews say. They'd rather be pilgrims and the descendants of slave owners than be themselves. The Jews over here ain't the real Jews anyway" (56). Shrank implies here that he knows just what "all the Jews" are like--better in fact than many "unreal" Jews themselves know. Reed suggests that any consideration of the external is necessarily simplistic; only through investigation of the self--as in Shrank's early writing or O'Reedy's consideration of Studs Lonigan as a fellow Irishman--are complex and valuable insights possible. Thus the gap represented by the individual/general split can be bridged by ethnic literature through focus on individual experience. Rather than providing a general label or "fact," such writing offers some far looser yet more real ethnic touchstone. Cut off from this, O'Reedy sees only the generalization--all Irishmen are losers--but misses how the expression of an individual experience can spark self-understanding for the equally individual reader in a way which the generalizations O'Reedy automatically looks for cannot.

Beyond encouraging the simplistic and generalized understanding of ethnic groups by severing individuals from their own ethnicity, American society provides specific "labels" for such groups. O'Reedy's attitudes toward black men offer the novel's clearest examples of such socially given generalizations about ethnic groups: "Well, maybe that black jogger was innocent, but it was dark the morning he shot him. He couldn't see so well, and besides there had been a number of rapes in that park. Everybody knew that all black men did was rape white women, so too bad for the jogger, but, well, the way O'Reedy looked at it this was war, and in war a lot of innocent people get killed" (8). Yet, as his self-assuring tone in this passage and hauntings throughout the novel suggest, some of the socially given generalizations on which O'Reedy relies are becoming less certain. O'Reedy makes evident his discomfort with changing black/white relations in his statements about police department reforms: "The force certainly had changed. Along about the mid-seventies some meddlesome wimp of a judge had decreed that every time a white policeman achieved a promotion, they had to promote a black. Sure, police brutality complaints were on the decline, but that wasn't the point. In the old days you roughed them up so that they'd realize that white men were in charge" (21). That O'Reedy may be left a bit confused by the undermining of these once universally accepted ethnic stereotypes is perhaps most clear in the line, "He thought of all the P.R.'s and nig--or blacks, as they were calling them these days--he'd arrested" (8). The hesitation evident here and the insecurity already noted in O'Reedy's denunciation of the "wimp of a judge" explain why he enjoys Tremonisha's play so much. "His wife had insisted that he see her play, *Wrong-Headed Man*. She thought that he'd fall asleep, but it turned out that he rather enjoyed it. Especially the scene where the big black ape throws his missionary wife down the stairs" (9). What O'Reedy finds so attractive in Tremonisha's play is the bolstering of his stereotypes about black men. O'Reedy's name is, after all, "Loathesome" rather than "Loathsome" Larry--implying less a tendency to inspire hatred in others than for he himself to hate, literally to loathe some people. Like Studs Lonigan, O'Reedy is a victim of change--in his case, of changing labels. This challenging of stereotypes leaves him guilt-ridden over his penchant for loathing others--which, given his disparaging of the Irish, must include himself--and unsure of the terms in which he is to understand members of ethnic groups. We see in O'Reedy a man who sold his ethnicity for social acceptance, but who now finds less than secure the stereotypes which caused him to desert his ethnic group and by which he has defined himself as other than Irish.

Wrong-Headed Man reinforces O'Reedy's stereotypes. This literary scenario is Reed's central and most complex demonstration of the dangers of falling away from the ethnic basis for social interaction. Further, this example is particularly important since it reveals most clearly how Reed subordinates gender politics to his larger cultural critique. Feminism, broadly conceived by Reed as a movement valuing issues of gender and willfully blind to their ethnic context, is Reed's most explicit target in the novel and the specific issue through which he reveals the politics of the de-ethnicization of America. Seen in this context, feminism is important to the novel as a force that *maintains* the gross generalizations out of crude self-interest. It is a particularly destructive form of racism in that its prejudices are not only allowed but exalted by liberal consciousness. Yet such racism, encouraged by the generalizations that come with the devaluation of the ethnic, also lies at the very heart of American society's drive to "go for it." As already noted, it is his very desire to "succeed" which causes O'Reedy to perpetuate the stereotypes of the ethnic group from which he would seek to distance himself. Tremonisha makes explicit the role feminism played in connection with *Wrong-Headed Man:*

> "I was writing about some brutal black guys who I knew in my life who beat women, abandoned their children, cynical, ignorant, and arrogant, you know these types, but my critics and the people who praised them took some of these characters and made them out to be *all* black men...I thought they were my fans, those feminists, but some of them would have drinks and ask me about "raw sex" and how black men were, you know. Others used my black male characters as an excuse to hate all black men, especially some of these white women." (129-30)

This passage suggests that racism and sexism are both based on a human, and particularly "American" tendency to seek stereotypes, especially when they provide a tool for social advancement of self. Yet even in this passage about sexist stereotypes, Reed accentuates issues of ethnicity rather than gender. Despite Reed's obvious desire to defend the black male, the solution to the problems of both kind of generalizations lies for Reed in the reassertion of the ethnic in general and ethnic literature in particular because, as noted above, it is this movement away from ethnic individuality that encourages a general acceptance of stereotypes. Reed sees America as discouraging any sense of ethnicity by associating all such traits with those "dislocated" and setting up as the model for success the perfectly assimilated, non-ethnic person that Ball seeks to become in New York. Such a perceived lack of ethnicity causes mainstream America not only to look down on the ethnic, but to be more willing to accept stereotypes in general. Tremonisha's resolutions at the end of the novel attest to the primacy of ethnic over sexist stereotypes. Having realized how stereotypes contributed to her own success, Tremonisha clearly makes no attempt to rectify or avoid gender stereotypes--she plans to "get fat" and "have babies" (130)--but, like O'Reedy, instead seeks her own ethnicity. In going to Yuba City she returns to her roots; as she says, "I grew up in a town like this" (129).

We should end this section by noting that Reed's subordination of gender to ethnic issues plays on one other "stereotype"--readers' assumptions about Reed's own sexism. Reed's antifeminism remains a powerful force in his writing in part because it instances the crucial issue of the subordination of the individual and all other cultural issues to an overarching ethnic basis for society. Yet, more important for our overall evaluation of Reed's rhetorical strategies, Reed's attack on feminism in *Reckless Eyeballing* plays to his critics, intentionally seeming to satisfy the stereotypes attached to his own work. Ultimately I will argue that Reed uses this apparently typical sexism in order to trick his readers into reading the novel in a way meant to reveal their own cultural assumptions about the African-American tradition. We cannot, however, understand this strategy until we have addressed directly how Reed's two forms of two-headedness interact in the novel.

2

Henry Louis Gates's discussion of "signifying" and intertextuality in black literature provides a starting place for understanding how these two highly divergent forms of two-headedness interact in *Reckless Eyeballing*. The term "signifying" in African-American culture has the specialized meaning of repeating another's discourse with some difference and with the purpose of parody and revision. Gates applies the concept of signifying to the black literary tradition in general: "It is clear that black writers read and critique other black texts as an act of rhetorical self-definition. Our literary tradition exists because of these precisely chartable formal literary relationships, relationships of signifying" (693). According to Gates, the black literary tradition has developed because of an implicit intertextuality such that, as a matter of course, any text must in some way modify the tropes and forms used by its precursors to represent black experience.

In the context of such a tradition, Reed clearly seems to be signifying in *Reckless Eyeballing* on the received trope of double-consciousness. The implicit individual/general split of two-headedness (2) signifies on the explicit, double-consciousness based version of this split--it repeats the traditional form with a difference such that it implies a criticism of that received trope. This critique, however, goes far beyond the traditional parodistic revisionary use of signifying; the very nature of that new two-headedness (2) denies the possibility of any trope representing universally *the* black experience. It is exactly this universal label that O'Reedy looks for in Studs Lonigan and which blinds him to the text's value as the description of an individual experience in all its complexity. Any trope retards self-understanding when it claims, like double-consciousness, to "sum up" such an ethnic experience. Universal tropes infect the invaluable wellspring of ethnicity in literature with the labels such ethnic writing should help to avoid.

Reed's alteration of the term "double-consciousness" to "two-headedness" suggests how this revision of the trope reaffirms Reed's antagonism toward the literary establishment. Robert Elliot Fox notes in connection with Reed's earlier work that two-headedness is equated with the "hoodoo man" of the Haitian hoodoo religion (46). By moving from double-consciousness to two-headedness (1), Reed changes the focus of the trope from psychology based on the logos of western civilization to the African-American roots in hoodooism. This move out of the western tradition toward the hoodoo parallels Reed's rejection of the forms he sees inflicted on black literature by the literary establishment, and suggests that Reed's novel somehow represents a more "black" approach to literature. In another sense, however, Reed's renaming of double-consciousness as two-headedness (1) also carries with it the purposeful *misreading* of both the original Haitian concept and Reed's previous use of the term in his own work. Two-headedness traditionally provides a way of being in touch with the loas, the spirits of the hoodoo religion. As Papa LaBas says in *Mumbo Jumbo,* "Evidence? Woman, I dream about it, I feel it, I use my 2 heads" (25). This original meaning of the term suggests how literally and logically the explicit trope of Ball's two-headedness (1) adapts and misreads the original black term-- simplifying it, giving it a single meaning, making it comprehensible to a white society afraid of the nonrational. Reed has simplified and rationalized, and in the process destroyed, the original Haitian meaning of two-headedness in two-headedness (1). By associating this destruction of the original ethnic meaning of two-headedness with the traditional trope of double-consciousness, Reed applies this general critique of universal tropes to the African-American literary tradition, arguing that even the trope of double-consciousness tames and regularizes African-American literature until it bears little resemblance to individual ethnic reality.

Despite the importance for *Reckless Eyeballing* of signifying in this intertextual sense, we can understand the need for the presence of *both* forms of two-headedness in the novel only when we realize that Reed's primary methods also includes a slightly different facet of signifying--that which sets up black vernacular as distinct from and inaccessible to white mainstream society. As I have already noted, Reed's primary artistic concern in the past has been those literary conventions and expectations imposed on black writers by the predominantly white literary establishment. Reed helps to provide a locus for black writing, to aid in "rhetorical self-definition," not by searching for a trope of black experience but by undermining such generality and the limitations on expressions that go with it. The "toast" of "The Signifying Monkey and the Lion," a traditional African-American oral tale that takes many different forms, draws attention to how signifying can function in relation to an outsider. This provides a model of Reed's methods for dealing with pressure for homogeneity in black writing from the white literary establishment.

The toast tells how the Signifying Monkey tricks the Lion. The Lion is, of course, the "king of the jungle," and by his physical superiority has exiled the Monkey to the trees and into subservience. For Gates, with the Monkey's marginal position come the marginal uses of language--nonstandard and figurative speaking. The monkey lyingly tells the Lion that the Elephant has insulted him:

> He said, "Mr. Lion," he said, "a bad-assed motherfucker down your way."
> He said, "Yeah! The way he talks about your folks is a certain shame.
> I even heard him curse when he mentioned your grandmother's name."
> (Abrahams 113)

Ignoring his own size disadvantage and even the Elephant's warning, the Lion seeks revenge and is trounced. The tale, of course, is a story of the dethroning of the powerful by the subservient:

> He [The Monkey] said, "Damn, Mr. Lion, you went through here yesterday, the
>   jungle rung.
> Now you come back today, damn near hung." (Abrahams 114)

This use of signifying as a way to overthrow the powerful is at the heart of Reed's method in *Reckless Eyeballing*. Reed himself noted and stressed this tradition of reversal in a recent interview: "If you look at our traditions all the way back to the plantations you see that satire and signifying are widely used. It's a way of subverting the wishes of the people in power (Watkins 610). Specifically, such signifying uses another's expectations and (particularly rhetorical) blindnesses; thus the Monkey plays up to the Lion's pride and uses language in a nonliteral way unsuspected by the Lion. As Gates says, "The Signifying Monkey is able to signify upon the Lion only because the Lion does not understand the nature of the Monkey's discourse" (691).

Reed, I suggest, sets himself as an artist in the same position and with the same possibilities for signifying and "dethroning" as the Monkey. (Indeed, he may have specifically had Gates's work in mind; in Mel Watkins's interview with Reed during the writing of *Reckless Eyeballing*, Reed specifically mentions Gates's work as "a kind of Rosetta stone" [610].) Just as the Monkey rebels against the Lion's role as king of the jungle, so too in the past has Reed rebelled against the right of the white literary establishment to read and judge his work according to traditional forms and criteria. Like the Monkey, however, Reed is also very conscious of his own practical subordination to the literary establishment which controls most publishing outlets and accepts only a very conventional form of minority writing. As Reed states in his "Introduction" to *19 Necromancers from Now*:

> Perhaps at the roots of American art is a rivalry between the oppressor and the oppressed, with a secret understanding that the oppressor shall always prevail and make off with the prizes, no matter how inferior his art to that of his victims. Art in America may even be related to sexual competition. In the beginning was The Word and The Word is the domain of the White patriarchy. Beware. Women and natives are not to tamper with The Word. (n. pag.)

A great many critics and reviewers have misread *Reckless Eyeballing*. I suggest that these mistakes are the result of Reed's intentional "trickery" of his audience, the need for which derives from the circumstances of "Art in America."

Two aspects of the Lion lead to his being duped--pride and an inability to understand the Monkey's nonliteral language. Both of these have analogues in the overall rhetorical strategies of *Reckless Eyeballing*. Just as the Monkey tricks the Lion by playing up to his proud concern for reputation, Reed dupes his readers by appearing to fulfill their condescending and limited expectations of black literature through two-headedness (1). Like the Monkey, Reed relies on misleading "language"--the novel's narrative style and structure--in order to encourage the audience to trust the obvious meaning of his message. While the Monkey effortlessly relies on the Lion's prideful blindness and automatic reaction to the besmirching of his reputation, Reed works much harder to ensure that his readers, at least the first time through the novel, get caught up in the novel's clarity, and pridefully take the explicit trope at face value and as the "point" of the novel. This duping of the reader will become much clearer by examining in some detail how Reed uses the style and structure of his narrative to invite such trust in the explicit trope of Ball's two-headedness (1).

Throughout the work, Reed employs a noticeably clear narrative style--of which the opening chapters provide the best examples. The novel opens with Ian Ball's dream. Yet, rather than this being a disorienting section grounded closely in Ball's own mind and associations, Reed uses this dream as a way to present the characters to the reader in a clear and explicit fashion. Not only does he give the full names of Tremonisha Smarts and Becky French, Ball's two main antagonists, but, to guarantee the reader's understanding, Reed makes explicit that the work opens in Ball's dream with the phrase "he'd gathered from the logic you get in dreams" (1). Even more helpfully, only two pages after Ball awakens, Reed provides a call from Ball's mother through which the reader learns all the necessary background information about the protagonist. Structurally, too, Reed stresses clarity, emphasizing Ball's central position in the narrative not only by opening in Ball's dream and following his actions to the relative exclusion of other characters (only nine of the twenty six chapters do not include Ball), but also by connecting Ball's name and the name of his play with the title of the novel.

This stylistic and structural clarity of the work obviously calls for a "neat" ending, which the revelation of Ball's two-headedness (1) seems to fulfill well. The novel ends with the revelation that Ball is the mysterious Flower Phantom, who has throughout the novel shaved the heads of prominent feminists. Ball's split personality comes about, we discover, because he was "born a two-head" (146)--the result of the curse mentioned earlier--thus neatly resolving the mystery and again repeating the theme of Ball's victimization at the hands of women. That Shrank is mistakingly identified as the Flower Phantom complements this fulfillment, and in the process suggests how hard Reed works to reinforce the clarity of the narrative. Reed offers an obviously unsatisfactory resolution to the mystery of the Phantom in Shrank's death--by comparison stressing the appropriateness of the later revelation of Ball's two-headedness (1) and corresponding identification as the Flower Phantom. Further, hints dropped throughout the work suggesting that Shrank may imitate the Phantom out of admiration ("Damn. Why didn't I think of that?" [55]) encourage immediate doubt about his identification as the Phantom. Thus the confirmation of the readers' suspicions about Shrank reaffirms the appropriateness of Ball's identity as the Phantom. As the completeness of the novel's closure suggests, Reed does more than simply provide a clearly structured and focused novel; he manipulates that structure to encourage the reader's overwhelming sense of resolution at the end of the work. This resolution is, as I have noted at the end of the first section of this essay, further supported by readers' expectations of Reed's own sexism, expectations substantiated by the ending's condemnation of women. Such a sense of resolution should lead the reader to accept the traditional, double-consciousness trope of Ball's two-headedness (1) as the Lion accepts the Monkey's report--without a thought to the possibility of being mislead.

Whether or not individual readers come to the novel expecting the trope of double-consciousness, through the use of this clarity Reed encourages them to accept that explicit trope of two-headedness (1) and thus to associate themselves with the traditional expectations of African-American literature, expectations that stress the generality of black experience and the universal application of simple tropes to explain that experience. The frustration that readers find when trying to apply that satisfying final trope to the novel as a whole in order to unify and explain the strivings of its characters makes obvious how useless and misleading simple "labels" in general, and traditional expectations of universal black literary forms in particular can be. At the same time that the readers realize the danger of generalized statements and the extent to which society provides specific "labels" for ethnic groups, they recognize that the belief created by the literary establishment in the traditional and generalized representation of black experience is wrong and had, in fact, lead to their initial misreading of the novel.

3

Although *Reckless Eyeballing* has been called "an instance of the diminution of power [Reed's] work of the 1980s has manifested, compared to his truly innovative work of the 1960s and 1970s" (Fox 79), my discussion of the novel suggests that *Reckless Eyeballing* may be more complex and innovative than his much-praised early work. What differentiates these two styles, I would like to suggest, is how Reed uses signifying to interrelate the African-American and mainstream literary traditions. In this final section I will try to characterize that use.

Henry Louis Gates uses Reed's early *Mumbo Jumbo* as a paradigmatic example of signifying in the African-American literary tradition. This is possible because the novel relies heavily on references to and parody of previous black texts. While he obviously fears the reification of "black experience" into some neat trope or form, in such early work he seems to suggest that the artist can avoid this problem simply by clarifying his or her individual vision against this tradition. As Reed says in *Mumbo Jumbo,* "I am saying Open-Up-To-Right-Here and then you will have something coming from your experience that the whole world will admire and need" (152). In this novel, signifying is for Reed a means of clarifying and criticizing the vision that he has inherited from other African-American writers, and of thus establishing his individual place within that tradition.

In *Reckless Eyeballing*, however, we see a very different understanding of signifying and the role of the African-American novelist. As the increased presence of the literary establishment makes clear, in *Reckless Eyeballing* there is no hermetically sealed African-American tradition and no chance at a purely "black" vision. Suggestions of this insight are already implicit in Reed's earliest work, but come to the fore only in his most recent fiction. Here Reed is confronted not simply with an African-American tradition, but with the mediation and interpretation of such a tradition by an establishment. In *Reckless Eyeballing,* Ball is by no means a straightforward hero attempting to establish a clear voice; he is, instead, constantly caught within traps as he attempts to find a medium by which to use such a voice. Striving after self-actualization too easily leads to ossification of the vision of both self and others. If Reed continues to hope that simple consideration of self can lead to art, it is with increased recognition of the complexities of the move from production to dissemination of art, and the effects that such dissemination will have on future production. An individualization and message will not be "safe" or meaningful until mainstream society receives that vision without simplification or overgeneralization.

In such a situation Reed cannot simply establish his own position in relation to the African-American tradition; he must establish his relation to the media which carry that tradition and his own response to it. In this sense signifying changes from a parodic response to what has gone before to a rhetorical anticipation of the reception of this work, particularly the reception by an audience that is outside of that tradition. Such a concern for how the hearer will react is implicit in signifying in general, but downplayed in Gates's discussion of the role of signifying in the black literary tradition. If any audience to a literary text is addressed at all, it is an audience thoroughly involved in this tradition, indeed, the audience in Gates's form of signifying is the tradition itself, since rather than anticipating an actual response, the rhetoric of such signifying functions only at a general level. This understanding of signifying does not draw a distinction between the inherited tradition against which the author reacts and the readers who will receive such a reaction. Conversely, Reed's rhetoric is not simply a way of establishing his stylistic relation to the African-American literary tradition; instead it takes as central the reaction of an audience only problematically conscious of this tradition.

We should note that this rhetorical turn is not simply a matter of Reed's thematizing the hearer/teller relation, as Robert B. Stepto observes in several African-American narratives; it involves a fundamentally different sense of what constitutes the content of the work. In the types of signifying that Gates examines, the rhetorical methods that the author employs must be read in terms of their references to black experience, even though stylistic revision often overshadows this representational goal. As Gates says, "Much of Afro-American literary tradition can, in a real sense, be read as successive attempts to create a new narrative space for the recurring referent of Afro-American literature--the so-called black experience" (698). Although Reed's writing at some level applies to such experience, he rejects this "reference" as the basis of his style and the content of the novel. Indeed, Reed's recent style shifts attention from what it is about (its referent) to what it does (its effect on this audience). In this sense, the rhetoric of Reed's style is not primarily a new way of representing experience and breaks free from the backdrop of representation against which more traditional African-American "rhetoric" must be read. Reed's rhetoric becomes, through the effects that it produces, the "point" of the novel itself. Perhaps the clearest example of this shifted understanding of the novel's content is Reed's antifeminism. Many reviewers took Reed's attack on feminism in *Reckless Eyeballing* as content of the work. Yet as the foregoing discussion suggests, the "content" of the work is much more the responses that this attack elicits. Reed's methods are playful and his own stance on issues such as the status of women often frustratingly slippery; he structures the novel to reflect back on his readers' expectations and ways of reading and uses such controversial material as a way to involve them and strongly elicit their reactions.

This rhetorical focus is just as much a way for Reed to locate himself in tradition as the signifying that Gates addresses. Reed's concern with what happens when a writer tries to take his or her personal, ethnic message to a general audience is relevant to the configuration of that ethnic group. Because the definition of such a group plays such a key role in writing, such external definitions cannot be disregarded for the sake of a hermetic writing within the group. (Consider for example the title of Shrank's book, *My Secret Enemy: Me*, which we have seen above is Reed's example of ethnic self-investigation. Shrank's writing is not only "secret" but also presupposes an "enemy"--that is, an outside position from which to see himself. Similarly, in projecting such external definitions of themselves, ethnic groups are easily entangled in wrong-headed generalization.) Reed's concentration on the means of the reception of his work acts not only as an important means of safeguarding his message from blind mass consumption, but also helps to clarify his own stance toward a tradition which is saturated with misreadings and limitations by a foreign audience. Reed's ability to "clear a space" for himself and future African-American writers relies just as much on what happens to his message as it does on what has gone before. By anticipating the response of the mainstream literary culture, Reed addresses those forces which have problematized and redirected black writing in the past. The tradition resides as much in the dynamics of this reception as in what the writers themselves were trying to do.

Reed's recent work demands, therefore, a very different type of reading and a very different sense of tradition. This tradition represents an opening outward toward the forces which have helped to form the tradition itself. Signifying here is just as crucial as it is in Gates's account of the intrareferentiality of the black literary tradition, but now it becomes more explicitly rhetorical and concerned with its reception. Signifying for Reed is a way of relating two or more very different cultures, and of carving out a place for African-American writing in the simplifying and open hostile arena of its reception.

WORKS CITED

Abrahams, Roger D. *Deep Down in the Jungle....: Negro Narrative Folklore from the Streets of Philadelphia.* Chicago: Aldine, 1970.
Du Bois, W. E. Burghardt. *The Souls of Black Folk: Essays and Sketches.* Chicago: A. C. McClurg, 1903.

Emerson, Ralph Waldo. "Nature." *Selections from Ralph Waldo Emerson: An Organic Anthology.* Ed. Stephen E. Whicher. Boston: Houghton Mifflin. 1957. 21-56.

Fox, Robert Elliot. *Conscientious Sorcerers: The Black Postmodernist Fiction of LeRoi Jones, Amiri Baraka, Ishmael Reed, and Samuel R. Delany.* New York: Greenwood, 1987.

Gates, Henry Louis, Jr. "The 'Blackness of Blackness': A Critique of the Sign and the Signifying Monkey." *Critical Inquiry* 9 (1983): 685-723.

Reed, Ishmael, ed. *19 Necromancers from Now.* Garden City, NY: Doubleday,1970.

---."Ishmael Reed--Self Interview." *Shrovetide in Old New Orleans.* Garden City, NY: Doubleday, 1978. 129-44.

---. *Mumbo Jumbo.* Garden City, NY: Doubleday, 1972.

---. "Neo-HooDoo." *Los Angeles Free Press* 18 Sept. 1970: 42.

---. *Reckless Eyeballing.* New York: St. Martin's, 1986.

---. *Yellow Back Radio Broke-Down.* Garden City, NY: Doubleday, 1969.

Stepto, Robert B. "Distrust of the Reader in Afro-American Narratives." *Reconstructing American Literary History.* Ed. Sacvan Bercovetch. Cambridge, MA: Harvard, 1986. 300-22.

Watkins, Mel. "An Interview with Ishmael Reed." *The Southern Review* 21 (1985): 603-14.

College English 54.4 (April 1992): 446-461. "Copyright 1992 by the National Council of Teachers of English. Reprinted with permission."

Female Troubles: Ishmael Reed's Tunnel Vision

Michele Wallace/Article

Ishmael Reed appeared on *Tony Brown's Journal* last summer to discuss the question of "whether black feminist writers are victimizing black men." The provocation was twofold: controversy over the movie of *The Color Purple*, based on Alice Walker's book, and the publication of Reed's novel *Reckless Eyeballing*, which explores the notion that black women writers are hapless pawns of manipulative white feminists. Although the television format implied that Reed was debating the possibility of black female disloyalty with the other guest on the show, literary critic Barbara Smith, they seemed to be articulating mutually exclusive perspectives from parallel worlds.

Smith edited a black feminist studies anthology called *All the Women Are White, All the Blacks Are Men, but Some of Us Are Brave.* Reed, seemingly unaware of the implications, paraphrased the title as "All the women are good and all the men are bad." In his world, such a substitution is as inevitable as the law of gravity, although Neo-Hoodoo, as it occurs in Reed's poetry, fiction, and essays, rejects the stifling duality and reification of Western rationalism in order to question the automatic devaluation of the black male, as well as other nonwhite males. But it does not confront the preeminent social instance of binary opposition: gender roles.

Last winter Ishmael Reed calmly explained to me that there was a media-wide conspiracy to blame black men for male chauvinism; mainstream feminists, consolidating a reconciliation with white men, needed a scapegoat--black men were it. (He might have added that he was doing everything in his power to assist this process.) Reed continued his obsessive ruminations on the Tony Brown show. A black male in the audience asked, "Isn't feminism about that spoiled white woman in Scarsdale?" Contending with a shouting Reed, Smith answered: "What *black* feminism is about is that black woman trying to raise her children on welfare in Harlem. It's about our sisters who are in the SROs right now surrounded by rats and drugs...."

To which Reed never responded. Instead, he cited FBI statistics for July 1985, which he said attributed 80 per cent of sex offenses to white males (in fact, according to the FBI, the annual figure for white males is 52 per cent). "Black men have been chosen to take all of this heat...we're not the only men who are male chauvinists," Reed insisted. "Why don't they make movies about that?" Of course, they do make movies about that. From priest to rapist, in *The Godfather* to *The Deerhunter* to *Blue Velvet*, the white male is symbolic everyman of first and last choice. So what is Reed really beefing about?

The problem appears to be that Reed doesn't relish the idea of black women making public judgments about black men, although black men in the know, from the ubiquitous Dr. Poussaint (psych consultant for the Cosby show) to Reed himself, insist on their right to define and describe black women. Reed's inflexibility undoubtedly has something to do with the "double oppression" of black women; their double disqualification for the exercise of power makes it all the more likely that black women intellectuals will be hypercritical of black men (and white women as well, but nobody seems much interested in this).

Reed fears that the double negative of being black and being a woman in this society adds up to a positive advantage. In the grotesque world of mass media, sometimes the double negatives appear to turn positive. Consider the proliferation of black women fashion models, news broadcasters, opera singers, and rock stars. Still, Janet Jackson's energetic performance in "Control" should be read as a cautionary tale: in our culture, control doesn't proclaim itself. Here, the sign of the black woman draws upon its own peculiar malleability: it is doubly divested of meaning, and therefore particularly well suited to enigma without content.

In the "real" world of pressing economic, political, and social consequences, the double negatives don't cancel each other out. They line up, one behind the other, like a combination punch, or the way black women line up in downtown streets all across the country to sell or display their bodies--extending interminably into the nether world of what Ralph Ellison once called "invisibility."

When Alice Walker described herself as a "womanist" in a 1984 essay, I wondered about her obsessive need to dissociate herself from white feminists. But the feminist-baiting of Reed and his cohorts makes me think Walker had the right idea after all. Black feminists are preoccupied with basic issues of survival. Their writing tends to stress the precise occasion of application, leaving the theorizing to somebody else--not because their engagement with feminist thought is less intense, but because black feminism is firmly grounded in a "real life" preoccupation with a black female population that is disproportionately poor and voiceless.

The problem with feminist theory, in general, is its failure to be concerned with palpable alternatives to conventional living arrangements because of its fondness for generalizations that will encompass us all. The problem with black feminists is the tight space they are forced to occupy as the "Other" of both black men and white women, who are "Other" themselves. This means that alternative models are essential to black women writers; expressive acts are unthinkable without them. Walker makes these points when she compares Virginia Woolf to slave poet Phillis Wheatley, who lacked not only a room, but a *life* of her own.

Being the "Other" of the "Others"--and thus twice removed from power-- also means that black women writers have to be careful not to offend. As they focus more and more on the patriarchy's decline, they become simultaneously frightening and provocative. On one hand, people don't want to change; on the other hand, they know they have to.

Once upon a time, the black male was preeminent "Other." He seemed to epitomize free expression, profligate sexuality, organic society--all the opportunities lost under modern industrial capitalism. In Norman Mailer's "The White Negro," for example, the white male becomes "hip" in an attempt to appropriate the liberating essence of black maleness. Increasingly--with a leg up from Black Power and Civil Rights--black male writers have found ways to render their position an articulate and critical presence. Before the work of Ishmael Reed, there was work by Richard Wright, Ralph Ellison, James Baldwin, John A. Williams, John Edgar Wideman, and Amiri Baraka in which the "Other" spoke protest, and everybody seemed satisfied for a time.

Yet his preeminence as "Other" was not secure. Just one of these writers, Ralph Ellison, achieved validation by the American literary establishment (and not only hasn't he written a second novel, but he's unpopular with blacks for his political conservatism). Lately, it seems more insecure than usual. Reed was next up for inclusion in the canon in the '70s, but his career seems to be in decline--precipitated, in no small part, by his perversely misogynistic views. Despite his popularity among black male critics, his novels receive less and less media attention, and all of his books except *Reckless Eyeballing* are now out of print, which doesn't bode well for canon inclusion.

Predictably, Reed sees himself as being in direct competition with white women. Part of his attack on black feminists is to claim that white feminists do their thinking for them ("Gloria Steinem has become some modern-day daughter of Dracula, claiming victim after victim, to carry out her orders," Reed says). Among the many advantages of white male privilege is the occasional luxury of role reversal--think of the mock drag of white male rock stars. As a black male writer, Reed is saddled with a more limited vision. When the black woman, the "Other" of the "Other," insists on having a voice, his status quo is profoundly disrupted. For the upwardly mobile black male intellectual, role reversal is neither tenable nor entertaining.

If the articulate black male deals with the way white males have divided up the world in which communication between us occurs--and he has to deal with it to get ahead materially and/or intellectually--then he is bound to be highly skeptical of attempts to scale down male privilege, because it means that when he does finally "get over," there's going to be less to get. I'm not saying that black men sit down and reason these things out. In fact, the black men who do think about them tend to come to different conclusions. With Reed, we're considering a kind of knee-jerk nonperceptiveness in which he mindlessly competes with white women for the number two spot, and will brook no interference from black women or anybody else. Even if it's to tell him the game has changed.

In Reed's work, characters and centuries come and go like color combinations in a kaleidoscope. Critics praise his narrative speed and abruptness. It's like watching Fellini, they say. It's like bebop. The man has his fingers on the pulse of the times.

Unencumbered by the uptight strategies of mimesis, this "cowboy in the boat of Ra" improvises plots that are perversely eventful parodies of the stodgy predictabilities of the bildungsroman (*Free-Lance Pallbearers,* 1967), the Western (*Yellowback Radio Broke-Down,* 1969), the detective story (*Mumbo Jumbo,* 1972), Greek tragedy (*The Last Days of Louisiana Red,* 1974), the slave narrative (*Flight to Canada,* 1976), the Gothic mystery (*The Terrible Twos,* 1982), and the epic (*Reckless Eyeballing,* 1986). And yet Reed never quite parodies the most important foregone conclusion of the originals.

These genres have in common their validation of the white male center. Reed attempts to displace only the color of the center (like trying to peel the white off snow!), leaving intact, even confirming, the notion of centers and therefore peripheries. Parasitic relations are inherently unstable; if the same observation can be made about relations of domination in texts, then it may explain the frantic energy Reed brings to an increasingly elaborate mythology about the black female.

Reckless Eyeballing (St. Martin's, $12.95) is the most extreme literary enactment so far of Reed's female trouble. The novel is talky, bitter, complicated, accusatory--the opposite of a charming text. It opens with protagonist Ian Ball's dream that he is being tried as a witch in Salem. His judges, the Puritan fathers, bear the face of Tremonisha Smarts, a black feminist whose successful play *Wrong-Headed Man* transparently echoes *The Color Purple*, and Becky French, a prominent and manipulative white New York feminist. Ball's nightmare ends in metaphorical castration--"A snakeskinned hand was about to cut off a rattler's head with a large, gleaming blade"--after he realizes that the guard who will lead him to the gallows is his mother.

Here the Neo-Hoodooist falls back on a reassuring Neo-Freudian geometry. The castrated female is so much an inevitability of this narrative that a man must occupy that space if a woman won't. The Salem witches condemned to death were almost all women. Ian Ball, therefore, is cast in a female or "feminine" role. The presence of the mother as executioner evokes "the suffocation of the mother"--a popular name in the 17th century for the choking sensation considered a common symptom of "feminine" hysteria, a symptom used to confirm the diagnosis of witchcraft. This painfully inarticulate text is a recurrence of that symptom. The snake in the dream, it is worthwhile to remember, seems to be chopping off his own head.

Ian Ball, clearly a stand-in for Reed, doesn't know his ass from his elbow when it comes to American feminism--which, I suppose, makes him yet another Afro-American trickster figure, like PaPa LaBas in *Mumbo Jumbo* and *The Last Days of Louisiana Red*, like Raven Quickskill in *Flight to Canada*, like Black Peter in *Terrible Twos*. In Afro-American folklore, tricksters are characters steeped in motherwit who turn the shortcomings of powerlessness to advantage. Reed has grafted on this agenda the conflicting demands of an edenic triangle that owes most of its inspiration to patriarchy. Consequently, his tricksters have been undergoing a fierce process of degeneration and an identity crisis that won't wait.

Ball--his arteries sluggish with gin and McDonald's burgers--is plagued by the burden of a strong mother with second sight, whom he suspects of watching his every move. The only candidate for an influential father figure, Jake Brashford, is famous for a single play, *The Man Who Was an Enigma*. Though unable to write another play, Brashford keeps on receiving prizes, chairs, and grants.

Ball's first play puts him high on the "theater feminists sex list" because its protagonist wants to be gang-raped; he attempts to clear his name with black feminists by writing another play called *Reckless Eyeballing*, which gives all the best roles to black female actors. In it, a white woman named Cora Mae has caused the lynching of a black Southern youth named Ham Hill. Twenty years later, Cora Mae, who has become a radical lesbian feminist (Reed's code for Totally Unreasonable Person), gets a court order to have Hill's body exhumed and tried for "reckless eyeballing," which her white female attorney calls "eye rape."

At the heart of *Reckless Eyeballing*--coddled within concentric subplots about Nazism, anti-Semitism, rape, lynching--lies Reed's perception that American feminism says white women are not responsible for bigotry and racism.

From the last quarter of the 19th century until the middle of the 20th, white Americans, mostly men, justified their lynching of black Americans, mostly men, by claiming that they were protecting white women from rape. Another early explanation of the lynchings was that white women were the cause of it all because of a deeply rooted psychological tendency to desire rape, which they communicated to their rope-toting men as an actuality. Reed, who cites Wilhelm Reich's *The Mass Psychology of Fascism* elsewhere and therefore ought to know better, is stuck at this stage of the dialogue.

He's not alone; the castrating woman (which is her tendency when she's not being castrated) has become a centerpiece in avant-garde Afro-American literature's attempt to personify the broken promises of America--from the red, white, and blue whore of Ellison's "Battle Royal" to the bitch goddess of Amiri Baraka's *Dutchman*.

In the "real" world, the black male has obviously had a hard time politically and economically, but he repeatedly portrayed his difficulty as a ritual of castration. His humiliation in a phallocentric culture is his feminization. It was thus that the rape of the white woman became a key trope in the rhetorical strategy of compensation--which was part of what Reed was objecting to, presumably, in his caricature of Black Power in *The Last Days of Louisiana Red*. In his 1981 essay "Black Macho, White Macho: The Stale Drama" (you said it!), Reed observes, "While black male macho might be annoying, white male macho could be the death of us." I thought he saw the connections as well.

Reed's determination to see feminism as a historical error reduces his black feminist characters to hand puppets mouthing his inane views. In *Reckless Eyeballing,* Tremonisha Smarts's opinions about Josephine Baker are particularly revealing (Baker, a potent symbol for Reed, is also on the cover of *Mumbo Jumbo*, in double images to evoke the two sides of the Haitian Voudoun goddess Erzulie). Here Smarts explains to Ball why Hitler slept with a picture of Baker over his bed the night of his Austrian campaign:

> *"He was getting even with his mother...He had her picture on the wall of his bedroom, but the night that he's away from his room, sort of a shrine to his mother, he fantasizes about sleeping with the demon princess, the wild temptress Lilith, Erzulie, the flapper who brought jazz dance to the Folies....Jesus Christ had the same experience with a prostitute on the road, away from his prying mother whom* [sic] *some say was the prostitute A Lilith or Erzulie of her time. He had the same*

problem. Jesus, Hitler, both had weak fathers and strong, manipulative mothers."

How are we supposed to distinguish this "suffocation of the mother" from garden variety Puritanism, which Reed once counted chief among sins?

Neo-Hoodoo harbors an intrinsic shortcoming. Borrowed in part from Zora Neale Hurston's anthropological investigations in the '30s, arguably literary in its intentions, Neo-Hoodoo is Reed's version of a syncretic creed based on New World adaptations of African religions. Manifestations of Neo-Hoodoo includes the blues, bebop and the lindy, North American Hoodoo, Haitian Voudoun, and Mardi Gras--mostly occasions of dance, music, and religion in the New World.

The point is that Western rationalism and capitalistic uptightness don't really bear imitation. Neither Afro-Americans nor other ethnic Americans (or any thinking WASP for that matter) should be forced to live in these square holes. On the other hand, it doesn't make sense to look back nostalgically on an African/ethnic, primitive/rural past of greater simplicity and purer motives. Instead, Reed's Neo-Hoodoo suggests that the focus of speculation should be the improvisational nature of the diaspora--or, in other words, how it works when it works.

The fly in the buttermilk here, however, is Neo-Hoodoo's basis in religion, which has been laying its eggs of phallocentrism wherever it goes at least since Egyptians had a choice between the worship of Osiris and Isis. Feminist anthropologists warn us that even the worship of female gods was a reflection of the rising social need to set women apart as unfathomable, threatening, and "Other."

The potential appeal of Neo-Hoodoo is that it offers the possibility of intellectual alternatives for nonwhites committed to aggressive adaptation rather than passive assimilation or blending in. The religious syncreticism of New World non-white populations, Reed intends, will serve as a guide to completing the process of East meets West which was aborted by racism--not by innocuous paste, but by making it into Gumbo.

Or has Neo-Hoodoo already entered another stage? The myopic philosophy Reed is currently bandying about is structurally unable to acknowledge the rise of sexism as an essential chapter in the story of all religious development in the West, in Africa, in the New World. Precisely because of Reed's inflexibility in these matters, the demoralization of the patriarchy seems an inevitable consequence in his world.

In *Mumbo Jumbo* and *The Last Days of Louisiana Red*, PaPa LaBas (also the name of the loa of U.S. Hoodoo) seems surefooted and persuasive as representative of the transcendent powers of Neo-Hoodoo--part Old World patriarch, part New World hougan. In *Mumbo Jumbo*, there's only a minor problem with one of Labas's devotees being possessed by Erzulie. Hurston mentions Erzulie as having two incarnations in Voodoo--one as a love goddess, one as the "terrible Erzulie" of Sect Rouge. Reed has become obsessed with the latter.

In *The Last Days of Louisiana Red*, an Erzulie-possessed Minnie, queen of the counterproductive Moochers, occupies the focal point of the text. Minnie the Moocher, after the Cab Calloway original, parodies Angela Davis's involvement in the Black Power Movement; she's a whiny, self-indulgent Afro-American version of Antigone. She was ruined by an ersatz Aunt Jemima called "Nanny," who made her flapjacks, sang blues "depicting negro men as brutish wayfaring louts," and told her "Louisiana Red" stories in which black women outsmart black men. *Louisiana Red* and *Reckless Eyeballing* are the only Reed novels with women as a primary subject. Yet there is a definite tendency in all his books, beginning with *The Free-Lance Pallbearers*, to blame women characters for every evil that comes into the world.

With each book, Reed's tricksters become more schizophrenic, comfortable in the role of neither father nor son. In *Flight to Canada*, the able leadership of PaPa Labas is nowhere in evidence. Instead, there's Uncle Robin--Uncle Tom reconceived as a crafty, literate old slave who rewrites his Master's will--and Raven Quickskill, whose subversive trickery goes no further than a poem that announces his escape and that prompts his Master to continue trying to recapture him even after the Emancipation. A woman, as usual, is on the wrong side; Mammy Barracuda, who as a kind of Sapphire/Lilith demonstrates a perverse loyalty to the slave master by bogarting the proto-feminist plantation mistress into wifely submission. In the underrated *Terrible Twos*, Black Peter is a more quixotic figure still--perhaps the secret ingredient behind the subversive mythology of St. Nicholas, that suspiciously Dionysian rival to Christ. We are left in the not-so-capable hands of Nance Saturday--no relation to Black Peter, and never more than one clue ahead of the reader.

Reed's tricksters seem to flip-flop back and forth like fish out of water reflecting increasing ambivalence about their relation to power. In the process, women become the only reliable scapegoat, and this obtuseness radically undermines the strategic basis of his whole oeuvre, which denounces reductivism and yet embraces it. In *Reckless Eyeballing*, male authority degenerates into unreconstituted hysteria. Jake Brashford explodes in a drunken rage of denunciation upon seeing Ball's new play, in which the skeleton of Ham Hill occupies the only male role: "I'm your literary father, you shit," he screams at Ball, whereupon he launches into a raucous rendition of Hambone--perhaps to shame Ball into memory of a time when black men didn't publish--slapping his thighs, singing grotesquely in dialect, until he is ejected by black male security guards.

What has become of the noble trickster? Mother Nature has overwhelmed him. In *Reckless*, black feminists are manipulated by white feminists. White feminists are slaves to the racism of white men. And white men are hamstrung by their ambivalent attachment to the Great Mother. Is Reed proposing a game of the dozens as the final solution to the Woman's Question? Is he terror-struck by his relative proximity as a black male to the castration complex of femaleness? Is he smarting over black feminist appropriation of the life and work of Zora Neal Hurston? Or is he sleepwalking? If any or all of these are the case, I suggest that a brief hibernation might not be totally unwarranted.

The Village Voice Literary Supplement 51 (Dec. 1986): 9, 11.

THE TERRIBLE THREES (1989)

The Terrible Threes

Peter Nazareth/Review

Ishmael Reed's eighth novel, *The Terrible Threes*, is a sequel to the *The Terrible Twos* and indications are that there will be yet a third volume, perhaps *The Terrible Fours*. Thus we find an incompleteness to *Threes* that one would expect of sequels. I laugh less at Reed's new novels than I do at such earlier ones as *Flight to Canada*, but he is as inventive as ever and continues signifying on everything and everyone, including other novels, other art forms, critics, et cetera. *Twos* signified on Dicken's *Christmas Carol*. The new novel carries the process further. Nance Saturday, a detective in both works, thinks, "But now he felt like Scrooge must have felt after his long night of the soul, a character in the novel by the English novelist whose last name, Dickens, was a variation of the name Nicholas."

It is impossible to sum up a Reed novel, because several things are happening at once. However, it is clear what is important to Reed: 1) the action is quick and simultaneous; 2) he is not interested in building up character but rather in giving us people, and creatures, by quick reference to prominent features, literary figures, or movie actors; 3) he tests the truth of everything and everyone by putting all into the text and letting the fiction judge, as with Lawrence's enjoinder to trust the tale and never the teller; 4) he believes in conspiracies, as well he should, since he knows his history and he reads; 5) people and society are haunted by the past and by past crimes; 6) most important of all, he seeks to save the people, to let them find redemption from their crimes against humanity. Though people are cursed by their own actions, Reed shows them what is haunting them--not to curse but to save. This explains why he would be drawn to Santa Claus and his black helper (some say master), Black Peter: both figures get a lot of play in *Twos* and *Threes*, though Black Peter has more of a say (there also being an imposter black Peter) in new work.

Many of the characters in *Threes* remind us of people from real life whom we read about in the papers. In some cases they have the same names, in others *Mad Magazine* variations of those names. Among the individuals Reed seeks to save: the Japanese woman critic who longs to be white, the famous black musician who was once a great trumpeter but has been squandering his talent making money to support a drug habit, the famous young singer who spends millions looking for pygmy dinosaurs, the anti-feminist alcoholic woman Supreme Court justice, and the non-Italian pope reading Chuck Berry's autobiography.

Some critics have been dumping on Reed, presenting him as a bad-tempered, small-minded, paranoid, unbalanced writer. That is a misreading. Even Reed's least powerful works are worth reading; one can learn something from them. It was on my third reading of *Threes* that I found the novel does work and is not a failure. Reed is not small-minded; the text always understands and tries to save, even those characters whom Reed himself attacks outside the text. He seeks to liberate us through opening up our imagination, letting us read in a way that is not linear.

World Literature Today 64.2 Spring, 1990: 310-311.

Still Subverting the Culture

Gerald Early/Review

In the introduction to his 1978 book of essays, *Shrovetide in Old New Orleans*, Ishmael Reed writes, "Maybe I should become a 'stand-up' comedian as some critics suggest." Although he goes on to blast those critics, there is a certain validity to the suggestion: perhaps we might better understand what Mr. Reed has been up to all these years if we concede that he has been a stand-up comic all along.

Like all great American comic spirits, from Louis Armstrong to Curly Howard of the Three Stooges, from Richard Pryor to Zora Neale Hurston, Mr. Reed relentlessly deciphers his culture, subverts it really. Comics do this partly to puncture the culture's pretensions and to reveal its dishonesty, but more because great comedians cannot help thinking of the world they live in as a palimpsest, a series of submerged texts and acts that must be made intelligible. In all the disorder that the comedian seemingly creates it is actually his cry against unintelligibility that is the center of his art. In his humane quest for intelligibility, the comedian condemns unintelligibility as inhuman. And the most unintelligible thing of all is a popular acceptance of a brutal and menacing world as inevitable.

The Terrible Threes, Mr. Reed's eighth novel, seems a work that he could not avoid writing. He had appraised and mediated, exploded and exposed tensions in American culture so brilliantly in some of his earlier novels by exploiting marginal pop-culture literary forms. His "western," *Yellow Back Radio Broke-Down* (1969), subverts the dime novel, the cowboy movie and both the Frederick Jackson Turner and Henry Nash Smith theories of the American West. *Mumbo Jumbo* (1972), which Mr. Reed says "has come to be regarded as a manifesto," is the best of his "detective" fiction--recapitulating and emulating Zora-Neale Hurston the anthropologist-cum-novelist, parodying the myth of America's cross-cultural origins (by combining the story of Moses with Rob Syrian) as well as the Chester Himes black tough guy as American soothsayer. ("[Himes] taught me the essential difference between a black detective and Sherlock Holmes," Mr. Reed once wrote.) *Flight to Canada* (1976) examines the relationship of the white editor to the black writer through the story (which, admittedly, Mr. Reed does not tell accurately) of Harriet Beecher Stowe and the slave narrator Josiah Henson while examining the very creative foundation of African-American letters in this country: the autobiography.

But after having deconstructed American culture, Mr. Reed, in his latest book, turns to mediating while simultaneously exposing the tensions of his own conception of a novel. The major problem with *The Terrible Threes* is that it seems to vaporize even as you read it; the very telling artifices that held together Mr.Reed's novelistic art in previous works, the cunning combination of boundless energy and shrewdly husbanded ingenuity, are missing here. The essences of the Reed narrative making, the pulling together of discrete, seemingly unconnected shreds of culture into complex secret conspiracies and patterns of knowledge, become the elements of his undoing here. The power of Mr. Reed's previous novels is that, like Raymond Chandler's or William Faulkner's at their best, the work only *seems* to make no sense. Mr. Reed in his latest novel finally reached the impasse of actually writing a novel that truly does not make sense.

Frankly, *The Terrible Threes* will be incomprehensible to anyone who has not read *The Terrible Twos* (1982), Mr. Reed's previous novel which was a deconstruction of two major American holidays, Thanksgiving and Christmas, using a small portion of Saint Nicholas myth (concerning Nickolas's relationship with Black Peter, who does not figure in all versions of the myth) while combining a mock Erik Erikson critique of the first Reagan term (America is analyzed as if it were a two-year-old child). Virtually all the characters of *The Terrible Twos* are back, although precisely what they are doing is unclear. The summaries of events of *The Terrible Twos* are provided in *The Terrible Threes*, but they would not help someone who has not read the earlier work. It might even be helpful to read Mr. Reed's 1986 novel, *Reckless Eyeballing,* a bitingly satirical critique of bourgeois feminism that comes close to being a *roman à clef* (many of Mr.Reed's novels seem close to that). Mr. Reed continues his criticism of bourgeois feminism in *The Terrible Threes,* although it seems unconnected to the novel's major theme.

And that is precisely what is intriguing about this book: it has no real point or theme. It rambles as episodically as a drunken man's speech. It seems to be nothing more than a series of addenda about such things as toleration, epiphany, self-acceptance and all manner of pop-culture throwaways from television evangelists to a send-up of such movies as *Conan, The Terminator, The Brother From Another Planet* and the like. In some sense the disconnected and dislocating feel of *The Terrible Threes* may very well be its points. After having written novel after satiric novel, many of which were outstanding, telling the reader of the interlocking grids of culture, of the narrative of culture as a quest for its hidden intelligibility, in his newest work Mr. Reed demonstrates at last that culture lacks cohesion, that his own compelling synecdoches never signify a whole. The novel becomes a strikingly got-up parody of a collection of Op-Ed pieces.

I like *The Terrible Threes*, but it seems more a work for Reed fans among whom I count myself. Newcomers to Mr. Reed should read *The Last Days of Louisiana Red* (1974), *Mumbo Jumbo, Yellow Back Radio* or *The Terrible Twos*. Or they may listen to the record album *Conjure,* which has a number of jazz and pop artists supplying musical settings to some of Mr. Reed's texts. Shades of Charles Mingus and Langston Hughes, of Run-DMC and the Last Poets, Mr. Reed mediates another art-form. At this point in his career, perhaps to stretch his imagination, Mr. Reed might take the opportunity to write for film; it is exciting to imagine him scripting a John Sayles or Spike Lee project. Or he might consider a book-length nonfiction project. A biography of the amateur-ethnologist J.A. Rogers or the New Orleans jazzman King Oliver would be right up his alley.

1990s

JAPANESE BY SPRING (1993)

Japanese by Spring

Peter Nazareth/Review

With his ninth novel, Ishmael Reed proves again that he is not afraid to plunge into the maelstrom. *Japanese by Spring* is full of contemporary issues plaguing the American consciousness: Rodney King, Anita Hill/Clarence Thomas, the U.S. attack on Iraq, and so on. As he moves through his fifties, has Reed lost his fictional abilities? No. For Reed, the novel is supreme. If you want to understand anything, put it into a novel and let the novel decide. And so Reed himself is also a character in the work: "He sometimes went around with a tacky beard in order to appear to be a man of the people. He sometimes wore clothes so long that they became ragged and his family would have to go to Macy's to buy him new clothes."

The protagonist is Benjamin Puttbutt, a black junior professor at white Jack London College. He is being nice to the English and Women's Studies departments and attacks black men for not shaping up--one of his heroes being Thomas Sowell--because he wants to get tenure. He even turns a blind eye to the outrageous racist actions against him by a student, Robert Bass, whose father is a rich contributor to the college. A radical in the sixties, he will do anything that goes over: "Now that the writer was considered as obsolete as a 1960s computer, he could share in some of the profits of the growth industry of the eighties and nineties. Criticism. All you had to do was string together some quotes from Benjamin, Barthes, Foucault, and Lacan and you were in business. Even a New Critic like himself could make some cash." However, he is double-crossed and denied tenure.

Puttbutt has been studying Japanese because he sees it as the wave of the future. Suddenly, the college is bought by a Japanese group, and his Japanese teacher becomes acting president and makes him his right-hand man. While the Japanese do to the Eurocentrics what the latter have done to others, Puttbutt makes Crabtree, an English professor, teach freshman Yoruba. Crabtree changes. "I have learned a language that transports me to a culture that's two thousand years old," he says. "Have they ever produced a Tolstoy? They have produced Tolstoys. Have they produced a Homer? They have hundreds of Homers. We were just too lazy and arrogant to find out."

The novel presents true multiculturalists versus hostile right-wing groups and "cause pimps" and opportunists. Reed and his group, Glossos United, have been fighting for multiculturalism for twenty years. "Fighting" is right: Reed enters the novel at the same time as an anti-Glossos point man from India named D'Gun ga Dinza, clearly based on Dinesh D'Souza, whom Reed identified as Destar D'Nooza, Santa's elf, in *The Terrible Threes* (see WLT 64:2, p. 310) and whom he pins down again for his illiberal education; naming is very important in the Yoruba American tradition.

Why is Reed studying Yoruba? "Perhaps it was Peter Nazareth's catching Ishmael Reed red-handed anglicizing Yoruba (Yoruban)" (see WLT63:3, p. 483). Like his detectives PaPa LaBas and Nance Saturday, he is out to make a psychic arrest. Reed is giving English a transfusion from Japanese and Yoruba. The struggle to learn each language, the successful use of expressions from each language, and concepts and ideas expressed through each language become part of the novel: the novel itself becomes multicultural. Reed believes racism is learned, so it can be unlearned. Bass is punished by his father (who wants access to the Japanese market) by having to act as Puttbutt's servant: the experience of getting to know a black American changes Bass.

Puttbutt is another I. Ball, the protagonist of Reed's *Reckless Eyeballing*, a sexist (see WLT 60:4, p. 631). Puttbutt's sexism leads to the murder of his Japanese lover by her husband. Lest we say he is Reed, as readers did with I. Ball, Reed enters the text and reads his game: "All about binary this and that. Liberal quotes from Walter Benjamin, Lacan, Foucault, Barthes (but his reviews fell back on Freud and Tate)." Puttbutt had read Reed earlier: if he had taken him seriously, he would have found his moral center. While Puttbutt dishes out his textbook, *Japanese by Spring*, Reed is springing his larger version.

Jack Only, an updated version of Swille the multinational in *Flight to Canada*, comes to see Reed for help, because, thanks to financing people who are single-visioned, mono-cultural, anti-Semitic, and racist, he has been losing business: Reed gives him a lesson on multiculturalism. Once again Reed is helping to save Western Civilization.

Japanese by Spring is full of plots and counterplots. It pulls together all of Reed's previous work and prepares us for more to come. It is his funniest novel since *Flight to Canada.* With Reed, humor is life-affirming.

World Literature Today 67/3 Summer (1993): 610.

Clever Satire, Inspired Nonsense

Merle Rubin/Review

Fans of Ishmael Reed's pungent, fast-paced prose have understandably (if predictably) likened it to jazz. His writing has a spontaneous, improvisational feel: It's full of quick turns, surprises, and inventive digressions, mixing the arcane and the down-to-earth in the unforced style of a man who can think on his feet.

His new novel, *Japanese by Spring* offers a guided tour of the groves--more aptly, the jungles--of contemporary academe, seen through the eyes of one hapless black junior professor struggling to achieve tenure.

Benjamin "Chappie" Puttbutt III is the first in a long line of Puttbutts stretching back to the American Revolution not to have followed the family tradition of volunteering for military service.

Benjamin's choice of a career in the humanities has been a severe disappointment to his father, who is a two-star Air Force general, and his mother, a dashing intelligence officer. They have told him time and time again that the United States military provides the best prospects for African-Americans in search of a genuinely integrated, equal-opportunity career.

Harry Truman, who ordered the military to integrate, is one of their heroes, along with the Puritan poet and polemicist John Milton (they like his emphasis on training and discipline). "That's not the only attitude they shared with Milton," we're informed, as the narrative slides deftly from clever satire into inspired nonsense: "With their continuous need for enemies, their motto could have been taken from Milton's panegyric for Cromwell: 'New Foes Arise.' Their favorite blues singer was 'Little Milton.' Their favorite comedian was Milton Berle."

Their peace-loving son is finding the academic terrain quite as arduous, despite his seeming flair for self-advancement:

> "When the Black Power thing was in, Puttbutt was into that. When the backlash on Black Power settled in, with its code words like reverse discrimination, he joined that. He'd been a feminist when they were in power. But now they were on the decline...and so for now he was a neo-conservative...."

As the story opens, this unabashed but appealingly unruthless opportunist is studying Japanese with a tutor who promises results "by spring," by which time the ever-enterprising Puttbutt hopes to speak the language well enough "to take advantage of new global realities."

Teaching at predominantly white Jack London College in Oakland, Calif. (named for the racist, socialist author of *The Call of the Wild)*, however, is a lot like picking one's way through a minefield. The feminists want to eliminate his modest $30,000 a year position to beef up their budget for enticing a chic, overpaid feminist poet from back East. The African-American Studies department is divided by rivalries between Africans and African-Americans, and between proponents of Swahili and champions of Yoruba.

The entire campus is plagued by a bunch of neo-Nazi students who continually harass and torment Puttbutt, even though he continues to defend their right to free speech and excuse their racism as an understandable response to the excessive "demands of black students."

While the aging white radical dean and many of his black colleagues consider him a sellout, the conservative old guard of the English department--Miltonists and the like--also close ranks against him.

Puttbutt is worried that he soon may be reduced to the same impoverished income level "as the black writers he wrote his lectures about."

Things take an unexpected turn for the better when a mysterious consortium of Japanese interests takes over the college. Dr.Yamato, Puttbutt's humble-seeming Japanese tutor, is installed as college president. Puttbutt, his right-hand man, is now able to repay his old enemies.

Puttbutt even accomplishes some good from his new position, sending his old nemesis, the Miltonist Crabtree, off to study Yoruba. (Worn out by years of chewing over the same old subject, Crabtree is rejuvenated by learning something new!)

In due course, however, Puttbutt discovers that this particular Japanese invasion is not a benign case of multicultural cross-fertilization, but rather is part of a plot to restore an ancient tradition of Japanese militarism. Before long, it's hard for anyone to know what to believe.

Confusing? Yes, and in more ways than one. Some of the confusion deliberately mimics the sheer lure to which academic politics can sink. ("Why is it that crazed serial murderers are usually white men?" demands a black professor. "Last I heard, Idi Amin wasn't a white man," replies his white colleague. "Oh, yeah." "Yeah." "Oh yeah." "Yeah.")

But a rather different kind of confusion ensues from the fact that Puttbutt is both the novel's hero and an object of its satire. Perhaps to alleviate this confusion, the author introduces a character called Ishmael Reed and keeps interrupting the story to let the reader know exactly where this gentleman stands on the many issues raised in the course of the book.

Summarized briefly, the targets of Reed's satire include out-and-out racists, xenophobes, Japan bashers, and neo-conservative defenders of Western Civilization courses, as well as tenured radicals, feminists, and other groups trying, as it were, to steal the thunder of the black civil rights movement by claiming to be equally, if not more, victimized. Nationalism in any form is identified as the chief foe, and cultural diversity the internationalist antidote to any one culture's attempt to dominate others.

All of which raises some questions: Is everyone who favors teaching Western Civilization merely, as this novel seems to suggest, a racist in disguise? Is "cultural diversity" a panacea for nationalism or a potential hothouse for new outgrowths of ethnic chauvinism?

And, while it's easy to make fun of well-heeled feminists claiming to be as victimized as blacks trapped by systemic discrimination and poverty, Reed's seeming inability to comprehend the pervasive oppression of women in almost every culture is a blind spot that undermines the force of an otherwise shrewd, funny, and instructive satire.

Christian Science Monitor (9 March 1993): 14.

The Improvisations of an "Ethnic Gate Crasher"

Joye Mercer/Interview

Interviewing the writer Ishmael Reed and reading his novels is a lot like listening to a jazz set: You never know when he'll go off on a tangential riff or strike a divergent chord.

Mr. Reed, a lecturer in the English department at the University of California at Berkeley, knows this about himself. And he likes the comparison.

"I free-associate like musicians do. And my language is very rhythmic," says Mr. Reed. who has published nearly 20 books of fiction, poetry, plays and essays. His latest novel, *Japanese by Spring,* was released this month.

"I know the structure and the technique, but I'm always improvising."

Mr. Reed, one of the country's most controversial writers on race relations, is a frequent social commentator in newspapers and magazines. Sometimes the notes he hits can be jarring.

He has parried with feminists in a variety of publications. He has lashed out at black woman novelists whose books do little more, he says, than vilify black men.

He has challenged those who jumped to support the University of Oklahoma law professor Anita Hill against then-Supreme Court nominee Clarence Thomas. Critics of Justice Thomas, Mr. Reed contends, were too eager to perpetuate the worst beliefs about black men, and to use a black woman to do their bidding.

In addition, Mr. Reed, who also has taught at Harvard and Yale University, Dartmouth College and the University of Washington, regularly criticizes the media as the main conduit of racial stereotypes in this country.

He sometimes goes to grotesque and bizarre lengths, particularly in his fiction, to make a point. Plots take the kind of turns that make the reader wonder: Where did *that* come from?

He says it's part of a style he developed as a student at the State University of New York at Buffalo in the 1950s.

"I'm more interested in synchronizing different strands of data than in character development," observes Mr. Reed, whose writing is often satirical and mischievous. "So my stuff is closer to a collage."

Take *Japanese by Spring*, which has a couple of twists: Without warning, the book shifts from English to phrases in Japanese and Yoruba, and Ishmael Reed enters the novel, as a character, carrying on conversations, challenging his real-life critics, and preaching the value of multiculturalism.

"This is the first time I have myself in a book engaging other characters," he says. "I've been criticized for putting myself in. But other artists have done it and do it all the time. Painters, for example. Alfred Hitchcock, Spike Lee. Woody Allen."

True to form, several themes appear in his latest book. They are entangled like spaghetti in a bowl.

The novel's central character is Chappie Puttbutt, a black professor in Oakland who teaches in the English, Humanities and African-American Studies departments at Jack London College, but has tenure in none.

Chappie is a neo-conservative "black pathology merchant" who advances his career by lambasting affirmative action and the "black underclass" on the lecture circuit. His book *Black America's Misfortune,* is a best-seller. He is a loner on campus--despised by blacks and not accepted by whites.

The book allows Mr. Reed to take swipes at the type of black conservative who he says is confined, ironically, to a kind of "separate but equal" conservatism. Such conservatives are expected to have views only on issues related to being black in America. But that confinement contradicts their central thesis: that race is of declining significance.

"White conservatives can discuss a number of issues, but black conservatives, or neo-conservatives, if they want to be published, must confine their observations to black subjects," he says.

"If Shelby Steele had written a book that said white women were corrupted by affirmative action, nobody would have published it."

Japanese by Spring also lets Mr. Reed, a self-described "ethnic gate crasher," examine racial strife. He makes the point that all ethnic chauvinism and fear of multiculturalism are misguided.

In the epilogue, he talks about walking through an Oakland park during a festival, and of being part of a mosaic of people and cultures: "In the battle of multiculturalism, California has fallen to the enemy," he writes sarcastically.

The novel also allows Mr. Reed to explore, often caustically, tensions between Japan and America--tensions that have grown in proportion to the shifting trade balance between the countries. He posits that the real issue may not be Japanese imperialism, but American greed.

The make-believe campus that is the backdrop of Mr. Reed's ideas is filled with an assortment of characters: a president who secretly supports a right-wing racist group, traditionalists stuck in the past, and "cause pimps" who cling to their principles as long as they are useful.

Throughout, Mr. Reed also takes jabs at William J. Bennett, Catherine MacKinnon, Dinesh D'Souza (here named D'Gun ga Dinza), and Gen. Colin Powell, to name a few.

All of this in a 225-page book.

"I try to pack everything in there," he jokes.

Mr. Reed's works have been called diatribes by fans and critics alike. He expects the response to his newest book to be no different.

"Hawthorne preached all the time. But the guy could write. I think we need some preaching," he says. "There are kids running around here in the city and in the suburbs who don't know what's good or bad."

Does Mr. Reed bring those didactic methods to the classroom?

"Sometimes you have to undo the damage done by teachers devoted to ethnic chauvinism," he says.

That, says Mr. Reed, may be the toughest gig of all.

The Resurrection of Olódùmarè: Ishmael Reed's Vision of Renewal in *Japanese by Spring*

Leon Lewis/Article

Ishmael Reed has shown little reluctance to express what are often unconventional, unpopular or counter to mass-trend opinions and ideas in his work. In spite of the detrimental effect that this has had on his career as a writer, he has continued this practice with a particular relish in *Japanese by Spring*. His gleeful demolition of various poses, postures, self-serving strategies, exploitive agendas, neurotic manipulations and mendacious calculations by a gallery of distasteful characters representing the worst of contemporary social, political and academic institutions is designed to discomfort his detractors and delight those readers who share his iconoclastic perspective. But in the tradition of classical satire, Reed's rampaging take-no-prisoners assault on what he considers to be those responsible for the wretched condition of life in the United States for many people in the last decade of the twentieth century is balanced by the presentation of a positive philosophical structure built on a strong moral and spiritual base. The narrative direction of the novel is controlled by the wayward "progress" of the protagonist, Benjamin "Chappie" Puttbutt, from an attempt to establish alliances with various schemers and power-hustlers toward a vague understanding of and tentative reconciliation with the forces that are actually responsible for the shape of his character and the survival of his soul. Reed sees Puttbutt with a mixture of sympathetic understanding and exasperated disappointment; sympathy based on mutual experience as an African-American intellectual in a hostile university setting and disappointment at the failure of black men like Puttbutt to work beyond the necessity for defensive wrath and reclusive avoidance toward a life-enhancing vision available through a knowledge of history--a black heritage reclaimed from centuries of racist distortion--and the eternal powers of art (in this case, the creative energy latent in language) which can reanimate a withered spirit.

The first part of *Japanese by Spring* depicts the social spectrum of the academic battleground where Puttbutt is struggling for security and self-respect. Puttbutt's family has a long history of very successful service in the United States military and he has been named for two of the most celebrated African-American soldiers in the country's history by his father who is a high-ranking officer known as "The Black Puma." After some involvement with the Black Power movement of the 1960's, Puttbutt has chosen pacificism as a personal theology following an intense romantic experience with a Japanese woman whose Buddhist practices have touched him deeply. Approaching middle age, essentially friendless, he is trying to win tenure at Jack London College in Oakland by espousing a neoconservative position designed to appear courageous and outspoken but calculated to court favor with those currently in power. By rejecting the black consciousness of the 1960's and by choosing to study Japanese in order to be in touch with the latest trends in global gamesmanship, Puttbutt has denied so much of what he instinctively feels that he has essentially lost any true center of being. Thus, he is effectively helpless in the academic power struggle with people who have no scruples and no moral basis to begin with.

In this section of the novel, Reed isn't concerned with the psychological plausibility of the "characters" Puttbutt has to deal with. His interest is in drawing a gallery of devastating caricatures revealing the hollowness and corruption of various currently fashionable positions in contemporary society. The thrust of Reed's satire is that the competing academicians and administrators at Jack London (named for an author who Reed laconically observes was a racist, a jingoist and a crypto-fascist) are either diminished to puniness and pettiness by inherent hypocrisy or bloated to grotesquery by vicious immorality. Most of the semi-realistic characters are of the first order: Jack Milch, the chair of the Humanities Department, is committed to every worthwhile cause he comes across in theory while keeping his wife and child locked in a cellar; Marsha Marx is a feminist who has consistently betrayed feminist principles to build an empire; Matata Musomi is a professional Africanist entertaining society gatherings with pseudo-African song and dance routines; Robert Hurt, the Dean of Humanities, is an old-left liberal trapped in stereotypical conceptions of ethnic diversity; Charles Obi, the chair of the Black Studies Department, is an academic diplomat and candid careerist who is primarily concerned with his own privileges and reputation. These people are depicted with some semblance of understanding since they have been controlled by a social system where they have almost no power.

The second group of people are powermongers devoid of the slightest vestiges of consideration for anyone else in their lust to carry out agendas of personal aggrandizement. Here Reed is directly attacking versions of enemies who have plagued his life for decades. The President of the college is called Bright Stool, his "name" signifying his nature. He is a corporate criminal reeking of racist bile. Dr. Yamato, who Puttbutt meets as a teacher of the Japanese language, is actually the agent of forces determined to restore the Tokugawa Shogunate which ruled Japan for three centuries. He stands for a fundamentalist fanaticism not satisfied short of a total control of a nation's thought and customs. The aptly named "lick-ass" D'Gun ga Dinza (a servant of colonial masters like Kipling's Gunga Din) is an open assault on Dinesh D'Souza, the neoconservative advocate of theories of racial inferiority who Reed calls "the point man in the fight to wipe out the multikults" (188). The poet April Jokujoku is described as a "good writer" but is also presented as a "cause pimp" blaming white women and black men for social dysfunction and demanding lavish remuneration while "her whole pitch was about the oppression of underclass females in the ghettos" (32). Reed's depiction of her as a threat (who never actually appears in the text) to Puttbutt is a kind of revenge for a disparagement of his ideas from some feminist factions.

The little whores and large jackals that inhabit the landscape of Puttbutt's life partially excuse Puttbutt's alterations of identity. Although he recognizes that he is a loner, sees himself as a survivor, and feels momentarily pleased that he is capable of resisting his impulses to retaliate with justification when he is insulted, belittled, scorned or betrayed, Puttbutt's endless rationalizations are an indication that all of his posturing and squirming have failed to satisfy some very fundamental human needs. While he is often the focus of Reed's satire for his shifting and shuffling, Puttbutt's instinctive decency, his very able mind, his solid grasp of his discipline and his reflective temperament make him a sympathetic character as well. Reed suggests that he is an appropriate figure for an African-American man compelled to constantly adjust to the realities of life in late twentieth-century America and the weight of American history while attempting to maintain some sense of integrity and self-respect. The contradictions in his given name, honoring General Benjamin O. Davis and General Chappie James, Jr. ("the great Black Eagle") and his ludicrous family name, a bizarre legacy from some slave owner's insulting sneer, reverberate through his life, personal pride undermined by a burden of past indignities still lethal and damaging. At his best, when discussing the character of Othello, debating geopolitics with his father, appreciating the demons afflicting his rivals or moved to grief by the loss of his true love, Puttbutt suggests the possibilities of humane discourse inherent in his character. When he adopts the mask of a faux feminist, ingratiates with the patter of an intellectual hustler, suppresses the "warrior in his genes" (66) or apologizes to himself for his neoconservative politics, he exhibits the worst features of a rootless striver. The schism in his character is a manifestation of the double consciousness black Americans have often been forced to adopt. Reed registers the complexity of the situation Puttbutt faces as the narrative progresses by introducing counter-arguments to every position taken by all of the characters, justifying the Japanese critique of American life and then recalling in detail the Japanese history of imperialism; supporting Puttbutt's pacifism and giving Puttbutt's father a convincing argument about the necessities of applying force in certain conditions; parodying lock-step liberalism and fascist feminism like Catherine MacKinnon's censorship crusade while providing a powerful endorsement of many classic liberal doctrines and quoting with admiration feminist thinkers like bell hooks. Reed's intention is to undercut the "smelly little orthodoxies" (as Orwell put it) of every dogma-driven zealot whose resort to a mind-closing mantra (like the title) promises instant salvation without any true understanding of human experience.

In addition to the almost casual introduction of a stream of supportive data and information which Reed provides in short paragraphs that are interlaced within the narrative, the satirical attack of the first part of *Japanese by Spring* is also altered toward a more reflective consideration of the issues Reed addresses by the appearance of a character named Ishmael Reed. Contrary to some critical contentions that this is a self-promoting manipulation of the reader's sympathy, Reed uses this device both as a type of gentle self-effacement (the character is described as a "modest merchant" working to produce "quality literature and videodramas" for society) and as a means of negotiating the gap between Puttbutt's limits and a positive vision of a cultural community of decency and justice. Puttbutt's struggle to win tenure (which is drawn from Reed's own experiences at UC Berkeley) indicates how important it is to have a solid sense of what one believes and what really matters so the self is not driven by the contradictions constantly generated by a public posture clashing with private convictions and instincts. Puttbutt senses this. He decides not to take down a portrait of Booker T. Washington--"Booker T. was complex"--after his neoconservative strategy fails, but he has lost contact with something so fundamental that he cannot exist without depending on some programmatic ideology grasped from an outside source. Puttbutt's father and mother are powerful warriors, their righteous anger justifying their choices and Reed understands that after centuries of oppression, there is an exhilaration in standing up, fighting back and living with the pride of a newly formed black consciousness. For Puttbutt, though, the era of Black Power of the 1960s has shifted so that a liberating resistance is not entirely sufficient. Although he seems content with his Japanese expertise as he fades out of the narration, his dependence on an extraneous cultural construct implies a continuing fragility. As the character named Ishmael Reed moves to the foreground, a vision of a multicultural community of tolerance, creative energy and life-enhancing contributions by a diverse variety of people from many ethnic traditions begins to take shape. This social construct is based on the Yoruba civilization of West Africa, those ancestors who Reed feels "must have been geniuses to be able to communicate in a language which was not only of great charm, beauty and poetry" but whose subtle, supple language expresses the core Yoruba values of "devotion to the family, to honor and respect" (120, 123).

The gradual interpolation of Reed's authorial consciousness through the employment of observations and asides amidst the account of Puttbutt's travails deliberately adjusts the focus of *Japanese by Spring* from the lacerating satire of the first part to the description of a Yoruba resurrection ceremony in the epilogue. Reed concludes the novel with an optimistic depiction of a people gathered in joy and harmony. Puttbutt's attempt to learn Japanese and his practice of pacificism adopted from Buddhist teachings are laudable efforts to transcend the limits of a Western European imperialist perspective, but Reed's endorsement of Yoruba is based on a reclamation of a lost heritage ("As he delved into the study of Yoruba he found that some of his views were no different from those of that generation of Africans who disembarked from the dreaded slave ships.") (120). And, rather than disavowing the American elements of his character, "Mongrelized," Reed emphasizes his background blending of Cherokee, Tennessee pioneer, Irish and black African strains so that no single-race theory of dominance is encouraged. The festival of celebration that Reed evokes is based on a belief in the spiritual qualities of a universal deity, a cosmos beyond Western rationality. For "homefolks Ishmael Reed" who is " a democrat and a populist" the idea of worship even in a Yoruba temple seems unnatural, although he acknowledges the nurturing nature of the Black Christian church during the days of slavery, but since his own special God is language, he is able to accommodate the instructions of his teacher, Ogun Sanya, a sort of Yoruba seer. What is most crucial here is that Reed is open to the possibilities of a new way of seeing and thinking. This is the ultimate measure of character in *Japanese by Spring.*[1]

The festival that Reed attends at the novel's close takes place in early June--the full flowering of the spring season. His teacher Ogun Sanya is dedicating a temple to the Yoruba deity Olódùmarè, resurrecting and reanimating the god/spirit which "lies dormant in the African-American experience" (217). The proper name Olódùmarè is an honorific for Olorun--Olo for owner; run for heavens. Following the formal but friendly ritual, Reed passes a park which he uses as a place for meditation. Here, a yearly Festival of the Lake is taking place, attended by 98,000 people. This festival is the living incarnation of the spirit of Olorun, a tangible manifestation of the true meaning of Yoruba thought and a suggestion of an earthly paradise; the human way to be an owner of the heavens. Using his capability as a poet, Reed captures the marvelous range of human possibility and creativity, listing the enticing array of foods available, then the full scope of entertainment featuring musicians and dancers from every continent. The mingling of languages themselves contributes to the ethos of wonder:

> They dance. Sun Eagle drummers & Fancy Dancers, Zydecdo Flames, Salsa, Charanga Tumbao Y Guerda, Cuban Salsa. Soca/Calypso/Reggae. Kotoja, Modern Afro Beat. Flamenco. Traditional Flamenco. Rhumba Flamenco. Vietnamese Music Ensemble. (224)

Ishmael Reed's aspirations as a social activist and as an artist coalesce in his admiration for and fascination with the Yoruba language. It is the core of a cultural matrix which he sees as a remedial redirection for a social system way off course. The elements of the Yoruba language which Reed cites includes an absence of a formal critical terminology, encouraging individual, personal responses beyond any privileged position supporting a particular aesthetic; a reliance on tonal inflection enhancing the nuance and subtlety of any kind of communication; a doubling of meaning so that the word for thief (ole) is similar to that for idler (ole), assuming that an idle person will steal, thus emphasizing the importance of productive work; an inclination to pronounce words with a lengthening and gliding of syllables, the basis Reed feels for the vocal styles of jazz singers and jazz poets [among whom Reed includes Amiri Baraka, Anne Waldman, and John Gould Fletcher(!)]; and a vocabulary that stresses particular values which Reed believes in, but which also reflects a market economy that operated for two thousand years, resulting in "one of the most complex numerical systems known to man" (123). Reed's presentation of his discovery and pursuit of knowledge of Yoruba is purposefully cast in a tone of reflective enthusiasm, a contrast to the contemptuous dismissal of the objects of his satirical wrath in the rest of the book. His modesty before a nearly lost civilization of imposing dimensions indicates his willingness to learn. This is the moral corrective for the rigid fixidity of the zealots and extremists. Reed suggests that the ancient West African society conventionally considered a backward jungle of savages is a much better example of enlightened tolerance and reason than many facets of modern America. The Festival at the Lake is a gathering of plural possibility, a challenge to any doctrine of racial superiority. Reed's last image, the black butterfly with yellow spots that collides with his chin (225), is an attractive hybrid supporting his belief that the richness of human experience depends on a blending of attributes and that no one individual has the best or only approach to anything.

NOTES

1. One of the participants in the temple dedication is Professor Crabtree of Jack London, a classical scholar of literature teaching a Sir John Suckling seminar and a course in Old Norse with three students attending. He has written an article dismissing non-European literature by saying "if Yoruba would produce a Turgenev he would be glad to read him"--a variant of Saul Bellow's similar comment on a Swahili Tolstoy. Puttbutt in his momentary ascendancy to power requires Crabtree to teach a Freshman Composition course in the Yoruba language, since he must know Yoruba well enough in light of his comment. In a delicious reversal, Crabtree approaches Yoruba with the same energy he brought to Milton scholarship decades ago and finds that "I haven't had so much fun since I learned to play poker. I have learned a language that transports me to a culture that's two thousand years old. Have they ever produced a Tolstoy? They have produced Tolstoys." Crabtree not only learns to speak Yoruba, "... unlike many non-native speakers, he was getting all of his tones right." He is like the officer in Hemingway's "In Another Country" who recognizes the value in precise mastery for the sake of the act alone.

Previously unpublished article (1998). Printed by permission.

Post-Modern Realism: Ishmael Reed and *Japanese by Spring*

Mark Vogel/Article

Yes, Yes. If you wanted to bad enough you could run Ishmael Reed right into a dirty hole in the ground. Consider his diatribes against feminists in *Airing Dirty Laundry* or his parodies in *Japanese by Spring* and call him a misogynist. Call him a political dinosaur as he defends Clarence Thomas. Call him uncontrolled as he portrays a "fictional" Ishmael Reed, a character given free rein to explore, and view his (the real Reed's) war with critics, as well as with academic, political, and military partisans blinded by ethnic, racial, and cultural ideologies. If Reed didn't show you so clearly the brazen aggressiveness of his enemies, it would be easy to say he is paranoid. See Reed as thin-skinned as he caricatures political figures, shallow professors, and media personalities. Yes. If the goal is to use bits of evidence to back a thesis there's no doubt it can and has been done. Reed, the trickster, the master of Hoodoo, provides plenty of evidence in *Japanese by Spring* as he forces the reader to see multiculturalism with new eyes. His surrealistic collage contains shock tactics to get a reaction, to destroy the cliches so blithely pushed by editorials, by public officials, and much of the public. Reed illustrates brilliantly the problems that ensue when those in power mistake the part for the whole.

The trickster has many personas, and thus can't easily be summed up. As poet, musician, editor, essayist, novelist, and political revolutionary, Reed has been active in race and culture wars for more than thirty years saying the things that need to be said--the funny, the brutal, the obscene. His ninth novel reinforces the persona of Reed as a source of energy and humor piecing together the commonplace into a collage of new forms. Reed has explained how his style comes into being:

> I think one of the things I have going for me is synthesizing and synchronizing. Synthesizing by combining elements into the same time, making them run in the same time together. (Johnson 53 in *Conversations*)

In *Japanese by Spring* the goal is to mix the public and the private, the banal and the beautiful. His juxtaposing of political and academic talk, of fictional and "real" characters, of scenes (like the Clarence Thomas hearings) which are engrained in American cultural consciousness, is the background for Chappie Puttbutt's story. In the process Reed presents a vision of society cleansed by his corrosive, loving eyes. *Japanese by Spring* shows Reed as a trickster, a hocus-pocus man, one of Quincy Troupe's "Unconstructed Negroes." As Reed suggests, he and his friends "are like the old conjure men out on the edge of the forest who were not part of the plantation system" (*Airing Dirty Laundry* 60). Reed as a West Coast transplant, part African American, part Irish, part Native

American, borrows and steals from whatever culture he chooses. He openly admits his penchant for borrowing.

> I can be influenced by and I can share culture, I don't say I own it or invented it....Around 1977 I went through a new period because I found that some of my Hoodoo ideas meshed with the trickster notions of the Native Americans.... But I'm not calling myself a black shaman. I use ideas borrowed from other cultures to reinforce my own culture. (Zamir 286 in *Conversations*).

That's what a trickster does. He reshapes the reader's notions of what is "real" about Reed and about society. In *Japanese by Spring* Reed revels in the chaos, in the discordant rhetoric of politics, intellectual life, and the street. His hodge-podge of "fact" and fiction rearranges our notion of story. The mix of cultures, the shock of the real world intrusions, the contemporary events, produces a peppery mixture of gumbo literature.

Because *Japanese by Spring* reveals Reed's current reading, his interest in jazz, and the writing of diverse friends and enemies, it is a welcome look at the contemporary scene. Reed's characters are literate readers, immersed in reviews, movies, public speeches, even cable tv. Strange guest appearances by characters resembling Robert Bennett, George Bush, and other both loved and unloved characters (ranging from Colin Powell to Robert Lowell) creates the surreal awareness that Miles Davis and George Bush can exist on the same planet.

Naming is a powerful weapon for Reed. As a consummate name dropper, Reed, in essays and his fiction lets us know the figures to be respected and reviled. In many cases these are true to life characters, like Colin Powell and Ronald Reagan. Naming, of course, is another trait prized by the trickster. To name is to obtain the power of another. To bestow names is to instill characters with power and establish their role. In Reed's fiction naming often is used to upset the current balance of power, to remove the respect given to authorities or those with unexamined credentials. Thus key negative figures like President Stool Bright of Jack London College, Marsha Marx, the head of Women's Studies, and "political" figures like D'Gun ga Dinza possess names that put them squarely in their place.

The stage for *Japanese by Spring* is Jack London University, a right-wing haven. Jack London, Reed quickly suggests, was the "apostle of the blond beast, the Nietzschean Übermensch...a brunette just as his fellow beast admirer, Adolf Hitler" (7). It is a dangerous time, when the larger political world has its greasy paw in the academic world, also when "the feud between the Paleolithic Right and the Neoconservative Right was expanding" (48). Enter into this scene one Chappie Puttbutt, an African American English professor searching for survival and tenure. Though he has taken on many roles, currently he is a feminist who has "memorized every mediocre line by Zora Neale Hurston" (11).

Puttbutt knows how to tiptoe in the superficial, power-hungry academic world. He has learned to mimic the chameleon and survive. He stays humble even as his colleagues taunt him with their literary power plays.

> You black guys had your chance. Wright and Baldwin were once the canon, but Zora overthrew them. Sent them hurling from the literary firmament. (93)

In his latest preservation tactic he is studying Japanese. "Puttbutt figured that with Japanese under his belt he would adjust to the new realities of the coming postsettler era, a time when the domination of the United States by people of the same background would come to an end" (47). The textbook from which he is learning the language is entitled, *Japanese by Spring*. Thus, from the beginning Reed presents a novel within a novel, and little separation between the fictional and non-fictional worlds. When the character, Ishmael Reed, appears, the reader knows traditional notions of narrative fiction have been supplanted by the aesthetics of collage making.

Puttbutt must compete with April Jokujoku, "a firebrand radical lesbian ecologist activist...[whose] poetry collected causes the way some people collect stray cats" (9). In addition, he finds himself pitted against feminists like Marsha Marx, who could spew "language in rapid-fire bursts....mowing down whatever man found himself unlikely to be in its way" (108-109). As Puttbutt deals with egos and convoluted reasoning, he learns the dangers of trusting English Department colleagues. The author's comments in an essay, "The Great Tenure Battle of 1977" show how his history of problems at Berkeley served as an inspiration for Puttbutt's experience.

> Well, I think King Kong is probably more civilized than some of these people teaching in English departments. Gorillas are very fastidious, very aware of hygiene, they're vegetarians. (Ewing 126 in *Conversations*).

Presiding over the small, fragmenting university is Dr. Bright Stool, who "saw the world in terms of losers and gainers." In his opinion "Humanity people were losers" (42). Puttbutt also deals with entrenched disnosaurs like Dr. Obi, head of African American Studies, whose "blackness had the irredescent beauty of a San Antonio grackle" (30). Obi had been president of "the Maoist Student League in the sixties. Now, all he talked about was his Volvo and his summer home on the Russian River" (35).

> The African American program, like all departments on campus, has become a mere satellite of Women's Studies. The new power merchants focus on literary criticism and ideology and treat living artists as if they don't exist. "All you had to do was string together some quotes from Benjamin, Barthes, Foucault and Lacan and you were in business" (49). Academia is seen as a narrow minded alignment of groups engaged in elitist war and endless jockeying for position. In the battle zone over which knowledge is to be

cherished, the "antidiversity movement's main war rooms were the history departments, those who had covered up the most, distorted the most and had the most to be defensive about" (125).

Though beaurocratic programs and lockstop ideologies are part of the collage Reed creates, the focus is on the absurd personalities and points of view of single minded grasping merchants of power. Layered into the story are characters who only get a scene or two, just enough to reveal the simple stupidity of their lives. Their names label them as mere caricatures mouthing cardboard tired slogans. Thus, we meet characters like Robert Hurt (a sixties do-gooder), Marsha Marx, and Himmlar Poop.

Into this mix arrives Puttbutt's family--patriotic, active, and visionary. Chappie is the only male in this civic-minded family who has failed at the military life.

> If they were pianists, [Chappie] would be Billy Taylor, a competent survivor, his grandfather, Errol Garner, given to flourishes and exaggerations, and his father--his father would be an accompanist for the Mills Brothers. (63)

His mother is her own special case. She is held by terrorists in the Middle East for much of the book. When she is released CNN produces photographs of her ordeal. "One showed his mother, sitting at a piano, playing 'Onward Christian Soldiers,' as the terrorists stood, singing. His mother was smoking a cigarettte and had a shotgun lying across her lap" (202).

But Puttbutt is a mere survivor. His family has been interceding in his life behind the scenes for years. Though he thinks of himself as autonomous, the most important decisions have been manipulated by his family. In their lofty and arrogant positions of power they mix personal and public needs, seeing both Middle East policy and Puttbutt's tenure as their realm of decision making. Puttbutt is aware of the differences between himself and those making the big decisions as he struggles with his academic colleagues.

> Why couldn't he, Puttbutt, be like his father, General Puttbutt and General Colin Powell?.... His father had always talked of the necessity of degrading the enemy....Why couldn't he get into a Desert Storm state of mind? (139-140)

When the Japanese buy the university, Puttbutt is elevated in power, and given the opportunity to exact revenge upon those who have pushed him around. The arrival of the Japanese is a blow to the old order, the "Miltonians." At first Puttbutt eagerly implements the orders of the new regime and routinely fires selected colleagues. He tells other primadonnas what they will have to do to survive. "Teach. That's what we hired you for, to teach. Not the TAs. Graduate students. But you" (116).

With Puttbutt as chief advisor to the president (his former teacher of Japanese), it seems an enlightened new world is inevitable. But a wholesale change in who holds the reins of power will not ensure a cohesive world, especially when warring factions in the multiculturist movement seem bent upon blindly seizing new territory and establishing fiefdoms of Black Culture or Feminist Thought rather than borrowing freely from many disciplines. Puttbutt, like Reed, sees through the lipservice liberal groups have paid to multiculturalism. He helps to put these groups in their place in the new hierarchy. But gradually Puttbutt also sees the new reality--that his Japanese leaders are as racist and as culturally claustrophobic as the "white masters had been." As Puttbutt works to mediate between the battling factions, Crabtree, a former Miltonian, impassionately tells his self-destructive colleagues how they have failed to embrace multiculturalism.

> It was my stupid arrogance, my devotion to these standards that we're always talking about that almost prevented me from embarking on this wonderful adventure.... We should be the ones to lead our students and our country to new intellectual frontiers. Instead, we're like the archaic Dixiecrats of the old South, but instead of yelling segregation forever, we're yelling Western culture forever (155).

Puttbutt, himself a collage of ideologies, disciplines, and self-serving rationalization, listens, and quietly makes decisions, helping to save the university by bringing together former Nazis, racists, and threatened departments.

Following in paths that intersect with Puttbutt's rise to power is a character known as Ishmael Reed. Reed the character, not surprisingly, resembles Reed the author. The character is a writer who lectures and teaches and thinks seriously about how multiculturalism ideally should work to reflect the diversity in American (and world) culture. Like Reed the author, the character has strong feelings about which authors and which texts should belong in the "new" literary canon. Reed the character has met Puttbutt at conferences, and spoken at least once on the campus of Jack London University. The topic of his campus lecture, like the plot of author Reed's novels, "merely provided a theme on which his mind could improvise, sort of like a jazz musician stating a song and then dancing around it elliptically" (129). When Puttbutt sees Reed on campus, he approaches him, and waves *Japanese by Spring*, announcing, "This is the book that got me to where I am now" (131).

But Reed, as a character, is part of the patchwork quilt of ideas and personalities, that Reed, as author, presents. He is a counterpoint to Puttbutt and the opposite of a political chameleon. The new language he studies is Yoruba, a "forgotten" language of "great charm, beauty and poetry" (120). According to Reed, "Yoruba had influenced the lengthening and gliding of words practiced by the great oral poets, the preachers of the Black Church; it influenced the vocal styles of Anita Baker and Sarah Vaughan"(121). Reed studies Yoruba not to bolster his career choices, but as an intellectual, spiritual, and cultural bringing together of the past and the present. By learning the language Reed also learns about Olódùmarè, owner of the heavens, "a god with whom African Americans lost contact after the breakup of the Yoruba empire and slave trade" (217). Reed's brand of multicultural forays complicate his world, providing new information and viewpoints, not facile answers to age-old problems. Learning Yoruba, Reed rewrites as a classicist would do, producing a new cosmology by reviving the dead, bringing back a "forgotten" spirituality embedded in a concrete culture.

Ultimately, Reed's heart is always in the right place. The fictional Reed mirrors the real Reed's ability to use language powerfully. Unlike the self-serving academics, he uses language to explore the needs of the varied culture he lives in.

> If, of all of the indexes of a nation's health, the condition of the children was the most important, then the United States was deeply troubled. Black male children were killing each other. White children and Native American children were killing themselves. Millions of children were mired in poverty and had no health care. Olódùmarè and his daughters would have their work cut out for them. (225)

Thus, for Reed and other multiculturalists the knowledge, spirituality and poetry gained from other cultures must be put to work to reflect the world as it exists. Rather than retreating into the cultish world of pat-on-the-back knowledge, Reed knows that cultures colliding produces friction and insight. At novel's end, his spiritual guru, Ogun Sanya, threatens to take his Yoruba knowledge to the public. "No more deception. No more speaking in codes. That would be the test. Were blacks ready for Olódùmarè, were whites?" (220) In the end, despite the small minded games he and Puttbutt have witnessed, and the viciousness of the racist attacks, Reed remains optimistic. Reed, more than any other character, can articulate the need for broadening the cultural and political market place, and put Puttbutt's struggle in perspective. Because the Ishmael Reed character is a writer first, and an academic second (much like the "real" Reed), he is never subservient to the ever shifting winds of academic power. Thus he can blast those he sees as responsible, and he does so routinely.

> Reed believed that racism was learned. That racism was a result of white leaders of Western nations placing little value on nonwhite life, or indeed, projecting violent impulses upon those who lived under constant fear of white terror. (209)

Reed often publishes fiction and nonfiction at the same time and each work enlightens the driving themes of the other. In *Airing Dirty Laundry*, a book of essays which was published alongside *Japanese by Spring* in 1993, Reed also suggests the blame for the chaos surrounding multiculturalism can be tied to political and media elites.

> Instead of fostering awareness between different groups, the media and the political intellectual and cultural elite often seem to be engaged in rumor mongering, spreading what amounts to gossip and faulty intelligence about members of our multiethnic civilization and dividing Americans into hostile groups. ("Beyond Los Angeles" 46)

The essay argues that until members of the "majority" culture actually know how members of minority groups live, they will continue to judge blacks and other multicultural unknowns by what they see on television.

Author Reed's collage delights in forcing the "majority" and the "minority" individuals to confront each other. The glue for his collage is his own unique and biting humor, which he uses as part of the trickster's bag of tricks. Bawdy, biting humor teaches and transforms the perspective of the reader. Reed's humor is drawn from a long tradition. As Reed explains in a 1993 interview, oppressed people have often used humor as the underpinning of their literature. The tales told by African Americans on plantations weren't designed to masquerade as "serious literature." The tales "used comedy to make serious points though. The situations are comic but they say something else. In Jamaica they call it serious comedy" (Dick 350 in *Conversations*).

Ultimately, Reed's stylistic collage of playful elements seems a form of realism. As the novel ends the character Ishmael Reed takes us to a city park to illustrate how the fringes of groups, ideas, and cultures merge around him. What he sees serves as a potent argument that multiculturalism is a reality, not a choice. "Cambodians, Laotians, Vietnamese, Chinese, Japanese, Africans, Latinos (there are parts of Oakland now that resemble Mexico City....In the battle of multiculuralism, California has fallen to the enemy" (224).

Reed as critic, poet, essayist, lecturer, inveterate reader, and aficiando of music, is equipped to show us how the common, the banal, the high, and the low of culture mix and influence each other. In the swirl of this mix Reed's characters are larger than life reflections of the contemporary scene in all its complexity. In this cacophony of these competing voices, Reed, as modern trickster, deflates facades, and pokes at everything that threatens to congeal into rigidity. Reed's goal is to merge story and being, making the lines between what is real and fiction fuzzy, bringing into question the reader's perspectives on, literally, reality. He evokes reactions, either anger on the part of feminists, academics, and politicians, or brief flashes into Reed's world perspective. The trickster laughs with you if you get it. Let the warts show.

WORKS CITED
Dick, Bruce. "Ishmael Reed: An Interview." (1993), in *Conversations with Ishmael Reed*, Eds. Bruce Dick and Amritjit Singh (Jackson: University Press of Mississippi, 1995), p. 126.
Ewing, Jon. "The Great Tenure Battle of 1977" (1978), in *Conversations with Ishmael Reed*, Eds. Bruce Dick and Amritjit Singh (Jackson: University Press of Mississippi, 1995), p. 126.
Gaga [Mark S. Johnson]. "Interview with Ishmael Reed" (1973), in *Conversations with Ishmael Reed*, Eds. Bruce Dick and Amritjit Singh (Jackson: University Press of Mississippi, 1995), p. 53.
Reed, Ishmael. "Beyond Los Angeles." In *Airing Dirty Laundry*. Reading, MA: Addison-Wesley (1993), p. 46.
---. *Japanese by Spring*. New York: Atheneum (1993).
Zamir, Shamoon. "An Interview with Ishmael Reed" (1988), in *Conversations with Ishmael Reed*, Eds. Bruce Dick and Amritjit Singh (Jackson: University Press of Mississippi, 1995), p. 286.

Previously unpublished essay (1998). Printed by permission.

The Next Round: Ishmael Reed's Battles in the 1980s and 1990s

Darryl Dickson-Carr/Article

Ishmael Reed's novels and essays of the 1980s and 1990s are direct reflections of the changing faces of African American and general American politics in those decades. Although Reed repeatedly focuses upon racial politics in *The Terrible Twos, Reckless Eyeballing, The Terrible Threes* and *Japanese by Spring*, the overarching gist of his novels' satire is a skewering of the new mean-spiritedness that has overtaken the American social and political landscape like an invading army of spite. Reed exposes neoconservatives of all stripes and their dupes most frequently, inasmuch as their goals are to reverse the social progress made in the decades following the passage of Civil Rights and other social legislation of the 1960s and 1970s. Reed makes one message starkly clear about this all-too-powerful segment of the population: Its attacks on social progress are (mis)guided by the usual human failings of greed and self-interest, rather than higher moral purposes. Additionally, although Reed's earlier novels act as tools with which we may take a richly referential look at history, a look that questions the foundations of Western discourses about history, his most recent works do not reach the sort of historically referential frenzy of his earlier works. Instead, Reed's primary concentration seems to be on two general topics: The aforementioned advent and effects of neoconservatism as marked by the policies and politics of the Reagan and Bush administrations and the horrific philosophical relativism of a multiculturalism mishandled by inept academics and naïve African American artists.

Reed's cynicism is a product of an era in which much of the promise of 1960s Black politics has been apparently squandered, ranging from the aforementioned social gains to the fervent intellectual and artistic activity of the Black Aesthetic, an important product of 1960s Black Nationalism. An effective metaphor for the lost potential in African American arts and politics may be found in Michael Omi and Howard Winant's Gramscian outline of several models for current reactions to changes in Black political and economic conditions:

> In the pre-World War II period change in the racial order was epochal in scope, shaped by the conditions of "war of maneuver" in which minorities had very little access to the political system, and understood in a context of assumed racial inequalities.... Today all of this has been swept away.... Racial politics now take place under conditions of "war of position," in which minorities have achieved significant (though by no means equal) representation in which the *meaning* of racial equality can be debated, but the desirability of some form of equality is assumed. (83; italics in the original)[1]

In the aftermath of the Civil Rights Movement, then, African-Americans face the challenge of articulating a new meaning for "race" and creating this definition's subsequent effects upon Black political and economic life. Some factions within and outside of African-American politics have argued vehemently and eloquently that virtually all of the barriers to Black success have been removed and that the failures of African-Americans to move into the American cultural mainstream may no longer be blamed on social structures but on African-American culture and the composition of individual or group morals. Other factions, however, argue that the same social structures that inhibited Black success in the past still exist, but have taken on new, more coded (and therefore more difficult to detect) forms. In contemporary Black politics, the choices African-Americans must make to redefine "race" are virtually always between or within one of these positions. True to his calling as a satirist and a Neo-HooDoo griot, Reed's recent novels frequently straddle all of these positions, though he is most consistently arguing that racism is becoming increasingly more coded. Reed's goal, then, is to *crack* the codes neoconservatism has constructed in the post-Civil Rights era.

The Terrible Twos (1982) and its sequel *The Terrible Threes* (1989),[2] together comprise an elaborate, futuristic vision of American neoconservatism in the 1980s and 1990s. The novels' plots are fantasies resembling George S. Schuyler's *Black No More*, the first complete African American satirical novel, in terms of their mixture of science fiction, HooDoo, and frequent interpolations of journalistic satire. Written and published early in or prior to the decades they satirize, *The Terrible Twos* and *Threes* predict America's political tenor with frightening accuracy. The principles underlying American politics, most prominently capitalism and jingoism, are stripped of their coded manifestations and placed within characters who cynically understand what the American mainstream really wants and are relatively successful at satisfying those demands. Put simply, the American people and their leaders are the equivalent of a spoiled two-year-old (hence *The Terrible Twos'* title):

> He throws tantrums until he gets what he wants. You'd like to whack him good across the bottom but your wife is reading childrearing books which advise against this. They counsel patience. As the child grows he tells you things. He tells you about nations and individuals. About how civilizations come into being. You're glad that two-year-olds don't have access to ICBMs the way the responsible leaders in your government do.... The terrible twos are twins to the terrible nos.... Human beings at two harbor cravings that have to be immediately quenched, demand things, and if another human being of their size and age enters the picture, there's war. (Reed, *Twos* 23-24)

The metaphor of the two-year-old as representative of American political and social concerns continually resurfaces throughout the text, primarily through the presence of Dean Clift, a composite of James Dean, Montgomery Clift and Presidents Ronald Reagan and John F. Kennedy. A former actor elected to the United States vice-presidency not for his political skills, which are nonexistent, but for his good looks, Clift ascends to the presidency when his running mate, former General Walter Scott, dies in office. Clift subsequently finds himself acting as a figurehead for the reactionary politicians who bankrolled his election campaign.

Via the hilarious ineptitudes of Clift, Vice President Jesse Hatch, Bob Krantz and the ultraconservative Reverend, Reed argues that the American people have continually chosen political and spiritual leaders who are best able to maintain an intricate architecture of illusion. The maintenance of this architecture is of such importance that a politician's platform will inevitably take second place to his or her carefully orchestrated image. The platform undergirding Clift's presidential cabinet not only becomes the novel's central device for exploring American racial politics; it also bears a disturbing similarity to the Reagan and Bush cabinets, despite the fact that the novels were written before either administration was fully formed. For example, "Operation Two Birds," the wildly elaborate conspiracy that would consolidate power for a small, fascist elite of white men while decimating the world's population of "surps" or people of color, is intended to parallel the retrograde racial politics of the Reagan-Bush era.[3] The plot depends on convincing the American public that the "surps," or surplus people, are destroying both the country and the world (Boyer 36). Given the frequent and sustained attacks on Affirmative Action, immigration and privacy in the 1980s and early 1990s by conservatives and neoconservatives, the outlandish genocidal Operation Two Birds doesn't seem particularly far-fetched. As Reginald Martin posits, "Reed's point is that 'facts' from history are often either fabricated or too biased or incredible to be believed. Fact overlaps with fiction, and only when the two are juxtaposed can one see the similarities" (89-90). Although Reed uses a more prophetic juxtaposition in the *Terribles*, the effect is similar, inasmuch as the majority of Reed's predictions of a government ruled by right-wing politicos and religious fanatics proved correct in the 1980s and appear to be doing the same in the 1990s.

The novels' conspiratorial milieu, however, in which clandestine government officials and organizations wage secret war against people of color, appears in some critics' eyes as paranoid, delusionary and therefore unworthy of Reed's talent. Stanley Crouch, for instance, avers that "for all the literary appropriations in *The Terrible Twos*, it hasn't the level of invention that made his best work succeed...*The Terrible Twos*, unfortunately, is mostly a shadow of his former work, and a shadow that tells us little that we didn't already know" (qtd. in Boyer 39). Similarly, Darryl Pinckney argues that "Reed's campaign to mention everything that has gone wrong in America results in a narrative that is all over the place, as if he were trying to work in everything from crime against the environment to offenses against the homeless. Instead of suspense or satire one is confronted with an extended editorial rebuttal" (*CLC* 314).

While each of these criticisms have considerable merit, with Pinckney's being the most persuasive, they fail to account for the fact that however vitriolic and cynical Reed's critique of American politics in the 1980s may seem, most of his predictions of the arc of American politics came true, though not necessarily to the apocalyptic extent his novels foresee. Furthermore, Pinckney errs in declaring the novels bereft of satire inasmuch as they resemble "an extended editorial rebuttal" which still manages to be "all over the place." The error here is Pinckney's conflicting assessments. While the narrative in the two novels does touch upon a panoply of political and social issues, it does not do so to the same degree as Reed's previous novels. It would be more accurate, in view of Leon Guilhamet's categorization of satirical rhetoric, to say that Reed's satire moves toward a model that combines the judicial with the deliberative while retaining the use of folk elements as the text's countervailing forces.

Guilhamet describes deliberative satire as that which "look[s] to the future" insofar as it examines a problem and proposes a course of action. In other words, "[a]fter a central question is asked somewhere early in the [text], the remainder...is devoted to answering it" (Guilhamet 33-4). The central question of *The Terrible Twos* and *The Terrible Threes* is apparently "What hope is left for the United States (and by extension the rest of the world) when immense greed coexists comfortably with abject poverty?" *The Terrible Twos'* first chapter thus contrasts the wealthy who "will have any kind of Christmas they desire," with "gifts rang[ing] from $100 gold toothpicks to $30,000 Rolls Royces" to the seven point eight million people [who] will be unemployed and will do without poinsettias tied with 1940 pink lace or chestnut soup. They will be unable to attend the ski lessons this year, but they will be fighting the snow, nevertheless. On Thanksgiving Day, five thousand people line up for turkey and blackeye peas in San Francisco. In D.C., four men freeze to death during inaugural week, one on the steps of a church. The church's door is locked"(Reed, *Twos* 5).

The essential dilemma implicit in the skiff of American wealth adrift in a sea of poverty provides the novels with their central question; their judicial element comes into play through the answer, which avers that a small cadre of rich, privileged men will attempt to eliminate all but the wealthiest whites from the face of the planet, an attempt aided by an excessively self-interested populace. Guilhamet describes the judicial element of satire as an "apparent disbelief in justice in our world or the hereafter...[that] places a grave responsibility with the satirist who must discover a basis for satire and then, himself, become the chief dispenser of justice"(65).[4] The problem of this particular satirical model is that the satirist's idea of justice can be especially bleak and harsh, which is "increasingly dependent on [the satirist's] personal wit. If the satirist is able to reconstruct an adequate sense of genre, his audience is unwilling or unable to do so" and is likely to reject the satirist's solutions (Guilhamet 65-6).

For the *Terribles*, though, the problem is not so much that Reed has instilled an inadequate sense of wit and satire, but that the satire could have been equally effective with a less polygenetic plot. Though Reed is at his best attacking buffoonery at every level of society, the novels would not have been lessened by a concentration on the nation's political and intellectual elite. Reed's brief resuscitation of old grudges against narrow and racist feminists via Beechiko Mizuni in *The Terrible Threes*, seems particularly gratuitous given the group's controversial treatment in *Reckless Eyeballing*. One of the novel's strengths is its incorporation of Neo-HooDoo, which Reed utilized so successfully in his earlier novels. In the *Terribles*, the figure of St. Nicholas, long since evolved into Santa Claus in the popular consciousness, is reunited with his erstwhile black partner, Black Peter. As a picaresque team, the pair set out to stop the cataclysmic Operation Two Birds with magic derived from HooDoo and conjure. Yet this team is insufficient in the fight against an evil born of complacency in American society. As Jay Boyer writes,

> Reed seems unable artistically to envision a hero with suitable powers to fend off [Operation Two Birds]. It's as if Reed's faith in the magic he's embraced for so long has begun to diminish...as if the weight and momentum of the historical forces in these novels is of such dimension that Reed can't envision a magic great enough to stop them. (38)

Indeed, the novel's satire derives its rhetorical force less from St. Nicholas and Black Peter's picaresque roles than it does from the juxtaposition of the caricatures of Operation Two Birds' conspirators upon the canvas of a world mad and deluded enough to allow their continued existence and oppressive policies. The nation's salvation, therefore, does not depend so much upon the intervention of otherworldly forces as it does upon the public's self-determination, intelligence and desire to entertain alternatives to narrow ideologies. On the one hand, Reed's argument for alternative belief and political systems is a continuation of the thematics that dominate his earlier novels. The stress upon self-determination, however, foregrounded towards the end of the *Terribles* and Reed's other later novels, represents a slight shift in the tenor of his narratives. Extraordinary forces are mere catalysts for social and political change; it is the individual and group's introspection that ultimately proves to be the decisive factor in limiting the chaos in the novels' satiric environments.

Thus we encounter similar environs within both *Reckless Eyeballing* (1986), which was published in the interim between the *Terribles,* and the more recent *Japanese by Spring* (1993). Both of these novels act as satiric extensions of Reed's disquisitions of American politics practiced in his essays and articles. The former novel is closely tied to and partially based upon the essays Reed published in *Writin' is Fightin'* and is, moreover, easily his most controversial novel; *Japanese by Spring* bears many resemblances to the coincidental *Airing Dirty Laundry*. Reed's satirization of certain types of feminisms and feminists (including, in utterly thin disguise, Alice Walker) as cynical, manipulative women, equally as enthralled by misanthropy and racist images of Black men as the men they critique are enthralled by misogyny, created an uproar and backlash against his work that, upon examination, is not entirely deserved. Boyer observes, correctly, that

> [a] closer look at [Reed's] female characters suggests that there isn't a feminist to be found in the lot. Reed's main [Black] characters....want...to make it in a world dominated by whites, and they'll take any political stance and mouth any political rhetoric they think will speed up this process. Feminism happens to be in vogue when Reed's protagonist, Ian Ball, is trying to get his second play...produced; and to see that the play does make it to the stage, he discovers that he's willing to do almost anything. He's willing to let Becky French, a white lesbian producer, turn his black hero into a malicious villain. He's willing to cow-tow to Tremonisha Smarts, herself a black writer who'll do anything to stay in favor.[5] He's willing to do anything that will make him marketable. (41)

Ian Ball and Tremonisha Smarts, then, find themselves playing roles that are unnatural to them in order to assimilate and achieve bourgeois status, two goals that are ultimately hollow insofar as they require a malevolent strain of tricksteristic behavior that benefits only the individual. Ball and Smarts must subsume their own desires as African-American artists for the sake of a party line that can only choke the vitality of their readings of Black experience. Reed issued similar warnings previously in *Yellow Back Radio Broke-Down* and

Mumbo Jumbo, but here the enemy is not Black nationalism. Rather, it is the materialism of the Black middle class in the post-Civil Rights era and the overwhelmingly materialistic 1980s that indirectly causes Black art and culture to suffer. The result is a stark double-consciousness more severe than any Du Bois could have imagined.

In the text's denouement, we discover that Ian Ball has been leading a double life as a vigilante who humiliates feminists, including Becky French, who disparage the image of Black men. This double life is a simultaneous manifestation of the "two-headedness or two-facedness" of Ian's Caribbean heritage and of his American upbringing and the source of the novel's final, greatest irony (Reed, *Reckless* 147). By virtue of his birthright, Ian contains within himself the potential to be a trickster in the traditions of Black Caribbean folk culture and HooDoo that his mother tries to sublimate via assimilation into mainstream American society. It is precisely this assimilation, however, that causes Ian to manifest his trickster heritage. Inasmuch as he is imbued with such a strong sense of American materialism, Ian struggles to achieve his material goals yet retain loyalty to his race and gender, two virtually irreconcilable goals in the novel's milieu. His split identity becomes another sign of the importance of African-Americans' (especially Black men's) need to keep culture intact at all costs. The alternative is to become truly "wrong-headed" and watch Black culture be coopted and therefore destroyed by mainstream America.

Tremonisha Smarts, on the other hand, functions as a paradigm for the integrity that Black people, especially Black artists, have lost and need to reify. She reveals that

> "I was writing about some brutal black guys who I knew in my life who beat women, abandoned their children, cynical, ignorant, and arrogant, you know these types, but my critics and the people who praised me took some of these characters and made them out to be *all* black men. That hurt me. The black ones who hated me and the white ones who loved me were both unfair to me....I thought they were my fans, those feminists, but some of them would have drinks and ask me about the 'raw sex' and how black men were, you know. Others used my black male characters as an excuse to hate all black men, especially some of these white women. Then they wouldn't feel so guilty for taking their jobs." (Reed, *Reckless* 129-30)[6]

After this revelation, Tremonisha decides she will leave the world of the intelligentsia and "just...get fat, have babies, and write write write," free of the ideological limitations that crop up among American intellectuals. The best artistic course for her and other Black artists to take is to remain true to the concerns that reflect their experience, rather than engage in an innately dishonest romanticism:

"Though the critics and the white feminists fell for it, I knew that those working class characters that I tried to write about and their proletariat voices I attempted to mime were phony. All of us who grew up in the middle class want to romanticize people who are worse off than we are....It won't be long before some of these teenage mothers will begin writing about places like Bed-Stuy themselves, and then all of us debutantes will have to write about ourselves, will have to write about our backgrounds instead of playing tour guides to the exotics." (Reed, *Reckless* 131)

Thus Reed offers his prescription for the maintenance of Black artistic integrity: attention to and writing about experiences relevant to one's self that reveal the richness of small, yet important niches of Black ontology. This allows a wider representation of Black experiences, thereby discouraging critics from engaging in the callous delimitation of African-Americans as a whole, no matter those critics' race or gender.

Japanese by Spring is largely a revision of *Reckless Eyeballing* as far as the structure of its plot is concerned. It simultaneously updates the problems of academic racism and intellectual cooptation for the cultural warriors of the 1990s and makes Reed's ideology increasingly explicit via the introduction of Reed himself as a major countervailing character in the satirical plot, one who actively contributes invective material to the novel's discourse. This is Reed's method of confronting the reader with the same type of hard, historical evidence that buoys his previous novels, but without the mediative function that his other characters have served. Moreover, this stratagem is perhaps a sardonic attempt to make Reed's personal views entirely lucid to a critical audience that continuously misreads his satire. *Japanese by Spring* represents Ishmael Reed's concatenation of the intensely fierce debates over the meaning of multiculturalism in United States academia in the late 1980s and early 1990s. It offers in novel form Reed's vision of what multiculturalism should be, as opposed to what it has tragically become, and his satiric assessment of the inanities of the most extreme poles in the debates. Set at fictional Jack London College in Oakland, California (an institution remarkably similar to the University of California at Berkeley, where Reed teaches), the novel utilizes pseudonymous characters and Reed's particular brand of reductio ad absurdam to represent the most visible scholars in the so-called "culture wars." These devices have the purpose and effect of satirizing the presence of established, nearly unquestioned racist beliefs, as well as a marked lack of moral courage and basic intelligence, in the multicultural debates' primary players. The solution to these debates is for the public at large to realize how mainstream American culture is always already multicultural. This realization may be what ultimately saves the United States from a race war, and is, to all appearances, possible only insofar as the public (including public intellectuals) is briefed on the fact surrounding events that clearly involve race.

Jack London College's central problem (which, besides possessing its pseudonymous value, acts as a synecdoche for American academia in general) is the existence of a dangerous relativism surrounding issues of race, class and gender among the campus' denizens, fostered primarily by incompetent administrators and neo-conservative gadflies. The novel's central figure is Benjamin "Chappie" Puttbutt, a Black English professor who, out of his own interest in safely obtaining tenure, mindlessly refuses to declare atrocious acts against Black students the racist acts they are and horrifically becomes a ludicrous apologist for the white perpetrators in front of the press:

> "The black students bring this on themselves," [Puttbutt] said, sucking on a menthol cigarette. Frowning to indicate gravity. Being careful not to leak any of the ashes on his blue blazer or gray slacks. "With their separatism, their inability to fit in, their denial of mainstream values, they get the white students angry. The white students want them to join in, to participate in this generous pie called the United States of America. To end their disaffiliation from the common culture. Black students, and indeed black faculty, should stop their confrontational tactics. They should start to negotiate. They should stop worrying these poor whites with their excessive demands. The white students become upset with these demands. Affirmative Action. Quotas....And so it's understandable that they go about assaulting the black students. The white students are merely giving vent to their rage. This is a healthy exercise. It's perfectly understandable. After all, the whites are the real oppressed minority. I can't think of anybody who has as much difficulty on this campus as blondes." (Reed, *Japanese* 6-7)

Reed intends Puttbutt's discourse to simultaneously demonstrate the intellectual contortions he must go to in order to become an apologist for racists and to create a thinly veiled parody of the ideology of Shelby Steele, whose book, *The Content of our Character* (1990), received lavish praise from innumerable conservatives and many liberals for its moderate stance on contemporary racial issues and its condemnation of Affirmative Action and other racial remedies.

Through this parodic illustration, Reed satirizes the wave of Black neoconservatives who emerged in the late 1970s and 1980s and their apparent *modus operandi* of crass careerism. It is, morever, Reed's version of one of essayist Derrick Bell's "Rules of Racial Standing":

> Few blacks avoid diminishment of racial standing, most of their statements about racial conditions being diluted and their recommendations of other blacks taken with a grain of salt. The usual exception to this rule is the black person who publicly disparages or criticizes other blacks who are speaking or acting in ways that upset whites. Instantly, such statements are granted "enhanced standing" even when the speaker has no special expertise or experience in the subject he or she is criticizing. (114)

Bell's rule is a fairly accurate assessment of the quality of intellectual discourse emerging from the sort of Black and other neoconservatives parodied in *Japanese by Spring*, insofar as Puttbutt/Steele is concerned. The novel levels numerous criticisms against neoconservatism, but they are all based on a central premise: opposition to multiculturalism and ethnic studies is grounded in racist, victim-blaming (il)logic that seeks to perpetuate the exclusion of people of color from mainstream university curricula.

We encounter further examples of neoconservatives attempting to delimit the breadth of discourse by and about people of color throughout the text. Reed's rhetoric rests comfortably on the devices of pseudonymity and reductio ad absurdum, as in the case of D'Gun ga Dinza, who is a caricature of Dinesh D'Souza,[7] author of *Illiberal Education: The Politics of Race and Sex on Campus* (1991) and, more recently, *The End of Racism* (1995), two of the most controversial texts in the so-called "culture wars." Dinza's role as a "high-pitched and high-strung" advocate of "antidiversity on panels and talk shows" reifies a premise that has run throughout Reed's work: muliticulturalism has always been an integral component of the American cultural fabric, and still is, despite the negative connotations attached to the term today (126-7). As evidence, Reed provides the following anecdote:

> Glossos United, an organization of artists, were using the term "multicultural" in the middle seventies, a few years before the right brought Dinza from India, and before its cooptation by the academic planting machine. Look at it this way, using the central antidiversity argument that freedom and democracy are Western inventions.
>
> Suppose that André Derain, Maurice de Vlaminck, Henre Matisse, Pablo Picasso, [et al.] denied themselves the opportunity to borrow from the art of Africa, because the countries which contributed the African sculpture which influenced their art had no history of democracy. Or suppose Bud Powell, considering a concert of Bach music, said, "I can't play this music because the Germans have had little experience with democracy"....If artists had paid attention to the central antidiversity argument, the tanka and the haiku would never have been introduced into American poetry, and so on. (127)

Thus Reed foregrounds several conspicuously troubling problematics of the "culture wars." First, most of the opponents of curricular and cultural diversity in the American university have extremely flimsy credentials vis-à-vis artists, including Reed, who actually produce the texts so hotly contested. Second, the tradition of intellectuals and artists borrowing from other cultural paradigms in order to create their own may be found in all cultures and is particularly well established in Western arts and letters. Third, academicians have had a long-standing habit of coopting the terminology of different egalitarianistic ideologies, such as multiculturalism, without either attempting to understand the implications of those terms or applying them properly to academia itself; they become merely fashionable bywords for career advancement or uncritically accepted shibboleths.

Each of these problematics continually weaves its way throughout *Japanese by Spring*, especially the latter problematic of intellectual cooptation, which in many ways contains the former two. Insofar as Puttbutt is the logical extension of *Reckless Eyeballing's* Ian Ball--both are upwardly mobile Black men striving for the material gains of the petty bourgeoisie despite the cultural costs-- cooptation remains a primary danger in each case since it causes each character to defy any sense of racial loyalty or self-respect. Ian Ball allows his identity as a Black man to be continually undermined; Puttbutt permits overtly racist students and administrators to heap racial slurs upon his person in order to maintain his image as a moderate, non-confrontational Black man in order to inch one step closer to tenure, which his department denies him, ironically, due to an article against *Othello* he'd written in his younger, more nationalist days (Reed 93-4).

Japanese by Spring, however, differs from *Reckless Eyeballing* in at least one facet. Puttbutt, unlike Ball, eventually finds himself in power as the "special assistant to the acting president of Jack London College" (Reed, *Japanese* 94) via the graces of a Japanese firm that purchases a controlling interest in the institution. After suffering the humiliation of his denial of tenure, Puttbutt proceeds with a thorough purging of the humanities departments' radicals and racists, two groups who are not, ironically, completely opposed in their ideologies. In each case, Puttbutt purges on the bases of personal revenge and a rediscovered sense of moral outrage. So long the player who refused to take the moral stance of defending other Black people in his career, Puttbutt, like Ian Ball before him, puts on a different face and adopts a second consciousness not unlike the one he possessed as a young nationalist. Subsequently, Puttbutt reorganizes the university into components that reflect each discipline's ideological pursuits, such as placing the Women's Studies department in the European Studies department as an ironic "reward" of sorts for statements the department chair, Marsha Marx, had made:

> "Europe is the source of our law, our values, and our culture, yet little had been done to recognize the role of women, the establishment of this great civilization," [Puttbutt] quoted from an MLA speech she'd made. "The way we see it, there's no significant difference between your aims and those of your patriarchal allies. You just wanted in." (Reed, *Japanese* 105)

The university's reorganization, however, eventually goes too far. The Japanese owners soon rename Jack London College after the infamous General Tojo and require the faculty to endure various humiliations that reinforce Japanese supremacy. These humiliations are, ironically, virtually identical to the sorts of humiliations that students and faculty of color endured when the university was funded and run by whites, and have the effect of showing the faculty, especially its white members, the folly of their previous beliefs in white supremacy or the other bigotries. Eventually the Japanese administration is ousted by the government, but not without a generous dose of gratuitous patriotism on the part of the faculty and students; they have reentered the cycle of jingoism.

Thus Reed returns to the hobby-horse of satirizing fey academicians, especially feminists, who fail to sincerely and fully support the ideals they profess due to their own aspirations for class mobility. The satiric thrust here demonstrates that while the problem of African-Americans pursuing middle-class material values, thereby bringing dangerous relativistic and neo-conservative philosophies to the university, is indeed perilous, it is not exclusive to that particular marginalized group. The case of the Women's Studies department further illustrates the text's overarching metaphor of power exchange. In other words, what happens when an individual or group previously excluded from the social mainstream suddenly gains access to power? Almost invariably, that power is squandered on frivolous ideologies and materials while the newly empowered try to hold onto what little power they have or gaining more power rather than enacting the social changes that engendered the original push for power. It is Omi and Winant's idea of a "war of maneuver" writ large and writ tragicomically.

Eventually, however, Reed does posit a solution to the stalemate engendered by rampant materialism among the text's marginalized groups via the character who bears his name. Put simply, Reed's argument is that a multiculturalism that is neither faddish nor materialistic will help restore the integrity and strength of progressivistic racial and cultural politics. This multiculturalism would mean that intellectuals would need to "stop moving in swanky company" and become "dogged populists" who "no longer would associate with cultural bigwigs in the establishment" (Reed, *Japanese* 191). Rather, they'd become involved in folk rituals, such as the humble service Ishmael Reed attends at the text's end to celebrate the resurrection of Olódùmarè, a god who lies dormant in the African-American experience. A god with whom African Americans lost contact after the breakup of the Yoruba empire and the slave trade which the people at Whittle Books [publishers of Arthur Schlesinger's *The Disuniting of America*, a neo-conservative critique of multiculturalism and Afrocentrism] blame on what they refer to as "African chieftains" (Reed, *Japanese* 217).

At this service and a festival on the following day, Reed watches as African-Americans revive a lost portion of their spirituality and observes people from all races exchanging food, clothing and other cultural artifacts, respectively. These combined events represent Reed's view of the point from which any reconciliation of American cultures and the easing of racial tensions must begin: recovery of individual cultures and their subsequent exchange via social and educational institutions.

As our reading of Reed's latter novels indicates, however, these recoveries and exchanges must always be honest and bound by neither crass materialism nor reductionist romanticism. Reed repeatedly avers that Americans' collective reluctance to acknowledge the potential within different cultures is a product of this dishonesty, one which resembles Ralph Ellison's conception of "blindness" in *Invisible Man*. In the satirical milieu of each author's works, America's reluctance will lead it to the brink of an apocalyptic self-destruction. Moreover, in Reed's case, the metaphor for this reluctance extends slightly beyond the plane of the physical world. It is as if Reed wishes us to acknowledge not only the potential within other cultures in a material sense; through the figures of Saint Nicholas, Black Peter, Ian Ball and NeoHooDooism, he is arguing that a variegated *spiritual* plane must become part of a collective national consciousness.

NOTES

1. Omi and Winant use Antonio Gramsci's terms "war of maneuver" and "war of position" to help describe the transformation of the status of African-Americans within the American political landscape. In Omi and Winant's summary of the terms, 'war of position' is 'predicated on political struggle--on the existence of diverse institutional and cultural terrains upon which oppositional political projects can be mounted, and upon which the racial state can be confronted" (74). "War of maneuver," on the other hand, "describes a situation in which subordinate groups seek to preserve and extend a definite territory, to ward off violent assault, and to develop an internal society as an alternative to the repressive social system they confront" (Omi and Winant 74).

   In other words, African-Americans are constantly in a state where they are forced to continually negotiate and renegotiate their social and economic status. At those points when the forces against which African-Americans have had to struggle, such as Jim Crow laws, are clearly defined, they undertake a war of position. When those forces and structures become more subtle and difficult to define, as has occurred in the post-Civil Rights era, the strategy of a war of maneuver is most commonly adopted as the best means to maintain a relative equilibrium (Omi and Winant 80-81).

2. Since *The Terrible Threes* is indeed a continuation of the events begun in *The Terrible Twos* and, as Jacob Epstein argues, is "almost impossible to understand without first having read *The Twos*, even though Reed provides a précis of the earlier book" (311), I shall discuss the novels together here, making distinctions between them only in the citations except where absolutely necessary.

3. *The Terrible Twos* tracks the unraveling of this plot and the efforts of numerous characters to derail it; *The Terrible Threes* is the chronicle of the plotters' attempts to hide the plot from the public, who learn of it at the end of the first novel.

4. The characteristic of an absence of justice in the hereafter, however, does not apply to *The Terrible Twos* or *The Terrible Threes*. In one pivotal scene that parodies Charles Dickens' *A Christmas Carol*, Dean Clift has a vision of the afterlife in which Harry S. Truman and Nelson Rockefeller are tormented for their acquiescence to brutality via their approval of the atomic bombings of World War II and the raid of Attica State Prison, respectively.

5. Smarts' play, *Wrong-Headed Man*, closely resembles certain aspects of Walker's *The Color Purple*, especially its oppressive Black men, though Reed greatly exaggerates the amount of domestic and sexual abuse in *Wrong-Headed Man* for his parodic purposes.

6. In addition to being a reference to the Trueblood episode of Ralph Ellison's *Invisible Man*, in which the narrator takes the rich white philanthroper Mr. Norton on a tour of the poor Black section of a Southern town, Tremonisha's notion of young, middle-class Black artists writing about their own experiences has been taken to heart, especially in Trey Ellis's novels, *Platitudes* and *Home Repairs*.

7. D'Souza also receives Reed's satirical treatment as Destar D'Nooza, sycophant of Saint Nicholas and Western Civilization, in *The Terrible Threes*.

WORKS CITED

Bell, Derrick. *Faces at the Bottom of the Well: The Permanence of Racism*. New York: Basic (1992).

Boyer, Jay. *Ishmael Reed*. Boise, ID: Boise State University Press (1993).

Fox, Robert Elliot. *Conscientious Sorcerers: The Black Postmodernist Fiction of LeRoi Jones/Amiri Baraka, Ishmael Reed, and Samuel R. Delany*. Westport, CT: Greenwood Press (1987).

Guilhamet, Leon. *Satire and the Transformation of Genre*. Philadelphia, PA: University of Pennsylvania Press (1987).

Martin, Reginald. *Ishmael Reed and the New Black Aesthetic Critics*. London: Macmillan (1988).

Omi, Michael and Howard Winant. "Racial Transformation in the United States: from the 1960s to the 1980s." Ed. Michael W. Apple. *Critical Social Thought*. New York: Routledge (1986).

Pinckney, Darryl. "Trickster Tales." *The New York Review of Books* (October 1989): 20, 22-4. Rpt. in Matuz, *CLC* 311-15.

Reed, Ishmael. *Japanese by Spring*. New York: Atheneum (1993).

---.*Mumbo Jumbo*. 1972. New York: Atheneum (1988).

---,Ed. *19 Necromancers from Now*. Garden City, NY: Doubleday (1970).

---.*Reckless Eyeballing*. New York: St. Martin's Press (1986).

---.*The Terrible Threes*. New York: Atheneum (1989).

---.*The Terrible Twos*. 1982. New York: Atheneum (1988).

Previously unpublished essay (1998). Printed by permission.

OVERVIEW

A Conversation with Ishmael Reed

Bruce Dick/Interview

The following interview was conducted by polycom telephone August 1 and September 20, 1997.

DICK: You've been writing fiction for over thirty years now. Looking back over your career, how would you assess the critical response to your novels?

REED: Some critics have made a genuine effort to study the different cultures from which my writing arises. Others have found it difficult to undertake the kind of intellectual adventure necessary to do so. When I invoked HooDoo as a reference for my early work, I was signaling to readers and critics that my work would be a modern interpretation of African American folklore. That I would depart from the modernist writing which had been the vogue from the turn of the century to the 1950s--these huge, sprawling things full of heavy-handed characterization, Freudian psychoanalysis, cryptic symbolism, and devoted to Western-bound political, aesthetic, and philosophical issues. Larry Neal spoke for our generation when he invoked the oral tradition in his introduction to *Black Fire,* an anthology he co-edited with Amiri Baraka.

Among African American writers, this took the form of these imitative works that were devoted to mimicking Hemingway and Faulkner, who, in turn, were imitating French models like Proust, according to Malcolm Cowley. I think this debate goes back to the one between George Schuyler and Langston Hughes. Schuyler, in "The Negro Art Hokum," saying that black writers should imitate Western literature, whatever that might mean, and Langston Hughes, in "The Negro and the Racial Mountain," saying that folklore could be the model for African American writers. Of course, Zora Neale Hurston went further than Hughes, or Du Bois, for that matter. And, of course, feminists are trying to adopt Hurston but she wasn't one. I wrote that in the introduction to her masterwork, *Tell My Horse,* but Henry Gates, Jr., deleted it at the request of a woman at Harper Row who was having a panic attack about black misogyny-- she was white. Gates said that my remarks would wave a red flag in front of the feminists, which to me indicated that by the summer of 1989, he had already made up his mind to go after the very lucrative women's studies market. You'll notice that the cover of the book has a black man riding a black woman's back. I asked Gates what this had to do with the book, and he told me to take it up with the publisher. He had no opinion about this black male-hating cover.

Getting back to the critical response, to my surprise, Darryl Pinckney and a few other African American critics reacted to this material with tirades and hatchet jobs, while white critics like Robert Fox, Sämi Ludwig, and Anna Chupa actually did their homework and were able to "make sense" of the experiments I was undertaking. I think that Pinckney is a good writer, but he and others who've done hatchet jobs on African American writers are mono-literate. They believe that the best African American writers are those who imitate Western models. For them, it's okay for writers to copycat the folklore of Homer, but to explore the folklore of other cultures is to be backward. It's okay for Darryl Pinckney to base his work with Robert Wilson on Assyrian folklore, but in the hatchet job he did against me, on behalf of powerful segments of the New York literary establishment, he said I shouldn't use African American folklore.

Another establishment hatchet man who believes the same thing is David Bradley. PEN/Faulkner liberals have told him that he's a great writer and as a result, the guy is insufferably arrogant. He has done hatchet jobs on Cecil Brown, John A. Williams, and Richard Wright, all of whom can write circles around the guy. He's writing a book now that criticizes the so-called founding fathers for holding slaves, which, as you can see, is an original observation. Some guy named Zukerman invited me to Penn to appear on a panel with Bradley, because they wanted their boy to go up against an "older, more establishment writer." I figured that it was a setup but had some business to take care of in the East so I accepted. This guy Zukerman was very rude to me, and the guy who introduced me at the beginning of the panel, a well-known poet whom other Irish American intellectuals refer to as a stage Irishman, wove in some sarcastic remarks about me. He tried to insult me by calling me a preacher, but on the way to the lectern, I reminded him that Nathaniel Hawthorne was a preacher and referred him to "The Minister's Black Veil." This was all done to make Bradley look good and to make me look bad. During the panel Bradley criticized my novel *The Free-Lance Pallbearers* in an attempt to get me into a head-butting contest with him for the entertainment of these white men who were all rooting for him. I was restrained because I have seen tokens come and go. Bradley is the kind of guy who goes to the right-wing *Chronicle of Higher Education*, which every week has some article jumping on black people, and assures these people that black people are unhappy in African American Studies because they'd rather be teaching Shakespeare. Don't these people get enough Shakespeare? The *Chronicle of Higher Education* recently featured a piece endorsing Nazi genetics, that appeared in *Commentary*, which, I guess, means that Norman Podhoretz and his son, John, are Übermenschen. The Pioneer Fund financed Charles Murray's Nazi attack on black people.

What Bradley doesn't know is that they call so many African American writers great that the word has lost its meaning. Henry Gates, Jr., has called about ten black women writers "great." When Gates and Bradley used voodoo as a term of derision, I figured that they were sending signals to the establishment and they were safe and weren't going to make white readers uncomfortable, which is the way you get over these days. Gates, in that bizarre fourth renaissance piece he did for *Time* magazine, seemed to be saying that. That black artists shouldn't make audiences "anxious," and that which sells the most is the best.

Do you think that Bradley and Gates, Jr., would get away with using terms like "Christian Scholarship" and "Christian Sociology" as terms of ridicule? On the other hand, when I invoke voodoo or African American religion, it signals that I could care less about what the Northeastern establishment thinks about me and whether they think of my work as "Mumbo Jumbo." You'll recall that on the jacket of *Mumbo Jumbo*, I included all of the hostile quotes that establishment critics and their African American gofers said about my work. These assimilationists are also uncomfortable because we went outside of the Western curriculum, their church, in order to find inspiration for our work. While they're worshiping Thomas Mann, André Malraux (exposed in a recent *New York Review of Books* to be a fraud) and other Western literary icons, we're hanging out in the woods. When you read their interviews and reviews, all they know are books by Western authors. All of the theorists in philosophy and other disciplines are Western. Everything.

Both the HooDoo and Yoruba religion emanate from an agricultural experience. They're country. It was the old people in the country who kept the old stories alive; in Nigeria it was the people from the backwoods, and it was country people in the South who did the same. William Bascom says that when he invited rural tradition-bearers to deliver the Yoruba stories about Olódùmarè and his family of "Saints," his servants were embarrassed because they were considered "rustic." These House Negroes are of the sort that the establishment sends out to put out literary brushfires among natives. Notice how the black writers of the 1960s are treated in books like this feminist propaganda volume that Gates put his name to called *The Norton Anthology of African American Literature*. He says that the black writing revolution of the 1960s was short-lived, when some of those he named produced some of their best work after the 1960s. The 1960s black writers were the most influential writers since the Imagists of the turn of the century. How can you put out an anthology of African American literature and leave out William Melvin Kelley, Lorenzo Thomas, Askia Muhammed Toure, Calvin Hernton, Cecil Brown, David Henderson, and John O'Killens, whose *And Then We Heard the Thunder* is as good as or even superior to Ellison's book, *Invisible Man*? When you decipher the propaganda line in Gates's *Norton*, it proposes that black men were "valued" and then, all of a sudden, a renaissance of black women writers occurred. Valued? If the establishment valued Richard Wright, Langston Hughes, and Chester Himes, who were desperately seeking funds toward the end of their lives, it had a funny way of showing it. Look at the way they treated O'Killens, who wrote the best book to come out of World War II, and John A. Williams, probably the best of African American pure novelists. When I made the speech honoring John A. Williams at Rutgers, I said that he should receive the Nobel Prize, and the white feminists were so rude and made such a commotion when I said that, that the African American faculty had to reprimand them. You can see why the establishment is pushing Northeastern Ph.D. intellectuals as the new black intellectuals. They serve a missionary function. The establishment is tired of being burned by extra-curricular and autodidactic intellectuals like Malcolm X, George Jackson, Eldridge Cleaver, Huey Newton, and John Henrik Clarke, and so they create a new intellectual rump regime.

Neo-Hoodoo begins in 1967, when I began to read about Marie Laveau's work in New Orleans. The manifesto was first published in the *Los Angeles Free Press*. Steve Cannon, Curtis Lyle, Jr., Quincy Troupe, Tom Dent, and I met in New Orleans about that time and made the traditional "Xs" on her tombstone. While her contemporary Creole academics were in France copycatting French culture, she kept a tradition alive that extends back to the rain forests. She saw herself as the descendant of Yemoja. ("She danced with the fish.") I am part of this tradition. I wrote the "Neo-HooDoo Manifesto" in 1969 and in the *Village Voice* last year, David Henderson, Steve Cannon, and a younger writer, the brilliant Darius James, were calling themselves Neo-HooDoo writers.

DICK: Is there a term you would apply to your fiction today? Through the years, you've used words interchangeably--gumbo, collage, hoodoo, Neo-HooDoo.

REED: All of those.

DICK: Let's return to the critical response. Most critics and scholars usually point to *Mumbo Jumbo* as your greatest literary achievement. Do you agree with this assessment?

REED: Many critics and scholars stopped reading me after the 1970s. I think that my work is more sophisticated now. The late Darwin Turner, who wrote some very favorable comments about my 1970s work in the *Parnassus Review*, said of my later work that it was too direct. He and other critics prefer the early work, which was heavily weighed down in symbolism and classical allusions. I think that the shift in my work began with *The Terrible Twos*, which used some of the socio-realist techniques that I had disdained in previous work. I was inspired by David Madden's *The Proletariat Writers*. I also became interested in black iconography in European myths. I found the relationship between St. Nicholas and Black Peter to be fascinating. But most of all, in 1979, we moved into a neighborhood that people at Harvard would call "underclass." I was able to see that many of the assumptions about these neighborhoods, including some of my own, were false. Gates wouldn't use terms like "a culture of poverty," which he used in *Forbes*, if he actually lived in one of these "underclass" districts. Nobody could live on the kind of checks that the welfare department provides for these families. They either have to work other jobs or hustle. And the criminal operations are so devoted to a work ethic that if the Fortune 500 were as devoted as they, there would be no trade deficit. Maybe what the government should do is to provide these criminal operations with cash incentive to go into legitimate business, like they're always encouraging farmers in South America to switch from growing coca leaves. The kind of corporate welfare that politicians extend to their campaign donors regularly. I recall one incident that occurred shortly after I moved here. A right-wing publication was requesting that I write a rosy piece about how beneficent the United States was toward the people of the world. I told them that a few blocks away from my house, people were lined up for food that a church was dispensing.

You know, I was writing about black-on-black crime, individualism, and personal responsibility long before the rise of the Talented Tenth regime. That was easy to do under Carter. But when Reagan was elected, I knew that the political climate would shift. That there would be trouble ahead. I wasn't going to be caught on the wrong side. *The Terrible Twos* and the subsequent books and plays were a response to a mean-spirited climate in which blacks, especially black men, would become the scapegoats for all that has gone wrong in American society. With the election of Reagan, millions of whites declared war on black Americans, and popular culture and intellectuals were enlisted to do the propaganda job. The movie version of *The Color Purple* was a good example of the offensive that took place in popular culture. *The End of Racism*, by Dinesh D'Souza, who has made a fortune from right-wing sponsors by using his dark face to make KKK remarks about black people, exemplified the assault on blacks that has emanated from think tanks. The media and the think tanks began to search for black faces to push this line. People who would say that the problem for many blacks was behavioral. In 1981, I was approached by the *Bill Moyers Show* to come on camera and endorse Reagan, because a famous black woman writer said that I would do so. I refused to do it.

DICK: What would be some examples of these "sophisticated" works that you mention?

REED: All of the novels I've written since *Mumbo Jumbo*, the poetry, and the theatrical works. I'm very satisfied with my most recent novel, *Japanese by Spring,* and my plays. The hatchet men who hounded me for my fiction can't follow me there because they don't know anything about theater. They can't do anything about my libretti because they don't know opera.

DICK: *Japanese by Spring* was well received here in the United States. How did you perceive the reactions in other parts of the world? In Japan, for example?

REED: In June 1996, I traveled to universities all over Japan and the critics and scholars were impressed that I would make some effort to study Japanese culture. When I signed autographs in Hiragana, the people who owned copies of the book were enthralled. In 1994, I received the Suszukini Hanayagi Award from the Osaka Community Foundation, an award that this Japanese group makes to American artists. It's very important that African American writers travel to Asia, Africa, and Europe. African Americans are under a propaganda assault of unprecedented proportions. The Committee on Responsible Philanthropy reports a 200 million-dollar war chest that's been used by the right wing to assault black people in the media and elsewhere. D'Souza has been made a millionaire for his efforts. He has received fellowships totaling $485,000 alone. I told an audience in Tokyo that they shouldn't believe these stereotypes that are beamed into Japan by places like CNN. I was on a show in Zimbabwe and said the same thing. I complained about the coverage of Africa by CNN. So, though we've been cut out of the dialogue, which is dominated by whites who say that racism no longer exists, or by feminists like Gloria Steinem, who says that sexism and racism have equal weight, diluting the oppression of millions of blacks, we can still take the discussion abroad.

DICK: There was a negative review that came out in *MELUS* by a Japanese scholar.

REED: I think that this guy was influenced by the badmouthing of my reputation by white feminists who've made Alice Walker into some kind of cult figure. One of these screwballs called in during one of her radio appearances and referred to her as the living Buddha. Trudier Harris wrote a devastating review of *The Color Purple* in *Black American Literature Forum*, in which she said its popularity was white feminist-generated. She received such hostility from them that she stopped writing about it. They tried to run me out of business after I criticized Stephen Spielberg's *The Color Purple*, which was the kind of movie that Nazis made about Jews in Hitler's Germany. They were also upset with my novel *Reckless Eyeballing*, which seems prophetic now. Pat McGee, author of *Ishmael Reed and the Ends of Race,* says that he interviewed some of these women and they hadn't even read the book. At least when Hitler arranged his show of degenerate art, he'd examined the work. These women are fascists. But why should Bob Fox be surprised that there would be fascist elements in the feminist movement? Their founding mother, Simone de Beauvoir, wrote for Vichy publications, and there were feminist elements in the Nazi Party and the 1920s Indiana Klan. I examined feminist fascism and racism in *Reckless Eyeballing* way before Tammy Bruce tried to take over NOW, using a racist attack on black men in order to make an appeal. She's been successful too. Many women have signed up for L.A. NOW because they have mixed-up emotions about black men. Anyway, Gates, Jr., and some of the others just about called me and others crazy for criticizing the movie *The Color Purple.* Said I was given to "bizarre overstatements" in a piece that was little more than a performance on his part for the purpose of impressing the feminist market. His remarks on *Reckless Eyeballing*, printed in *African American Writers*, edited by Valerie Smith, Lea Baechler, and A. Walton Litz, was a disgrace. He had to distance himself from me in order to have credibility among feminists. He said that critics like me were misguided for criticizing *The Color Purple*, which made it okay for feminists like his friend Catherine MacKinnon to launch racist attacks on people like Clarence Thomas. *The Color Purple* made it possible for white feminist racism toward black men to come out of the closet, where it had been stored since the Anglo-Saxon supremacists who led the suffragette movement. Feminist agitation led to the placing of a statue in the Capitol Rotunda that included a white supremacist, Elizabeth Cady Stanton. Black women protested and demanded that Sojourner Truth's image be added, and they were ridiculed by white feminists. Now that Ms. Walker has essentially made the same criticism of the movie as mine in her book, *Stepping into the Same River Twice*, I'm wondering whether Gates is going to call her "misguided." For her part, Ms. Walker said that she felt that with my criticism of *The Color Purple,* I was stalking her. Well, every day on t.v. somewhere, they're running *The Color Purple.* As a black man, I feel that I'm being stalked. Stalked by white directors, script writers, and producers who are using properties by black women in order to carry on a vindictive campaign against black men. Bell hooks has a good essay about how these guys are turning gifted literary projects by black women into propaganda pieces against black men in her book *Reel to Reel.* We're supposed to just keep quiet, and not engage in what Henry Louis Gates, Jr., calls "divisive polemics" against a feminist movement, elements of which, I continue to maintain, are the most serious threat to black male survival since the Klan. C. Carr, Valerie Burgher, Tammy Bruce, and Maureen Dowd are even to the right of David Duke when it comes to discussing black men.

Anyway, this Japanese critic was influenced by this sort of tabloid atmosphere that characterizes discussion of race and gender issues on American campuses by these femirazzi. He accused me of disparaging black women writers in *Japanese by Spring.* There's not a single line in the book disparaging of black women writers. This guy is one of those male critics from other ethnic backgrounds who've piled onto the maligning of black men that's a multi-billion-dollar market these days. Yet we seldom hear these guys talk about how they treat women of their own ethnic backgrounds. When I was in Tokyo, I met only one feminist. One! If he's so hot on women's liberation, why doesn't he lead a drive for women's lib in Japan? See how far he gets. I'm still waiting for Spielberg to do a movie about the mistreatment of women in American Jewish households, an issue that, according to some Jewish feminists, is a cover-up by the community. He could do one about the battery of women in Israel, also treated with silence. According to a spokesperson for a battery center in Haifa, one out of six Israeli women has been battered. He said that when he read *The Color Purple*, all he could think of was rescuing Celie. But what about rescuing Naomi and Rachel?

DICK: *The Critical Response to Ishmael Reed* is broken down into decades. Do you feel, judging by the critical response that you've read or know about, that the 1970s is your strongest decade? And the 1980s the most difficult?

REED: I think that my work is getting stronger. I can thank my feminist critics for this. When I was dumped on by white feminists and their African American divas, I made up my mind that never again would my career be impeded by special-interest cultural fascism. I began studying non-Western languages in 1989, and I haven't let up. I was bad at languages during my so-called formal education, but by the end of the 1980s, after years of financial insecurity, I was able to afford tutors, and the African Center at Berkeley awarded me two fellowships to study Yoruba. I'm translating works from the African oral tradition, which stand up next to the world's great literary epics. And from an examination of these works, I have concluded that this hemisphere's Africans may be Americans but they are still Africans as well. Africans came to this hemisphere with not only chains and shackles, which is what we hear about to death, but with stories, philosophies, psychologies, and aesthetics. They obeyed a work ethic that made the Calvinists seem lazy. They invented family values. You still find these elements in African American arts. Anyway, there may have been an attempt to cast me out of the literary community in the 1980s until now, but I'm gaining audiences elsewhere. When I traveled to Africa last year, critics and scholars over there were acquainted with my work. The next issue of my magazine *Konch* will feature works by some of the African writers I met there. I think that I've done my best work since the 1980s.

DICK: There are a few new scholars included in this collection who apparently view things the same way. Darryl Dickson-Carr, for example, who treats the last four novels pretty favorably. There is also a scholar named Daniel Punday, which brings me to my next question. In his article on *Reckless Eyeballing*, Punday discusses "the politics of literary reception." He says that you're aware of this politics.

REED: Absolutely.

DICK: And that what you're doing in your writing is actually baiting your audience, knowing beforehand what their response will be. If that's the case, don't you feel that some of this media response that you say judges your work for your audience is only natural, and that you actually bring some of this reaction and criticism on yourself?

REED: I'm getting a better break from the younger generation of scholars. A young woman from Martinique did the best work on *The Terrible Twos*. And Daniel Punday's piece on *Reckless Eyeballing* was first rate. He wasn't just poking around for evidence of misogyny, or trying to get over by grandstanding before some special-interest audience at my expense. I've had a good exchange with some critics who've been challenged by my work, and I've taunted some of them deliberately in my books, but to say that I bring this reaction on myself is too simple. Some of those who've written the most vicious reviews about me provide no evidence in these reviews that they've even read the books under review. This was true of those by Crouch and Pinckney. Pinckney dismissed my *New and Collected Poems* with one word: contentious. Certainly things are more complicated than that. People find my work offensive or insulting because I raise issues that others are reluctant to raise. Charles Johnson says that he would have been scared to write *Reckless Eyeballing*.

DICK: You've been saying that all along, haven't you? That just because something is fashionable or a fad, the other side's not going to go away.

REED: One of the roles of the trickster fiction is to raise issues that others won't raise. This has its hazards, because once in awhile you'll do a send-up exposing the foibles of a powerful special-interest group. Let me give you an example. I had a chance to see the headnotes about my work before the Gates *Norton* came out. They were so bad that I submitted some information to Barbara Christian, co-editor. In my notes about *Reckless Eyeballing*--a book that got Barbara Christian so incensed that she made such a scene at a party I left--I reminded them that some feminist scholars praised the book. In the final version of the headnotes, they not only left those women out, but in order to really do me in, and play to special-interest consumers, women's studies, etc., they said that Susan Brownmiller had also condemned the book. This never happened. In fact, I once received a letter from Ms. Brownmiller saying that she was a fan of mine, and that she liked *Yellow Back*. This *Norton* is an expression of Gates's view that black women writers are superior to black male writers, which is what he pronounced in his notorious review of an anthology edited by Mary Helen Washington. His announcement that he had capitulated to the feminist movement, and that from that time on, he'd be little more than their literary cheerleader. In this showbiz piece he made some remarks about my use of the word "bimp." Bimp is a word that I coined to denote a buppie who pays uncritical obeisance to the feminist movement, usually to push a product or for intimate favors. One of these guys, a brilliant young writer, tried to off me as a sexist in *Essence*. When a Hollywood movie that he co-wrote and produced came out, it was full of sexist language and shot in a sexist manner. There were close-ups of women's behinds and the whole number. Gates even embraces Andrea Dworkin, who believes that all men are evil and that even the instances of lesbians battering each other is the fault of men. He came close to endorsing Catherine MacKinnon's censorship proposals. I ran into him at J.F.K. shortly after the Washington review (*Times*, Oct 5, 1987) appeared, which was a result of black feminist pressure on him to share some of the women's studies loot, and, by coincidence, we were on the same plane to San Francisco. I challenged some of the assertions he made in the review and he was unable to defend them. I later asked Rebecca Pepper Sinkler, who was the editor of the book review, why white male and women writers weren't pitted against one another as black men and women were in the Gates review. Speaking of "divisive politics." They'd run a review of Jewish American literature along about the same time, and very few women were even mentioned, even though Jewish American women have been producing superior literature from the turn-of-the-century Yiddish writers to the present day. Ms. Sinkler indicated that the Gates review was a response to an article written by Mel Watkins, which was critical of some black women writers.

That review was the beginning of Gates's decline as a critic. He got into a real show-me-the-money mode. Now he's a tabloid writer for the *New Yorker* magazine. He's sort of a colored Rex Reed. I think that he's been upset by my criticisms of him. When he wrote that disingenuous piece for the *Times,* saying that the last vestiges of anti-Semitism were present among African Americans, adding another social pathology to the list that politicians and the Nazi media had aimed at African Americans, at a time when anti-Semite Pat Robertson and his millions of white followers were seizing the Republican Party, my response in *Airing Dirty Laundry* got to him. I pointed out that *A.D.L* at the time was saying that anti-Semitism among blacks was on the decline. He hadn't even read the poll that his conclusions were based upon. He said that he'd read about it in an article written by a Jewish feminist in the black male-hating *Nation* magazine. He didn't dispute my argument, but reminded me that he'd been generous to me. He wrote some very generous comments about my novel *Mumbo Jumbo*, but by 1982, according to the bibliography compiled by Settle and Settle, I was only 40 pages short of Richard Wright's. Skip Gates didn't discover me. Since the establishment has made him the H.N.I.C., people are afraid to criticize him. Bell hooks said that she was afraid to criticize him. For this deference, Gates has made her a member of his Talented Tenth cabinet. Somebody's got to keep the guy honest. Letters criticizing him are suppressed by the editors of these right-wing magazines he's working for. John Henrik Clark wrote a letter to the *Times* replying to Gates's charge that he was anti-

Semitic, and the *Times* refused to publish it. Martin Kilson wrote a letter to the *New Yorker*, in an attempt to engage Gates in a debate, and they said they were going to publish it, only to mysteriously back out.

He recently gave a blurb to a book by Abigail Therstrom, this woman who is a mole for the Manhattan Institute, a neo-Nazi think tank founded by William Casey, the late C.I.A. director. The late Charles Davis, his mentor, and my friend, told me to keep an eye on him, and so I'm just doing my job.

DICK: What about your relationships with other critics? Are you friends with Pat Holt, who reviewed some of your books in the past?

REED: She's a big Alice Walker fan. After her words of praise for *Reckless Eyeballing*, some members of the Walker cult apparently got to her, and so some of her comments about me since then have been nasty. Her book review has become a black male-bashing outfit like the *Village Voice,* National Public Radio, Pacifica Radio, and the *Nation*, now that Katrina Vanden Heuvel has taken over. Bell hooks was right when she said that white feminists have a different misogyny standard for white men and black men. And so Pat Holt dismissed Claire Bloom's book about the psychotic misogyny of Phillip Roth. She said it was Bloom's fault for being attracted to such men. Other publications which have given black men a hard time have hired women to criticize books by Adele Mailer and Mia Farrow, about the misogyny of Norman Mailer and Woody Allen. Michiko Kakutani tried to run me out of business for *Reckless Eyeballing*, a book she reviewed in her column for the *New York Times*. She falls all over herself kissing up to powerful white misogynists. While Kakutani gives black men a hard time, writing in one review that a Toni Morrison book proved that black men treated black women, during slavery, worse than the slave master treated blacks, she praises some white male writers for their "jazz" writing, while genuine black jazz writers have never been reviewed in the daily book column that she runs for the *Times*. She's like Terry Gross of NPR. She runs shows on black misogyny, but adored Phillip Roth, who once said in *Esquire* "Fuck the feminists," and then she has the nerve to give credit to white men for forms created by black men. She says that rock and roll is a white invention. She says that Elvis Presley changed American music. How? Because he mixed black music with country-western music? She thinks country-western music is white when some of the originators of country-western music were black. As for mixing these genres, she's never heard of Chuck Berry or Allen Toussaint. It was a black man who created the term "Grand Ole Opry," and he's never been elected to the Grand Ole Opry Hall of Fame. Even the banjo, that's used in country-western music, is an African invention.

I've watched all-white panels discuss why progressive feminists haven't come to Paula Jones's aid as readily as they did Anita Hill's. The one possibility that is never discussed is that it's easier for feminists to do-in black men than to hit a powerful white man. After all, this is a movement that has been accused of racism by black women for over a hundred years. Ironically, right-wing women have taken positions more favorable to black men than these "progressive" women like Gloria Steinem, who said that *The Color Purple* told the truth about black men, which is the kind of generalization that has hounded Jews for centuries. By contrast, Linda Chavez said that the women's movement was trying to bring down Clarence Thomas by using ancient sexual stereotypes about black men. Kate O'Beirne of the *National Review* said that if black drill sergeants are going to be sent to prison for having consensual sex with white women, then the women should be sent to prison as well. Contrast that viewpoint with that of Gates, who has signed on to every feminist agenda since 1989. He uncritically accepted all of the charges made against Sgt. Gene C. McKinney, even though some of these women contradicted themselves and lied. He must believe with his buddy Anita Hill that the woman must always be believed. He made no attempt whatsoever to present McKinney's position. It's obvious that when it comes to black men, feminists are engaged in hypocrisy and chicanery and obey a double standard. Pat Holt is now exhibiting all of the symptoms of post-traumatic stress when it comes to black men. She can't get Clarence Thomas or Mike Tyson or O.J. off her mind. She recently interviewed Maya Angelou, and all she could think to ask her was about Thomas and Tyson. She reviewed a book by Paula Barbieri, in which Paula Barbieri said that O.J. was bad at sex. You'd think that this would end it, but I doubt it.

DICK: Some well-known African American writers continue to commend your work. When Nikki Giovanni was on our campus two or three years ago, she praised your writing.

REED: Nikki and I go back to the 1960s. She included a chapter about my work in her new book, *Shimmy, Shimmy, Shimmy Like My Sister Kate*. I have a very good relationship with many black women writers. Thulani Davis, Joyce Carol Thomas, Lucille Clifton, and Baraka Sele all give me credit for assisting them during the early stages of their careers. We were the first to publish excerpts from Ntozake Shange's *Colored Girls*. Terry McMillan was my student at Berkeley, and we were the first to publish a work of fiction by her. The attacks on me as a misogynist emanate from powerful factions in the feminist movement, and from white males and from black men who try to get in good with feminists by stomping me. In the grandstanding piece by Gates, he challenged *Reckless Eyeballing* because it proposed that powerful white feminists were supporting the attack on black men by a few divas. Recently, Michele Wallace said the same thing in the *Village Voice*. That corporate feminists at *Ms.* were backing the divas. In an interview with Cecil Brown, Toni Morrison methodically laid out the tactics that Gloria Steineim used to get *The Color Purple* over. And bell hooks, before she became a *Ms.* magazine diva, said that white feminists told her that in order to get over, she had to write for them. Michele Wallace told me that white *Village Voice* feminists were always trying to get her to hit black men, which explains why Ed Bullins, John O'Killens, James Baldwin, Bill Gunn, and other black male writers, including myself, get hit in the *Voice* for our misogyny, while white writers like William Burroughs are always praised by white feminists at the *Voice*. Burroughs murdered his wife. Ultimately, I get my problems from white feminists. About two years ago Joe Wood, who was at the *Village Voice* at the time, asked me to do a piece about Oakland. When he submitted it, Karen Durbin, who was the radical feminist editor at the *Voice* then, and who takes credit for creating Gates as a public intellectual, wouldn't even read it. She said that I was a misogynist. This was ironic because my first experience with feminist censorship occurred at the same publication in 1979.

When white feminists in San Francisco asked Ntozake Shange to condemn me she refused, and when two white feminists successfully prevented me from appearing on a panel sponsored by the National Writers' Union, Gwen Carmen, editor of a black lesbian magazine, cussed them out, publicly.

DICK: The references seem endless.

REED: When they say that I have some feud with black women writers, on the basis of what Margo Jefferson, Barbara Smith, and a few others have said about my work, they're engaging in racist thinking. Margo Jefferson commented about misogyny in my books in *Newsweek* (Dec 20, 1976) and elsewhere, and when I gave a party in N.Y. to celebrate our publication of Calvin Hernton's *Medicine Man*, she showed up and made such a scene, accosting me publicly with charges of misogyny, that I thought we'd have to call the police. She went out, screaming and shouting all over the place. In an edition of the *New York Times* (Sept. 17, 1997), she praised John Wayne, a man who said that he was all for women's lib as long as they had his dinner ready when he got home. She gets on my case but writes a soppy, goofy valentine for John Wayne, the very symbol of American macho. She talks about his "beauty," and she says that she can't watch his films without feeling that "John Wayne is a dangerous, savage Other whom I must destroy or be destroyed by. But I can no longer dismiss the lure and force of his screen presence." Remarkable! I guess that Anne Rice was right. You got to treat them rough. But John Wayne wasn't all that rough. I knew his black mistress. She ran a restaurant in Berkeley. She used to wear a blond wig. She said that on the night that he received an Oscar, he wept in her arms like a baby.

DICK: A couple of minutes ago you mentioned that you're part of the trickster tradition. You've been saying that for a long time too. One of the things revealed in *Conversations with Ishmael Reed* is that you are repeatedly compared to white writers. You also mentioned how much of a global world it is now. Are you still writing out of the trickster tradition? That vein? Is this something you're conscious of now when you write?

REED: I invoked the trickster because some Native American scholars identified my work as such. When Punday says that I engage in an exchange with critics, he's right. Critics like Peter Nazareth have influenced my work. They write constructive criticism. *Reckless Eyeballing* is my consummate trickster novel. But there are differences between the Native American trickster and the African trickster. They both can change shapes, but the Native American trickster sort of shows up and injects irony into a scene. The African trickster is very busy, accomplishes a number of tasks, and serves as Olódùmarè's enforcer. Though some critics associate him with indeterminacy, his judgments about good and evil are cut-and-dried. He knows a lot, having dwelled among the dead for one hundred years, and he is a hunter, which requires patience. Esu-Kekere-Ode, the little hunter. The main difference between the Native American trickster and the Esu figure is that the Native American trickster doesn't engage in didacticism. The African works I've read in the original are very didactic.

DICK: We've talked before about Michele Wallace's critical article on your work, especially *Eyeballing*. What is it that she has said recently that makes you think she's changed her mind about your writing, or what have other African American women critics and scholars done to indicate their change?

REED: The second part of your question indicates the success that white feminists have had in smearing my reputation. White feminist writers, scholars, and reporters have maintained that I am engaged in a feud with African American women critics and scholars on the basis of a few black women writers and critics badmouthing me. This shows that these women are incapable of exploring the complex and diverse works by black women other than those of *Ms.* magazine, ordained by divas. They like the work that bashes black men, which justifies their racist attitudes toward black men. Joyce Ann Joyce is one of the best critics writing in America today, but they don't support her because she fails to hew the party line, and because she's had a run-in with Henry Gates, Jr., who's tried to corner the feminist market by lambasting black male writers, even Richard Wright and Ralph Ellison. They're dead and can't defend themselves. In the last two years, even white feminists have broken ranks in their appraisal of my work. Women's bookstores are inviting me to appear, and places like Mills College, a hotbed of feminist power, have also invited me to appear on programs. This is because my former critics have begun to re-examine *Reckless Eyeballing*, the work that got me into trouble. I was the first to write about fascist and racist elements in the modern feminist movement. Feminist reaction to Clarence Thomas and O.J. Simpson and the rise of a Klan faction in NOW have proven my point. Michele Wallace was the master of ceremonies when I received the Langston Hughes Medal at City College in 1995 and was extravagant in her praise for my work. The only person who brought up this black woman-hating charge was a black male professor who dredged up a statement that Barbara Smith had made about my work twenty years ago. His statement was treated unfavorably by my black women fans who were in the audience. He thought that he was going to grandstand on me, and it backfired. Incidentally, when Barbara Smith was used by *Ms.* magazine to hit me, I wrote Robin Morgan, who was then editor, demanding that I receive as much respect as the men who owned their publication. When she resigned as editor of *Ms.*, whom did she hit? Not the misogynists in the Pentagon who bombed an Iraqi baby food factory, killing hundreds of her colored sisters. Not the white men involved in Tailhook, during which women were assaulted and raped. Not the men in Congress and their allies, who used Anita Hill to justify their candidacies, both of whom voted for a welfare bill that cuts poor women--black, white, and brown--off of food stamps, but Mike Tyson and Clarence Thomas. *Ms.* magazine, according to a *Nation* writer who used to work there, kept black women off the cover because it was felt that their appearance on the cover would "depress" sales, but ran a number of articles lambasting black men which, I guess, boosted sales. That's another reason for the assault on black men by the feminist movement, Hollywood, and infotainment news industry. It's big business. The guy at the Langston Hughes ceremony was trying to get in good with women in order to score points with women.

Some white males are thrilled by this black male-bashing for obvious reasons. It takes the heat off them. Two white male critics, writing for San Francisco newspapers, jumped on my play *Savage Wilds* about the entrapment of Marion Barry, in which the government's role was that of a pimp, as a misogynist play, yet black media feminists in Washington, D.C., raised the money for a staged reading that occurred there.

DICK: Some of the writers in this collection who do "overuse" the word misogyny are male.

REED: Yes, well, I haven't read your book, but I'm sure that these critics, if they are white, haven't done a thorough job in investigating the misogyny that takes place in their own ethnic groups and view it as a black thing, and if they're black, they're probably hypocrites like Gates. He talks about my misogyny, yet I didn't see him resigning from the *New Yorker* when Jamaica Kincaid was fired. He hangs out with Marty Peretz, who said that black women were "culturally" deficient. Why hasn't he jumped on Peretz the way he did on Farrakhan? Why doesn't he insist that progressive Jews be given space in these neo-conservative publications where he has power? Why doesn't he ask his friends at the *New Republic* to hire progressive Jewish women writers? Why doesn't he criticize the *New Yorker*, where his colleague is Joe Klein, the biggest liar of the 1990s, who recently had the moxie to write an article suggesting that the inner cities be turned over to the churches? Somebody ought to turn him over to a religious institution. Why doesn't Gates criticize Klein's racist book, *Primary Colors*? The book did reveal his idea of an ideal black male--a spineless, cultureless, impotent nerd. The *New Yorker* uses Gates to front issues about crime in which all of the faces are black, the kind of propaganda that the Nazis used against the Ost-juden. The fact that some Jewish Americans have a hand in creating these kinds of images of black people in New York magazines, Hollywood, and television must come under the banality of evil. It shows what assimilation can do to you. Erase the memory of your group past. Ironic, no?

Bob Fox, who used to call me a misogynist, recently said that he did so in order to score brownie points with the feminists. He's honest. The others are not so honest.

DICK: Fox is a serious scholar and one of the first to write about your work. Many other scholars allude to his work.

REED: Fox knows more about African and African American literature than the assimilationalists who they trot out to blast Afrocentricity. I invited one of these Talented Tenthers to debate Mauluna Karenga in the pages of my magazine *Konch*, and he never replied to my offer. He knows that in a debate with Karenga about African civilization, he'd get his clock cleaned. Karenga would waste Gerald Early, who carries on about Afrocentricity in some Eurocentric publication called *Civilization*. Contrast Fox's serious attempt to understand the African American folklore upon which our work is based and that of Neil Schmitz, whom they're always quoting when they want to put me down. He said that the material I was working with was arcane. A number of magic realist novelists include allusions associated with Yoruba religion in their work. They're praised by the same people who criticize me for using arcane material. I was told by the Nigerians, when I was in Ghana last year, that they have an Orisha festival in Nigeria, attended by people from all over the world. I attended an Hispanic film festival the other day, and saw a film called *Santera*, directed by Solveig Hoogesteijn, about Yoruba religion in Venezuela! I always thought that Venezuela was white and Indian. Apparently the Africans took their religion wherever they arrived, attracting Indian and white converts. This is a culture that Neil Schmitz calls arcane. This is the problem with white supremacy. It encourages an isolated perspective that damages us all, and the best example of this isolated perspective is the so-called American school curriculum. And they give you these SAT scores, administered by this company that has been accused of covering up widespread cheating by whites for years.

DICK: Stanley Crouch has also been critical of some of your work for a number of years. His piece on *The Terrible Twos* is included in this volume.

REED: He was assigned to do *Twos* by Elizabeth Pochoda, a notorious black-male hater. She hates my guts. She also sponsored a racist hatchet job on me that appeared in the *New York Post*. He reviewed the book without any evidence in the review that he had read it; he conducted an "interview" with me in which he did all of the talking, and he wrote about the publishing record of my publishing company, and the history of the Before Columbus Foundation, without asking me or my associates a single question about either. You'll notice that he hasn't reprinted that essay in any of his books. Quincy Troupe made the same complaint about Crouch. He told Quincy that he admired his Miles book, only to go out and do a hatchet job for the *Village Voice*. I think that Stanley has matured since those days. He no longer feels the need to be a literary assassin for hire. He's passed that to Dinesh D'Souza admirer Gerald Early, who even did a number on Langston Hughes. You know, Steve Cannon and I got into trouble for interviewing George Schuyler, a conservative, but this new crowd makes Schuyler seem like a flaming progressive. Anyway, the *Nation* feminists have had it in for me since that review. They never reviewed any of my books after the Crouch review in 1982. I asked the guys at the *Nation*, who are always asking me to write articles, why no review of my book has appeared in that publication since 1982. They say they don't run the book review. The same thing has happened at other publications, where white feminists have control, including the *American Book Review*, which, ironically, I co-founded and where a feminist, Rochelle Ratner, is executive director. White feminists at the *Detroit News* prevented a review of *Reckless Eyeballing* from appearing there. In the 1950s, you had the blacklist, and I'm sure that the parents of some of these women were on it. Now you have the sexist list. I'm on that one.

DICK: Do you think this criticism might have something to do with what you said to Walt Shepperd in a 1968 interview? You mentioned then that when a "black man tries to be a satirist, tries to look at the whole universe...all these cats get uptight." And later you mentioned that white writers have more freedom to be avant-garde than black writers do.

REED: Sure, black writers are confined to realism. They are also handicapped by the puny range of intellectual and cultural life in this country. If you examine the tastes of many white intellectuals and writers, you'll discover that their reading habits are confined to the works of those who resemble them--other white men. When they enjoy non-Western forms like Native American poetry, or black music, they don't feel comfortable with them unless they manufacture white invention of these forms. I remember a famous review that appeared in the *Times* in which the white reviewer said that Stan Getz was better at Brazilian music than the Brazilians. I enjoy Getz's music, which was influenced heavily by Lester Young, but to make that claim is merely an expression of white nationalism. These are the people who set the standards. And they spend millions of dollars and take up a great deal of media time, taking anti-intellectual positions, like opposing the study of other cultures and bilingualism, and designing I.Q. tests that are favorable to people like them. (*A.D.L.* recently revealed that the man who designed most of the I.Q. tests, Raymond B. Cattell, was a Hitler admirer.) But there's nothing wrong with realism. I'm taking drawing lessons now, in connection with the O.J. book, and I've decided that maybe abstract expressionists are people who can't draw. Some of them. Pollock could draw, if you look at his early work, but some of the others can't. What I'm saying is that black artists should explore as many forms as there are available to other artists.

DICK: So you still think, as you've said before, that white, black, and other critics and writers still want blacks to write about how much they "suffer"?

REED: Yes, I still think so. For the women. And so a mediocre book like *Their Eyes Were Watching God* gets canonized because these people have given Gates so much power, yet her masterwork, *Tell My Horse*, is ignored. That's because the women who back Hurston are Christian missionaries who write books about how men should atone. Apparently they need no atonement. They're perfect. I thought that Tremonisha from Scott Joplin's opera was a perfect symbol for these types. You'll notice that in the libretto she stands for enlightenment (assimilation) and opposes the HooDoo men of the forest.

Gates was giving the establishment hell before he made a deal with the feminists. He was accusing them of treating black intellectuals and writers the way they would the people who served them drinks. But then he compromised. Said that if they'd admit a couple of black divas to the canon, he'd call off the dogs. He then began picking on welfare mothers and even told one audience that multi-generational welfare dependency was a problem, when such situations are rare and the majority of welfare recipients are only on welfare for a short time. He engages in this sort of talk show-type rhetoric about black teenage pregnancy without mentioning that dramatic drop in teenage pregnancy that was recently reported by the Center for Disease Control. For the males, it's the Horatio Alger story about how they succeeded where other African Americans failed, due to their character flaws. His book *Colored People* is a good example of that. If the Talented Tenth continues to mimic the insidious trend rightward, soon it'll be because of their genes. The kind of talk that's coming out of *Commentary* these days. We prefer the pre-1987, early Gates, the intellectual warrior and ass-kicker to the one we have now.

DICK: So this is not only something that white critics have said but black critics too?

REED: Sure. The women get away with these novels in which flawless, virtuous women protagonists triumph over male evil, not only because of white women book buyers' mixed-up emotions about black men and their need for sexual voyeurism, but because the establishment needs to blame all of the social problems on black men. I believe that these divas have the right to write whatever fiction they desire, and the academic femirazzi, who've distorted my views about *The Color Purple,* forget that I called the novel "gifted," but their remarks about black men in the press merely promote old stereotypes.

DICK: I'd like to shift now to some of the fiction you're currently working on. Two years ago when I saw you in New York, you said that you were not only working on *The Terrible Fours* but another novel, on O.J. Simpson, which you were calling *Making a Killing.* Could you talk a little about both books?

REED: I'm working on a novel about the O.J.Simpson case. It's very difficult because the case is still a developing story. Writing it is like trying to capture a comet. The hysteria in this case, driven by white feminists who've used black men like Clarence Thomas and Mike Tyson to score points for their agendas, while ignoring the sexist crimes of the men from their own ethnic groups, will make it difficult to get this novel published. One thing that is clear about trickster fiction is that it challenges, provokes, and even infuriates. My O.J. novel will raise some sand. Toni Morrison stuck her neck out with *Birth of a Nation'hood.* Even though she's won all of these prizes, the book was ignored by the media. One of the best reviews appeared in a Toronto newspaper, which shows how reasonable some whites can be when they're not prone to white settler-hysteria. Seeing themselves surrounded by millions of dark people, etc. The fear of the "Other" among white people in the U.S. is at an all-time high, and it's exploited by the press, the popular culture, public relations intellectuals, think tanks, and academics. Can you imagine a book edited by a white Nobel Prize winner being ignored?

DICK: Why do you suppose?

REED: Because writers in *Birth* depart from the line promoted by the media and the commentary that O.J.Simpson was guilty or that he received a fair trial. The civil trial, with its all-white jury, was a disgrace and the judge had made up his mind about O.J.'s guilt before the trial even began. The same commentators who are accusing the judge in the Marv Albert case of shepherding the decision, ignore the fact that the judge in the civil case did the same thing. Geraldo Rivera and other Simpson-haters, who are crying over the fact that 85% of the defense evidence was left out of the Albert case, rejoiced when the civil judge in the Simpson case threw out the defense's case. The press didn't castigate the all-white civil jury, which included six white women, as much as it did the criminal jury, because they agreed with their decision. I saw a panel of lawyers who were mostly against O.J., and when asked by Alan Dershowitz whether they thought that the decision against O.J. Simpson was unjust, agreed with Dershowitz that it was, but they doubted whether a California appellate judge would have the guts to overturn the verdict. The hostility against black people in this state under Pete Wilson is like that against black people in Mississippi of the 1920s. Contemporary Mississippi is enlightened in comparison to California. Cecil Brown was called a "nigger" on the streets of counterculture Berkeley, this so-called radical town, and Janice Edwards, a local newscaster, was called a "nigger bitch" in the same town. The case against O.J. was driven by public hysteria, whipped up by the press, especially that of white feminists who've lost their minds over black misogyny. The press not only controls the political system but the judicial system as well. I suggested at one point that we should have a system here like Canada's, where the press can't comment on a case until the jury makes a decision. Of course I have organized boycotts and panels about the media since 1990. Jesse Daniels, in her book *White Lies*, says that she studied the Nazi press, and that their image of blacks is no different from that of the mainstream press, and in fact, uses images from the mainstream press to promote its arguments. In my O.J. novel, Ishmael Reed will be discussing this history.

DICK: When you used the Reed character in *Japanese by Spring*, was this a conscious attempt to straighten out what critics have said about the real Ishmael Reed?

REED: Writers and artists including themselves in their work is nothing new. My aim in the book was to engage in a dialogue between the author and a fictional character.

DICK: When is the O.J. book coming out? Is it finished?

REED: I don't know. It will include drawings and newspaper photos and other graphics.

DICK: Anything else?

REED: It's going to be a big hell-raiser.

DICK: And *The Terrible Fours*?

REED: *The Terribles* have built up a following, especially in Europe. It's interesting to watch the American critics' response to the book. Gerald Early successfully killed the book sales for *The Terrible Threes* with his comment in the *New York Times* that the book didn't make sense. I've never seen a review like that before. If someone sent me a book to review and it didn't make sense to me, I'd send it back so that another reviewer could review it. Early is Stanley's one convert. As in the Crouch *Twos* review in the *Nation*, Early made no attempt to delve into the novel's narrative, no mention of the characters--just a lot of remarks and grandstanding. He then spent a lot of time in another book criticizing me for my devotion to boxing in his book about boxing. Odd, huh?

I salvaged *The Terrible Threes* by buying a sizable amount of the inventory. And so *The Terrible Twos* and *The Terrible Threes* are still in print. Sooner or later these hatchet men that they send after me will realize that the only thing that can stop me is a debilitating illness, or death, and after that my daughters, both of whom can write and have published, will take over.

DICK: And *The Terrible Fours*?

REED: The *Fours* are underway. It begins with scenes taking place in another galaxy. Some critics are having difficulty with this series because they can't have the final word on these books. They don't know what's going to happen next.

DICK: Some people have said that the *Terribles* series is too esoteric and some say it's your most accessible work. How do you feel about this response?

REED: The *Terribles* are straightforward in comparison to the early work.

DICK: I'd like to shift focus once again. As you know, mainly because of space limitations, this collection of criticism focuses on your fiction. But you've written in several other genres, including drama. Would you care to discuss some of this work and what you've recently been writing for the theater?

REED: My first full length work was a play. It was called *Ethan Booker* and dealt with conflict between Muslims and Christians on a southern campus. It was written in about 1961. I acted in Buffalo theater before I went to New York. I've always had an interest in theater and was writing little plays in second grade.

DICK: Has all of your drama been staged?

REED: Everything but *Mother Hubbard* that was written in the late 1970s. But now some high school students in Berkeley have chosen it for production. I'm pleased with this, because these kids aren't power brokers, or chose this play because it sends out a neo-conservative message to blacks, or because they're friends of mine. There was a staged reading of this play at Dartmouth, and Actors' Studio and I tried to shoot a video production of it, but a technician messed up the sound. A woman from CBS asked me to write a film script for *The Free-Lance Pallbearers*. I went way beyond the original novel.

DICK: How was that received?

REED: Very well. At the Actors' Studio, Clarence Williams III, played the lead. And Bill Cook directed a reading at Dartmouth. Since *Mother Hubbard*, four plays--*Savage Wilds*, *Hubba City*, *The Preacher and the Rapper*, and most recently, *The C Above C Above High C*--were produced at the Nuyorican Poets Cafe. Three plays were just published by Scribner's Touchstone. They include *Savage Wilds*, *The Preacher and the Rapper*, and *Hubba City*. The title of the volume is *Action: Plays from the Nuyorican Theatre Festival*. It's edited by Nuyorican producer Miguel Algarin. *Hubba City* and *Savage Wilds* were originally staged in Berkeley, Oakland, and San Francisco. The Black Repertory Theater in Berkeley did *Hubba City*, and Ed Bullins's BMT theater in Oakland did *Savage Wilds*. In 1992, Bobbie McFerrin selected me to be the librettist for an opera he wanted to score for the SF Opera Company. After about three drafts, I completed the libretto in 1994. It took him two years, after we had all signed off on the final version, to decide that he was unable to provide music for the piece, and then he chose Tony Kushner to write a libretto for a play that had been written in the 1700s. They had a press conference and said that my libretto was rejected because it was more like a dramatic oratorio. Nobody mentioned that this is what I was asked to do--write a dramatic oratorio based on Bach's "Saint Matthew's Passion." I didn't make an issue of this. I didn't want to embarrass McFerrin. I had a libretto, and the Opera officials treated me very well. I learned a lot. For example, most of the operas that I saw were very political. Now, we're told by some pretentious critics that politics and art don't mix. Yet some of the most famous operas are very political, and opera is supposed to be the highest form of Western art. I also met Kathleen Battle and was able to watch her perform at a rehearsal. It was like a command performance. My libretto, *Gethsemane Park*, is a people's opera. It deals with contemporary issues like homelessness, and the kind of Spencerian Darwinism that characterizes the attitude of the boomers, Reagan's children, toward the poor. Berkeley's Black Repertory Theater, a community theater, will produce this opera in the spring. This is the perfect place for it. Carman Moore, one of our best composers, with whom I've worked on other projects, is writing the music. This opera will bring this form to the African American community of the East Bay, and it will give black singers who don't get roles in the uptown opera scene a chance to do their stuff. People who can't afford opera tickets will be exposed to opera. This is what my plays have accomplished. Dozens of African American actors and actresses, directors, etc., have been able to perform in roles that are usually off-limits to them. Roles that are not demeaning like the terrible things they have to do in order to get over in Hollywood or television.

Selected Bibliography

Book Reviews, Articles and Books

Ambler, Madge. "Ishmael Reed: Whose Radio Broke Down?" *Negro American Literature Forum* 6 (1972): 125-31.

Baker, Houston. "Books Noted: *The Last Days of Louisiana Red.*" Rev. of *Last Days of Louisiana Red. Black World* (1975): 51-52, 89.

Bamberger, W. C. "The Waxing and Waning of Cab Calloway." *The Review of Contemporary Fiction* 4.2 (1984): 202-204.

Baraka, Amiri. "Afro-American Literature and Class Struggle." *Black American Literature Forum* 14.1 (Spring 1980): 5-14.

Boccia, Michael. "Ishmael Reed's *Mumbo Jumbo*: Form of the Mystery." *Journal of Popular Literature* (Spring/Summer 1987): 98-107.

Boyer, Jay. *Ishmael Reed.* Boise, ID: Boise State University, 1993.

Bryant, Jerry H. "Books and the Arts: Who? Jes Grew? Like Topsy? No, Not Like Topsy." Rev. of *Mumbo Jumbo. The Nation* (September 1972): 245-247.

---."Old Gods and New Demons: Ishmael Reed and His Fiction." *The Review of Contemporary Literature* 4.2 (1984): 195-202.

Bush, Glen. "Ishmael Reed: Post-Modern and Narrative Architecture in *Mumbo Jumbo.*" *MAWA Review* (June 1990): 1, 20-23.

Bush, Roland E. "Werewolf of the Wild West: On a Novel by Ishmael Reed." *Black World* (1974): 51-52, 64-66.

Byerman, Keith E. *Fingering the Jagged Grain: Tradition and Form in Recent Black Fiction.* Athens: University of Georgia Press (1985).

Byrne, Jack. "White Men with Three Names (Or) If Sam Has Kidnapped Checkers, Then Who Is in the John--Reed's Journey from Scat to Scatology." *The Review of Contemporary Fiction* 4.2 (1984): 195-202.

Cade, Toni. "*The Free-Lance Pallbearers.*" Rev. of *The Free-Lance Pallbearers. Liberator* 9 (June 1969): 20.

Cannon, Steve. "The Search for the Baaad America." Rev. of *Flight to Canada.*

Boston Phoenix (5 August, 1977): 18, 20.

Carter, Steven R. "Ishmael Reed's Neo-HooDoo Detection." In *Dimensions of Detective Fiction.* Eds. Larry Landrum, Pat Browne, and Ray B. Browne. Bowling Green, OH: Popular Press, (1976): 265-90.

Charyn, Jerome. "*Flight to Canada.*" Rev. of *Flight to Canada. New York Times Book Review* (September 1976): 5, 12.

Colter, Cyrus. "Red-Hot Gumbo-Jumbo by Ishmael Reed." Rev. of *The Last Days of Louisiana Red. Chicago Daily News* (1974): no pagination.

Cowley, Julian. "What If I Write Circuses? The Space of Ishmael Reed's Fiction." *Callaloo: A Journal of African-American and African Arts and Letters* 17.4 (Fall 1994): 1236-1244.

Davis, Robert Murray. "Scatting the Myths: Ishmael Reed." *Arizona Quarterly* (Winter 1983): 406-420.

De Arman, Charles. "The Black Image in the Black Mind, or *Flight to Canada.*" *CLA Journal* 33.2 (December 1989): 157-177.

De Filippo, Bernard J. *HooDoo, Voodoo and Conjure: The Novels of Ishmael Reed.* Ph.D. Dissertation, Carnegie Mellon University (1987).

Desraj, Shubsheel. "Fabulation as a Literary Mode in the Fiction of Ishmael Reed." *Panjab University Research Bulletin* 21 (1990): 59-67.

Dick, Bruce and Amritjit Singh, Eds. *Conversations with Ishmael Reed.* Jackson: University Press of Mississippi, 1995.

Duff, Gerald. "Ishmael Reed." *American Novelists Since World War II.* Eds. Jeffrey Helterman and Richard Layman. Detroit: Clark/Gale, (1978): 4, 17-22.

Fleischer, Leonore. "Black Magic Under Blue Skies." Rev. of *Yellow Back Radio Broke-Down. Chicago Tribune Book World* (10 August, 1969): 3.

Fontenot, Chester J. "Ishmael Reed and the Politics of Aesthetics, or Shake Hands and Come Out Conjuring." *Black American Literature Forum* 12 (1978): 20-23.

Ford, Nick Aaron. "A Note on Ishmael Reed: Revolutionary Novelist." *Studies in the Novel* 3 (Summer 1971): 216-218.

Fox, Robert Elliot. "The Logic of the White Castle: Western Critical Standards and the Dilemma of Black Art." *Obsidian* 3.2 (1977): 18-27.

---.*Conscientious Sorcerers: The Black Postmodernist Fiction of Leroi Jones/Amiri Baraka, Ishmael Reed, and Samuel R.. Delany.* Westport, CT: Greenwood Press (1987).

---."Blacking the Zero." *Masters of the Drum: Black Lit/oratures Across the Continuum.* Ed. Robert Elliot Fox. Wesport, CT: Greenwood Press, 1995.

Gates, Henry Louis, Jr. "Parody of Forms." *Saturday Review* 5 (March 1978): 28.

---."'The Blackness of Blackness': A Critique of the Sign and the Signifying Monkey." *Critical Inquiry* 9 (June 1983): 685-723.

---."On 'The Blackness of Blackness': Ishmael Reed and the Critique of the Sign." *The Signifying Monkey: A Theory of African American Literary Criticism.* New York: Oxford University Press, 1988.

Gayle, Addison, Jr. "Reed, Ishmael." In *Contemporary Novelists.* Ed. James Vinson. New York: St. Martin's Press (1972): 1053-54.

---.*The Way of the New World: The Black Novel in America.* Garden City, NY: Anchor Press/Doubleday (1975).

Graham, Mariemma. "Ishmael Reed and the Neo Black Aesthetic Critics." *Black American Forum* 24.3 (Fall 1990): 59.

Green, Geoffrey. "Reality as Art: *The Last Days of Louisiana Red.*" *The Review of Contemporary Fiction* 4.2 (1984): 233-237.

Hardack, Richard. "Swing to the White, Back to the Black: Writing and 'Sourcery' in Ishmael Reed's *Mumbo Jumbo.*" *Arizona Quarterly* 49 (1993): 117-139.

Harris, Norman. "Politics as an Innovative Aspect of Literary Folklore: A Study of Ishmael Reed." *Obsidian: Black Literature in Review* (1979): 41-50.

---."The Black University in Contemporary Afro-American Fiction." *CLAA Journal* (September 1986): 1-13.

---."The Gods Must Be Angry: *Flight to Canada* as Political History." *Modern Fiction Studies* 34.1 (Spring 1988): 111-123.

Hernton, Calvin. "A Fiery Baptism." In *Amistad I.* Eds. John A. Williams and Charles F. Harris. New York: Vintage Books (1970): 200-225.

Herron, Carolivia. "Milton and Afro-American Literature." *Milton: Essays on the Texts and Traditions.* New York: Methuen (1987).

Hoffman, Donald. "A Darker Side of Grail: Questing as the Crossroads in Ishmael Reed's *Mumbo Jumbo.*" *Callaloo* (1994): 1245-56.

Holt, Pat. "Humorous Modern Novel of Black Voodoo." Rev. of *The Last Days of Louisiana Red. San Francisco Chronicle* (December 1974): no pagination.

Houston, Helen Ruth. "Ishmael Reed." In *The Afro-American Novel 1965-1975: A Descriptive Bibliography of Primary and Secondary Material.* Troy, NY: Whitson Publishing Co. (1977): 140-49.

Hower, Edward. "*Japanese by Spring.*" Rev. *New York Times Book Review* (7 March 1993): 11.

Hume, Kathryn. "Ishmael Reed and the Problematics of Control." *PMLA* 108.3 (May 1993): 506-18.

Johnson, Carol Siri. "The Limbs of Osiris: Reed's *Mumbo Jumbo* and Hollywood's *The Mummy.*" *MELUS* 17.4 (1991-1992): 105-15.

Johnson, Lemuel A. "'Ain'ts,' 'Us'ens,' and 'Mother-Dear': Issues in the Language of Madhubuti, Jones, and Reed." *Journal of Black Studies* 10.2 (1979): 139-66.

Jones, Robert W. "Language and Structure in Ishmael Reed's *Yellow Back Radio*

Broke-Down." *Notes on Contemporary Literature* 8.2 (March 1978): 2-3.

Katzman, Allan. "Books." Rev. of *Yellow Back Radio Broke-Down. East Village Other* (July 1968): 14.

Klinkowitz, Jerome. *Literary Disruptions: The Making of a Post-Contemporary American Fiction.* Urbana: University of Illinois Press (1975).

---."Reed's Slapstick History." Rev. of *Flight to Canada. Chicago Daily News Panorama* 25-26 (1976): 11.

---.*The Life of Fiction.* Urbana: University of Illinois Press, (1977): 117-27.

La Polla, Franco. "*The Free-Lance Pallbearers,* or: No More Prescenium Arch." *The Review of Contemporary Fiction* 4.2 (1984): 188-195.

Lehman-Haupt, Christopher. "Will the Real 'Black Esthetic' Please Stand Up?" Rev. of *Yellow Back Radio Broke-Down. New York Times* (1 August 1969): 31.

---. "Decline and Fall of Jes Grew." Rev. of *Mumbo Jumbo. New York Times* (9 August 1972): 35.

Lindroth, James R. "From Krazy Kat to Hoodoo: Aesthetic Discourse in the Fiction of Ishmael Reed." *The Review of Contemporary Fiction* (1984): 227-233.

---."Generating the Vocabulary of Hoodoo: Zora Neale Hurston and Ishmael Reed." *Zora Neale Hurston Forum* 2.1 (Fall 1987): 27-34.

---."Images of Subversion: Ishmael Reed and the Hoodoo Trickster." *African American Review* 30.2 (1996): 185-196.

Link, Franz. "In Search of the Future in the Carpet of History: Thomas Pynchon, Ishmael Reed, and Umberto Eco." Engler, Bernd (Eds.). *Historiographic Metafiction in Modern American and Canadian Literature.* Padenborn: Ferdinand Schoningh (1994): 185-96.

Lock, Helen. "A Man's Story Is His Own Gris-Gris: Ishmael Reed's Neo-HooDoo Aesthetic and the African-American Tradition." *South-Central Review: The Journal of the South-Central Modern Language Association* (1993): 67-77.

Ludwig, Sämi. "Diabolic Possession in Ishmael Reed's *Mumbo Jumbo*: Bakhtin, Voodoo, and the Materiality of Multicultural Discourse." *The Black Columbiad: Defining Moments in African American Literature and Culture.* Cambridge, MA: Harvard University Press (1994): 325-36.

Mackey, Nathaniel. "Ishmael Reed and the Black Aesthetic." *CLA Journal* 21 (March 1978): 355-366.

Major, Clarence. "*Mumbo Jumbo.*" Rev. of *Mumbo Jumbo. Black Creation* (Fall 1972): 59-61.

Martin, Reginald. "Ishmael Reed's *Mumbo-Jumbo.*" *Explicator* (1986): 55-56.

---."Ishmael Reed: Re-writing America." *Kwartalnik Neofilologiczny.* Warsaw, Poland (1986): 499-511.

---.*Ishmael Reed and the New Black Aesthetic Critics.* London: Macmillan

(1988).

Mason, Theodore O., Jr. "Performance, History and Myth: The Problem of Ishmael Reed's *Mumbo Jumbo.*" *Modern Fiction Studies* 34.1 (Spring 1988): 97-109.

McConnel, Frank. "Ishmael Reed's Fiction: Da Hoodoo Is Put on America." Lee, Robert A., Ed. *Black Fiction: New Studies in the Afro-American Novel Since 1945.* New York: Barnes and Noble (1980): 136-48.

McGee, Patrick. *Ishmael Reed and the Ends of Race.* New York: St. Martin's Press, 1997.

McKenzie, James. "Pole-Vaulting in Top Hats: A Public Conversation with John Barth, William Gass, and Ishmael Reed." In *Modern Fiction Studies,* West Lafayette, IN. (1976): 131-51.

Melnick, Jeffrey. "What Are You Looking At? Ishmael Reed's *Reckless Eyeballing.*" *The Black Columbiad: Defining Moments in African American Literature and Culture.* Cambridge, MA: Harvard University Press (1994): 298-311.

Mikics, David. "Ism: Postmodern Ethnicity and Underground Revision in Ishmael Reed." *Essays in Postmodern Culture* (1993): 297-324.

Musgrave, Marian E. "Sexual Excess and Deviation As Structural Devices in Gunter Grass's *Blechtrommel* and Ishmael Reed's *Free-Lance Pallbearers.*" *CLA Journal* 22.3 (1979): 229-239.

Mvuyekure, Pierre-Damien. "Signifyin(g) Revisions, Pretexts, Subtexts, and Posttexts: Elements of Multiculturalism in Ishmael Reed's Writing." Ph.D. Dissertation, University of Iowa Vol. 54, No. 8 (February 1994).

Nadle, Marlene. "Ishmael Reed Conjures Up a Voodoo Cure for Black America." *Politics and Other Human Interests* (April 1978): 22-23.

Nazareth, Peter. "Time in the Third World: A Fictional Exploration." In *The Awakened Conscience.* Ed. C. D. Narrasimhiah. New Delhi, India: Sterling (1978): 195-205.

---.*In the Trickster Tradition: The Novels of Andrew Salkey, Francis Ebejar and Ishmael Reed.* London: Bogle - L'Ouverture Press (1994).

Olderman, Raymond M. "American Fiction 1974-1976: The People Who Fell to Earth." *Contemporary Literature* (1978): 497-527.

Paravisini, Lizabeth. "*Mumbo-Jumbo* and the Uses of Parody." *Obsidian II: Black Literature in Review* (Spring 1986): 113-127.

Parks, John G. "Mining and Undermining the Old Plots: Ishmael Reed's *Mumbo-Jumbo.*" *The Centennial Review* 39.1 (Winter 1995): 163-70.

Pinckney, Darryl. "Trickster Tales." *New York Review of Books* (12 October 1989): 19-29.

Rao, R.M.V. Raghavendra. "Afrocentricity in *Mumbo-Jumbo* and the System of Dante's Hell." *The Literary Griot: International Journal of Black Expressive Cultural Studies* 5.1 (Spring 1993): 17-32.

Reed, Ishmael. "The Writer as Seer: Ishmael Reed on Ishmael Reed." *Black World* 23.8 (June 1974): 20-34.

Reilly, John. "The Reconstruction of Genre as Entry into Conscious History." *Black American Literature Forum* (Spring 1979): 3-6.

Rushdy, Ashraf H.A. "Ishmael Reed's Neo-HooDoo Slave Narrative." *Narrative* 2.2 (May 1994): 112-139.

Schmitz, Neil. "The Gumbo That Just Grew." *Partisan Review* 42 (1976): 311-316.

Schwenk, Katrin. "Lynching and Rape: Border Cases in African American History and Fiction." *The Black Columbiad: Defining Moments in African American Literature and Culture*. Cambridge, MA: Harvard University Press (1994): 312-34.

Settle, Elizabeth A. and Thomas A. Settle, Eds. *Ishmael Reed, A Primary and Secondary Bibliography*. Boston: G.K. Hall & Co. (1982).

Simon, Myron. "Two Angry Ethnic Writers." *MELUS* (1976): 20-24.

Staples, Brent. "Media-Lashed and Sex-Listed." Rev. of *Reckless Eyeballing*. *New York Times Book Review* (5 April 1986): 12.

Stepto, Robert B. "Distrust of the Reader in Afro-American Narratives." *Reconstructing American Literary History*. Ed. Sacvan Bercovitch. Cambridge, MA: Harvard (1986): 300-322.

Turner, Darwin T. "Black Fiction: History and Myth." *Studies in American Fiction* 5.1 (1977): 109-226.

Uphaus, Suzanne Henning. "Ishmael Reed's Canada." *Canadian Review of American Studies* (1977): 95-99.

Walsh, Richard. "A Man's Story is His Gris-Gris: Cultural Slavery, Literary Emancipation and Ishmael Reed's *Flight to Canada*." *Journal of American Studies* 27 (1993): 57-71.

Weixlman, Joe. "Politics, Piracy, and Other Games: Slavery and Liberation in *Flight to Canada*." *MELUS* (1979): 41-50.

---."Ishmael Reed's Raven." *The Review of Contemporary Fiction* 4.2 (1984): 205-208.

---."African-American Deconstruction of the Novel in the Work of Ishmael Reed and Clarence Major." *MELUS* (1991-1992): 57-79.

---."Culture Clash, Survival, and Transformation: A Study of Some Innovative Afro-American Novels of Detection." *Mississippi Quarterly*. (Winter 1994-95): 24-27.

Young, Al. "Fiction: Introduction." *Iowa Review* (Spring 1975): 42-44.

Zamir, Shamoon. "Ishmael Reed." *Callaloo: A Journal of African-American and African Arts and Letters* 17.4 (Fall 1994): 1129-1256.

Index

BRUCE ALLEN DICK is Associate Professor of English at Appalachian State University. His previous books include *Conversations with Ishmael Reed* and *Conversations with Rudolfo Anaya.*

PAVEL ZEMLIANSKY is a doctoral student in English at Florida State University.

ISBN 0-313-30025-9

90000>

EAN

9 780313 300257

HARDCOVER BAR CODE